ALSO BY ROBERT M. PARKER, JR.

Parker's Wine Buyer's Guide

The World's Greatest Wine Estates

*Bordeaux: A Consumer's Guide
to the World's Finest Wines*

Wines of the Rhône Valley

*Burgundy: A Comprehensive Guide to the
Producers, Appellations, and Wines*

PARKER'S WINE BARGAINS

The World's Best Wine Values Under $25

ROBERT M. PARKER, JR., AND CONTRIBUTORS TO *THE WINE ADVOCATE*

SIMON & SCHUSTER PAPERBACKS

NEW YORK   LONDON   TORONTO   SYDNEY

To the women of my life,
Maia-Song Elizabeth Parker,
Patricia E. Parker, Aunt Betty Jane,
and my late mother, Ruth "Siddy" Parker

Simon & Schuster
1230 Avenue of the Americas
New York, NY 10020

Copyright © 2009 by Robert M. Parker, Jr.

First Simon & Schuster trade paperback edition November 2009

SIMON & SCHUSTER and colophon are
registered trademarks of Simon & Schuster, Inc.

For information about special discounts for bulk purchases, please contact Simon & Schuster Special Sales at 1-866-506-1949 or business@simonandschuster.com.

The Simon & Schuster Speakers Bureau can bring authors to your live event. For more information or to book an event contact the Simon & Schuster Speakers Bureau at 1-866-248-3049 or visit our website at www.simonspeakers.com.

Designed by Joel Avirom and Jason Snyder

Manufactured in the United States of America

10   9   8   7   6   5   4   3   2   1

Library of Congress Cataloging-in-Publication Data
Parker, Robert M.
    Parker's wine bargains : the world's best wine values under $25 / Robert M. Parker, Jr.
        p.   cm.
    Includes bibliographical references and index.
    1. Wine and wine making.   I. Title.   II. Title: Wine bargains.
TP548.P286   2009
    641.2'2—dc22   2009015662

ISBN 978-1-4391-0190-2
ISBN 978-1-4391-2324-9 (ebook)

ACKNOWLEDGMENTS

First and foremost, to my team of contributors, who have added their areas of expertise, which has benefited the book enormously: David Schildknecht, Antonio Galloni, Dr. Jay Miller, Mark Squires, and Neal Martin, my profound thanks for your exceptional efforts.

To the tiny staff at *The Wine Advocate,* who were heavily involved in gathering information and putting it into some sort of sensible arrangement, I owe a great deal of thanks. Despite Joan Passman's officially retiring at the end of 2006, her heartfelt loyalty and concern for my mental well-being has her still working several days a week and has helped expedite the book's completion. Her full-time replacement, Annette Piatek, did as much as anybody, and I can't thank her enough for her hardworking and conscientious efforts in gathering information, sorting through it, and trying to make some sort of sense of everything all of us have written. She was assisted very capably by the other *Wine Advocate* staffer, Betsy Sobolewski.

At the professional publishing level, my editor, Amanda Murray, deserves an enormous amount of credit for making sense of our verbose commentary, cleaning it up, and assisting all of us in making certain ideas clearer. In short, her enormous efforts have made the book significantly better, and we all deeply appreciate it. I would also like to thank the rest of the Simon & Schuster crew, including Kate Ankofski, Josh Karpf, Mike Kwan, and Nancy Singer.

Every author requires plenty of psychological support, and I suspect I receive more than most. The love of my life, my beautiful wife, Patricia, always provides wisdom and counsel, and is an encouraging voice when things seem gloomiest. I must not forget my wonderful daughter, Maia. Now that she is in college, I actually see less of her these days than of my two furry companions, Buddy, a three-year-old English bulldog, and Hoover, his favorite friend (and mine too, for that matter).

I also want to acknowledge a longtime friend, bon vivant, and exceptionally wise man by the name of Dr. Park B. Smith, a spiritual elder brother whose love of wine and laserlike thinking have provided enormous wisdom to me over many years.

Finally, to the following friends, supporters, and advisers, a heartfelt "million thanks"—all of you have taught me valuable lessons about wine and, more important, about life: Jim Arseneault, Anthony Barton, Ruth Bassin and the late Bruce and Addy Bassin, Hervé Berlaud, Bill Blatch, Thomas B. Böhrer, Barry Bondroff, Daniel Boulud, Rowena and Mark Braunstein, Christopher Cannan, Dick Carretta, Jean-Michel Cazes, Corinne Cesano, Jean-Marie Chadronnier, M. and Mme Jean-Louis Charmolue, Charles Chevalier, Bob Cline, Jeffrey Davies, Hubert de Boüard, Jean and Annie Delmas, Jean-Hubert Delon and the late Michel Delon, Dr. Albert H. Dudley III, Barbara Edelman, Fédéric Engérer, Michael Etzel, Paul Evans, Terry Faughey, the legendary Fitzcarraldo—my emotional and quasi-fictional soulmate—Joel Fleischman, Mme Capbern Gasqueton, Dan Green, Josué Harari, Alexandra Harding, Dr. David Hutcheon, Barbara G. and Steve R. R. Jacoby, Joanne and Joe James, Jean-Paul Jauffret, Daniel Johnnes; Nathaniel, Archie, and Denis Johnston; Ed Jonna, Elaine and Manfred Krankl, Robert Lescher, Bernard Magrez, Adam Montefiore of Carmel Winery, Patrick Maroteaux, Pat and Victor Hugo Morgenroth; Christian, Jean-François, and the late Jean-Pierre Moueix; Bernard Nicolas, Jill Norman, Les Oenarchs (Bordeaux), Les Oenarchs (Baltimore), François Pinault, Frank Polk, Paul Pontallier, Bruno Prats, Jean-Guillaume Prats, Judy Pruce, Dr. Alain Raynaud, Martha Reddington, Dominique Renard, Michel Richard, Alan Richman, Dany and Michel Rolland; Pierre Rovani and his father, Yves Rovani; Robert Roy, Carlo Russo, Ed Sands, Erik Samazeuilh, Bob Schindler, Ernie Singer, Elliott Staren, Daniel Tastet-Lawton, Lettie Teague, Alain Vauthier, the late Steven Verlin, Peter Vezan, Robert Vifian, Sonia Vogel, Jeanyee Wong, and Gérard Yvernault.

CONTENTS

INTRODUCTION

What Is This Book?

One of the most gratifying aspects of being a wine critic is discovering those under-the-radar, superb wine bargains that taste as if they should cost two or three times the price but don't. I taste thousands of wines every year, and most of my colleagues have been tasting wine for twenty or more years. This book has long been in the works, and it seems that it could not come out at a more appropriate time, given the world economic crisis and the downsizing of everyone's net worth. This book focuses on wines that, given current exchange rates with the dollar and what domestic wineries are charging, are priced at $25 or below per bottle. The selections that we have proposed, with a thumbnail sketch of what to expect from these wines in a good- to above-average-quality vintage, represent a tiny percentage of all the wines we taste. The myth is that wines that cost $25 or less are worth just what you pay for them and are never terribly interesting. This is totally untrue, and with work, one can unearth these small treasures that deliver seriously good wine at remarkably fair prices. Obviously, some viticultural areas of the world provide more value than others. Spain, southern France, southern Italy, South America, and Australia certainly lead all other areas in terms of the wealth of wine values that exist in those regions. Yet even in prestige areas such as Bordeaux or in northern California, there are wineries that can and do produce very high-quality wines for a song. Therefore, this book is only about the world's greatest wine values, and no bottle should cost more than $25. Many of these wines actually sell for between $10 and $15. But as a wine consumer for over thirty years, I always felt that the sweet spot for wine bargains has to be defined with some limit, and we have chosen $25 and under.

The Concept of Value

One can certainly argue that a nearly perfect, famous Bordeaux château turning out a wine for $50 would represent a good value, when many of the most renowned wines of that hallowed wine region cost from $250 to as much as $1,000 a bottle, and thus the $50 wine would be a "good value" in the context of that category. The same argument can apply to Burgundy, where most of the best-known classified grands crus and premiers crus of Burgundy sell for well in excess of $50 to $100 a bottle. We reject that. We have set value as a top-flight wine that can be purchased at a retail shop for under $25. To reiterate, most of these wines are actually available for a lot less. We also realize that prices vary from state to state, and certainly imports reflect the value of the dollar at the time an importer purchased the wine. We define the concept of value as wines under $25, and this book is strictly confined to those wines that fit that category.

Vintage Smarts and Drinking Curves

In each chapter, there is a section called "Vintage Smarts." This gives readers a synopsis of the best and worst vintages of late that a region has experienced. "Drinking Curves" sections will give readers an idea of how soon the wines must be consumed. Most of these value wines are meant for near-term consumption. This doesn't mean within thirty minutes of purchase, but within 1 to 2 years for most of the white and rosé wines, and 3 to 5 years for most of the red wines. White and rosé wines, not having any of the tannin content that most red wines have, even at the low end of the price hierarchy, are best consumed in their exuberant, fresh, vigorous youth, and the duration of that stage is usually only 1 to 2 years. Even the least expensive red wines can actually improve for a year or two and, where stored in a refrigerator or wine storage unit, can sometimes last well past 4 or 5 years without losing their fruit and becoming boring and uninteresting.

The Entries

For each area of the world covered, we have listed the finest wine values (under $25) in alphabetical order, giving a short summary of the style and character of the wine that you are likely to find in a reasonably good vintage for that region. Hopefully, this will help you understand what to look for and what you personally enjoy the most. All of the producers who have been briefly profiled in this book are the best in the world at producing good value wines, and we think the pleasure of discovering a wine for $10, $15, or at the very highest end, $25, that performs at the level of wine selling for three to five times that price, will be an enormously gratifying experience for all wine consumers.

Each chapter of this book is written by the writer who covers that particular region for *The Wine Advocate*. In my case, that means Bordeaux, the Rhône Valley, and California. David Schildknecht has written the chapters on Austria; Alsace, the Savoie, and the Jura; Burgundy and Beaujolais; Languedoc and Roussillon; the Loire Valley; Provence; France's Southwest; Germany; and South Africa. Antonio Galloni has provided information on every wine region of Italy. Dr. Jay Miller has written the chapters on Argentina, Australia, Chile, Oregon, Spain, and Washington State. Mark Squires contributed the sections on Greece and Portugal, and Neal Martin provided the chapter on New Zealand.

—*Robert M. Parker, Jr.*

A note about Champagne's Best Values

No wine in the world can match the sheer pleasure and excitement that a great Champagne can add to a celebration. Unfortunately, Champagne is one of the few regions in the world where value is hard to come by. The big, historic houses have succeeded in creating an image of luxury, which has resulted in a large number of Champagnes that are priced like luxury handbags rather than wine. Readers willing to do a little searching should be able to find a number of delicious Champagnes between $30 and $50, but because that price point is above our limit in this book, we weren't able to include them. If you're interested in bargain-priced sparkling wines from around the world, you'll find an index of them on page 479.

—*Antonio Galloni*

KEY TO SYMBOLS	
$	*$8–$15*
$$	*$16–$20*
$$$	*$21–$25*
♟	*Red*
♈	*Rosé*
♈	*White*
♈	*Sparkling*
S	*Sweet*
SD	*Semidry*

PARKER'S
WINE
BARGAINS

ARGENTINA

ARGENTINIAN WINE VALUES

by Dr. Jay Miller

Argentina is the world's fifth-largest wine producer (behind France, Italy, Spain, and the United States). Sales of Argentina wines continue to explode despite economic hard times in the USA. It's not just about the seemingly ideal bond between the Malbec grape and Mendoza *terroir*. Inexpensive labor and land (roughly $30,000 an acre, compared to $300,000 in Napa Valley) plus an ideal climate and a good water supply from the Andes make for low production costs.

Regions

While Mendoza is not Argentina's only wine-producing region, it is far and away the most significant. It features a high desert climate, with most vineyards planted at elevations of 2,500–4,500 feet (and some even higher), resulting in intense sunshine but cooler air temperatures. This results in physiologically ripe grapes in almost every vintage, without elevated sugars and high alcohol levels. There are almost no wines noted here with alcohol levels over 14.5%. With Mendoza's desert climate there is very little rainfall, but there's no shortage of water thanks to its proximity to the Andes mountains (which can be seen from every vineyard and appear to be next door because of their immense size). Irrigation is the rule. Phylloxera is not an issue, so most vines are planted on their own roots. Soils at these high elevations are poor in organic material, so the vines must develop deep roots, thus intensifying flavors. Pesticides and herbicides in this climate are rarely used and hand-harvesting is the rule. The only significant weather risk is hail (13% of the annual crop is typically lost to this problem), so most vineyards are netted for protection.

Grapes

Argentina's most important grape by far is Malbec. It is a French variety that has had limited success in the Old World but produces magnificent reds in Argentina. Characterized by its spicy dark fruit character,

Argentinian Malbec flourishes at a level of quality unparalleled anywhere else in the world. Cabernet Sauvignon is also important and frequently blended with Malbec. The other Bordeaux varietals (Cabernet Franc, Petit Verdot, even Carménère) exist, but are used almost exclusively for blending. Pinot Noir is just beginning to make an appearance and appears to have some potential. Syrah and Tempranillo can be found but play subsidiary roles.

There are two other grapes that are virtually indigenous to Argentina. The red grape is Bonarda, originally from Lombardy in Italy, where ripening is typically an issue. In Mendoza it makes juicy, flavorful, vibrant wine. Moreover, it rarely sells for over $15 a bottle. The white grape is Torrontés, most of it grown in Cafayate in northern Argentina. Research has shown that it is a cross of Muscat Alexandria and the Mission grape once planted widely in California. When well grown, it is remarkably fragrant, with the fruit nicely buttressed by zesty acidity. For those looking for Chardonnay alternatives, this is a variety worth exploring. Even better, they rarely sell for more than $15 a bottle.

Vintage Smarts

Argentina is on the rise. Recent vintages, particularly 2008, 2007, 2006, and 2005, have been excellent to outstanding, and this country's improved viticultural and winemaking practices as well as the arrival on the scene of quality-conscious boutique wineries foreshadow an extremely bright future.

Drinking Curves

All of Argentina's white wines are meant to be drunk in their youth—within 3 years of the vintage. The red wines can also be enjoyed within this time frame but some of them will last for a decade or more.

Argentina's Top Wine Values by Winery

ALAMOS *(Mendoza)*

Bonarda ♟ $ The Bonarda offers up plum and blackberry aromas and flavors meant for drinking during its first 3 years of life.

Cabernet Sauvignon ♟ $ The Alamos Cabernet is a spicy, medium-bodied red for near-term drinking.

Chardonnay ♀ $ The Alamos Chardonnay exhibits a bouquet of spiced apple, pear, and tropical aromas leading to a smooth-textured, tasty wine meant for near-term drinking.

Malbec ♀ $ The Malbec offers layers of black cherry fruit, good weight on the palate, and a pure, fruit-filled finish. It can be enjoyed during its first 4 years.

Malbec Selección ♀ $$ The Selección is sourced from older vines and has a bit more new oak along with a lovely bouquet of smoke, spice box, earth notes, and black cherry. Enjoy it during its first 5 years of life.

Torrontés—Cafayate ♀ $ Fragrant with an attractive perfume of spring flowers, honey, and tropical fruits. Dry, crisp, and well balanced; meant for drinking during its first 12–18 months.

ALTA VISTA *(Various Regions)*

Atemporal Blend—Mendoza ♀ $$ This fragrant blend is composed of Malbec, Cabernet Sauvignon, Syrah, and Petit Verdot. On the palate it reveals a restrained personality, some elegance, ample savory fruit, and excellent length.

Cabernet Sauvignon—Mendoza ♀ $ Aromas of black currant and cassis are followed by an easygoing, forward, uncomplicated effort offering layers of fruit and savory flavors for drinking during its first 4 years.

Malbec—Mendoza ♀ $ An expressive floral and black cherry–scented bouquet leads to a supple-textured, forward wine with good flavors and no hard edges. Drink it over its first 3 years.

Torrontés Premium—Cafayate ♀ $ Fragrant Muscat and tropical fruit aromas are followed by a dry, medium-bodied, smooth-textured wine for drinking during its first 12–18 months.

ALTOS LAS HORMIGAS *(Mendoza)*

Malbec ♀ $ The entry-level Malbec has always been a superb value. It exhibits a smoky, spicy, black cherry bouquet leading to a medium-bodied wine with surprising depth and savory fruit. Forward and easygoing, it will provide much pleasure during its first 4 years of life.

Malbec Reserva Vineyard Selection ♀ \$\$\$ The Reserva offers up a spicy perfume of wood smoke, mineral, black cherry, and blackberry followed by a structured wine with good ripeness, balance, and depth. It will benefit from a few years of cellaring but will ultimately offer no more pleasure than its less expensive sibling.

ANDELUNA CELLARS *(Mendoza)*

Cabernet Sauvignon Winemaker's Selection ♀ \$ This Cabernet reveals an attractive nose of spice box, cassis, and black currant along with plenty of spicy fruit, an easygoing personality, soft tannin, and moderate length.

ANTONIETTI *(Mendoza)*

Malbec ♀ \$ Antonietti's Malbec is made in a lighter, forward, elegant style with plenty of ripe cherry fruit for near-term drinking. It is a good introduction to the delights of Malbec.

ARGENTO *(Various Regions)*

Cabernet Sauvignon—Lujan de Cuyo ♀ \$ The Argento Cab delivers a perfume of cedar, tobacco, cassis, and blackberry. Medium bodied and restrained, it has enough stuffing to improve for 1–2 years but can be enjoyed now.

Malbec—Agrelo ♀ \$ The nose of the Malbec reveals spice box, cedar, earth notes, and black cherry. Fruity, forward, and easygoing, it can be enjoyed during its first 3 years of life.

AVE *(Salta)*

Malbec Premium ♀ \$ The Malbec Premium is dark ruby colored, with an enticing nose of cherry and plum. This leads to a forward wine with plenty of sweet fruit, good depth and concentration, and a long, pure finish.

Torrontés ♀ \$ The medium-straw-colored Torrontés has a fragrant, floral, mineral, and lemon-scented nose. On the palate it is dry with good acidity, some elegance, and a medium-long finish.

BELASCO DE BAQUEDANO *(Mendoza)*

AR Guentota Malbec ♟ $$$ The AR Guentota Malbec is sourced from 100-year-old vines in Agrelo and Perdriel. The bouquet offers wood smoke, spice box, black cherry, and blackberry. Savory on the palate, it will evolve for at least 2 years and drink well for 6 years thereafter.

Llama Malbec ♟ $ The Llama Malbec has an appealing nose of cedar, tobacco, spice box, and black cherry leading to a smooth-textured, spicy wine with excellent depth and concentration.

BENEGAS *(Various Regions)*

The specialty of the house is Bordeaux-style wine from their old-vine parcels.

Finca Libertad—Maipu ♟ $$$ Finca Libertad is a blend of Cabernet Sauvignon, Cabernet Franc, and Merlot. It exhibits a complex aroma leading to an elegant wine with savory flavors, considerable complexity, and enough structure to evolve for another 2–3 years.

Malbec—Mendoza ♟ $$$ The Malbec's aromatics offer enticing notes of cedar, spice box, blueberry, and black raspberry leading to a smooth-textured, flavorful, well-balanced Malbec with 2–3 years of aging potential.

Sangiovese—Mendoza ♟ $$$ The Sangiovese is dark ruby colored, with a lovely red cherry perfume, notes of cedar and mineral, and an elegant personality. This smooth, friendly wine could easily pass for Tuscan in a blind tasting.

Syrah Estate—Maipu ♟ $$$ The purple-colored Syrah offers an alluring perfume of toasty blueberries leading to a full-bodied, layered wine with gobs of succulent fruit, outstanding depth, and a fruit-filled finish.

BENMARCO *(Mendoza)*

BenMarco is the label of Pedro Marchevsky, one of the more prominent viticulturalists in Argentina.

Cabernet Sauvignon ♟ $$$ The nose offers up fragrant baking spices, black cherry, and black currant leading to a wine with an elegant personality, succulent fruit, a lush texture, and outstanding length. It will offer prime drinking from 2010 to 2018.

Malbec 🍷 $$$ The Malbec exhibits a kinky perfume of black cherry, wild black raspberry, earth notes, and leather. On the palate there is plenty of jammy fruit, bright acidity, excellent balance, and a lengthy finish.

VALENTIN BIANCHI *(Mendoza)*

Malbec Famiglia Bianchi 🍷 $$ Delivers an excellent perfume of cedar, spice box, violets, and black cherry. This is followed by a full-bodied wine with savory black fruit flavors, solid depth, and good length.

LUIGI BOSCA *(Various Regions)*

Malbec Reserva Single Vineyard—Lujan de Cuyo 🍷 $$$ An expressive bouquet of black cherry, mineral, and spice box leads to a palate that is both mouth coating and elegant, with plenty of sweet fruit, excellent depth, and a long, pure finish.

Pinot Noir—Maipu 🍷 $$$ Enticing varietal aromas of raspberry and strawberry lead to a friendly, velvety-textured, sweetly fruited Pinot with attractive flavors and good length.

BODEGA BRESSIA *(Cafayate)*

Torrontés 🍸 $ Bodega Bressia's Torrontés offers a floral, lemon-lime perfume in a more elegant style than is the norm for this grape. The wine has good concentration, a smooth texture, and a medium-long finish.

BUDINI *(Mendoza)*

Chardonnay 🍸 $ The light-gold-colored Chardonnay delivers attractive apple and pear aromas and flavors within its medium-bodied personality. Easygoing and well balanced by bright acidity, it should be consumed during its first 12–18 months.

Malbec 🍷 $ The Malbec is dark ruby colored, with a bouquet of spice box and black cherry. Supple and friendly on the palate, this uncomplicated effort can be enjoyed during its first 2–3 years.

HUMBERTO CANALE *(Patagonia)*

Malbec Gran Reserva ♉ $$ The Malbec Gran Reserva has an expressive nose of smoke, black cherry, and mineral along with good depth and grip and enough structure to evolve for 2–3 years.

Pinot Noir Estate ♉ $ The Pinot Noir Estate is medium ruby colored, with a varietal nose of cherry, raspberry, and rhubarb. Light and pleasant on the palate, it is a good introduction to Pinot Noir at a fair price.

Pinot Noir Gran Reserva ♉ $$ The Pinot Noir Gran Reserva is barrel fermented and aged in new oak. It has a more expansive nose and sweeter fruit than its less expensive sibling. It is worth the extra $5 investment.

CATENA ZAPATA *(Mendoza)*

Chardonnay ♉ $$ Catena Zapata's Chardonnay offers a sophisticated bouquet with a touch of toasty oak, mineral, poached pear, and tropical notes. This is followed by a smooth-textured wine with spicy, savory white fruits, bright acidity, excellent concentration, and a fruit-filled finish.

Malbec ♉ $$$ The Malbec's aromatic array displays toasty black cherry, black raspberry, and violet notes leading to a smooth-textured, layered, rich wine bordering on opulence. It manages to achieve this while retaining an elegant, light-on-its-feet personality. On the palate, spice notes and a hint of chocolate emerge. There is enough structure for the wine to evolve for 2–3 years, although it can be enjoyed now.

FINCA LA CELIA *(Uco Valley)*

Chardonnay ♉ $ La Celia Chardonnay offers aromas of toast, apple, pear, and white peach. On the palate the wine is crisp and vibrant with good integration of oak and acidity. It has plenty of ripe fruit and a clean finish.

Kamel Malbec ♉ $ The dark-ruby-colored Kamel Malbec delivers an attractive nose of black cherry and blueberry leading to a forward, smooth-textured, easygoing wine meant for immediate enjoyment.

Malbec Reserva 🍷 $$ The Malbec Reserva raises the bar a bit. The aromatics reveal greater complexity and the wine has enough structure to evolve for 1–2 years.

CHAKANA *(Mendoza)*

Cueva de las Manos Cabernet Sauvignon 🍷 $$ The Cabernet Sauvignon exhibits a classy perfume of smoke, mineral, violets, and black currant. Layered and nearly opulent, it has plenty of succulent black fruit, good focus, and solid length.

Cueva de las Manos Malbec 🍷 $$ The Cueva de las Manos Malbec reveals a brooding bouquet of cedar, pencil lead, spice box, and black cherry. Layered on the plate, it has good depth and grip, savory flavors, and excellent length.

Estate Selection 🍷 $$$ The wine is composed of Malbec, Syrah, and Petit Verdot. The nose exhibits elements of toast, pencil lead, black cherry, blackberry, and plum. Firm on the palate, it has ample ripe fruit, a forward personality, and several years of aging potential.

Maipe Cabernet Sauvignon 🍷 $ This wine has a bouquet of spicy black currant, black fruit flavors, and a forward personality. Drink it over the next three years.

Maipe Malbec 🍷 $ This purple-colored wine is soft, forward, tasty, and easy to understand.

CLOS DE LOS SIETE *(Vista Flores)*

Clos de los Siete 🍷 $$ There may be no finer red wine value in Argentina than this superb blend of Malbec, Merlot, Syrah, and Cabernet Sauvignon. The wine coats the glass while offering up a superb bouquet of toasty oak, violet, mineral, black currant, blueberry, and black cherry. This is followed by a layered wine with gobs of ripe fruit, a plush texture, outstanding balance, and several years of aging potential.

VIÑA COBOS *(Mendoza)*

El Felino Cabernet Sauvignon 🍷 $$ This purple-colored wine offers up spicy black currant and blackberry. Smooth textured and layered, it has excellent balance and a lengthy, pure finish. It's hard to think of a better value in Cabernet Sauvignon.

El Felino Chardonnay ♀ $$ This wine is medium gold colored, with a bouquet of toasty apple, poached pear, and tropical fruit aromas. Smooth and seamless on the palate, it has surprising depth, ripe flavors, and a pure finish.

El Felino Malbec ♀ $$ This Malbec is a splendid introduction to this grape variety. The nose is redolent of wild black cherry, leading to an elegant, ripe wine with gobs of flavor and 1–2 years of aging potential. Drink this hedonistic effort through 2015.

El Felino Merlot ♀ $$ This Merlot is dark ruby colored, with a classy perfume of spice box, cedar, red currants, and cherry. On the palate it has surprising concentration as well as some elegance. It's what Merlot is supposed to be about but seldom is.

COLOMÉ *(Valle Calchaquí)*

The Colomé estate vineyards are organically farmed and biodynamically certified.

Torrontés ♀ $$ The medium-straw-colored Torrontés offers a floral, spicy, Muscat-like perfume leading to a ripe, smooth-textured, dry wine with excellent balance and length. Some Torrontés can be a bit heavy but this rendition is light on its feet.

CRIOS DE SUSANA BALBO *(Mendoza)*

Cabernet Sauvignon ♀ $ The Cabernet Sauvignon reveals an expressive perfume of cedar, spice box, black currant, and black raspberry. This is followed by a wine with lots of savory black fruit, excellent balance, and a long, fruit-filled finish.

Malbec—Agrelo ♀ $ The Malbec offers an enticing bouquet of spice box, cedar, black cherry, and black raspberry. Medium bodied and full flavored, on the palate it has gobs of spicy, savory fruit, soft tannins, and a lengthy finish.

Rosé of Malbec ♀ $ The Rosé of Malbec exhibits a fragrant bouquet of cherry and wild strawberries leading to a medium-bodied, dry, concentrated wine with lots of spicy red fruits and excellent balance. Drink it over the next 12–18 months.

Syrah-Bonarda ♀ $ The Syrah-Bonarda contains 50% of each component. It delivers an alluring nose of baking spice, blueberry, plum, and black raspberry. On the palate it has loads of spicy dark fruit, a forward personality, good balance, and a pure finish.

Torrontés—Cafayate ♀ $ The Torrontés offers up an alluring perfume of spring flowers, peach, apricot, and a hint of citrus. On the palate the wine is dry, smooth textured, layered, and succulent while retaining a sense of elegance.

BODEGA DANTE ROBINO (Mendoza)

Bonarda ♀ $ The Bonarda is deep ruby colored, with an intense perfume of blueberry and earth notes. Layered and ripe on the palate, it has no hard edges.

Malbec ♀ $ The purple-colored Malbec exhibits a spicy, black cherry–scented nose, a smooth texture, and an easygoing personality.

FINCA DECERO (Agrelo)

Cabernet Sauvignon Remolinos Vineyard ♀ $$ This Cabernet is deep crimson colored, with an alluring bouquet of cedar, cinnamon, allspice, cassis, and black currant. Supple and elegant on the palate, it has excellent depth and grip, and a lingering finish.

Malbec Remolinos Vineyard ♀ $$ The purple-colored Malbec Remolinos Vineyard offers up aromas of smoke, spice box, violet, blueberry, and black cherry leading to a smooth-textured wine with excellent concentration and some elegance. It has plenty of spicy, savory fruit, excellent balance, and a pure finish.

BODEGA DEL FIN DEL MUNDO (Patagonia)

Malbec Reserva ♀ $$ The Malbec Reserva has an attractive bouquet of cedar, mineral, spice box, red cherry, and raspberry. On the palate it is elegant, with complex spice notes and lovely red fruit flavors.

DOÑA PAULA (Argentina)

Malbec—Lujan de Cuyo ♀ $$ The opaque purple Malbec reveals a brooding black fruit bouquet, ripe flavors, excellent depth and grip, and 2–3 years of aging potential.

Naked Pulp Viognier—Uco Valley ♀ **$$$** The Naked Pulp Viognier has an alluring perfume of melon, apricot, guava, and kiwi. Full bodied, ripe, and round, it has good acidity, superb depth and concentration, and a lengthy finish.

Sauvignon Blanc—Tupungato ♀ **$$** The Sauvignon Blanc has a superb bouquet of spring flowers, fresh herbs, a touch of mineral, citrus, and green apple. On the palate it is viscous, smooth, and complex.

Shiraz-Malbec Estate—Mendoza ♥ **$$** The Shiraz (60%)–Malbec (40%) raises the bar considerably. It has an enticing nose of spice, chocolate, wood smoke, earth notes, blueberry, and black cherry. Ripe and layered, this rich effort will evolve for 1–2 years and provide pleasure through 2015.

FLECHAS DE LOS ANDES *(Uco Valley)*

Gran Malbec ♥ **$$$** The Gran Malbec is a glass-coating purple with a superb bouquet of cedar, mineral, black cherry, and black raspberry. This leads to a full-bodied, layered, ripe wine with enough structure to evolve for 2–3 years.

FINCA FLICHMAN *(Various Regions)*

Expresiones Malbec–Cabernet Sauvignon—Mendoza ♥ **$$** A blend of Malbec and Cabernet Sauvignon with an enticing bouquet of black cherry and black currant. This leads to a mouth-coating wine with plenty of spicy black fruits, ripe tannin, excellent grip, and 1–2 years of aging potential.

Gestos Malbec—Mendoza ♥ **$** The Gestos Malbec exhibits a bright black cherry–scented aroma, sweet fruit, soft tannins, savory flavors, and a friendly personality.

Paisaje de Barrancas—Maipu ♥ **$** The purple-colored Paisaje de Barrancas is composed of Shiraz, Malbec, and Cabernet Sauvignon. The aromatics offer a hint of game, earth notes, and blueberry. On the palate it is chunky, with a firm finish to its rustic personality.

Paisaje de Tupungato—Uco Valley 🍷 $$ The Paisaje de Tupungato is a blend of Cabernet Sauvignon, Malbec, and Merlot. The attractive perfume includes notes of cedar, violets, black currant, and cassis. This leads to a supple, medium-bodied wine with savory red and black fruit flavors and excellent balance. It can be enjoyed now.

BODEGA ENRIQUE FOSTER *(Mendoza)*

Bodega Enrique Foster makes only old-vine Malbec.

Reserva Malbec 🍷 $$$ The Reserva Malbec offers an attractive bouquet of cedar, mineral, plum, and blueberry. This leads to a forward wine with some elegance, good depth, and a pure finish.

O. FOURNIER *(Mendoza)*

B Crux Blend 🍷 $$$ A blend of Tempranillo, Malbec, and Merlot, the B Crux reveals a fragrant bouquet of cedar, violets, blackberry, black raspberry, and licorice. It has layers of savory fruit, cinnamon, and chocolate, good balance, excellent concentration, and a lengthy, fruit-filled finish.

DON MIGUEL GASCON *(Mendoza)*

Malbec 🍷 $ The purple-colored Malbec exhibits an attractive nose of black cherry with a hint of blueberry. Smooth textured, savory, and nicely balanced, it will drink well for another four years. It overdelivers for its humble price tag.

BODEGA GOULART *(Lunlunta)*

Both Bodega Goulart wines are sourced from 95-year-old high-elevation vineyards.

Malbec–Cabernet Sauvignon Reserva 🍷 $$ The Malbec–Cabernet Sauvignon has an alluring nose of cedar, smoke, espresso, black cherry, and black currant. This leads to a wine with excellent balance, tasty flavors, and a medium-long finish.

Malbec Reserva 🍷 $$ The Malbec Reserva is a saturated purple color with an attractive perfume of violets, black cherry, and black raspberry. On the palate it is medium bodied, balanced, and ripe, with enough structure to evolve for 2–3 years.

KAIKEN *(Mendoza)*

Cabernet Sauvignon ♟ $ Dark ruby in color, it reveals an excellent bouquet of cedar, cassis, and black currant. Ripe and forward on the palate, this seamless effort can be enjoyed during its first 4 years.

Cabernet Sauvignon Ultra ♟ $$ The Cabernet Sauvignon Ultra has a nose of cedar, tobacco, black currant, and blackberry. On the palate, this medium- to full-bodied effort reveals some silky tannin; spicy, savory fruit; and excellent length.

Malbec ♟ $ The Malbec exhibits an alluring perfume of spice box, violet, and black cherry. This leads to a wine with layers of ripe, spicy black cherry fruit and surprising depth, and concentration for its humble price, as well as a fruit-filled finish.

Malbec Ultra ♟ $$ The Ultra has an enticing perfume of toast, pencil lead, mineral, violet, and black cherry. This is followed by a layered wine with plenty of ripe fruit, a firm structure, excellent concentration, and a lengthy, pure finish.

BODEGA LAGARDE *(Mendoza)*

Cabernet Sauvignon ♟ $ The Cabernet Sauvignon is dark ruby colored, with a spicy, floral, and black fruit–scented bouquet. This medium-bodied effort has solid depth, savory flavors, and excellent length.

Malbec ♟ $ The purple-colored Malbec offers up a fragrant nose of spice box and black cherry. On the palate it reveals an easygoing personality with plenty of soft, spicy black fruits, good depth, and a fruit-filled finish.

Malbec DOC—Lujan de Cuyo ♟ $$$ The dark ruby colored Malbec exhibits an enticing bouquet of cedar, tobacco, spice box, black cherry, and black raspberry. On the palate it has good density; lingering, savory flavors; and a fruit-filled finish.

Syrah ♟ $ The Syrah is dark ruby colored, with an attractive perfume of pepper, game, and blue fruits. This leads to a supple, easygoing wine with moderate intensity, savory flavors, and good length.

CASA LAPOSTOLLE *(Colchagua & Casablanca Valleys)*

Chardonnay Cuvée Alexandre Apalta Vineyard—Casablanca Valley ♀ $$$ A refined wine with nuances of vanilla, buttered toast, butterscotch, and tropical fruit flavors along with well-integrated oak. This nicely balanced, layered wine should drink well during its first 4 years of life.

Merlot Cuvée Alexandre Apalta Vineyard—Colchagua Valley ♟ $$$ This Merlot has an attractive nose of black currant, blueberry, vanilla, and clove. The wine has good weight on the palate with layers of black fruits and a firm structure. Drink it during its first 6 years of life.

Cabernet Sauvignon Cuvée Alexandre Apalta Vineyard— Colchagua Valley ♟ $$$ Similarly styled but with the focus on black currants. It has enough structure to evolve for 2–3 years in the bottle and will drink well during its first 8 years of life.

FRANÇOIS LURTON *(Mendoza)*

Chardonnay Reserva ♀ $ The Chardonnay has aromas and flavors of poached pear and apple. Round and easygoing, the wine is nicely balanced for drinking during its first 2 years.

Gran Lurton Corte Friulano ♀ $$ A unique white wine, the Gran Lurton Corte Friulano is a blend of 70% Tokay Friulano, 20% Pinot Gris, 8% Chardonnay, and 2% Torrontés. It has a fragrant bouquet of spring flowers, lemon zest, and a hint of tangerine leading to a smooth-textured wine with vibrant acidity, complex flavors, some elegance, and a lengthy finish.

Gran Lurton—Uco Valley ♟ $$$ A blend of 80% Cabernet Sauvignon and 20% Malbec, this wine's nose reveals smoke, tobacco, blackberry, and black currant leading to a wine with an elegant personality, tasty red and black fruit flavors, and a lengthy, fruit-filled finish.

Malbec Reserva ♟ $ This wine offers up a fragrant bouquet of cedar, spice box, and black cherry followed by a forward, smooth-textured wine with plenty of cassis and black fruit flavors and a lengthy finish.

Pinot Gris ♀ $ The Pinot Gris has an enticing bouquet of orange peel, tangerine, and white peach. On the palate it exhibits finesse, crisp flavors, good balance, and a fruit-filled finish.

LAMADRID *(Vista Alba)*

Malbec Gran Reserva ♀ $$ This wine has an excellent nose of spice box, mineral, black cherry, and blueberry. It has excellent richness and depth and superior length for its price point.

Malbec Reserva ♀ $ A spicy, black cherry–scented perfume leads to a chunky wine with good depth, savory flavors, excellent balance, and a pure finish.

MAIP *(Mendoza)*

Bonarda ♀ $ The Bonarda offers an enticing bouquet of smoke, mineral, and blueberry. Round and ripe on the palate, it has surprising depth and length for its humble price.

Cabernet Sauvignon ♀ $ The nose offers up pure black currants and blackberry with some earth notes in the background. The wine is slightly austere on the palate but is likely to round out with another year or two in the bottle.

Malbec ♀ $ The Malbec has a striking perfume of violets, black cherry, and black raspberry. Exhibiting surprising complexity for its price category, the wine has gobs of fruit, savory flavors, and excellent depth and length. It is an outstanding value for drinking its first 3–4 years.

Sauvignon Blanc ♀ $ The Sauvignon Blanc has a grassy citrus nose leading to a crisp wine with grapefruit and lemon-lime flavors. It should be drunk during its first 12–18 months.

Torrontés—Salta ♀ $ The Torrontés exhibits a fragrant, floral, honey-accented perfume followed by a dry wine with a smooth texture and ripe flavors.

MAPEMA *(Various Regions)*

Malbec—Mendoza ♀ $$$ The Malbec has an attractive nose of cedar, spice box, and black cherry. On the palate it is claret-like, with an elegant personality and ripe, racy flavors.

Sauvignon Blanc—Tupungato ♀ $ Offers an enticing perfume of fresh herbs, grapefruit, and lemon-lime leading to a medium-bodied, smooth-textured wine with plenty of citrus flavor balanced by bright acidity.

MASI *(Tupungato)*

Passo Doble Corbec ♟ $$ The Passo Doble Corbec has an excellent bouquet of jammy black cherry and blackberry liqueur. Forward and easygoing, this tasty effort should drink well for several years and pair well with southern Italian cuisine.

BODEGA MONTEVIEJO *(Uco Valley)*

Lindaflor Chardonnay ♀ $$$ This wine has an attractive bouquet of toast, butterscotch, apple, poached pear, and pineapple. Full bodied and smooth textured, it has plenty of ripe fruit, excellent concentration, and balancing acidity.

Petite Fleur ♟ $$$ A blend of Malbec, Cabernet Sauvignon, Merlot, and Syrah, it offers a superb nose of smoke, spice box, mineral, violets, cassis, black currants, and black cherry. This is followed by a wine with layers of savory fruit, spicy flavors, and a 45-second finish.

FINCA LAS MORAS *(San Juan)*

Malbec Black Label ♟ $$ Offers a fragrant black cherry bouquet, a smooth texture, forward fruit, and good balance. This easygoing wine will drink well over the next 4 years.

Shiraz Black Label ♟ $$ Exhibits enticing meaty, gamy notes along with wild blueberries. The flavors are tasty but the wine is a bit compact in the finish.

NIETO SENETINER *(Mendoza)*

Bonarda Reserva ♟ $$ The nose delivers wood smoke, mineral, earth notes, blueberry, and blackberry. Dense and layered, the wine has impeccable balance and a plethora of fruit. Lively acidity gives the finish a vibrant lift. Drink this brilliantly rendered Bonarda from 2012 to 2025.

Chardonnay-Viognier 🍷 $ The Chardonnay (60%)–Viognier (40%) offers up notes of tangerine, peach, and assorted white fruits. On its dry, fleshy palate mineral and spice elements emerge, leading to a moderately long, fruit-filled finish.

Don Nicanor Blend 🍷 $ The blend is composed of equal parts Malbec, Cabernet Sauvignon, and Merlot. It exhibits an enticing perfume of cassis, black cherry, and black currant leading to a succulent wine with 1–2 years of aging potential and a pure finish.

Don Nicanor Malbec 🍷 $ The nose reveals spicy blue fruits, black cherry, and floral aromas followed by a forward, flavorful, supple-textured wine with gobs of savory fruit and excellent length. It lacks only complexity, but at this price, who's complaining?

BODEGA NORTON *(Mendoza)*

Cabernet Sauvignon Reserve 🍷 $$ The Cabernet Sauvignon Reserve is dark ruby colored, with a nose of cedar, spice box, cassis, black currants, and blackberry. Slightly austere on the palate, it nevertheless has attractive flavors, decent balance, and a medium-long finish.

Malbec Reserve 🍷 $$ Exhibits a bouquet of smoke, spice box, violet, and black cherry. On the palate it has layers of spicy black fruit flavors, excellent depth, and a lengthy, fruit-filled finish.

Merlot Reserve 🍷 $$ Dark ruby colored, with an attractive nose of cedar, earth notes, cassis, and black currant. This leads to a forward wine with an easygoing personality designed for near-term drinking.

BODEGA NQN *(Patagonia)*

Malbec Lonko 🍷 $$ Offers aromas of cedar, spice box, a hint of violets, cola, and black cherry. Medium bodied with a touch of elegance, the wine has solid depth, savory flavors, and enough structure to evolve for 1–2 years.

Malbec Picada 15 🍷 $ The Malbec Picada 15 (a vineyard designation) is dark ruby colored, with a spicy black cherry and black raspberry perfume. This is followed by a medium-bodied, easygoing wine with ample fruit and no hard edges.

OBVIO *(Mendoza)*

Malbec ♟ $ The Obvio Malbec is dark ruby colored, with a pleasant nose of violets, a hint of mineral, and cherry. Forward and easygoing on the palate, this tasty Malbec is an excellent value meant for drinking during its first 2–3 years.

BODEGA POESIA *(Mendoza)*

Pasodoble ♟ $$ Pasodoble is a blend of Malbec, Syrah, Bonarda, and Cabernet Sauvignon. The nose reveals cedar, spice box, pepper, blueberry, and black cherry. On the palate, the wine has plenty of spicy, savory fruit, good balance, and a forward personality.

EL PORTILLO *(Mendoza)*

Chardonnay ♀ $ The unoaked Chardonnay is a straightforward effort delivering plenty of crisp, apple-flavored fruit. It should be consumed within 2 years of purchase.

Malbec ♟ $ The Malbec is supple, easygoing, and uncomplicated, offering a nice mouthful of black cherry–flavored fruit for drinking during its first 2–3 years.

Merlot ♟ $ The Merlot has surprising depth and concentration for a wine of its humble price. It offers plenty of cassis- and cherry-flavored fruit meant for near-term drinking.

Pinot Noir ♟ $ The Pinot Noir's nose reveals rose petal, raspberry, and strawberry aromas. Light on the palate but tasty, it is a fine value in Pinot Noir for enjoying during its first 1–2 years.

Sauvignon Blanc ♀ $ The light-straw-colored Sauvignon Blanc offers aromas of citrus, herbs, and a hint of tropical fruit. Smooth-textured, ripe, and clean, it will deliver pleasant drinking during its first 12–18 months.

EL PORVENIR DE LOS ANDES *(Cafayate)*

Laborum Torrontés ♀ $ This wine has an alluring bouquet of spring flowers, honey, lychee nuts, apricot, and pineapple. Concentrated and dry on the palate, it reveals lots of spice and layered fruit. It would be a great match for sushi and empanadas.

LA POSTA *(Mendoza)*

Bonarda Estela Armando Vineyard 🍷 **$$** Reveals an alluring nose of spice box, cedar, plum, and blueberry. This is followed by a round, easygoing, forward Bonarda with good length and no hard edges.

Malbec Angel Paulucci Vineyard 🍷 **$$** Delivers aromas of spice box, mineral, and black cherry, leading to a medium-bodied, elegant wine with savory, spicy flavors, good depth and balance, and a lengthy, pure finish.

Malbec Pizzella Family Vineyard 🍷 **$$** Exhibits an attractive perfume of cedar, leather, cinnamon, pepper, and black cherry. Medium bodied with good grip and depth, this round, savory effort has enough structure to evolve for 1–2 years.

PRODIGO *(Uco Valley)*

Malbec Classico 🍷 **$** The Malbec reveals aromas of plums and cherries leading to a ripe, forward, surprisingly rich wine for its humble price. Nicely balanced and lengthy, it can be enjoyed over the next 4 years.

Malbec Reserva 🍷 **$$** The Malbec Reserva has an enticing bouquet of cedar, tobacco, earth notes, black cherry, and spice box. It is more structured than the Classico, with 2–3 years of aging potential.

LA PUERTA *(La Rioja)*

Reserva Bonarda 🍷 **$$** The Bonarda delivers notes of spicy black fruits and damp earth in its attractive nose. This is followed by a medium- to full-bodied wine with ample ripe black fruit, savory flavors, good depth, and enough ripe tannin to hold the wine for several years.

Reserva Malbec 🍷 **$$** The Malbec has a spicy bouquet of black cherry and violet. On the palate it is full bodied, ripe, and chewy. What it lacks in complexity it makes up for in a pure mouthful of tasty fruit. Drink this easygoing, friendly effort during its first 4 years.

QUARA *(Cafayate)*

Cabernet Sauvignon 🍷 $ The Cabernet Sauvignon reveals slightly herbal-accented cassis aromas, soft fruit with surprising depth, and good balance and length.

Malbec 🍷 $ The Malbec offers a spicy, black cherry–scented nose, sweet fruit, no hard edges, and a friendly personality. This nicely balanced wine will drink well during its first 3 years.

BODEGA RENACER *(Mendoza)*

Punto Final Malbec Reserva 🍷 $ This Malbec is dark ruby colored, with an attractive nose of cedar and black cherry. Medium- to full-bodied, the wine has plenty of savory flavor, density, and excellent length.

FINCA EL RETIRO *(Mendoza)*

Bonarda Barrica 🍷 $ The Bonarda Barrica exhibits an attractive nose of spice box, blueberry, and blackberry. On the palate there is plenty of vibrant fruit, savory flavors, and an easygoing personality. Drink this tasty, well-balanced effort during its first 3 years.

Malbec Barrica 🍷 $ Offers a nice mouthful of mineral and black cherry flavors, good balance, and moderate length for near-term enjoyment.

Malbec Reserva Especial 🍷 $$ This wine raises the bar. It's considerably more expressive, with plenty of peppery, spicy black fruit aromas leaping from the glass. It possesses enough structure to evolve for 2–3 years but can be enjoyed now.

Syrah Barrica 🍷 $ Meaty, peppery, blueberry, and violet aromas emerge from the glass, leading to a richly flavored, forward, satisfying wine lacking only complexity. At this price, who's complaining? Drink it during its first 4 years.

Tempranillo Reserva Especial 🍷 $$ The Tempranillo Reserva Especial has plenty of black cherry and blackberry scents. On the palate it has gobs of ripe fruit and a pure finish.

RJ VIÑEDOS *(Uco Valley)*

Grand Bonarda Joffré e Hijas 🍷 $ This Bonarda offers up a spicy blue fruit bouquet leading to an easygoing, smooth-textured wine with plenty of uncomplicated, chewy fruit.

Malbec Reserva Joffré e Hijas 🍷 $$ This Malbec offers a bit more structure and complexity than its younger sibling but not as much pure pleasure. It will evolve for 1–2 years and can be enjoyed over the next 6 years.

Pasión 4 Malbec 🍷 $ The Pasión 4 Malbec exhibits an expressive, smoky nose accompanied by earth notes, violet, and black cherry. The wine has remarkable depth and concentration for its humble price and a lengthy, sweet finish.

ALFREDO ROCA *(San Rafael)*

Chenin Blanc 🍷 $ The Chenin Blanc offers up a pleasant nose of melon and floral notes leading to a smooth-textured, easygoing Chenin with decent acidity and modest length. Drink during its first 12–18 months.

Malbec-Merlot 🍷 $ The Malbec-Merlot has aromas of spice box, cassis, black cherry, and violet. This is followed by a medium-bodied wine with spicy, savory flavors, good balance, and a fruit-filled finish.

BODEGA RUCA MALÉN *(Mendoza)*

Cabernet Sauvignon Lujan de Cuyo 🍷 $$ Dark crimson colored, it exhibits an attractive nose of cedar, black currant, and cassis. This leads to a medium-bodied, elegant wine with ample spicy, ripe black fruits; good depth; and a medium-long finish.

Malbec 🍷 $$ The Malbec offers up aromas of cedar, smoke, blueberry, and black cherry, leading to an elegant expression of Malbec with light tannin, excellent balance, and 1–2 years of aging potential.

FELIPE RUTINI *(Tupungato)*

Cabernet Sauvignon 🍷 $$$ The Cabernet Sauvignon surrenders aromas of cedar, damp earth, cassis, and black currant, leading to an elegantly styled wine owing more to Bordeaux than California.

Smooth-textured and flavorful, it possesses enough ripe tannin to evolve for a year or two. This well-balanced effort offers a 6-year drinking window.

Chardonnay ♀ $$$ The Chardonnay exhibits an attractive perfume of mineral, pear, apple, and a hint of tropical fruits. This leads to a medium-bodied, smooth-textured wine with lively acidity, excellent flavors, and good balance.

Encuentro ♀ $$$ Is a blend of Malbec and Merlot. The nose exhibits a hint of green olives as well as black currant and blackberry. This leads to a structured wine with tannin to resolve, decent flavors, and moderate length.

Malbec ♀ $$$ The purple-colored Malbec emits scents of cedar, tobacco, blueberry, and black raspberry, leading to a firm, slightly muted wine. The flavors are savory and it has good grip but the finish is slightly compact. Consume it over the near term.

SALENTEIN *(Mendoza)*

Cabernet Sauvignon Reserva ♀ $$ This Cabernet exhibits a fragrant bouquet of cedar, tobacco, cassis, and black currant. On the palate spice notes emerge along with plenty of savory fruit. Elegantly styled and well-balanced, it will drink well for another 6–8 years.

Malbec Reserva ♀ $$ The Malbec Reserva offers up a bouquet of wood smoke, pencil lead, mineral, violet, and black cherry. Medium- to full-bodied, the wine has plenty of ripe fruit, enough structure to evolve for 2–3 years, and excellent balance.

Merlot Reserva ♀ $$ The Merlot Reserva is dark ruby colored, with an enticing perfume of spice box, cedar, cassis, and cherry. Although a bit lean on the palate, it still exhibits tasty flavors and good balance. Drink it over the next several years.

Pinot Noir Reserva ♀ $$ The medium-ruby-colored Pinot Noir Reserva offers an alluring nose of raspberry, cherry, and rose petal. This leads to a velvety-textured wine with ripe flavors, good depth, and enough structure to last for several more years.

BODEGAS SANTA ANA *(Maipu)*

Casa de Campo Cabernet Sauvignon Reserve 🍷 **$** The Cabernet Sauvignon delivers an attractive nose of smoke, lead pencil, cassis, and black currant. This leads to a wine with ripe red and black fruit flavors, excellent balance, and a forward personality.

Casa de Campo Malbec-Shiraz Reserve 🍷 **$** The Malbec (70%)–Shiraz (30%) Reserve exhibits an alluring bouquet of cedar, spice box, earth notes, blueberry, and black cherry followed by a wine with superb depth for its humble price, layers of flavor, and a fruit-filled finish. It may well evolve for a few years but there is no need to defer your gratification.

BENVENUTO DE LA SERNA *(Uco valley)*

Blend 🍷 **$$$** The purple-colored Blend is 60% Malbec and 40% Merlot. The bouquet of spice box, cedar, black cherry, and red currant is enticing, leading to a firm wine with attractive, spicy flavors and 1–2 years of aging potential.

SERRERA *(Mendoza)*

Malbec Perdriel 🍷 **$** The Malbec Perdriel exhibits an enticing perfume of cedar, earth notes, black cherry, and black raspberry. On the palate it is medium bodied with excellent depth of flavor, plenty of spicy fruit, and a lengthy, fruit-filled finish.

Serrera Syrah Tupungato 🍷 **$** The Syrah reveals an attractive blueberry-scented nose followed by a medium-bodied, smooth-textured, ripe, savory wine with excellent balance and good length.

FINCA SOPHENIA *(Tupungato)*

Cabernet Sauvignon Reserve 🍷 **$$** Presents an attractive nose of cedar, mineral, black currant, and blackberry. This elegantly styled wine offers ample sweet fruit, spicy black fruit flavors, good balance, and a medium-long finish.

Malbec Reserve 🍷 **$$** The Malbec Reserve presents a primary perfume of wild blueberry, blackberry, and black cherry leading to a layered, savory wine with complex flavors and enough light tannin to support 2 years of further evolution.

SUR DE LOS ANDES *(Mendoza)*

Bonarda ♦ $ The unoaked Bonarda has aromas of blueberry and blackberry. Medium bodied and substantial on the palate, it offers up plenty of spicy black fruits, excellent balance, and pure flavors.

Malbec ♦ $ The Malbec exhibits a nose of cedar, spice box, and black cherry. This leads to a forward, easygoing wine with savory fruit, good balance, and a fruity finish.

Malbec Reserva ♦ $$ The Malbec Reserva has an attractive perfume of cedar, spice box, leather, and black cherry. This is followed by a wine with good depth and concentration, savory flavors, and a pure finish.

Torrontés—Cafayate ♦ $ Medium straw colored, with an enticing perfume of spring flowers, honey, spice, and pit fruits. On the palate it is smooth textured, dry, and savory with ripe fruit, good balance, and a medium-long finish. Drink this wine during its first 12–18 months.

BODEGA TAPIZ *(Mendoza)*

Tapiz Cabernet Sauvignon ♦ $ The Tapiz Cabernet Sauvignon offers good Cabernet aromas and flavors in a slightly lean, racy style.

Tapiz Malbec ♦ $ The Tapiz Malbec offers greater depth and richness in its friendly personality and will deliver pleasure for at least its first 4 years.

Tapiz Syrah ♦ $ The Tapiz Syrah delivers an excellent bouquet of smoke, meat, game, and blueberry. Smooth textured with good depth of flavor, this friendly Syrah can be enjoyed now and its first 4 years.

Zolo Malbec ♦ $ The Zolo Malbec delivers a pleasant nose of violets and black cherry leading to a smooth textured, easygoing, tasty wine with plenty of up-front fruit and a spicy finish.

Zolo Reserve Cabernet Sauvignon ♦ $$ The nose gives up toasty oak scents along with mineral, spice box, and black currant. Medium bodied, on the palate it has savory flavors, moderate depth and concentration, good balance, and a fruit-filled finish.

Zolo Reserve Malbec 🍷 $$ The Zolo Reserve Malbec reveals an enticing aromatic array of wood smoke, spice box, violet, blueberry, and black cherry. On the palate it is firm, structured, and well balanced, with all components in harmony.

TERRAZAS DE LOS ANDES *(Mendoza)*

Malbec 🍷 $ The purple-colored Malbec offers a fragrant nose of black cherry and violets. This leads to a forward, ripe, fruity wine with savory flavors, good concentration, and a pleasing personality.

Malbec Reserva Vistalba 🍷 $$ The Malbec Reserva delivers more sophisticated aromatics, including cedar, spice box, violets, blueberry, and black cherry. On the palate it is smooth textured, mouth coating, and firmer than its less expensive sibling.

TIKAL *(Mendoza)*

Patriota 🍷 $$$ The Patriota is a blend of 60% Bonarda and 40% Malbec. It offers an alluring bouquet of spice box, black cherry, and blueberry. It is supple and flavorful on the palate, and additional notes of raspberry and chocolate emerge, accompanied by a complex, rich wine with good structure and length. It way overdelivers for its modest price.

TILIA *(Mendoza)*

Cabernet Sauvignon 🍷 $ The Cabernet Sauvignon is a bit lean but nevertheless possesses very good, spicy flavors and decent length.

Chardonnay 🍸 $ The Chardonnay offers a surprisingly complex bouquet of spring flowers, apple, pear, and tropical fruits. Made in a straightforward style with ripe, tasty flavors, it is ideal for drinking during its first 12–18 months.

Malbec 🍷 $ My favorite of the Tilia wines is the purple-colored Malbec. The nose reveals plenty of black cherry and black raspberry fruit, and it is medium bodied with a bit of structure.

Malbec-Syrah 🍷 $ The Malbec-Syrah has an attractive nose of black cherry and blueberry with a good core of fruit, a supple texture, and no hard edges.

Merlot 🍷 $ The Merlot reveals spicy red fruit aromas and flavors, purity, and excellent depth.

TITTARELLI *(Mendoza)*

Bonarda Reserva de Familia 🍷 $ This Bonarda exhibits a very good nose of toasty, smoky blueberry and blackberry that jumps from the glass. Medium bodied, on the palate it has vibrant acidity, gobs of black fruit flavor, surprising depth, and a lengthy finish.

TIZA *(Mendoza)*

Malbec El Ganador 🍷 $ Offers up an attractive nose of violet and black cherry. Supple, ripe, and easygoing on the palate, this excellent value has no hard edges.

Malbec Tiza 🍷 $$ The Tiza is more deeply colored with a bouquet of spice box, wood smoke, pencil lead, mineral, and black cherry. Layered, ripe, and intense, it conceals enough structure to evolve for 2–3 years.

MICHEL TORINO *(Cafayate)*

Don David Malbec 🍷 $$ Reveals notes of cedar, spice box, mineral, black cherry, and black raspberry in its pleasing nose. On the palate it offers elegance, spicy flavors, excellent balance, and a lengthy finish.

Don David Torrontés 🍷 $$ Offers up a superior bouquet of spring flowers, honey, and tropical aromas leading to a dry, elegant version of Torrontés. It has excellent balancing acidity, a smooth texture, and a lengthy finish. Torrontés does not get much better than this.

PASCUAL TOSO *(Mendoza)*

Malbec 🍷 $ The Malbec reveals an alluring nose of black cherry and blueberry, leading to a grapy, smooth-textured, forward wine with tons of flavor. It is an awesome value.

Syrah 🍷 $ The same can be said for the Syrah as for the Malbec. It presents intense blueberry and pepper aromas and flavors, a forward personality, and exceptional length for its humble price.

TRAPICHE *(Mendoza)*

Broquel Chardonnay—Mendoza ♟ $ The Broquel Chardonnay offers up toasty apple, pear, and tropical aromas leading to a medium-bodied, straightforward wine with lively acidity and moderate length.

Broquel Malbec—Agrelo and Uco Valleys ♟ $ The Broquel Malbec offers up aromas of smoke, mineral, spice box, blueberry, and black cherry notes. This is followed by a layered, spicy wine with excellent grip and depth, several years of aging potential, and a long, pure finish.

Broquel Torrontés—Cafayate ♟ $ A fragrant, floral-accented wine with crisp, refreshing acidity; dry, slightly tropical flavors with a hint of citrus; and a fruit-filled finish.

TRIVENTO *(Mendoza)*

Amado Sur ♟ $$ A blend of Malbec, Syrah, and Bonarda with an alluring perfume of blueberry, black currant, and black cherry, a touch of cedar, and a bit of damp earth. On the palate it is smooth textured, forward, and easy to understand.

Chardonnay Golden Reserve ♟ $$$ The Golden Reserve has an attractive nose of mineral, apple, and pear that jumps from the glass. This leads to a balanced, medium-bodied wine in which tropical fruits emerge, leading to a pure, fruit-filled finish.

Malbec Select ♟ $ The Malbec Select reveals aromas of blueberry and black cherry followed by a forward, easygoing wine with plenty of flavor and no hard edges. It is an excellent value and a pleasant introduction to the virtues of Malbec.

TRUMPETER *(Mendoza)*

Cabernet Sauvignon ♟ $ The Cabernet Sauvignon is a forward, tasty effort with cassis and black currant aromas, a supple texture, moderate depth, and good length.

Malbec ♟ $ The Malbec offers a pleasant nose of violet and black cherry leading to a forward, fruity, easygoing wine with plenty of flavor and a surprisingly long finish.

Malbec-Syrah 🍷 $ The Malbec-Syrah contains 50% of each variety. It reveals an excellent bouquet of smoke, earth, blueberry, and black cherry. Soft, forward, and tasty, this ripe crowd-pleaser can be enjoyed during its first 3 years.

VALENTIN BIANCHI *(Mendoza)*

Cabernet Sauvignon 🍷 $$ The Valentin Bianchi Cabernet Sauvignon emits aromas of cedar, spice box, tobacco, red currant, and black currant. It makes a firm entry onto the palate with ample savory fruit, good balance, and enough structure to evolve for 1–2 years.

Chardonnay Famiglia Bianchi 🍷 $$ This Chardonnay exhibits toasty tropical aromas leading to a smooth-textured, vibrant wine with lively acidity and good balance. Drink this tasty effort during its first 1–2 years.

Syrah Elsa Bianchi 🍷 $ The bargain-priced Elsa Bianchi Syrah delivers plenty of up-front blueberry and peppery flavors in an easy-to-understand package.

VENTUS *(Patagonia)*

Cabernet-Malbec 🍷 $ The Cabernet-Malbec reveals aromas of cedar, tobacco, cassis, and cherry leading to a forward, balanced wine with good depth, ripe flavors, and solid length.

Chardonnay 🍷 $ The unoaked Chardonnay delivers a fine perfume of white peach, pear, and a hint of tropicals. Smooth textured and forward, it will provide pleasure during its first 2 years.

Malbec 🍷 $ This Malbec exhibits aromas of cedar, tobacco, spice box, and black cherry. Focused and forward on the palate, it has a good layering of sweet fruit, savory flavors, good balance, and a pure, fruit-filled finish. It may well evolve for 1–2 years but can be enjoyed now.

Malbec-Syrah 🍷 $ The emphasis here is on black cherry and blueberry aromas and flavors in an easygoing package. This crowd-pleasing wine will perform well over its first 3 years.

VINITERRA *(Mendoza)*

Malbec 🍷 $ Viniterra's Malbec has an attractive nose of cedar, spice box, violets, and black cherry leading to a smooth-textured, easygoing wine with good concentration and depth.

Select Carmenere ♟ $$ The Select Carmenere is a pleasant effort with plenty of ripe cassis and blueberry fruit, a supple texture, and moderate length.

Select Malbec ♟ $$ This bottling is typically more structured and backward than the regular Malbec and will benefit from 1–2 years of additional aging after purchase.

BODEGA VISTALBA *(Mendoza)*

Corte C ♟ $ The Corte C is a blend of Malbec, Cabernet Sauvignon, and Bonarda. Surprisingly complex for its humble price, it has plenty of ripe fruit, a firm presence on the palate, good depth, and a medium-long finish.

Tomero Cabernet Sauvignon ♟ $ The Tomero Cabernet Sauvignon is a forward, sweetly fruited, tasty wine with plenty of cassis and currant fruit in a style meant for early drinking.

Tomero Malbec ♟ $ The Tomero Malbec emphasizes spicy black cherry aromas and flavors in its easygoing personality.

FAMILIA ZUCCARDI *(Mendoza)*

Cabernet Sauvignon Q ♟ $$ The Cabernet Sauvignon Q delivers earth notes, tobacco, spice box, and black currant. This leads to a medium-to full-bodied wine with good intensity and grip followed by a firm finish.

Chardonnay ♟ $$ The barrel-fermented Chardonnay has an attractive bouquet of vanilla, white peach, poached pear, and a hint of tropical fruits. This is followed by a smooth-textured, concentrated wine with excellent balance and a medium-long finish.

Malbec Q ♟ $$ The Malbec Q offers up notes of cedar, pencil lead, smoke, blueberry, and black cherry. Firm on the palate, the wine has plenty of savory, spicy fruit, good flavors, and an elegant personality.

Tempranillo ♟ $$ The dark-ruby-colored Tempranillo reveals aromas of smoke, mineral, violet, and blackberry. On the palate it offers lots of spicy black fruits, savory flavors, some elegance, and enough structure to evolve for 2–3 years.

AUSTRALIA

AUSTRALIAN WINE VALUES

by Dr. Jay Miller

You name it and the Australians no doubt grow it, make it into wine, blend it with something else, and give it an unusual name. And the good news is that much of it sells for less than $25 a bottle. The combination of quality and value that many Australian wines offer despite economic hard times and currency fluctuations is quite remarkable. Like California, and Alsace in France, Australia labels its wine after the grape (or grapes) from which it is made. All the major grapes are used here. While great wines are produced from most varietals, Syrah (called Shiraz in Australia) triumphs over all the others.

Regions

Adelaide Hills (South Australia): Located in southern Australia, this is a high-altitude, cooler-climate region. Chardonnay and Pinot Noir appear to be the varieties with the greatest promise.

Barossa Valley (South Australia): In southern Australia, this huge, well-known viticultural area north of Adelaide is the home of some of the quantitative titans of Australia's wine industry. It is the source for Australia's finest wines as well as some of its best values.

Clare Valley (South Australia): Located north of Adelaide and the Barossa Valley, this beautiful area is better known for its white than red wines. Some surprisingly fine Riesling emerges from this area.

Coonawarra (South Australia/Victoria): Coonawarra is among the most respected red wine–growing areas of Australia. It is situated in South Australia, west of the Goulburn Valley. Cabernet Sauvignon is the star here.

Heathcote (Central Victoria): Heathcote is well known for its Cambrian soils and deeply colored, rich Shiraz.

Margaret River (Western Australia): In the very southwestern tip of the country is the Margaret River viticultural zone. Australian wine experts claim that Australia's most European-style Cabernet Sauvignons and Chardonnays come from this area, which produces wines with higher natural acidities.

McLaren Vale (South Australia): Shiraz, Grenache, and Cabernet Sauvignon can be superb in this region located near Adelaide.

Yarra Valley (Victoria): This is Australia's most fashionable viticultural area, and its proponents argue that the climate and resulting wines come closest in spirit to those of Bordeaux and Burgundy in France. Pinot Noir and Chardonnay are the two most important grapes.

Vintage Smarts
Australia is a large and diverse country, making it difficult to generalize about vintages. Virtually all of the wines noted here come from the 2005, 2006, and 2007 vintages, with a sprinkling of 2008 white wines that do not require upbringing in oak barrels. These were all good to excellent vintages in South Australia and Victoria.

Drinking Curves
The vast majority of wines in the under-$25 category from Australia are meant to be drunk in their first few years of life. The notable exceptions are the Rieslings from Clare Valley, Eden Valley, and Western Australia. The best of these will reward several years of bottle aging and drink well for 10–12 years.

Australia's Top Wine Values by Winery
ANNIE'S LANE *(Clare Valley)*

Shiraz-Grenache-Mourvèdre Copper Trail 🍷 $$$ This SGM offers an expressive bouquet of cedar, spice box, earth notes, blueberry, and wild cherry. This easygoing, medium-bodied effort is nicely balanced with enough structure to evolve for 1–2 years and will drink well for 6–8 years.

D'ARENBERG *(McLaren Vale)*

The Broken Fishplate Sauvignon Blanc 🍷 $$

The Custodian Grenache 🍷 $$

d'Arry's Original Shiraz-Grenache 🍷 $$

The Dry Dam Riesling 🍷 $$

The Footbolt Shiraz 🍷 $$

The Hermit Crab 🍷 $$$

The High Trellis Cabernet Sauvignon 🍷 $$$

The Last Ditch Viognier 🍷 $$$

The Love Grass Shiraz 🍷 $$$

The Money Spider Roussanne 🍷 $$$

The Olive Grove Chardonnay 🍷 $$

The Stump Jump Red 🍷 $

The Stump Jump White 🍷 $

The d'Arenberg portfolio is loaded with values. The winery works with more than 140 growers to fashion their superb blends.

BALGOWNIE ESTATE *(Bendigo)*

Cabernet Sauvignon 🍷 $$$

Shiraz 🍷 $$$

Australian cognoscenti continue to regard Balgownie Estate as the leading winery in the thriving region of Bendigo.

BAROSSA VALLEY ESTATE *(Barossa)*

Chardonnay E Minor 🍷 $$ Offers green apple and pear aromas leading to a nicely balanced, smooth-textured wine with dry flavors, good acidity, and solid length. Drink it over 1–2 years following the vintage.

Shiraz E Minor 🍷 $$$ The Shiraz E Minor reveals a touch of cedar, blueberry, and black cherry. On the palate, pepper, spice notes, and plum and cherry flavors emerge. The wine has good depth, decent concentration, and moderate length.

JIM BARRY *(Clare Valley)*

The Cover Drive Cabernet Sauvignon 🍷 $$$

The Lodge Hill Riesling 🍷 $$$

The Lodge Hill Shiraz 🍷 $$$

In addition to making some of Australia's best (and most expensive) wines, Jim Barry also turns out several notable values.

ROLF BINDER *(Barossa)*

Cabernet Sauvignon–Merlot Halcyon ♥ $$$

Riesling Highness Eden Valley ♀ $$

Shiraz Hales ♥ $$$

Shiraz-Grenache Halliwell ♥ $$$

Shiraz-Malbec ♥ $$$

Viognier Veritas "Hovah" ♀ $$

Rolf Binder is one of Australia's leading vignerons. He works both as a consultant and as a winery owner. His single-vineyard Shiraz cuvées are among the most sought-after collectibles of Australia, but he takes just as much care with his less-expensive wines.

THE BLACK CHOOK *(McLaren Vale)*

Shiraz-Viognier ♥ $$ The Shiraz (96%)–Viognier (6%) is a crowd-pleaser, with the nose receiving an uplift from the Viognier component. Aromas of smoke, plum, and blueberry are enticing and lead to a full-bodied wine with a smooth texture, ripe flavors with depth, and a long finish.

Black Chook VMR ♀ $$ The VMR is composed of 80% Viognier and 10% each of Marsanne and Roussanne. It offers aromas of white peach and apricot followed by a medium-bodied wine with good depth, ripe fruit flavors, and a long, refreshing finish.

BLEASDALE VINEYARDS *(Langhorne Creek)*

Bremerview Shiraz ♥ $$$

Mulberry Tree Cabernet Sauvignon ♥ $$

Bleasdale has been a consistent overachiever through the years. Today it is one of the top wineries in the up-and-coming Langhorne Creek region.

BROKENWOOD *(Hunter Valley)*

Cricket Pitch White ♀ $$ A blend of 60% Sauvignon Blanc and 40% Sémillon. It offers up aromas of citrus, melon, and minerals leading to a crisp, dry wine with ripe flavors, good concentration, and a lengthy finish.

Sémillon ♀ $$ The Sémillon exhibits a bouquet of citrus, melon, and lemon sherbet. Crisp, intensely flavored, and long, it can be enjoyed over several years.

GRANT BURGE *(Barossa)*

Miamba Shiraz ♀ $$$ Grant Burge is a large winery that produces a decidedly mixed bag of wines. Occasionally they produce a real gem, such as their Miamba Shiraz.

CASCABEL *(McLaren Vale)*

Tipico ♀ $$$ Tipico is an estate-grown blend of Grenache, Shiraz, and Monastrell. It offers plenty of savory fruit, excellent depth, and a lengthy, pure finish.

CAT AMONGST THE PIGEONS *(Barossa)*

Cabernet Sauvignon ♀ $

Chardonnay ♀ $

Riesling ♀ $

Shiraz ♀ $

Shiraz-Cabernet ♀ $

Shiraz-Grenache ♀ $

Cat Amongst the Pigeons has followed up its brilliant debut with another fine set of wines. Two white wines have been added to the portfolio. The portfolio ranks among Australia's greatest wine values. They are all worth a try.

CHATEAU CHATEAU *(McLaren Vale)*

Skulls Red Wine ♀ $$ Chateau Chateau is a label created by importer Dan Philips and marketed under the R Wines umbrella. This is their entry-level Grenache and is highly recommended.

DE BORTOLI *(Yarra Valley)*

Chardonnay Vat 7 ♀ $

Petit Verdot Vat 4 ♀ $

Petite Sirah DB Selection ♀ $

Petite Sirah Vat 1 ♀ $

Pinot Noir Rosé ♀ $$$

Pinot Noir Vat 10 ♟ $

Shiraz Vat 8 ♟ $

Shiraz Vat 9 ♟ $

De Bortoli produces a substantial amount of wine (it has 4 winemaking facilities), but under the leadership of manager/winemaker Steve Webber this has not been a deterrent to high quality. The main winery facility, which I visited in September 2008, is located in the cooler climate of the Yarra Valley, where the focus is on Chardonnay and Pinot Noir. The value wines merit equal attention.

DEVIATION ROAD *(Adelaide Hills)*

Chardonnay ♀ $$$ The Chardonnay has an attractive nose of apple and pear, ripe flavors on the palate, good balance, and a fruit-filled finish.

Sauvignon Blanc ♀ $$$ Offers up a bouquet of fresh herbs, melon, citrus, and floral notes leading to a creamy, vibrant, intensely flavored Sauvignon with exceptional depth and length. It should be drunk within 2 years of the vintage.

DUTSCHKE *(Barossa)*

WillowBend ♟ $$$ WillowBend is a blend of Shiraz, Merlot, and Cabernet Sauvignon. Purple colored, it offers a fragrant bouquet of cedar, spice box, cassis, black cherry, and blueberry. Medium- to full-bodied on the palate, it has plenty of succulent fruit in its forward personality.

EARTHWORKS *(Barossa)*

Cabernet Sauvignon ♟ $$ An expressive nose of spice box and black currants leading to a medium-bodied, smooth-textured, easygoing wine with abundant sweet fruit, light tannin, and a long, fruit-filled finish.

Shiraz ♟ $$ The Shiraz exhibits aromas of smoke, sausage, bacon, and blueberry that jump from the glass. Medium-bodied, ripe, and sweet with no hard edges, it can be enjoyed for 4–6 years following the vintage.

FETISH *(Barossa)*

Playmates 🍷 **$$** The Playmates is a blend of Mataro and Grenache. It exhibits an attractive nose of underbrush, mineral, spice box, blueberry, blackberry, and a hint of chocolate. On the palate it has plenty of sweet blue and black fruit, succulent flavors, light tannin, and a lengthy finish.

Shiraz the Watcher 🍷 **$$$** The Shiraz the Watcher is all about pleasure. Uncomplicated but very flavorful, on the palate it exhibits loads of ripe blue and black fruits, an easygoing personality, and a seamless finish.

Viognier V Spot 🍷 **$$** Offers a nose of spring flowers, apricots, and white peach. On the palate it reveals a touch of oak, vibrant acidity, and racy flavors.

GLAETZER *(Barossa)*

The Wallace 🍷 **$$$** A blend of Shiraz and Grenache, this wine reveals a fragrant bouquet of cedar, scorched earth, pencil lead, black cherry, and blueberry. On the palate it has an elegant personality with racy, slightly tart fruit flavors, good concentration, and a silky finish.

HUGH HAMILTON *(McLaren Vale)*

The Rascal Shiraz 🍷 **$$$** The Rascal Shiraz reveals an attractive bouquet of smoked meat, blueberry, and blackberry. Layered on the palate, it has excellent depth and grip and enough structure to evolve for several years.

The Villain Cabernet Sauvignon 🍷 **$$$** The Villain Cabernet Sauvignon reveals notes of eucalyptus and black currant in its aromatics. On the palate it exhibits a racy style with good balance and moderate length.

RICHARD HAMILTON *(McLaren Vale)*

Gumprs Shiraz 🍷 **$$$** The Gumprs Shiraz, which contains 3% cofermented Viognier, exhibits a fragrant perfume of cedar, spice box, violets, blueberry, and blackberry. This medium-bodied Shiraz should be enjoyed through 2015.

ANDREW HARDY *(McLaren Vale)*

Little Ox Shiraz ♟ $$ Opaque purple in color with a superb nose of mineral, cedar, blackberry, and blueberry. Rich and layered, this Shiraz typically evolves for several years but can be enjoyed upon purchase.

HEGGIES *(Eden Valley)*

Chardonnay ♟ $$$ The Heggies Chardonnay has an excellent bouquet of toasty oak, mineral, pear, apple, and white peach. On the palate it is reminiscent of a midlevel white Burgundy in its medium-bodied style and elegance. Nicely balanced, it usually drinks well for several years.

HENSCHKE *(Adelaide Hills)*

Tilly's Vineyard ♟ $$$ A blend of Sémillon, Sauvignon Blanc, and Chardonnay. It offers up a fragrant nose of citrus and melon leading to a medium-bodied wine with complex flavors, good acidity, and a lengthy finish. In style, it could easily pass for a quality Pessac-Léognan from Bordeaux.

HEWITSON *(Adelaide Hills)*

Sauvignon Blanc LuLu ♟ $$ The Sauvignon Blanc LuLu offers a superb bouquet of melon, citrus, and mineral. That leads to a broad, full-flavored, intense Sauvignon for drinking over the 2 years following the vintage.

HOPE ESTATE *(Hunter Valley)*

Merlot ♟ $$

Shiraz ♟ $$

Shiraz-Malbec ♟ $$

Verdelho ♟ $$

Hope Estate offers some of the finer values coming out of Hunter Valley.

INNOCENT BYSTANDER *(Yarra Valley)*

Chardonnay ♀ $$

Pinot Gris ♀ $$

Pinot Noir ♀ $$

Innocent Bystander produces some of the better values coming out of the pricey Yarra Valley.

JIP JIP ROCKS *(Limestone Coast)*

Chardonnay ♀ $

Shiraz ♀ $$

Shiraz–Cabernet Sauvignon ♀ $$

These are well-made efforts that merit serious consumer attention. They are meant for near-term drinking, within 2–3 years of the vintage.

TREVOR JONES *(Barossa)*

Boots Grenache ♀ $$ Sourced from 65-year-old vines, this wine offers a lovely perfume of spice box, wild strawberries, and kirsch leading to a medium- to full-bodied, smooth-textured, tasty Grenache with layers of flavor and excellent length.

Boots Shiraz ♀ $$ Exhibits aromas of cedar, smoke, blueberry, and blackberry followed by a medium-bodied, lean, elegant wine with bright fruit and a slightly tart finish.

Virgin Chardonnay ♀ $$$ The Virgin receives no oak treatment. It offers an alluring bouquet of white peach, pear, and baked apple. Medium-bodied, with excellent concentration, the wine is mouth-filling, rich, and long in the finish.

KAESLER STONEHORSE *(Barossa)*

GSM ♀ $$$ The GSM is a blend of Grenache, Shiraz, and Mourvèdre with an attractive nose of cedar, spice box, earth notes, and black cherry. This leads to a forward, easygoing wine with savory red and blue fruit flavors, plenty of spice, and a silky finish.

Stonehorse Shiraz 🍷 $$$ This Shiraz emits an enticing aromatic array of balsam wood, spice box, blueberry, and black cherry. Dense and rich on the palate, it has the structure and fruit to evolve for 1–2 years following the vintage.

KOONOWLA *(Clare Valley)*

Riesling 🍷 $$ Exhibits floral notes, spice, poached pear, and lemon-lime aromas. On the palate it is medium bodied with superb concentration, vibrant acidity, and ripe flavors. In a good vintage it will evolve for 6–8 years and drink for 10–15 years.

KURTZ FAMILY VINEYARDS *(Barossa)*

Boundary Row GSM 🍷 $$$ Boundary Row GSM is a blend of Grenache, Shiraz, and Mourvèdre exhibiting an alluring bouquet of cedar, leather, earth notes, spice box, wild cherry, and blueberry. This leads to a mouth-filling wine that is layered, sweet, and expansive on the palate.

LANGMEIL *(Barossa)*

Shiraz-Viognier Hangin' Snakes 🍷 $$$ The purple-colored Shiraz (95%)–Viognier (5%) blend reveals aromas of violets, black cherry, and blueberry leading to a succulent, forward wine for drinking in its first 4 years.

LECONFIELD *(Coonawarra)*

Chardonnay 🍷 $$$ Leconfield's Chardonnay offers a nose of toasty oak, mineral, pear, and apple leading to a medium-bodied, elegant wine with a creamy texture and soft acidity. Nicely balanced, it should drink well for at least 4 years after the vintage.

LEEUWIN ESTATE *(Margaret River)*

Riesling Art Series 🍷 $$$

Siblings Shiraz 🍷 $$$

Leeuwin Estate is renowned for its (expensive) Art Series Chardonnay, but the rest of the portfolio is quite reasonably priced, and several of the offerings are superb values.

LENGS & COOTER (Clare Valley)

Riesling ♀ $$ Lengs & Cooter's Riesling has a fragrant perfume of
mineral, petrol, citrus, and honeysuckle. Dry and crisp on the palate,
slightly tart lemon-lime flavors emerge and lead to a moderately
long, refreshing finish. It will drink well for 3–4 years following the
vintage.

DE LISIO (McLaren Vale)

Quarterback ♀ $$ De Lisio's entry-level Quarterback is a blend of
Shiraz, Cabernet Sauvignon, Merlot, and Grenache. It offers serious
bang for the buck.

LONGWOOD (McLaren Vale)

The Shearer Shiraz ♀ $$ A spicy bouquet with notes of blueberry
and black cherry, followed by a medium- to full-bodied, smooth
Shiraz with ample ripe fruit; spicy, savory flavors; good balance; and
a fruit-filled finish.

MADCAP WINES (Barossa)

Cabernet Sauvignon ♀ $$ The Cabernet has an excellent perfume of
smoke, pencil lead, black currant, and blackberry. Supple and ripe on
the palate, the wine is nicely layered, full flavored, and well balanced.

Riesling ♀ $$ Madcap's Riesling is light straw colored, with an
expressive bouquet of mineral, lemon-lime, and melon. This is
followed by a dry, crisp wine with vibrant acidity, good concentration
and depth, some complexity, and a lengthy finish.

Shiraz Pastor Fritz ♀ $$ The Shiraz Pastor Fritz has aromas of
pencil lead, blueberry, and blackberry liqueur leading to a mouth-
filling, fruity, concentrated wine with gobs of flavor.

MAGPIE ESTATE (Barossa)

The Call Bag ♀ $$$ A blend of Mourvèdre and Grenache, this wine
has an enticing perfume of underbrush, mineral, wild cherry, and
blackberry leading to a glossy, ripe, intensely flavored wine with
enough structure to evolve for 2–3 years in a good vintage.

The Fakir Grenache ♥ $$$ The Fakir Grenache has a bouquet of earth, spice, and wild cherry elements. On the palate it has a velvety texture, plenty of ripe cherry-accented fruit, and a plush finish.

Salvation Gewurztraminer ♀ $$ The Salvation Gewurztraminer has a fragrant bouquet of baking spices, rose petals, and lychees. Crisp, ripe, and flavorful, it should be consumed with Asian cuisine.

The Magpie Estate wines are made by Rolf Binder.

MITOLO *(McLaren Vale)*

Jester Cabernet Sauvignon ♥ $$

Jester Shiraz ♥ $$

Jester Sangiovese Rosé ♀ $

The Mitolo wines are made by the talented Ben Glaetzer. The Jester label is the entry level for this high-quality portfolio.

MOLLYDOOKER *(McLaren Vale)*

The Boxer Shiraz ♥ $$$

The Maître D' Cabernet Sauvignon ♥ $$$

The Scooter Merlot ♥ $$$

Two Left Feet ♥ $$$

The Violinist Verdelho ♀ $$

Mollydooker is the label of the renowned winemaking team of Sarah and Sparky Marquis. These are among the greatest red wine values anywhere and should not be missed.

MR. RIGGS *(McLaren Vale)*

Shiraz the Gaffer ♥ $$$ The nose of the Shiraz the Gaffer reveals wood smoke, spice box, pencil lead, mineral, and blueberry. Structured on the palate, it typically requires 2–3 years to unwind and fill out in the finish.

GREG NORMAN ESTATES *(Eden Valley)*

Chardonnay ♟ $ Greg Norman's Chardonnay is made in the popular style exemplified by Kendall-Jackson. The nose offers some oak notes and aromas of white peach and pear. This leads to a smooth-textured wine with an excellent layering of apple and pit-fruit flavors with a hint of tropical fruits in the background.

OXFORD LANDING *(South Australia)*

Chardonnay ♟ $

Oxford Landing Merlot ♟ $

Oxford Landing Sauvignon Blanc ♟ $

Massive quantities of Oxford Landing are produced and usually steeply discounted. In the scheme of things, amongst much mediocrity, they offer solid value.

PENFOLDS *(South Australia)*

Bin 28 Kalimna Shiraz ♟ $

Bin 51 Riesling ♟ $$

Koonunga Hills Shiraz–Cabernet Sauvignon ♟ $$

Thomas Hyland Cabernet Sauvignon ♟ $

Thomas Hyland Chardonnay ♟ $

Penfolds is a giant producer that makes good-quality wines from the top to the bottom of the portfolio. The value wines are often heavily discounted and can offer significant value.

PENLEY ESTATE *(Coonawarra)*

Cabernet Sauvignon Phoenix ♟ $$

Cabernet Sauvignon–Shiraz ♟ $$

Merlot Gryphon ♟ $$

Shiraz Hyland ♟ $$

Penley Estate is a candidate (along with Majella) for top producer in the prestigious region of Coonawarra. Their top-end wines are superb, while these value-priced offerings are nearly as good. They are remarkable values.

PEWSEY VALE *(Eden Valley)*

Dry Riesling 🍷 $$ Pewsey Vale's Dry Riesling is light straw colored, with an alluring bouquet of honeysuckle, citrus, and apple. Medium bodied, with crisp, ripe, succulent fruit and buttressing acidity, this dry, tasty effort is capable of evolving for 3–4 years.

Prima Riesling 🍷 $$ The Prima Riesling is made in a slightly less dry style. It has an outstanding aromatic array of petrol, spring flowers, mineral, and citrus. Light bodied and semisweet, there is more than enough acidity to provide balance and a structure for further development in the bottle.

PIKE & JOYCE *(Adelaide Hills)*

Pinot Noir 🍷 $$$ The Pinot Noir has a reticent red cherry and raspberry perfume. This is followed by a forward, easygoing Pinot with ample fruit, good balance, and an elegant personality.

Sauvignon Blanc 🍷 $$ The Sauvignon Blanc offers an attractive bouquet of mineral and grapefruit leading to a smooth-textured wine with ripe citrus and melon flavors, lively acidity, and a crisp finish. Drink this Loire-styled Sauvignon within 1–2 years of the vintage.

PIKES *(Clare Valley)*

The Assemblage 🍷 $$$

Dry Riesling 🍷 $$$

Luccio 🍷 $

The Red Mullet 🍷 $$

Shiraz Eastside 🍷 $$$

Pikes is one of the top producers of the Clare Valley, known for their elegant style of winemaking. Although all of their wines are good, their particular specialty is ageworthy Riesling.

PILLAR BOX *(Padthaway)*

Red 🍷 $ The Pillar Box Red is a blend of Shiraz, Cabernet Sauvignon, and Merlot. It exhibits an expressive nose of spice box, earth notes, blueberry, and black currant. Ripe, sweet, and layered, this nicely rendered red has exceptional balance and length for its humble price.

Reserve Shiraz 🍷 $$ The Pillar Box Reserve Shiraz delivers an enticing nose of cedar, spice notes, violet, black currant, and blueberry. On the palate the wine is full bodied, plush, and layered, with notes of clove, briar patch, and road tar making an appearance. Round and velvety on the palate with excellent length, it can be enjoyed now but will evolve for several years.

White 🍷 $ Pillar Box White is a blend of Sauvignon Blanc, Verdelho, and Chardonnay. It offers up a fragrant bouquet of lime, grapefruit, and kiwi with a touch of fresh herbs. On the palate hints of pineapple and other tropical fruits emerge. This smooth-textured, crisp, refreshing wine overdelivers in a big way.

R WINES (South Australia)

R Wines encompasses four familiar labels—Marquis Philips, 3 Rings, Roogle, and Bitch—along with several others created especially for R Wines. Needless to say, the packaging of these wines is amazingly creative, but, more important, what is in the bottle consistently over-delivers from low end to high end.

Bon-Bon Rosé 🍷 $ Bon-Bon Rosé is made from 100% Shiraz. Medium pink, it exhibits fragrant aromas of strawberry and rhubarb. Barely off-dry and crisp, there is ample ripe fruit and a long, refreshing finish.

(Little) r Cabernet Sauvignon 🍷 $$ The (Little) r Cabernet Sauvignon has an expressive perfume of cedar, smoke, tar, and black currants. Ripe and layered on the palate, it has a medium- to full-bodied, fruit-driven personality with plenty of spicy black fruits, excellent depth, and a lengthy finish.

R Ose Rosé of Cabernet Sauvignon 🍷 $$ A 100% Cabernet Sauvignon rosé from McLaren Vale. It has a fragrant perfume of wild strawberries and cherries. Savory on the palate, it has very good depth and a long, pure finish.

Evil Cabernet Sauvignon 🍷 $ The Evil Cabernet Sauvignon reveals a fragrant bouquet of cedar and black currants. Fruit driven, full bodied, with tons of flavor, this Cabernet is an exceptional value.

Pure Evil Chardonnay 🍷 $ The Pure Evil Chardonnay has an attractive perfume of butterscotch, spice box, baked apple, and poached pear, more like the nose of a wine three times the price. It delivers intense, ripe, spicy flavors buttressed by good acidity and a long finish.

Bitch Grenache ♟ $ Bitch Grenache presents an alluring bouquet of earth, smoke, cherry, and strawberry. Supple, sweet, and tasty, this wine totally overdelivers for its humble price.

Roogle Red ♟ $ Roogle Red is composed of Shiraz, Merlot, and Cabernet Sauvignon. It offers attractive aromas of cedar, cassis, blueberry, and plum. Plush and fruit-driven on the palate, this is a ripe, tasty wine for casual quaffing with burgers and pizza.

Roogle Riesling ♟ $ The Riesling has a lovely perfume of mineral, spring flowers, and honeysuckle with a hint of tropical fruits in the background. Just off-dry, round, and intensely flavored, this is very sexy Riesling at a great price.

Roogle Rosé ♟ $ The Rosé has a fragrant perfume of pink grapefruit, strawberry, and rhubarb. Fleshy and intense on the palate, with excellent balance and length, this is a terrific value in rosé that overdelivers for its humble price.

Roogle Shiraz ♟ $ The Shiraz offers up a big whiff of cedar, blueberry, blackberry, and chocolate aromas. Full bodied, ripe, and sweet, it has enough structure to improve for 2–3 years in the bottle, but who is going to defer their gratification?

Marquis Philips Cabernet Sauvignon ♟ $$ The Cabernet Sauvignon offers aromas of cedar, spice box, plum, black currant, and blackberry. Full bodied, with spicy black fruit flavors, there is enough structure to support 2–3 years of additional bottle aging.

Marquis Philips Holly's Blend ♟ $$ The Holly's Blend is 90% Verdelho and 10% Chardonnay. It exhibits a fragrant bouquet of citrus, melon, lemon-lime, and a hint of tropical fruits in the background leading to a wine with plenty of ripe flavors balanced by crisp acidity.

Marquis Philips Sarah's Blend ♟ $$ Composed of 60% Shiraz, 28% Cabernet Sauvignon, and the balance Merlot and Cabernet Franc. It yields a complex aromatic array of cedar, spice box, clove, pepper, cassis, and blueberry. Full bodied, fruit driven, and intensely flavored, this layered blend has a 45-second finish.

Marquis Philips Shiraz 🍷 $$ The nose offers up fragrant aromas of cedar, smoke, tar, blueberry, and blackberry liqueur. Full bodied, opulent, and structured, this intense, well-balanced Shiraz will evolve for 2–3 years.

Marquis Philips Shiraz Tabla 🍷 $$ The Shiraz Tabla has a splendid aromatic profile of cedar, tobacco, smoke, saddle leather, and blueberry compote. Mouth filling, full bodied, and fruit driven, this Shiraz is ultrarich, intense, and very long.

Boarding Pass Shiraz 🍷 $$ The Boarding Pass Shiraz is very expressive, with a nose of smoke, spice box, blackberry, and blueberry jam. Layered, supple textured, sweet, and full bodied, this seamless, crowd-pleasing wine offers a remarkably long finish for its humble price.

Strong Arms Shiraz 🍷 $ The Strong Arms Shiraz has a nose of cedar, spice box, and blueberry. Fruit driven, supple textured, rich, and easygoing, the wine has remarkable class for its giveaway price.

Luchador Shiraz 🍷 $$ This Shiraz features first-class aromas of spice box, cedar, mocha, lavender, and blueberry. Velvety textured, fruit driven, and intense, the wine has excellent depth of flavor and a long finish.

Chris Ringland Cote Rotie Shiraz 🍷 $$ The Chris Ringland Shiraz delivers a brooding nose of cedar, tar, smoke, licorice, blueberry, and blackberry. Full bodied and massive, particularly for a wine in this price category, it offers succulent, savory fruit, great depth, and a 60-second finish.

Suxx Shiraz 🍷 $$ The Suxx Shiraz offers an expressive bouquet of espresso, mocha, licorice, blueberry, and blackberry liqueur. It is full bodied and voluptuous in the mouth, and all components are well integrated. Ripe and sweet with a blanket of soft tannins, the wine will evolve for 2–3 years but can be enjoyed now.

3 Rings Shiraz 🍷 $$ The 3 Rings Shiraz offers aromas of cedar, spice box, violet, blueberry, and blackberry. This leads to a surprisingly elegant wine with well-integrated tannin. This hedonistic effort will evolve for 3–5 years but can be enjoyed now.

CORRINA RAYMENT *(McLaren Vale)*

Shiraz Revolution 🍷 $$$ The Shiraz Revolution has a complex perfume of earth, mineral, sausage, game, truffle, and blueberry that borders on kinky. This leads to a full-bodied, plush, sweet, dense wine with exquisite balance and length.

Viognier Revolution 🥂 $$$ The Viognier Revolution has a very expressive aromatic array of mineral, peach, apricot, and mango. Medium bodied, it is smoothly textured with round, ripe, layered flavors, outstanding depth, and a long, fruit-filled finish.

REILLY'S *(Clare Valley)*

Dry Land Shiraz 🍷 $$$ Reilly's Dry Land Shiraz delivers a superb bouquet of smoke, game, bacon, espresso, and blueberry leading to a full-bodied, plush wine with layers of succulent fruit; savory, ripe flavors; outstanding integration of all components; and a lengthy, pure finish.

Barking Mad Cabernet Sauvignon 🍷 $$

Barking Mad Riesling 🥂 $$

Barking Mad Sparkling Shiraz 🥂 $$$

Barking Mad Shiraz 🍷 $$

The Barking Mad wines are favorably priced and offer exceptional value.

ROCKBARE *(McLaren Vale)*

Shiraz 🍷 $$ The Rockbare Shiraz's nose reveals scorched earth, smoke, espresso, blueberry, and blackberry. This leads to a full-bodied wine with gobs of black fruit flavors, excellent depth and concentration, and a long, pure finish.

ROSEMOUNT ESTATE *(Coonawarra)*

Cabernet Sauvignon Show Reserve 🍷 $$$ The Cabernet Sauvignon Show Reserve reveals an enticing bouquet of cedar, pencil lead, spice box, black currant, and blackberry with a hint of eucalyptus in the background. On the palate there are layers of savory flavor, good depth and concentration, and enough ripe tannin to evolve for 3–4 years.

ROSEMOUNT ESTATE *(Hunter Valley)*

Chardonnay Show Reserve ♉ $$$ Offers up aromas of toasty oak, pear, and caramel. This leads to a smooth-textured wine with pit-fruit notes, a hint of minerality, and poached pear flavors. Medium bodied and restrained, it is a pleasant offering meant for drinking 1–2 years following the vintage.

ST. MARY'S *(Limestone Coast)*

House Block Cabernet Sauvignon ♉ $$$

Shiraz ♉ $$$

The tiny St. Mary's winery is literally within spitting distance of the Coonawarra demarcation line, and its omission is a political hot potato. Be that as it may, proprietor-vigneron Barry Mulligan is making wine on par with most of the wineries in Coonawarra. The fact that the winery falls inches outside of the more prestigious Coonawarra region (technically they must be labeled with the more generic Limestone Coast) brings the price down to value level. Do not overlook them.

SHOTTESBROOKE *(Adelaide Hills)*

Sauvignon Blanc ♉ $$$ Shottesbrooke's Sauvignon Blanc delivers a fragrant bouquet of sage, baking spices, melon, gooseberry, and grapefruit leading to a crisp, dry wine with vibrant acidity and lingering, fruity flavors. Drink it within 12–18 months of the vintage.

SHOTTESBROOKE *(McLaren Vale)*

Shiraz ♉ $$$ The alluring nose reveals wood smoke, spice box, leather, game, and blueberry. On the palate the fruit has a slightly exotic wild-berry character, excellent depth, and an overall sexy personality.

SOLITARY VINEYARDS *(Clare Valley)*

Riesling ♉ $$$ The Riesling is sourced from the dry-grown Khileyre Vineyards in the Watervale region of Clare Valley, one of Australia's prime sites for this variety. It has a fragrant perfume of mineral, spring flowers, citrus, and lemon-lime followed by a dry, crisp, tightly wound, balanced Riesling that can evolve for at least 3–4 years and drink well for a decade.

SYLVAN SPRINGS *(McLaren Vale)*

Shiraz 🍷 $$ Sylvan Springs Shiraz has a pleasant perfume of cedar, pepper, and blueberry. Medium bodied on the palate, it is a straightforward wine with savory flavors, good balance, and a medium-long finish.

Hard Yards Shiraz 🍷 $$ The Hard Yards Shiraz offers more aromatic interest with its notes of cedar, spice box, mineral, game, and blueberry. Smooth textured on the palate, it has layers of sweet fruit, incipient complexity, fine balance, and a fruit-filled finish.

TAIT *(Barossa)*

The Ball Buster 🍷 $$ Tait has established a well-deserved reputation for full-blown, pleasure-filled wines. The Ball Buster is a blend of Shiraz, Cabernet Sauvignon, and Merlot with a nose of cedar, leather, spice box, and blueberry that leaps from the glass. This is followed by a plush, full-bodied wine with gobs of flavor and superior length.

THORN-CLARKE *(Barossa)*

Shotfire Cabernet Sauvignon 🍷 $$$ The Cabernet Sauvignon offers up a fragrant bouquet of cedar, spice box, earth notes, black currant, and blackberry. Bordering on opulent, it has gobs of savory black fruit, excellent balance, and a fruit-filled finish.

Shotfire Shiraz 🍷 $$$ The Shotfire Shiraz has a nose of wood smoke, bacon, mineral, and blueberry that leaps from the glass. Rich and intense on the palate, it has layers of flavor, excellent balance, and a pure finish. It way overdelivers for its humble price.

Milton Park Riesling 🍷 $

Milton Park Shiraz 🍷 $

Milton Park Chardonnay 🍷 $

Terra Barossa Cuvée 🍷 $$

Terra Barossa Merlot 🍷 $$

Terra Barossa Shiraz 🍷 $$

Terra Barossa Chardonnay 🍷 $$

The Milton Park and Terra Barossa wines are Thorn-Clarke's entry-level wines and they all offer superb value.

TORBRECK VINTNERS *(Barossa)*

Cuvée Juveniles ♟ **$$** The Cuvée Juveniles, a blend of Grenache, Mataró, and Shiraz, has a fragrant nose of black cherry and wild blueberry. Elegant and friendly on the palate with plenty of succulent blue and black fruits, it will provide pleasure over the 4 years following the vintage.

Woodcutter's Sémillon ♟ **$$** Offers up an enticing nose of mineral, candle wax, melon, and citrus. Creamy textured, balanced, and lengthy, this tasty effort should be drunk over the 2 years following the vintage.

Woodcutter's Shiraz ♟ **$$$** The Woodcutter's Shiraz reveals aromas of earth, spice, and blueberry in a straightforward, full-flavored style.

TSCHARKE *(Barossa)*

The Master Montepulciano ♟ **$$$** The Master Montepulciano offers up an intriguing nose of wood smoke, pencil lead, mulberry, and blueberry. Full bodied and structured on the palate, it has plenty of ripe, tasty fruit for enjoying during its first 4 years.

The Curse ♟ **$$$** The Curse is 100% Zinfandel from estate vineyards. It reveals briary, brambly black raspberry and black cherry aromas followed by a full bodied, velvety-textured wine with gobs of forward, sweet fruit, excellent balance, and good length.

Girl Talk ♟ **$$** Girl Talk is 100% Albariño. It exhibits aromas of mineral, spring flowers, citrus, and lemon meringue. This is followed by a full-flavored wine with lively acidity and a lengthy finish.

Only Son ♟ **$$** The Only Son is a blend of 70% Tempranillo and 30% Graciano. It offers a smoky bouquet of black currant and blackberry. Full bodied, the wine is ripe and sweet on the palate with a slightly roasted character and plenty of black fruit flavor interest.

VASSE FELIX *(Margaret River)*

Chardonnay ♉ **$$$** The Vasse Felix Chardonnay exhibits aromas of white peach, pear, and tropical notes. This is followed by a medium-bodied wine with ample ripe fruit, good balance, and a long, pure, fruit-filled finish. Drink it over the 2–3 years following the vintage.

WATER WHEEL *(Bendigo)*

Cabernet Sauvignon ♉ **$$**

Memsie Red ♉ **$**

Memsie White ♉ **$**

Shiraz ♉ **$$**

Water Wheel, located in the thriving region of Bendigo, consistently overdelivers on its superb quartet of wine values.

WINNER'S TANK *(Langhorne Creek)*

Shiraz ♉ **$$** A perennial best buy. It has a wonderfully expressive perfume of plum, black cherry, and blueberry compote. This leads to a full-bodied, seamless, rich wine with a long, pure finish. This is an ideal everyday wine worth buying by the case.

Shiraz Velvet Sledgehammer ♉ **$$$** The slightly more expensive Shiraz Velvet Sledgehammer exhibits smoky notes as well as plum, blueberry, and blackberry liqueur. It has a bit more depth and length than the "regular" bottling as well as several years of aging potential.

WOLF BLASS *(Adelaide Hills)*

Shiraz-Viognier Gold Label ♉ **$$$** The Shiraz-Viognier has a fragrant bouquet of violet, white pepper, ginger, cassis, and blueberry leading to a full-flavored, opulent wine with a silky texture and a forward personality. Sweet, ripe, and intense, with a long, pure finish, this pleasure-bent effort is capable of evolving for 1–2 years but can be enjoyed now.

Chardonnay Gold Label ♉ **$$$** The aromatics reveal notes of toasty oak, grapefruit, nectarine, and poached pear. Medium bodied on the palate, the wine is creamy textured, with solid depth and plenty of ripe fruit. Nicely balanced, it will provide pleasure during its first 2–3 years.

WOLF BLASS *(Barossa)*

Shiraz Gold Label ♀ $$$ The Shiraz Gold Label exhibits aromas of cedar, earth notes, spice box, blueberry, and blackberry. Layered on the palate, with enough stuffing to evolve for 2–3 years, the wine will drink well for 6–8 years after the vintage.

WOLF BLASS *(Coonawarra)*

Cabernet Sauvignon Gold Label ♀ $$$ This Cabernet from Coonawarra is a bit herbaceous aromatically but ripe and layered on the palate. Blackberry, black currant, and chocolate notes emerge, leading to a lengthy, fruit-filled finish. In a good year it will evolve for 1–2 years and drink well for a decade.

WOLF BLASS *(Eden Valley)*

Riesling Gold Label ♀ $$$ The Riesling's nose gives up notes of spring flowers, lime, green apple, and nutmeg. Crisp and dry on the palate with vibrant lemon-lime and citrus flavors, the wine is well balanced, firm, and long.

WOOP WOOP *(South Australia)*

Cabernet ♀ $ The Cabernet has an expressive bouquet of plum and black currant. With plenty of body, layered sweet fruit, and soft tannins, this is as good an entry-level Cabernet as you are likely to find.

Shiraz ♀ $ The Shiraz offers up a spicy, black fruit–scented nose followed by a succulent, savory wine with gobs of flavor and excellent balance.

"V" ♀ $ 100% Verdelho with a fragrant perfume of white peach, melon, and tangerine. In the mouth guava and other tropical flavors emerge. The wine is nicely balanced and has good length.

YALUMBA *(Barossa)*

Cabernet Sauvignon–Shiraz the Scribbler ♀ $$ This Cabernet Sauvignon–Shiraz has an attractive perfume of spice box, violet, black currant, cassis, and blackberry. Layered and ripe on the palate, it has plenty of savory fruit, good structure, and a medium-long finish.

Grenache Bush Vines 🍷 $$ The Grenache Bush Vines is medium ruby colored, with aromas of rose petal and cherry. Ripe and easygoing on the palate, it delivers plenty of savory fruit and a medium-long finish.

YALUMBA *(Eden Valley)*

Chardonnay Wild Ferment 🍷 $$ The Chardonnay Wild Ferment is medium straw colored, with toasty, tropical aromas. Medium bodied, the wine has a creamy texture, ripe fruit flavors, good balance, and a lengthy finish.

YALUMBA *(South Australia)*

Organic Shiraz 🍷 $$ The Organic Shiraz exhibits an enticing nose of wood smoke, violet, meat, game, and blueberry. This leads to a medium- to full-bodied, layered wine with spicy black cherry and blueberry flavors.

Y Series Riesling 🍷 $ The Riesling has an alluring perfume of mineral, spring flowers, and citrus. Nicely balanced with a lengthy, crisp finish, it will provide pleasure during its first 5 years.

Y Series Sauvignon Blanc 🍷 $ The Sauvignon Blanc has an attractive nose of citrus and gooseberry. On the palate the wine is dry, with lively acidity and ripe fruit providing balance.

Y Series Shiraz-Viognier 🍷 $ The Shiraz (94%)–Viognier (6%) has an enticing perfume of violets, spice box, and blueberry. This leads to a medium-bodied wine with a smooth texture, sweet fruit, good depth and concentration, and a fruit-filled finish.

ZONTE'S FOOTSTEP *(South Australia)*

Shiraz-Viognier 🍷 $$ The Shiraz-Viognier has an alluring, slightly kinky nose of wild blueberries, smoked sausage, and bacon. This is followed by a ripe, seamless, easy-to-understand wine with a lengthy, fruit-filled finish.

Verdelho 🍷 $$ Offers aromas of minerals and fruit salad leading to a wine with crisp, slightly tart, melon-like flavors, good balance, and a medium-long close.

Viognier 🍷 $$ The Viognier exhibits aromas of spring flowers, peach, and apricot. On the palate it has a smooth texture, ripe flavors, adequate acidity, and a fruity finish.

AUSTRIA

AUSTRIAN WINE VALUES

by David Schildknecht

Old-World Traditions and New-World Mentality

Austria's rise to international vinous stardom has accumulated momentum over the course of a quarter century, and few consumers who take time to sample this country's diverse and distinctive wines—many from grape varieties unfamiliar elsewhere, and many in styles unknown before the mid-1980s—will come away wondering why all the fuss or without adding one or another sort of Austrian wine to their home repertoire. Success abroad has been accompanied by an intensification of what was already arguably Europe's most enthusiastic wine culture. This has driven up prices for some wines, it's true, but a thirsty local populace also ensures that Austria remains an incredibly fertile source of value.

Grapes

Most Austrian wine is dry and white. The country's best-known viticultural ambassador is the variety **Grüner Veltliner**, which accounts for a third of vine acreage. The range of aromas and flavors of which Grüner Veltliner is capable is utterly striking, including lentil, green bean, snap pea, cress, beetroot, rhubarb, roasted red pepper, zucchini, tobacco, white and black pepper, fresh citrus, citrus zest, iris, nutmeg, caramel, and peach. There are two other notable gustatory features of this grape: its tactile, signature "bite"—a pleasant astringency that often segues into faintly sizzling notes of pepper—and its ability to achieve satisfying ripeness of flavor and harmonious completeness (albeit in distinctly different styles) at anywhere from 10.5% to 15.5% alcohol. **Riesling** is without question number two in importance among Austria's white grapes. The best specimens can hold their own with any wines from this grape, and fortunately there are numerous outstanding and highly affordable examples as well (although they are generally pricier, even if no more complex or delicious, than a corresponding Grüner Veltliner). Austrian excellence is demonstrated with a host of other white grapes too: internationally well-known ones like **Sauvignon Blanc, Pinot Gris** (Grauburgunder), or **Chardonnay** (here sometimes called Morillon); less familiar grapes like **Pinot Blanc** (Weissburgunder) or **Muskateller**; and indigenous and internationally unknown grapes like **Neuburger, Roter Veltliner**, or **Zierfandler**. In the south and east of Austria—as in most of Central Europe (under various names)—**Welschriesling** is ubiquitous and generally generates wines of simple refreshment.

Until relatively late in the last century, most Austrian wines were blends, but wine from a single grape and labeled with its name is now the norm. That applies, too, to the increasing acreage of diverse red grapes, although some are blends. The most exciting red wine potential accrues to another grape little grown or known outside of Austria, the black-fruited, nuanced, and site-sensitive **Blaufränkisch**. But the indigenous **Zweigelt** is a particularly good source of value. **Pinot Noir** (Blauer Spätburgunder) and its offspring fellow Austrian variety **St. Laurent** make up in intrigue for what (at least as yet) they lack in sheer acreage. **Cabernet Sauvignon** and **Merlot** are used in blends and sometimes solo, though increasingly less often nowadays. The eastern edge of Austria also has a proud tradition of nobly sweet wines, and the quality of the best of these (most notably from the hands of the late Alois Kracher) has been instrumental in the rise of the country's fortunes in world wine markets. The labors and selectivity associated with top-notch botrytis or ice wine, however, precludes these from meriting further mention within the price parameters of this guide.

Regions

Austria's vineyard area can be viewed as two great arms with Vienna (an official growing region in its own right) as the hub. To the north and west of the capital, the dominant grape is Grüner Veltliner, and virtually all of Austria's Riesling grows there, too. Clustered around Krems, a 45-minute drive west along the Danube from Vienna, are no fewer than five growing regions: the **Wachau, Kremstal, Kamptal, Traisental**, and **Wagram**. Of these, the Wachau, with its steep riverside terraces of so-called *Urgestein* (primordial rock), is the most prestigious (and pricey), but parts of the Kremstal downstream have exceptional potential too. And few places on earth render more diverse, superb wines growing in a wider variety of soils and microclimates than the Kamptal, localized around the town of Langenlois.

The growing pattern and wine character in each of these Danubian regions is influenced by the alternation of warm air from the Hungarian Plain funneling up the river each day and cold air from Austria's deep, mountainous forests and sub-Alps descending at night. Unique names are employed in the Wachau for dry wines of varying alcoholic strength and richness: Steinfeder, Federspiel, and Smaragd, this last named for the emerald-green lizards that sun themselves on rocky ledges even as the grapes ripen well into November or later. In neighboring regions one frequently sees the word "reserve" used to designate riper and fuller whites. In addition to *Urgestein* of volcanic origins, loess, the ocher-colored glacial dust of the last Ice Age, plays a major role in the propagation of Grüner Veltliner, especially in the Wagram and neighboring parts of the Kremstal. Sporadic but important viticultural outposts extend to the Czech and Slovakian borders in the vast arc known as the **Weinviertel,** dominated by Grüner Veltliner and an outstanding source of value.

The grape-growing metropolis of **Vienna** itself mirrors the transition from Danube-dominated viticulture in its hilly northwestern suburbs to warmer and more red wine–friendly microclimates in the south, which segue into the so-called **Thermenregion.** Red wine dominates in the **Carnuntum** region along the Danube east of Vienna. South along the entire length of the Hungarian frontier lies Burgenland (officially split into four growing regions: **Neusiedlersee, Neusiedlersee-Hügelland, Mittelburgenland**, and **Südburgenland**), whose climate is influenced by the juxtaposition of hills and the Pannonian Plain, as well as by a single, geographically anomalous, broad and shallow lake, near whose shores are grown most of Austria's important nobly sweet wines. Red wines dominate Burgenland, but the dry whites here are proving increasingly exciting, too. Along the Slovenian frontier in Austria's southeast lies **Styria** (Steiermark, officially consisting of three subregions), whose steep, undulating hills harbor a diverse and distinctive cast of dry white wines, headed by Sauvignon Blanc. Lighter, pungently refreshing whites rendered with little or no oak are called "Klassik" here and represent the sole Styrian category that falls within the price parameters of this guide.

Vintage Smarts

Austrian growers are assiduously working to adapt to any climatic challenges and ensure a ready supply in white or red of refreshing and crisp as well as rich and ample wines, but some years favor one or the other of these stylistic poles. Vintages 2004, 2007, and 2008 offer lots of refreshment, crispness, cut, and buoyancy, while 2005 and especially 2006 tend toward impressive volume, opulence, even power. Relish the refreshment offered by the aforementioned trio of vintages, but take advantage of a year like 2006 to buy wines that excel above their normal weight (and price) class, since ordinarily the wines featured most often in this guide (from the Wachau, for example, wines of the class Federpiel) are those in the lighter, 11.5–12.5% alcohol range. The red wines of Burgenland and nearby Carnuntum were challenged by cool, rainy early autumn weather in 2005, so approach with caution. Conditions were better in 2004 and 2007, promoting a high rate of success, while 2006 was virtually ideal for steady ripening, resulting in arguably the finest red wine vintage in the history of Austria's wine renaissance.

Drinking Curves

Even less expensive Rieslings and Grüner Veltliners can sometimes reward bottle aging. As a rule of thumb, the lightest and least expensive should be enjoyed within 2–3 years of harvest; single-vineyard and comparable special bottlings will generally hold up well to—and often truly reward—4–6 years in the bottle, the Grüner Veltliners (and occasionally the Pinot Blancs) more so than the Rieslings. The potential for Blaufränkisch has proven to be impressive, with wines that can be held for at least a half dozen years. The typical Zweigelt, St. Laurent, or blend mentioned in this guide is best enjoyed within 2–3 years, since the forte of those wines (at least in low-price brackets) is their sheer fruit.

Austria's Top Wine Values by Winery

PAUL ACHS *(Burgenland [Neusiedlersee-Hügelland])*

Blaufränkisch ♟ $$$ Loaded with black fruits, relatively full and firm, this basic bottling consistently delivers several years of satisfaction.

K. ALPHART *(Thermenregion)*

Veltliner & Co. ♟ $$ A blend of Grüner Veltliner with Neuburger and Welschriesling, this offers a mouthful of flowers, citrus, and greens, finishing with fascinatingly mineral savor and crunchy refreshment.

KURT ANGERER *(Kamptal)*

Grüner Veltliner Friesenrock ♀ $$$ Reflecting its loess origins in a display of lentil, herbs, clover, green bean, citrus zest, and chalk dust, this is creamily rich and consistently succulent.

Grüner Veltliner Kies ♀ $$ As wry and exuberant as its producer, if somewhat rough-hewn, this brims with flowers, citrus, and herbs and utterly belies its alcoholic fullness with a sense of finishing verve and lift.

BÄUERL *(Wachau)*

Grüner Veltliner Smaragd Pichl Point ♀ $$$ Johann Bäuerl of Joching (who, like an eponymous Wachau grower in Oberloiben, utilizes no first name on his label) offers here heady, ripe concentration of citrus and tropical fruits; volume with invigorating pungency; and rare value for such a prestigious region.

JUDITH BECK *(Burgenland [Neusiedlersee])*

Blaufränkisch ♥ $$ A, tart, black fruit–laden, subtly herbal and spicy introduction to the charms of Blaufränkisch.

E. & M. BERGER *(Kremstal)*

Grüner Veltliner ♀ $ From broad loess terraces that sit back from the Danube just east of Krems, this amazingly inexpensive basic liter bottling is a tartly invigorating and downright irresistible "refrigerator white."

Grüner Veltliner Lössterrassen ♀ $$$ Offering lentil, herbs, and suggestions of mineral salts, this puts the "grün" in Grüner Veltliner and will prove especially welcome drunk young with such wine-challenging fare as fresh tomatoes, asparagus, or garden greens.

WILLI BRÜNDLMAYER *(Kamptal)*

Grüner Veltliner Kamptaler Terrassen ♀ $$$ A combination of ripeness and polish with herbal, vegetable, and mineral interest reflects this wine's geologically and microclimatically diverse origins, as well as the talents of one of Austria's most celebrated vintners.

Riesling Kamptaler Terrassen ♀ $$$ This snappy, vivacious, adamantly dry Riesling will prove hugely versatile, though it only hints at the profundity of Bründlmayer's single-site bottlings.

EBNER-EBENAUER *(Weinviertel)*

Grüner ♀ $ This new wine from a talented young couple offers refreshingly citric, crisply vegetal, and invigoratingly mineral expressions of Weinviertel typicity at an amazing price.

ECKER (ECKHOF) *(Wagram)*

Grüner Veltliner Steinberg ♀ $$$ Here's a perfect introduction to this grape: light to the touch, whistle-clean, and refreshing, but generously filling the mouth with flavors of fresh green beans, lentil, and citrus.

Zweigelt Brillant ♀ $$ A classic introduction to Austria's best-known indigenous crossing and most widely planted red wine grape, this delivers intense aromas and sappy, palate-saturating flavors of ripe black cherry tinged with bitter notes of cherry pit and hints of herbs and humus.

BIRGIT EICHINGER *(Kamptal)*

Grüner Veltliner Wechselberg ♀ $$$ This typically offers a rich, relatively full-bodied example of its variety, loaded with pit fruits and herbs, but the site's high elevation helps lend refreshment and refinement.

FREIE WEINGÄRTNER (DOMÄNE WACHAU) *(Wachau)*

Grüner Veltliner Federspiel Terrassen ♀ $$ The generic wines labeled "Domäne Wachau" offer classic expressions of their grapes, region, and styles, as well as proof that a huge grower co-op can achieve excellence. Fresh green bean, snap pea, cress, rhubarb, lime, lentil, and white pepper are among the components in this extract-rich and texturally satisfying yet always lively and pungent value. (The corresponding Grüner Veltliner Smaragd can sometimes be found for not too much more money and should then not be missed.)

Riesling Federspiel Terrassen ♀ $$$ Here is a combination of floral aromatics, tactile citrus and mineral elements, bracing refreshment, and sheer finishing grip that can only be coaxed from this grape in a few Austrian regions, and not usually at such a low a price.

FRITSCH (*Wagram*)

Grüner Veltliner Windspiel ♀ $$ This "play of the wind"—from an estate better known for its serious reds—is indeed a breath of fresh, palate-cleansing, herbal and citric Grüner Veltliner virtues.

WALTER GLATZER (*Carnuntum*)

Blaufränkisch ♀ $$ Expect pepper and spice accenting tart black fruits and roasted meats, with a satisfyingly fine-grained tannic "chew" and considerable depth for its modest price.

Grüner Veltliner Dornenvogel ♀ $$ Tending toward the freshly-ground-pepper and fresh-green-vegetable side of its variety, this is satisfyingly juicy but quite powerful and pungent.

St. Laurent ♀ $$$ Representing one of the most modestly priced wines among excellent renditions of this indigenous grape, this offers soothingly mouth-coating black cherry and blueberry fruit with hints of smoked meats.

Weissburgunder Klassic ♀ $$ Versatile, vivacious, and refreshing variation on the too often unsung virtues of Pinot Blanc.

Zweigelt Riedencuvée ♀ $$ Tartly black fruited and spicy, but with a treble brightness and sappy, pure-fruited intensity typical of its grape.

SCHLOSS GOBELSBURG (*Kamptal*)

Grüner Veltliner Gobelsburger ♀ $$ Based on purchased fruit, this wine represents a consistently astonishing value, offering pungent citrus, herb, mineral, and spice in a delicate yet palpable extract-rich form.

Riesling Gobelsburger ♀ $$$ While less exciting than the corresponding Grüner Veltliner, this wine's combination of bright, focused intensity with light weight and complete dryness is still a winner.

STIFT GÖTTWEIG *(Kremstal)*

Rosé Messwein ♆ $$ An improbably delicious pink Pinot Noir from a newly revived monastic estate and local landmark.

GROSS *(Styria)*

Gelber Muskateller Steierische Klassik ♆ $$$ Low-toned richness and breadth are characteristic Gross virtues, and even with its satisfying herbal and citrus-zest pungency this is surprisingly gentle for its genre.

SCHLOSS HALBTURN *(Burgenland [Neusiedlersee])*

Koenigsegg Velt.1 ♆ $ This presents Grüner Veltliner at its most citric, lime-like, and bright—unadorned, simple, but infectious, and with pungent herbs and citrus zest, as well as considerable substance for its pittance of a price.

GERNOT HEINRICH *(Burgenland [Neusiedlersee])*

Blaufränkisch ♟ $$$ This is a model for its variety and region that smells and tastes of deeply rich black fruits and roasted meats accented by pepper and manages to flatteringly combine creaminess of texture with brightness of sappy, palate-staining fruit.

J. HEINRICH *(Mittelburgenland)*

Blaufränkisch ♟ $$ This early-bottled Blaufränkisch offers ripe black fruits with peaty, smoky, and saline inflections, fine-grained tannins, and a sappy, generous finish.

HIEDLER *(Kamptal)*

Grüner Veltliner Loess ♆ $$ An irresistible value from a master of its grape variety, this boasts a creamy yet delicate palate and fascinatingly diverse, refined persistence.

HIRSCH *(Kamptal)*

Grüner Veltliner #1 ♆ $$ Dynamo and innovator Johannes Hirsch's "intro-level" wine offers a satisfyingly juicy amalgam of citrus, cress, sweet pea, and lentil. (His single-vineyard offerings are some of the least expensive among Austria's top wines.)

H. & M. HOFER *(Weinviertel)*

Grüner Veltliner ♀ **$** This irresistible refrigerator white bottled in liters—from a neighborhood that oil derricks share with the vines—is full of green beans, fresh lime, and pepper, and represents a ridiculous value.

Grüner Veltliner Freiberg ♀ **$$$** Redolent of fresh lime, ginger, nutmeg, flowers, lentils, and pungent herbs, this sappy, bright Grüner clings with lip-smacking intensity yet buoyant refreshment.

Riesling ♀ **$$$** Loaded with floral aromas, citric, bright, brisk, and with an invigoratingly nippy bit of bitterness in the finish, this is what three generations of Austrian drinkers would call classic Riesling.

Zweigelt Rosé ♀ **$$** This deliciously confirms the experience of Austrian wine growers from Krems to the Neusiedlersee, namely that their best-known indigenous red crossing can taste more than merely pretty in pink. Brimming with sour cherry and rhubarb, it offers tart, thirst-quenching refreshment with an invigorating seasoning of cress, salt, and white pepper.

JOSEF HÖGL *(Wachau)*

Grüner Veltliner Federspiel Schön ♀ **$$$** Floral, sleek, pungently smoky, and briskly citric, this very treble wine really gets you salivating. (Other Federspiel bottlings from Högl, too, are unusually low-priced, high-quality exemplars of the Wachau.)

MARKUS HUBER *(Traisental)*

Grüner Veltliner Alte Setzen ♀ **$$$** This bottling from an ambitious young grower is satisfyingly juicy yet incipiently creamy, typically featuring beetroot, snap pea, red berry, citrus, herbs, and spices.

JURTSCHITSCH (SONNHOF) *(Kamptal)*

GrüVe ♀ **$** The three Jurtschitsch brothers—pioneers in the return to organic viticulture and tireless crusaders for the image of their region—bottle one of the U.S. market's least expensive and most often encountered Grüner Veltliners, garishly labeled but peppery, herbal, and satisfyingly refreshing.

Grüner Veltliner Loiserberg ♀ $$$ A versatile and serious value; lentil, citrus, herb, and orchard fruit filled.

KRACHER (WEINLAUBENHOF) *(Burgenland [Neusiedlersee])*

Pinot Gris ♀ $$ The dry Pinot Gris from this estate renowned for its nobly sweet wines exudes ripe melon and peach accented by smoky, meaty notes and is silky smooth, subtly creamy, and consistently refreshing.

LACKNER-TINNACHER *(Styria)*

Welschriesling Klassik ♀ $$$ A delightful introduction to a Styrian staple that is seldom seen stateside, this offers pineapple, flowers, and herbs in a refreshing, surprisingly silken-textured, sappily persistent manner.

PAUL LEHRNER *([Mittel]burgenland)*

Blaufränkisch Gfanger ♥ $$$ This exudes vividly ripe purple plum and blackberry; hints at brown spices, black pepper, cocoa, and saline, stony minerality; and finishes clear and vividly fresh, with no gummy sweetness, extraneous woodiness, or noticeable alcohol.

Claus ♥ $$$ Lehrner's versatile blend of Zweigelt and Blaufränkisch mingles black raspberry, plum, and smoky oriental tobacco and offers a bit of tannic chew en route to a lip-smacking, resinous, sappy finish.

LETH *(Wagram)*

Grüner Veltliner Brunnthal ♀ $$$ Displays considerable richness, density, and length, with lentil and diverse herbs often allied to an alluring suggestion of red fruits.

Grüner Veltliner Scheiben ♀ $$$ Palpably extract-rich and lushly textured, this offers an amalgam of pit fruits and citrus (often blood orange), along with a striking sense of peppery, saline, mineral pungency that signals Leth's best site.

Grüner Veltliner Steinagrund ♀ $$ Surprisingly lush for an entry-level bottling, this offers tart rhubarb, bitter citrus rind, pepper, and a satisfyingly refreshing finish.

LOIMER *(Kamptal)*

Grüner Veltliner Kamptal ♀ $$$ Offers modest body with plenty of herb, legume, fruit, and vegetable flavors, finishing with peppery pungency.

Lois ♀ $$ This green-labeled Grüner from one of Austria's best-known international ambassadors offers uncomplicated refreshment with a bit of its grape's trademark bite.

Riesling Kamptal ♀ $$$ Offers melon, pit fruits, and citrus in juicy profusion, finishing with hints of salt and stone.

MANTLERHOF *(Kremstal)*

Grüner Veltliner Lössterrassen ♀ $$ A biodynamically grown, midweight, classic exhibition of lentil, crunchy greens, and pepper.

Grüner Veltliner Mosburgerin ♀ $$$ This refined, juicy, delicate, floral Grüner subtly suggests sweetness even though by analysis the wine is truly dry.

GERHARD MARKOWITSCH *(Carnuntum)*

Pinot Noir ♟ $$$ The basic bottling from this Pinot specialist offers ripe, bright, oak-tinged fruit and excellent value in direct competition with far more expensive new-world Pinots of similar style.

MUHR–VAN DER NIEPOORT *(Carnuntum)*

Carnuntum ♟ $$$ The entry-level or, (as they put it, "village"-level) Blaufränkisch from Muhr and famed port producer Dirk Niepoort offers a ripe, silken-textured, fresh mouthful of cool, juicy black fruits accented with pepper and juniper and subtly underlain by suggestions of forest floor.

LUDWIG NEUMAYER *(Traisental)*

Grüner Veltliner Engelgarten ♀ $$$ This simplest wine from the Traisental's foremost grower is delicate, infectiously juicy, and redolent of snap peas, citrus, and herbs.

NEUMEISTER *(Styria)*

Gelber Muskateller Klassik ♗ **$$$** From southeast Styria's leading estate, a lovely display of flowers, citrus, and herbs that briskly fulfills in spades Muscat's duty to refresh, invigorate, and stimulate an appetite.

Sauvignon Blanc Klassik ♗ **$$$** With an almost Muscat-like pungency of citrus zest and herb, this high-spirited, saline, bright, invigorating, yet luscious Sauvignon is a model of clarity, complexity, and refreshment.

Weissburgunder Klassik ♗ **$$$** This highly versatile Pinot Blanc offers rich orchard fruit and nut oils, a creamy texture, admirable clarity and refreshment, and strikingly saline minerality.

NIGL *(Kremstal)*

Grüner Veltliner Kremser Freiheit ♗ **$$$** In this bargain from one of Austria's foremost growers, flowers, sweet pea, brown spice, and tart rhubarb play against honeyed richness, always managing to preserve lift and refreshment.

OTT *(Wagram)*

Grüner Veltliner Am Berg ♗ **$$** Offering invigorating, citric brightness and hints of flowers, red berries, and herbs that perfectly fit its relatively delicate frame, this sustainably grown Grüner offers consistent refreshment and versatility.

Grüner Veltliner Fass 4 ♗ **$$$** Lime, purple plum, pear, flowers, nut oils, spices, and herbs typically inform this polished, juicy, sappy, harmonious, and intriguing wine, confirming Ott's role as a leading Grüner Veltliner specialist.

PFAFFL *(Weinviertel)*

Grüner Veltliner Haidviertel ♗ **$$$** Displaying green bean, lentil, and lime accented by bitter hints of fruit pit, this wine's clarity and its deep stony, saline-savory dimensions illustrate Pfaffl's role as his region's leader.

DER POLLERHOF *(Weinviertel)*

Grüner Veltliner ♀ $ This light yet concentrated liter bottling offers classic traits of Austria's "national grape" and emphatic evidence that Poller's are among the most undervalued wines in all of Austria.

Grüner Veltliner Galgenberg ♀ $$ Full of lentil, fresh lime, and pungent herbs; subtly creamy, yet (at only around 12% alcohol) quite light, this offers a generous, refreshing, and persistent finish.

Grüner Veltliner Phelling ♀ $$$ Typically featuring sweet pea and lavender, melon and lime, with a peppery note to its irresistibly generous, lip-smacking finish, this lush yet elegant wine will amaze with its versatility.

PRIELER *(Burgenland [Neusiedlersee-Hügelland])*

Blaufränkisch Johannishöhe ♥ $$$ An ideal introduction to its grape and to a top red wine estate. Polished and bright (typically only 13% alcohol), this saturates the palate with bittersweet black fruits, herbs, peat, and nut oils.

Pinot Blanc Seeberg ♀ $$$ Toasted nuts, lemon cream, sweet corn, apple blossom, and herbs inform a palate that illustrates this grape's magic: density and creaminess of texture allied to delicacy and refreshment and infused with crustacean and mineral nuances reminiscent of great Chablis, and an astonishing value!

FRITZ SALOMON (GUT OBERSTOCKSTALL) *(Wagram)*

Grüner Veltliner Brunnberg ♀ $$ A, wine of purity, brightness, and penetration; laden with flowers, herbs, citrus, and tart red berries and sporting a fruit-filled and invigoratingly saline finish.

SALOMON-UNDHOF *(Kremstal)*

Grüner Veltliner Hochterrassen ♀ $$ Consistently juicy lime, lentil, and floral satisfaction, and glossy richness with clarity and refreshment, from an export-oriented estate that offers an unprecedented range of values.

Grüner Veltliner Wachtberg ♀ $$$ A Grüner that reserves clarity and elegance but offers chewy density, pithy concentration, and a wealth of elements than cannot be described as other than "mineral."

Riesling Kögl ♈ $$$ An affordable opportunity to sample wine from a top site, this tends toward a cool personality, with citrus, flowers, and overt suggestions of salt and crushed stone.

Riesling Pfaffenberg ♈ $$$ Strikingly marrying richness, bracing refreshment, and intrigue as only Riesling from a great site can, Salomon's Pfaffenberg emphasizes pit fruit and spice. (The estate's richer, more expensive "reserve" bottlings aren't always superior.)

Riesling Steinterrassen ♈ $$ This blend typically offers snappy tartness, a distinct sense of local minerality, and consummate refreshment.

SCHELLMANN *(Thermenregion)*

Muskateller ♈ $$$ Revived by new partners (led by the Kamptal's Fred Loimer), Schellmann offers a pungently herbal, sappy, zesty, and unusually full-bodied variation on Muscat.

UWE SCHIEFER *([Süd]burgenland)*

Blaufränkisch Königsberg ♉ $$$ Cool, fresh black fruits wreathed in smoke and crushed stone open to reveal amazing vistas of complexity for the price, confirming the potential of long-neglected South Burgenland sites.

Grüner Schiefer ♈ $$ Grüner in rather Muscadet-like garb: juicy, lightly floral, full of lemon, cress, and pungent finishing notes that can only be called mineral, delivering plenty of thirst-quenching satisfaction.

JOSEF SCHMID *(Kremstal)*

Grüner Veltliner Kremser Alte Reben ♈ $$$ This offers lush texture and considerable body yet infectious juiciness and refreshment.

Grüner Veltliner Kremser Weingärten ♈ $$ Saline and alkaline mineral suggestions allied to lime; honeydew melon; musky, narcissus-like floral perfume; peppery bite; and deep notes of root vegetables.

Riesling Vom Urgestein Bergterrassen ♀ $$$ Sauvignon-like gooseberry, citrus, and herbs; this can be counted on to finish with pungency and refreshment. ("Urgestein" may soon be dropped from the label.)

HEIDI SCHRÖCK *(Burgenland [Neusiedlersee-Hügelland])*

Weissburgunder ♀ $$$ This least expensive of Schröck's numerous fine dry whites positively drips with creamy hazelnut paste, apple jelly, and lemon cream, yet in the best fashion of Pinot Blanc offers a core of invigoratingly juicy fresh fruit as well as thought-provoking suggestions of carnal and mineral elements.

SCHWARZBÖCK *(Weinviertel)*

Gelber Muskateller ♀ $$$ A great opportunity to discover the amazing wiles of Austrian Muskateller: lemon zest and peppermint inform a wine with a snappy, saline, bright, face-slapping initial palate impact yet hidden creaminess and dark notes of coffee.

Grüner Veltliner Viergarten ♀ $$ Loaded with fresh apple, grapefruit, lentil, and herbs, this lithe, bright, Riesling-like Grüner finishes with citrus-zest pungency and invigorating salinity.

Riesling Pöcken ♀ $$$ From a high hill just outside Vienna, this offers a heady bouquet of lilac; irresistibly luscious, herb-tinged fresh lime; and a bright, saline finish.

SETZER *(Weinviertel)*

Grüner Veltliner ♀ $ This basic liter bottling delivers a startling degree of floral perfume, sheer citrus, and crunchy green refreshment and cannot be too highly recommended for any refrigerator.

Grüner Veltliner Vesper ♀ $$$ Characterized by the utmost delicacy and refreshment you can ask from this variety, with floral, herbal, and snap pea aromatics, a saline mineral cast, and a Riesling-like citricity.

SÖLLNER *(Wagram)*

Grüner Veltliner Hengstberg ♀ $$$ Consistently impressive wine from a pioneer in sustainable viticulture, featuring rhubarb, citrus, berry, pit fruits, and herbs, with frisky brightness and tactile pungency.

SPÄTROT-GEBESHUBER *(Thermenregion)*

Classic 🍷 **$$** Uniting St. Laurent, Pinot Noir, and (in most vintages) Zweigelt, this offers generous nut and red fruit flavors with a satiny texture and a polished, irresistible finish, and will embarrass countless pure Pinots that sell for two to three times its price.

STADLMANN *(Thermenregion)*

Zierfandler Classic 🍷 **$$** A local (grape) hero in the hands of its foremost champion: redolent of green tea, pungent flowers, quince, and citrus, this delivers a combination of textural richness with refreshing acidity and invigorating finishing salinity and bite.

WEINGUT DER STADT KREMS *(Kremstal)*

Grüner Veltliner Lössterrassen 🍷 **$$** This wine from the dynamic young team at the city winery of Krems is light yet not insubstantial and loaded with lentil and pepper.

Grüner Veltliner Sandgrube 🍷 **$$$** Green bean, lentil, lemon, and brine are among the elements in a wine that typically pushes 13% alcohol yet comes off refreshing and practically delicate.

TEMENT *(Styria)*

Sauvignon Blanc Klassik 🍷 **$$$** Gooseberry, lime, sage, and caraway typically inform this juicy and refreshing, texturally polished yet invigorating Sauvignon from south Styria's most renowned vintner.

ERNST TRIEBAUMER *(Burgenland [Neusiedlersee-Hügelland])*

Blaufränkisch 🍷 **$$$** The basic bottling from esteemed veteran "ET" brims with juicy, pepper-tinged black fruits and can serve as a highly affordable introduction to its great yet little-known grape.

UMATHUM *(Burgenland [Neusiedlersee])*

Zwiegelt 🍷 **$$$** Josef Umathum's basic Zwiegelt characteristically displays a lush depth of pure fruit, enticing ripeness, as well as vivacity, infectious juiciness, and a flatteringly glossy palate impression.

WENINGER ([Mittel]burgenland)

Blaufränkisch Hochäcker ♟ $$$ This veteran's take on Blaufränkisch from a classic site offers a complex amalgam of black fruits and dark, woodsy notes, sappy concentration, and a refined, rich yet refreshing back end.

WENZEL (Burgenland [Neusiedlersee-Hügelland])

Furmint ♀ $$$ This makes its case for the Wenzel's reestablishment of Furmint in Burgenland with honey; flowers; a faintly smoky, buckwheat-like note; and a combination of palate density and refreshment that puts one in mind of Loire Chenin.

RAINER WESS (Wachau and Kremstal)

Grüner Veltliner Terrassen ♀ $$$ Wess's Grüner Veltliner Terrassen typically features green beans, snap peas, coffee, and pit fruits; considerable fullness and a glossy-textured palate; yet plenty of lift and refreshment.

Grüner Veltliner Wachauer ♀ $$$ Sporting flowers, snap peas, and citrus, this offers a soft, luscious, yet still typically nippy example of Austria's national signature grape.

Riesling Terrassen ♀ $$$ Peach, lemon, and almond are key notes in this sleek, refined, richly textured and long-finishing Riesling value, which originates in some very fine, steep sites.

Riesling Wachauer ♀ $$$ No more expensive than its Grüner Veltliner counterpart, this finishes with lip-smacking generosity as well as smoky, saline minerality and faintly bitter fruit-pit complications that one has no right to expect for the price.

WIENINGER (Vienna)

Chardonnay Classic ♀ $$ This serves to refreshingly introduce a grape from which Wieninger also crafts serious, voluminous, and ageworthy (if, arguably, "internationally" styled) reserve wines.

Grüner Veltliner Herenholz ♀ $$ Amazingly—perhaps dangerously—this refreshingly light, beautifully balanced, infectiously drinkable wine brimming with flowers, herbs, cress, and lentil generally reveals itself to contain 13% or more alcohol.

Grüner Veltliner Nussberg ♀ $$$ Vienna's winemaking dynamo offers from the city's best-known hillside a consistently refreshing yet relatively robust wine expressing its grape's myriad virtues.

Wiener Gemischter Satz ♀ $$ You won't have to close your eyes and imagine yourself in the garden of a Viennese wine tavern to enjoy drinking this synergistic version of a classic, multigrape local blend, but you might want to anyway.

WIMMER-CZERNY *(Wagram)*

Grüner Veltliner Fumberg ♀ $$$ A typically delicate and restrained, pure and persistently refreshing wine from one of Austria's pioneers in biodynamic viticulture.

ZANTHO *(Burgenland* [*Neusiedlersee*]*)*

Blaufränkisch ♀ $$ A collaboration between noted vintner Josef Umathum and a local co-op, this offers a simple but delicious example of the primary blackberry fruit and subtly peppery, smoky notes that typify its grape.

St. Laurent ♀ $$ Displaying dark cherry, leather, smoke, and humus, quite thick in texture and rich in flavor, this unusually affordable St. Laurent finishes with carnal notes that betray its Pinot Noir ancestry.

Zweigelt ♀ $$ This offers intense fresh cherry and spice along with suggestions of salt and marrow, a model of balance that shows why even at a low price and with the unpretentious vinification it enjoys here, this grape is worthy of serious international attention.

CHILE

CHILEAN WINE VALUES

by Dr. Jay Miller

Like Argentina, its Andean neighbor, Chile has made enormous progress in recent years. At present, this South American country produces wines that can satisfy any consumer's desires, from cheap quaffing wines to world-class ageworthy reds.

What my tastings and three visits to Chile in the past several years reveal is that much progress has been made and much remains to be done. One encouraging sign is the amount of foreign investment, especially European, that has been taking place recently. Another positive sign is the exploration of new regions where high-quality Pinot Noir, Carménère, and Syrah can be grown successfully. Some names worthy of attention are the San Antonio Valley (which includes Leyda); the Aconcagua Valley, where much organic and biodynamic farming is being done; the Casablanca Valley for cool-climate varieties; and the Colchagua Valley for top-quality red wines.

Chile produces many of the standard grape varieties grown everywhere. Sauvignon Blanc and Chardonnay are ubiquitous. Among the reds, Merlot, Cabernet Sauvignon, Cabernet Franc, and Syrah are widely planted. Chile's unique grape is Carménère, a Bordeaux varietal that is nearly extinct in France. Some producers are hopeful that Carménère will become for them what Malbec has become for Argentina, something that will set them apart from everyone else. My tastings indicate that Carménère grown in the right microclimates can produce unique, unforgettable wines, the primary example being Concha y Toro's Terrunyo Carménère. However, most Carménères, especially those priced in the bargain category, turn out horribly green and vegetal. But when it's done right, this is remarkably exotic, hedonistic wine.

A couple of other cautionary notes: Most Chardonnay from Chile is overly oak flavored and unbalanced. However, Chile has a knack for producing some amazing values in Sauvignon Blanc from a variety of regions, mostly in a Loire Valley style, and these wines sell for a song. Among red wines, much of the production is overly acidified or picked underripe from huge yields, causing the wines to have gritty tannins in the finish. That said, wineries such as Montes, Cono Sur, Cousiño-Macul, and Casa Silva, among others, have figured out how to produce terrific red wines at bargain prices.

Vintage Smarts

Chile has had a series of excellent vintages in recent years. The wines you are likely to encounter—2005, 2006, 2007, and 2008—all have much to recommend them.

Drinking Curves

All of the white wines in the value category are ready to be drunk upon purchase. A handful of the reds may evolve for several years, but they can be enjoyed in their youth as well.

Chile's Top Wine Values by Winery

AGUSTINOS (Various Regions)

Cabernet Sauvignon Reserva—Aconcagua 🍷 $$ The Cabernet Sauvignon Reserva has a nose of cedar, earth notes, red currants, and black currants. On the palate it offers savory flavors and an overall elegant personality.

Pinot Noir Reserva—Bio-Bio 🍷 $$ Offers a bouquet of cherry and cranberry. The wine has good varietal character with silky fruit and solid length.

Sauvignon Blanc Reserva—Bio-Bio 🍷 $ Agustinos's Sauvignon Blanc Reserva offers fragrant citrus aromas leading to a crisp, intense, balanced wine with ample grapefruit and lemon-lime flavors. It has excellent balance and length. Drink it during its first 1–2 years.

ANAKENA (Casablanca Valley)

Sauvignon Blanc "Ona" 🍷 $$ This Sauvignon reveals a nose of fresh herbs and grapefruit that jumps from the glass. On the palate it has excellent depth and intensity, lively citrus flavors, vibrant acidity, and a crisp, clean finish. Drink it during its first 12–18 months.

HACIENDA ARAUCANO *(Central Valley)*

The Hacienda Araucano label is produced by the excellent firm of J. & F. Lurton.

Pinot Noir ♟ $ Araucano's Pinot Noir is medium ruby colored, with excellent varietal aromas of strawberry, raspberry, and rhubarb. On the palate it reveals an elegant personality, as manifested by its silky fruit and smooth texture. It could use greater depth and concentration but is a fine introduction to Pinot Noir.

Sauvignon Blanc ♟ $ The pale straw-colored Sauvignon Blanc is very fragrant, with notes of spring flowers, grapefruit, and lemon-lime. Smooth textured, with underlying vibrant acidity, this ripe, intensely flavored Sauvignon will drink well during its first 12–18 months.

ARBOLEDA *(Various Regions)*

Cabernet Sauvignon—Aconcagua ♟ $ The Cabernet Sauvignon has an enticing nose of cedar, clove, cinnamon, tobacco, and currants. Firm, with enough structure to evolve for 1–2 years, this ripe, layered Cabernet has good length and surprising grip.

Carménère—Colchagua ♟ $ Offers an alluring nose of violet, plum, and blueberry compote. Nicely extracted, chewy, and intensely flavored, this plush effort is a crowd-pleaser that should continue giving for another 4 years.

Chardonnay—Casablanca ♟ $ The Chardonnay is attractively fresh, with aromas of pear and apple and just a hint of toasty oak in the background. Smooth textured with moderately intense flavors, this medium-bodied wine has good depth and balance and a medium-length finish.

Merlot—Aconcagua ♟ $ The Merlot offers aromas of spice box, earth notes, red currant, and black currant. This leads to a medium-bodied, forward Merlot with plenty of up-front fruit, tasty flavors, and an easygoing personality.

Sauvignon Blanc—Leyda ♟ $$ Made in an attractive Loire Valley style, this medium-straw-colored wine exhibits a grass, herb, citrus, and apple–scented bouquet. Light to medium bodied with a crisp, refreshing feel on the palate, this nicely balanced wine has good depth and a pure, vibrant finish. Drink it during its first 12–18 months.

Syrah—Aconcagua 🍷 $ The Syrah is purple colored, with an aromatic array of lilacs and toasty blueberries. Surprisingly elegant on the palate with lively acidity, this nicely balanced effort has good length and a pure finish.

AZUL PROFUNDO (Bio-Bio Valley)

Pinot Noir 🍷 $$ Medium ruby colored, with enticing raspberry and strawberry aromas. Smooth textured, the wine has excellent depth, varietally correct flavors, and a lingering, sweet finish.

BIG TATTOO WINES (Colchagua Valley)

Big Tattoo Cabernet-Syrah 🍷 $ Exhibits an expressive nose of spice box, violet, black currant, and blueberry. On the palate it offers plenty of savory fruit, excellent ripeness, and enough structure to evolve for 1–2 years.

BOTALCURA (Rapel Valley)

Cabernet Franc Grand Reserve 🍷 $$ It has a perfume of cedar, tobacco, cinnamon, clove, and red currant. On the palate it is smooth textured and has good depth and an elegant personality.

Cabernet Sauvignon Grand Reserve 🍷 $$ The Cabernet Sauvignon Grand Reserve offers aromas of toasty oak, pencil lead, and black currant. It is a bit more structured than the Cabernet Franc and a bit longer in the finish.

BUTRON BUDINICH (Cachapoal Valley)

Cabernet Sauvignon Cumbres Adinas 🍷 $$ The Cabernet Sauvignon Cumbres Adinas reveals a bouquet of spice box, cedar, and black currant. It has a bit more structure than its cousins and may evolve for 1–2 years.

Malbec Cumbres Adinas 🍷 $$ The Malbec Cumbres Adinas offers aromas of cherry and red currant. Smooth textured and easygoing, it will drink well during its first 4–5 years.

Merlot Cumbres Adinas 🍷 **$$** The Merlot Cumbres Adinas is dark ruby colored, with a nose of spicy red fruits. Ripe, balanced, and forward, it can be enjoyed during its first 4 years.

CALITERRA *(Colchagua Valley)*

Cabernet Sauvignon Tribute 🍷 **$$** The Cabernet Sauvignon Tribute offers a nose of cedar, spice box, and currant. Balanced and forward, it can be enjoyed during its first 5 years.

Carménère Tribute 🍷 **$$** The Carménère Tribute, my favorite of the quartet, offers spice box and blueberry aromas, a smooth texture, excellent depth, and layers of flavor. When you find a well-made, value-priced Carménère, it's well worth a try.

Malbec Tribute 🍷 **$$** The Malbec Tribute reveals black cherry and blackberry aromas and flavors. It has excellent depth and concentration with the potential for 1–2 years of evolution.

Shiraz Tribute 🍷 **$$** The Shiraz Tribute offers meaty, gamy notes; ripe flavors; good grip; and a lengthy finish.

CARMEN *(Maipo and Casablanca Valleys)*

Chardonnay—Maipo Valley 🍷 **$$** The Chardonnay is unoaked. It offers up aromas of apple, pear, and white peach. On the palate it reveals lively acidity, good depth of flavor, and a medium-long finish.

Chardonnay Reserva—Casablanca Valley 🍷 **$$** The Chardonnay Reserva is a more substantial effort revealing a touch of oak and plenty of ripe apple- and pear-flavored fruit.

Chardonnay Winemaker's Reserve—Casablanca Valley 🍷 **$$$** Delivers spicy oak aromas along with butterscotch and tropical aromas. This leads to an intense, layered, creamy-textured Chardonnay with gobs of tropical flavors.

Pinot Noir Reserva—Casablanca Valley 🍷 **$$** The Pinot Noir Reserva exhibits aromas of spice box, raspberry, and cherry. Sweetly fruited, balanced, and tasty, this varietally correct Pinot Noir can be enjoyed during its first 4 years.

Reserva Syrah–Cabernet Sauvignon—Maipo Valley 🍷 $$ The Reserva Syrah–Cabernet Sauvignon has fragrant toasty blue and black fruit aromas. Supple, forward, and ripe on the palate, this forward effort may evolve for 1–2 years but can be enjoyed now.

Sauvignon Blanc Reserva—Casablanca Valley 🍷 $ The Sauvignon Blanc Reserva has an aromatic array of citrus, lemon-lime, and fresh herbs. Racy and crisp on the palate, this well-balanced effort has a vibrant, tangy finish.

CHONO *(Various Regions)*

Cabernet Sauvignon—Maipo Valley 🍷 $$ The Cabernet Sauvignon offers an attractive bouquet of black currant and blackberry. On the palate it is surprisingly lush for its humble price with plenty of flavor and excellent length.

Chono Riesling—Bio-Bio Valley 🍷 $$ Chono's Riesling has aromas of petrol, mineral, and spring flowers. On the palate intense white fruits intermingle with vibrant acidity.

Chono Syrah—Elqui Valley 🍷 $$ The Syrah offers up scents of blueberry and earth notes. Ripe and supple textured, it has enough stuffing to provide pleasure over the next several years.

CONCHA Y TORO *(Various Regions)*

Concha y Toro's entry-level lineup is called Casillero del Diablo.

Carménère Casillero del Diablo—Rapel Valley 🍷 $ This Carménère is an excellent introduction to the grape. Pleasant, ripe, and forward, it has plenty of blueberry and black raspberry flavors for casual quaffing.

Chardonnay Casillero del Diablo—Casablanca Valley 🍷 $ The Chardonnay reveals pear, apple, and pineapple in its fragrant perfume, leading to an intense, ripe, and lengthy wine for drinking 12–18 months.

Chardonnay Marques de Casa Concha—Pirque 🍷 $$ This Chardonnay offers up toasty oak, butterscotch, pear, and tropical fruit notes. Creamy-textured, round, and full-flavored, all of its components are well integrated in this serious, flavorful effort.

Chardonnay Maycas de Limari—Limari Valley ♀ $ The Chardonnay Maycas de Limari exhibits even more aromatic complexity, serious depth, and gobs of ripe, mineral-accented Chardonnay fruit.

Gewürztraminer Casillero del Diablo—Maule Valley ♀ $ The Gewürztraminer offers up an expressive bouquet of rose petal, lychee, and spice box. Off-dry on the palate, it has terrific intensity, unusual focus and delineation for its humble price, and superb length.

Palo Alto Reserva—Maule Valley ♀ $$$ The Palo Alto Reserva is a blend of Cabernet Sauvignon, Carménère, and Syrah. Aromas of cedar, tobacco, spice box, cassis, and blueberry are enticing. This is followed by a plush, crowd-pleasing wine with gobs of flavor and a fruit-filled finish.

Sauvignon Blanc Reserva Maycas de Limari—Limari Valley ♀ $$$ The Maycas de Limari is pale straw colored, with an exquisite bouquet of mineral, lemon-lime, grapefruit, gooseberry, and floral notes. Focused and layered on the palate, it has unusual richness and a long, pristine finish.

Sauvignon Blanc Reserva Palo Alto—Maule Valley ♀ $$ The Sauvignon Blanc is pale straw colored, with intense citrus aromas and flavors. Nicely balanced and lengthy, this tasty Sauvignon should be consumed during its first 12–18 months.

Sauvignon Blanc Trio—Casablanca Valley ♀ $ The Sauvignon Blanc Trio exhibits more aromatic complexity with its notes of freshly cut hay, herbs, citrus, and gooseberry. Balanced, vibrant, and long, it will provide pleasure during its first 1–2 years.

Shiraz Casillero del Diablo—Rapel Valley ♀ $ The Shiraz offers plenty of layered blue fruits for drinking over the 3 years following the vintage.

Syrah Marques de Casa Concha—Rucahue ♀ $$$ Medium purple colored, this Syrah's nose exhibits plum, blueberry, and black cherry aromas leading to an uncomplicated but ripe and flavorful wine for drinking over the next several years.

Syrah Maycas de Limari—Limari Valley ♀ $ The Syrah Maycas de Limari exhibits a more fragrant perfume and greater intensity on the palate. Nicely layered and flavorful, it may evolve for 1–2 years but can be enjoyed now.

Trio—Maipo Valley ♉ $ The Trio is composed of Cabernet Sauvignon, Syrah, and Cabernet Franc. The nose reveals cedar, spice box, clove, cinnamon, blueberry, and cassis leading to a plush, easygoing wine with no hard edges.

Trio Reserva—Casablanca Valley ♉ $ Not to be overlooked is the Trio Reserva, a blend of Chardonnay, Pinot Gris, and Pinot Blanc. It reveals an aromatic array of mango, tangerine, poached pear, and lemon zest. It is surprisingly complex, intensely flavored, and pure.

Viognier Casillero del Diablo—Casablanca Valley ♉ $ The Viognier exhibits petrol and pit fruits in its aromatics. Nicely balanced with a bit of complexity unusual for its price point, this lengthy effort will provide pleasure during its first 1–2 years.

CONO SUR *(Various Regions)*

Cabernet Sauvignon 20 Barrels—Maipo Valley ♉ $$ The Cabernet Sauvignon 20 Barrels offers up notes of earth, tobacco, plum, cassis, and blackberry. On the palate it shows an elegant personality, several years of aging potential, and a lengthy finish.

Cabernet Sauvignon Vision—Maipo Valley ♉ $ The Cabernet Sauvignon Vision has a bouquet consisting of spice box, damp earth, red currant, and black currant. It reveals a restrained personality, albeit with good savory flavors, solid balance, and a medium-long finish.

Chardonnay 20 Barrels—Casablanca Valley ♉ $$ The Chardonnay 20 Barrels offers greater depth, mouth-filling pear and tropical flavors, vibrant acidity, and a lush finish.

Chardonnay Vision—Casablanca Valley ♉ $ The Chardonnay Vision has a bouquet of white peach, apple, and a hint of tropical fruits in the background. It has good concentration, lively acidity, and a fruit-filled finish.

Pinot Noir 20 Barrels—Casablanca Valley ♉ $$ The Pinot Noir 20 Barrels has an expressive nose of cherry and raspberry along with an attractive earthiness. There is plenty of sweet fruit on the midpalate, good balance, and a lengthy, pure finish.

Pinot Noir Vision—Colchagua Valley 🍷 **$** Offers an enticing bouquet of strawberry and cherry. This leads to a wine with good varietal character, lively acidity, ample silky fruit, and good length.

Riesling Limited Release—Bio-Bio Valley 🍷 **$$$** This Riesling has a lovely perfume of spring flowers, citrus, and white peach. Made in a dry style, it is bright and lively on the palate, nicely balanced, and has a pure crisp finish.

Sauvignon Blanc 20 Barrels—Casablanca Valley 🍷 **$$** Delivers aromas of gooseberry, citrus, and fresh herbs. Round but not as focused as its less expensive sibling, it should be consumed over the next 2 years.

Sauvignon Blanc Vision—Casablanca Valley 🍷 **$** The Sauvignon Blanc Vision has precision aromatics featuring mineral, citrus, and lemon-lime. Balanced, vibrant, and long, it is meant to be enjoyed during its first 12–18 months.

COUSIÑO-MACUL *(Maipo Valley)*

Cabernet Sauvignon 🍷 **$** The Cabernet Sauvignon is cherry red in color with aromas of violets and black currants. Smooth textured with an elegant personality, it has plenty of spicy fruit and good length.

Cabernet Sauvignon Antiguas Reservas 🍷 **$$** The Antiguas Reservas has a slightly brooding nose of black currant and blackberry. This leads to a wine with some elegance, excellent depth, and savory flavors. It has enough structure to evolve for 2–3 years but can be enjoyed now.

Chardonnay 🍷 **$** The Chardonnay is made in a fruity, unoaked style. White peach and pear dominate the aromatics, leading to a round, ripe, tasty wine with good balance and length.

Chardonnay Antiguas Reserva 🍷 **$$** The Antiguas has a nose featuring green apple, honeysuckle, and tropical fruit aromas. Round and ripe on the palate, notes of hazelnut, grapefruit, and anise make an appearance. The wine has excellent depth and a lengthy finish.

Finis Terrae 🍷 **$$$** A blend of Cabernet Sauvignon and Merlot, the wine has a fragrant bouquet of wood smoke, cedar, leather, black currant, and blackberry. Bordeaux-like on the palate with an elegant personality, it has a smooth texture, succulent flavors, excellent depth, and a long, pure finish. It will evolve for 2–3 years and be at its best from 2011 to 2022.

Merlot ♀ $ The Merlot reveals an expressive nose of cherry and cranberry. Supple and ripe, on the palate notes of assorted red fruits, plums, and violets put in an appearance. The flavors are savory, and there is enough tannin to support 1–2 years of development.

Riesling Doña Isidora ♀ $ Offers a lovely floral, mineral, apple blossom, and white peach bouquet leading to a dry wine with fennel, apple, and lemon zest making an appearance on the palate. The wine has good balance and a medium-long finish.

Riesling Reserve ♀ $ The Riesling Reserve has a nose featuring mineral, spring flowers, apple blossom, and lemon-lime. It is medium bodied and just off-dry, and the slight sweetness gives an impression of richness and depth. It is nicely balanced by crisp acidity leading to a long, refreshing finish.

Sauvignon Gris ♀ $ Has an expressive nose of lemon-lime, grapefruit, and other citrus fruits. Crisp, lively, and refreshing on the palate, the wine offers plenty of citrus-flavored fruit, excellent balance, and a sprightly finish. Drink it over the next 12–18 months.

ECHEVERRÍA *(Central Valley)*

Carménère Réserve ♀ $ This is an easygoing, friendly wine with tons of ripe blueberry, black cherry fruit, a smooth texture, and excellent concentration.

LUIS FELIPE EDWARDS *(Colchagua Valley)*

Carménère Reserva ♀ $ The nose is an attractive bouquet of black cherry and blueberry. This leads to an easygoing, layered wine with gobs of savory fruit and no hard edges. It has good balance and a fruit-filled finish.

Doña Bernarda ♀ $$$ A blend of Cabernet Sauvignon, Shiraz, Carménère, and Petit Verdot, this wine's nose reveals notes of smoke, scorched earth, blue and black fruits, and allspice. It has enough structure to evolve for 2–3 years, some complexity, and ample savory fruit.

EMILIANA ORGÁNICO *(Casablanca Valley)*

Chardonnay Novas Limited Selection ♇ $ Made from organically grown grapes, it offers a fragrant perfume of poached pear, white peach, and pineapple. This is followed by a smooth-textured, easygoing Chardonnay with good balance and a lengthy, fruit-filled finish.

ERRAZURIZ *(Aconcagua Valley and Casablanca Valley)*

Cabernet Sauvignon Max Reserva ♇ $$ The Cabernet Sauvignon Max Reserva has an enticing nose of toasty black currants and allspice. This leads to a Cabernet with savory flavors and moderate length that should evolve and round out with another 1–2 years of cellaring.

Chardonnay Wild Ferment ♇ $ The Chardonnay Wild Ferment reveals notes of toasty oak, poached pear, and tropical fruit aromas. This leads to a medium- to full-bodied Chardonnay with nicely integrated oak, mango, pineapple, and butterscotch flavors, and good acidity.

Merlot Max Reserva ♇ $$ The Merlot Max Reserva has a nose of toasty red currant, cinnamon, and vanilla. Ripe, sweet, and elegant on the palate, this easygoing effort will provide pleasure during its first 4 years.

Pinot Noir Wild Ferment ♇ $ This Pinot reveals notes of cedar, vanilla, raspberry, and strawberry. On the palate it has a silky texture, sweet fruit, an elegant personality, good depth, and a pure finish.

Sauvignon Blanc Estate ♇ $ This Sauvignon exhibits a fragrant citrus and gooseberry perfume leading to a crisp, nicely balanced, vibrant wine with ample ripe, citrus-flavored fruit and a clean finish.

Sauvignon Blanc Single Vineyard ♇ $$ The Sauvignon Blanc Single Vineyard offers a more expressive bouquet of fresh herbs, new cut grass, snow pea, and citrus fruits. A bit more ample on the midpalate, it has a smooth texture, crisp flavors, lively acidity, and a pure, lengthy finish.

Shiraz Max Reserva ♇ $ It has an alluring perfume of blueberry, meat, and game. Made in a lighter, racy style, it delivers persistent spicy blue fruit flavors, good depth and balance, and a pure finish.

ESTAMPA *(Various Regions)*

Gold—Colchagua Valley 🍷 **$$$** The Gold is a Bordeaux-style blend of Carménère, Cabernet Sauvignon, Cabernet Franc, and Petit Verdot. It offers up a bouquet of cedar, tobacco, spice box, blueberry, and blackberry followed by a plush wine with gobs of succulent blue and black fruits, a smooth texture, and outstanding richness and depth.

Reserve Assemblage—Casablanca Valley 🍷 **$$** A blend of Sauvignon Blanc, Chardonnay, and Viognier, it exhibits a fragrant nose of fresh herbs, citrus, and white peach. This leads to a crisp, fruity wine with some complexity and ripe flavors.

IN SITU *(Aconcagua Valley)*

Carménère Gran Reserva 🍷 **$** The Carménère Gran Reserva has a bit more substance than the Winemaker's Selection. Richer, riper, and with greater depth, it may well evolve for 1–2 years.

Carménère Winemaker's Selection 🍷 **$** Tasty blueberry flavors take primacy on the palate leading to a medium-long, soft finish. This pleasurable effort will drink well for several years.

Chardonnay Winemaker's Selection 🍷 **$** The Chardonnay Winemaker's Selection has a bouquet of mineral, white peach, and tropical fruits; good depth; and a pure finish.

Syrah Winemaker's Selection 🍷 **$** The Syrah Winemaker's Selection has an attractive nose of pepper and blue fruits. Made in a forward, supple style, the wine has ample flavor, modest depth, and a fruity finish.

CASA LA JOYA *(Colchagua Valley)*

Carménère Gran Reserve 🍷 **$$** Exhibits aromas of cedar, spice box, blueberry, and black currant. This is followed by a structured wine with 1–2 years of aging potential. It has excellent intensity and depth as well as a fruit-filled finish.

Gewürztraminer 🍷 **$** The Gewürztraminer offers aromas of rose petal and lychee. The palate reveals plenty of spicy fruit and a hint of sweetness leading to a medium-long, clean finish.

Sauvignon Blanc Reserve ♈ $ The Sauvignon Blanc Reserve has a pleasant bouquet of fresh herbs, grapefruit, and lemon-lime. On the palate the wine has good depth of flavor, crisp acidity, and a vibrant finish.

KINGSTON FAMILY VINEYARDS *(Casablanca Valley)*

Pinot Noir ♈ $$ The Pinot Noir offers a bouquet of cherry and raspberry. On the palate there is plenty of savory fruit with ample Pinot varietal character.

Sauvignon Blanc Cariblanco ♈ $$ The Sauvignon Blanc has a fragrant nose of fresh grass, grapefruit, and gooseberry. This is followed by a crisp, clean wine with ripe citrus flavors, good balance, and a sprightly finish.

CASA LAPOSTOLLE *(Colchagua Valley and Casablanca Valley)*

Casa Lapostolle is French, owned by the proprietors of Grand Marnier.

Cabernet Sauvignon Apalta Vineyard Cuvée Alexandre ♈ $$$ The Cabernet Sauvignon Apalta Vineyard Cuvée Alexandre has an expressive bouquet of smoke, pencil lead, spice box, black cherry, and black currant. The wine's black fruit flavors linger into a medium-long finish.

Chardonnay ♈ $$ The Chardonnay offers toasty apple and pear aromas and flavors leading to a crisp, balanced wine with ample white fruit flavors, good balance, and a lively finish.

Chardonnay Atalayas Vineyard Cuvée Alexandre ♈ $$$ The Atalayas Vineyard Cuvée Alexandre has an attractive bouquet of toasty oak, poached pear, and butterscotch. This leads to a creamy-textured wine with tropical flavors and a hint of hazelnut. The wine has fine depth and length but could use greater complexity.

Merlot Apalta Vineyard Cuvée Alexandre ♈ $$$ The Merlot Apalta Vineyard Cuvée Alexandra has aromas of cedar, spice box, black cherry, and black currant followed by a smooth-textured, ripe Merlot with ample savory black fruits, good depth, and a moderately long finish.

LEYDA *(Leyda Valley and San Antonio Valley)*

Chardonnay Classic Reserva ♀ **$$** Made without oak. The nose offers up white peach and poached pear aromas. This leads to a crisp, vibrant, forward wine for drinking over the next 12–18 months.

Chardonnay Falaris Hill Vineyard ♀ **$$$** Reveals some toasty oak notes, an amalgam of white fruits, lively acidity, and surprising depth and length for its humble price.

Pinot Noir Las Brisas Vineyard ♥ **$$$** Offers up pleasant strawberry and cherry aromas. This leads to a forward, easygoing Pinot with adequate varietal character and savory flavors.

Pinot Noir Cahuil Vineyard ♥ **$$$** This Pinot Noir offers a similar personality but with greater depth, concentration, and length.

Sauvignon Blanc Classic Reserva ♀ **$$** Light straw colored, with an attractive nose of fresh herbs and citrus. This leads to a crisp, balanced wine with a pleasant, fruity finish. Drink it over the next 12–18 months.

Sauvignon Blanc Garuma Vineyard ♀ **$$$** This Sauvignon Blanc offers more focused aromatics with notes of gooseberry and mineral. It has plenty of lively acidity, ripe flavors, and a refreshing finish. It should be consumed over the next 2 years.

LOMA LARGA *(Casablanca Valley)*

Chardonnay B3-B4 ♀ **$$$** Medium straw colored, with a pleasing bouquet of white peach, apple, and pear. On the palate it is forward, with ripe, savory flavors; vibrant acidity; and good balance.

Pinot Noir B9 ♥ **$$$** Reveals a toasty, cedary perfume with notes of spice box, cherry, and black raspberry. On the palate it exhibits an easygoing personality and savory flavors but a lack of depth and concentration. This moderately lengthy effort will provide simple pleasures during its first 2–3 years.

MAQUIS *(Colchagua Valley)*

Calcu ♟ $ A blend of Cabernet Sauvignon, Carménère, and Cabernet Franc, the wine reveals a fragrant bouquet of clove, cinnamon, blueberry, and black currant. This leads to an easygoing, full-flavored wine with surprising depth and length for its humble price.

Lien ♟ $$ The Lien is composed of Syrah, Carménère, Cabernet Franc, Petit Verdot, and Malbec. It offers a bit more richness and structure than the Calcu, and a hint of chocolate on the midpalate. It is likely to evolve for 1–2 years in the bottle but can be enjoyed now.

VIÑA MAR *(Casablanca Valley)*

Sauvignon Blanc Reserva ♀ $ Viña Mar's Sauvignon Blanc Reserva is light straw colored, with a pleasant nose of grapefruit and fresh herbs. Crisp, ripe, and friendly, it will drink well during its first 12–18 months.

CASA MARIN *(San Antonio Valley)*

Cartagena Gewürztraminer Estate Grown ♀ $$$ The Cartagena Gewürztraminer Estate Grown has a superb perfume of spice box, rose petal, and lychee. Crisp, focused, and intense, the wine has layers of savory fruit and a lengthy finish.

Sauvignon Blanc Cypress Vineyard ♀ $$$ The Sauvignon Blanc Cypress Vineyard has a fragrant bouquet of freshly mown hay, grapefruit, and lemon-lime. Intense, crisp, and well balanced, it will drink well during its first 1–2 years.

Sauvignon Blanc Estate Grown ♀ $$ The Sauvignon Blanc Estate Grown offers a fragrant bouquet of fresh herbs, sage, citrus, and lemon-lime. Ripe, concentrated, and balanced, the wine will drink well during its first 1–2 years.

Sauvignon Blanc Laurel Vineyard ♀ $$$ The Sauvignon Blanc Laurel Vineyard offers a floral component, as well as gooseberry and kiwi. Complex, ripe, and lengthy, with buttressing acidity, it should drink well for several years.

MATETIC *(San Antonio Valley)*

Matetic is one of just a few biodynamically certified vineyards in Chile.

Sauvignon Blanc EQ ♀ $$$ The Matetic Sauvignon Blanc EQ offers up a nose of fresh herbs and citrus. Clean, crisp, and refreshing, it will provide pleasure during its first 12–18 months.

MONTES *(Various Regions)*

Alpha Cabernet Sauvignon Apalta Vineyard—Colchagua Valley ♀ $$$ The Alpha Cabernet Sauvignon exhibits aromas of cedar, spice box, tobacco, black currant, and blackberry. Layered yet elegant, it has enough structure to evolve for 2–3 years.

Alpha Chardonnay—Casablanca Valley ♀ $$ This Chardonnay's nose delivers an attractive perfume of apple, pear, and a touch of oak. This is accompanied by a smooth-textured wine with plenty of ripe fruit, good balance, and a lengthy finish.

Alpha Merlot Apalta Vineyard—Colchagua Valley ♀ $$$ Dark ruby/purple in color, this Merlot has a stylish nose of cedar, spice box, red currant, and black currant. Supple textured with ample ripe fruit, it has a bit of sweet tannin and attractive flavors leading to a medium-length finish.

Alpha Syrah Apalta Vineyard—Colchagua Valley ♀ $$$ The Alpha Syrah has an enticing nose of game, espresso, earth, and blueberry. This leads to an elegantly styled Syrah with spicy blue and black fruit flavors, good depth, and a fruit-filled finish.

Classic Series Sauvignon Blanc—Casablanca-Curico Valley ♀ $ Montes's Sauvignon Blanc Classic Series is a Loire Valley–inspired effort. It delivers aromas of freshly cut grass and citrus, lively acidity, a crisp palate-feel, and moderate length.

Sauvignon Blanc Leyda Vineyard—Leyda Valley ♀ $$ The Leyda Vineyard, a more serious effort, has an expressive bouquet of spring flowers, citrus, and fresh herbs. It exhibits lively white fruit flavors, vibrant acidity, and excellent balance.

MONTGRAS *(Colchagua and Leyda Valleys)*

Cabernet Sauvignon–Carménère Antu Ninquen 🍷 $$$ It has an enticing aromatic array of smoke, pencil lead, spice box, black currant, and blueberry. On the palate this complex effort has layers of fruit, savory flavors, excellent balance, and enough structure to evolve for 1–2 years.

Carménère Reserva 🍷 $ The Carménère Reserva has an expressive bouquet of spice box, black raspberry, and black cherry; lots of succulent blue and black fruits on the palate; a friendly personality; and a finish with no hard edges.

Chardonnay Amaral Barrel-Fermented—Leyda Valley 🍷 $$ This wine offers a toasty perfume of poached pear and tropical fruits. Creamy textured and savory, it is a well-balanced effort with very good length.

Quatro 🍷 $$ A blend of Cabernet Sauvignon, Malbec, Carménère, and Syrah, Quatro has a complex bouquet of cedar, spice box, black currant, blackberry, and a hint of blueberry in the background. This is followed by a layered wine with good depth and concentration with enough structure to evolve for 1–2 years.

Sauvignon Blanc Amaral—Leyda Valley 🍷 $$ The Amaral is sourced from the cool-climate Leyda Valley. It offers a fragrant bouquet of freshly cut hay, gooseberry, and mineral. This is followed by a beautifully balanced wine with layers of savory flavor, vibrant acidity, and a lengthy finish. Drink this Sancerre look-alike during its first 2–3 years.

Sauvignon Blanc Reserva 🍷 $ The Sauvignon Blanc Reserva exhibits aromas of fresh herbs and citrus. Medium bodied, this straightforward Sauvignon offers grapefruit and lemon-lime flavors, bright acidity, and a clean, refreshing finish.

Syrah Antu Ninquen 🍷 $$$ Offers up cedar, wood smoke, scorched earth, and blueberry aromas that jump from the glass. On the palate, it has attractive, savory flavors but is slightly compressed and tight.

MORANDÉ *(Various Regions)*

Carignan Edición Limitada—Loncomilla Valley 🍷 **$$$** Offers an attractive perfume of cedar, spice box, damp earth, and black cherry. On the palate it is firm and structured with a good balance of savory, spicy black fruits and a hint of mineral.

Carménère Edición Limitada—Maipo Valley 🍷 **$$$** Exhibits a fragrant perfume of blueberry, black raspberry, and black cherry. Silky textured with pure blue fruit flavors, this superbly balanced, nicely priced Carménère should drink well through 2018.

Chardonnay Gran Reserva—Casablanca Valley 🍷 **$$** The Chardonnay Gran Reserva provides a bit more complexity and the oak nicely frames the wine's white fruit aromas and flavors. Drink this harmonious effort 1–2 years.

Chardonnay Reserva—Casablanca Valley 🍷 **$** The unoaked Reserva offers ample apple, pear, and pineapple aromas and flavors. On the palate, it is medium bodied, vibrant, and fruity.

Sauvignon Blanc Reserva—Casablanca Valley 🍷 **$** The Sauvignon Blanc has an enticing bouquet of fresh herbs and citrus. This leads to a medium-bodied, crisp, grapefruit-flavored wine with good balance and a clean finish.

ODFJELL *(Various Regions)*

Cabernet Sauvignon Orzada—Colchagua Valley 🍷 **$$** The unfiltered Cabernet Sauvignon Orzada exhibits spicy red and black currant aromas. This leads to a forward, smooth-textured Cabernet with good balance and length but not much complexity.

Carignan Orzada—Maule Valley 🍷 **$$** The Carignan Orzada reveals aromas of earth, mushroom, plum, and blueberry. They lead to a layered wine with savory blue and black fruits, plenty of spice and earth notes, and enough silky tannin to improve for 2–3 years.

Malbec Orzada—Ribera del Rio Claro 🍷 **$$** The Malbec Orzada offers aromas of black cherry and blackberry. Made in a restrained, elegant style, the wine is balanced and has enough structure to evolve for 1–2 years.

Syrah Orzada—Maipo Valley 🍷 **$$** The purple-colored Syrah Orzada reveals a bouquet of smoke, game, and blue fruits. Forward and tasty on the palate, this easygoing wine will offer pleasure during its first 4 years.

VIÑA PEÑALOLÉN (*Maipo Valley*)

Cabernet Sauvignon 🍷 **$$** Viña Peñalolén's Cabernet Sauvignon has a nose of cedar, spice box, tobacco, red currant, and black currant. This is followed by a smooth-textured, easygoing Cabernet with enough structure to evolve for 1–2 years, savory red and black fruit flavors, cinnamon and earth notes, and a medium-long finish.

PÉREZ CRUZ (*Maipo Valley*)

Carménère Reserva Limited Edition 🍷 **$$** The Carménère Reserva offers a superb aromatic array of scorched earth, pencil lead, blueberry, and blackberry liqueur. On the palate spice, plum, and chocolate notes emerge followed by a lengthy, fruit-filled, pure finish.

Cot Reserva Limited Edition 🍷 **$$** The Cot Reserva has an attractive bouquet of cedar, spice box, cassis, and black cherry. Forward, supple, and uncomplicated, this tasty wine will round out with 1–2 years of cellaring but can be enjoyed now.

Syrah Reserva Limited Edition 🍷 **$$$** The Syrah Reserva Limited Edition offers up notes of game, wood smoke, and blueberry. This leads to a medium- to full-bodied wine with ample spicy, peppery blue fruits; a smooth texture; light tannin; and good length.

POLKURA (*Colchagua Valley*)

Syrah 🍷 **$$$** Polkura's Syrah has an excellent smoky, gamy, blue fruit perfume. Ripe and full flavored on the palate, this nicely balanced wine will evolve for 1–2 years and be at its finest through 2016.

PORTA (*Bio-Bio Valley*)

Pinot Noir Winemaker Reserva 🍷 **$$** The medium-ruby-colored Pinot Noir Winemaker Reserva reveals varietally correct strawberry, cherry, and cranberry aromas leading to a wine with modest depth and length.

Sauvignon Blanc Reserva ♟ $ Offers up a fragrant bouquet of mineral, grapefruit, and gooseberry. This is followed by a medium-bodied wine with intense citrus flavors, vibrant acidity, and a long, refreshing finish.

QUINTAY *(Casablanca Valley)*

Sauvignon Blanc Clova ♟ $ The nose reveals fresh herbs and citrus leading to a light- to medium-bodied wine with crisp, vibrant citrus flavors and a clean finish.

Sauvignon Blanc Quintay ♟ $ Offers a bit more class than the Clova and complexity with layered flavors and a lengthy, fruit-filled finish. It will provide pleasure over the next 1–2 years.

VIÑA REQUINGUA *(Curico Valley)*

Toro de Piedra Carménère–Cabernet Sauvignon ♟ $ Made in a forward style. Ripe and flavorful, this tasty effort has no hard edges. It can be enjoyed over the next several years.

Toro de Piedra Syrah–Cabernet Sauvignon ♟ $ Offers an attractive blue and black fruit nose leading to a wine with ample, spicy, savory fruit; good depth; and an easygoing personality.

CASA RIVAS *(Maipo Valley)*

Carménère Gran Reserva ♟ $ It has an excellent nose of spice box, blueberry, and blackberry. Concentrated, ripe, balanced, and long, it will provide pleasure over its first 4–5 years.

SANTA CAROLINA *(Various Regions)*

Chardonnay Reserva—Casablanca Valley ♟ $ The unoaked Chardonnay Reserva exhibits white fruit aromas, apple and pear flavors, and good depth.

Chardonnay Reserva de Familia—Casablanca Valley ♟ $$ This Chardonnay is a bit more substantial than the Reserva, with better depth and concentration.

Sauvignon Blanc Reserva—Rapel Valley ♀ $ Reveals an alluring bouquet of fresh cut grass and citrus. Light to medium bodied, it offers crisp grapefruit and lemon-lime flavors, vibrant acidity, and a fruity finish.

SANTA EMA *(Various Regions)*

Amplus Cabernet Sauvignon—Cachapoal Valley ♀ $$ Features an alluring nose of spice box, black currant, blackberry, and a suggestion of chocolate in the background. Smooth textured, forward, and easygoing, this nicely balanced wine has a lengthy, fruit-filled finish.

Amplus Sauvignon Blanc—Leyda Valley ♀ $$ Offers an excellent aromatic array of grapefruit, lime, gooseberry, and a hint of minerality. Crisp, with good depth of flavor, this nicely balanced, lengthy wine can be enjoyed during its first 12–18 months.

SANTA HELENA *(Various Regions)*

Cabernet Sauvignon Gran Reserva—Colchagua Valley ♀ $$ Offers up pleasant cassis and currant aromas. Forward and uncomplicated on the palate, it offers ample spicy red and black fruit flavors for enjoying during its first 2–3 years.

Sauvignon Blanc Gran Reserva—Leyda Valley ♀ $$ Reveals an alluring bouquet of mineral, grapefruit, and gooseberry leading to a complex wine with intense fruit flavors, serious depth, and a pure finish.

SANTA LAURA *(Colchagua Valley)*

Chardonnay Reserve ♀ $ This Chardonnay has a pleasant perfume of white peach and apple. Medium bodied, it has ample fruit, good acidity, and a medium-long, fruity finish.

SANTA RITA *(Various Regions)*

Cabernet Sauvignon Medalla Real—Maipo Valley ♀ $$$ The Medalla Real has an attractive bouquet of cedar, earth notes, cassis, and black currant. On the palate the wine is firm with enough structure to improve for 1–2 years. It offers ample spicy red and black fruits, good depth, and a medium-long finish.

Carménère "120"—Rapel Valley ♉ $ Forward, easygoing, and friendly, with plenty of ripe fruit and no hard edges.

Chardonnay "120"—Aconcagua Valley ♉ $ The unoaked Chardonnay "120" offers crisp apple and pear aromas and flavors for drinking during its first 12–18 months.

Sauvignon Blanc "120"—Lontue Valley ♉ $ Exhibits an attractive bouquet of spring flowers, citrus, and lemon-lime followed by a crisp, refreshing wine with a clean finish.

Sauvignon Blanc Floresta—Leyda Valley ♉ $$ Floresta, from the cool-climate Leyda Valley, is a first-class effort with an expressive bouquet of minerals, fresh herbs, grapefruit, and gooseberry. Round and complex, the wine has exceptional depth and concentration.

Sauvignon Blanc Reserva—Casablanca Valley ♉ $ It is a bit more aromatic, layered, and rich than the Floresta.

Shiraz "120"—Maipo Valley ♉ $ A pleasant, fruity, forward wine meant for near-term drinking. This easy-on-the-pocketbook effort has no hard edges.

Shiraz Reserva—Maipo Valley ♉ $$ A bit more substantial, with enough structure to improve over the next 1–2 years. However, this generously fruited wine can be enjoyed now.

CASA SILVA *(Colchagua Valley)*

Carménère Gran Reserva Los Lingues ♉ $$ Exhibits an alluring perfume of blueberry compote, black raspberry, and earth notes leading to a sweetly fruited, layered wine with excellent concentration and a forward personality.

Chardonnay Angostura Gran Reserva ♉ $$ The Gran Reserva adds toasty oak notes and has greater depth than the Reserva. This should be consumed over its first 1–2 years.

Chardonnay Reserva ♉ $ This unoaked Chardonnay exhibits attractive green apple and pear aromas and flavors in a straightforward style. It should be consumed over its first 1–2 years.

Petit Verdot Gran Reserva 🍷 $$ The Petit Verdot Gran Reserva offers up a perfume of smoke, scorched earth, pencil lead, black currant, and blackberry. Layered, full flavored, and discreetly structured, it will evolve for 3–4 years and drink well through 2025. It way overdelivers for its humble price.

Pinot Noir Reserva 🍷 $ The Pinot Noir Reserva offers raspberry and cherry aromatics. It has good varietal character, albeit without much depth or complexity.

Sauvignon Blanc Reserva 🍷 $ Offers an excellent nose of grapefruit and lemon-lime. Crisp, clean, and vibrant on the palate, this nicely balanced value can be enjoyed over the next 12–18 months.

Syrah Gran Reserva Lolol 🍷 $$ The Lolol has an enticing nose of spice box, blueberry, and earth notes. Supple textured, the wine has good depth and concentration as well as 1–2 years of aging potential. Drink it through 2015.

Viognier Lolol 🍷 $$ The Viognier Lolol delivers a bit more richness and a creamier palate-feel. It too is meant for near-term drinking.

Viognier Reserva 🍷 $ The Viognier Reserva offers fragrant peach and apricot notes leading to a lively, concentrated wine with ample spicy fruit meant for drinking during the first 1–2 years.

VIÑA GARCES SILVA (AMAYNA) *(Leyda Valley)*

Chardonnay 🍷 $$ The Chardonnay exhibits mineral, almond, white peach, and poached pear aromas. On the palate it displays elegance, a creamy texture, layers of flavor, and a striking resemblance to grand cru white Burgundy. It is a steal at the asking price.

Sauvignon Blanc 🍷 $$ The Sauvignon Blanc reveals a superb bouquet of fresh hay, grapefruit, lemon-lime, and floral notes. Smooth textured, the wine exhibits succulent fruit, outstanding depth and concentration, and a lengthy, pure, fruit-filled finish.

TABALI *(Limari Valley)*

Reserva Especial 🍷 $$$ The Reserva Especial is a blend of Syrah, Cabernet Sauvignon, and Merlot. It offers up an enticing nose of smoke, mineral, blue fruits, and black currant. Smooth textured, the wine has very good depth, savory dark fruit flavors, plenty of ripeness, and a medium-long finish. Drink it during its first 6–8 years.

VIÑA TARAPACA (*Maipo Valley*)

Cabernet Sauvignon Gran Reserva ♟ **$$** The Cabernet has an attractive aromatic array of toasty oak, blueberry, and black cherry. Forward on the palate, it exhibits a friendly personality, sweet flavors, light tannin, good depth, and a pure finish.

Carménère Gran Reserva ♟ **$$** The succulent Carménère offers up an alluring perfume of cedar, mineral, and blue fruit. Layered and ripe on the palate, it has plenty of ripe blueberry and blackberry flavors, excellent depth and length, and enough structure to evolve for 2–3 years.

TERRUNYO (*Casablanca Valley*)

Sauvignon Blanc Block 27 ♟ **$$** A superb bouquet of freshly cut hay, grapefruit, lemon-lime, and gooseberry, is followed by a lush, ripe, focused Sauvignon with layers of flavor, superb balance, and a pure, fruit-filled finish.

MIGUEL TORRES CHILE (*Curico Valley*)

Sauvignon Blanc Santa Digna ♟ **$$** The Santa Digna offers focused aromas of fresh herbs, cut grass, and grapefruit. Crisp, flavorful, and well balanced, it will drink well during its first 12–18 months.

LOS VASCOS (*Colchagua Valley and Casablanca Valley*)

Chardonnay ♟ **$** The unoaked Chardonnay's nose exhibits lively white fruits with a hint of tropical fruit in the background. It has decent acidity and enough ripe fruit to provide pleasure during its first 2 years.

Los Vascos Reserve ♟ **$$** The Reserve is a blend of Cabernet Sauvignon, Carménère, Syrah, and Malbec. It reveals an enticing bouquet of spice box, cedar, tobacco, cassis, and black cherry leading to a wine with plenty of savory fruit but also some hard tannin in the finish.

Sauvignon Blanc ♀ $ Offers an expressive nose of fresh herbs and citrus. Ripe, balanced, and made in a round, pleasing style, this tasty Sauvignon should be enjoyed over the next 12–18 months.

VENTISQUERO *(Maipo Valley and Casablanca Valley)*

Cabernet Sauvignon Gran Reserva Único Luis Miguel ♀ $$ This Cabernet exhibits an expressive bouquet of spice box, cassis, black currant, and blackberry. This is followed by a medium- to full-bodied, structured wine with plenty of fruit but also substantial tannin.

Sauvignon Blanc Gran Reserva Queulat ♀ $$ This Reserva adds a touch of minerality and earth notes to the citrus aromas and flavors.

Sauvignon Blanc Reserva ♀ $ Offers up pleasant grapefruit and lemon-lime aromas leading to a crisp, refreshing wine for drinking during its first 12–18 months.

Sauvignon Blanc Root 1 Reserva ♀ $$ The Port 1 Reserva is sourced from ungrafted wines, hence the name. It has just a bit more weight and depth than its grafted sibling.

Shiraz Gran Reserva Queulet ♀ $$ It delivers an alluring blueberry, peppery perfume along with a variety of other spice notes. Supple and easygoing, with the tannin in check, this tasty, concentrated wine can be enjoyed over its first 5 years.

VERANDA *(Casablanca Valley)*

Cabernet Sauvignon–Carménère Apalta ♀ $$$ The Cabernet Sauvignon–Carmenère exhibits an attractive perfume of cedar, blueberry, and black currant. Ripe and forward on the palate, the wine displays an elegant personality with enough stuffing to evolve for 1–2 years.

Chardonnay ♀ $$ Veranda's Chardonnay offers up baked apple and pear aromas along with a touch of oak. Crisp and lively on the palate with the wood nicely integrated, this is a Chardonnay to enjoy during its first 1–2 years.

Pinot Noir ♀ $$ The Pinot Noir reveals excellent cherry and raspberry perfume. On the palate it is a bit firm, but it is likely to round out and provide outstanding drinking.

VILLARD *(Casablanca Valley)*

Chardonnay Expresión Reserva ♀ **$$** Delivers pear and apple-blossom aromas followed by a wine with moderate depth, ripe white fruits, and a clean finish.

Pinot Noir Expresión Reserva ♟ **$$** Offers up bright cherry and rhubarb aromas with a hint of cinnamon in the background. On the palate it is a bit tart but has decent varietal character, modest depth and concentration, and a crisp finish.

Le Pinot Noir Grand Vin ♟ **$$$** This wine has an alluring perfume of spice box, strawberry, raspberry, and rhubarb. It exhibits an elegant personality marked by a silky texture and a fruit-filled finish.

Sauvignon Blanc Expresión Reserva ♀ **$$** The Sauvignon Blanc has an excellent nose of citrus, gooseberry, and fresh herbs. This leads to a crisp, intensely flavored, well-balanced wine with good depth and a fruit-filled finish.

VIU MANENT *(Leyda Valley)*

Sauvignon Blanc Reserva ♀ **$$** It offers an attractive bouquet of mineral, fresh herbs, citrus, and lemon-lime. This leads to a medium-bodied wine with vibrant acidity; concentrated, fresh flavors; excellent depth; and a clean finish.

VIÑA VON SIEBENTHAL *(Aconcagua Valley)*

Carménère Reserva Single Vineyard ♟ **$$** The Carménère Reserva Single Vineyard delivers an expressive bouquet of cedar, leather, blueberry, and black currant. This leads to a smooth-textured wine with layers of spicy black and blue fruits, succulent flavors, excellent depth and balance, and enough structure to evolve for 1–2 years.

FRANCE

ALSACE, THE SAVOIE, AND THE JURA WINE VALUES

by David Schildknecht

Alsace, the Savoie, and the Jura are each mountainous wine-growing regions of eastern France, many of whose bewilderingly diverse but splendid wines (some from grapes scarcely known elsewhere) are high priced and drunk largely within their regions of production. Yet all three harbor some amazing values that will come as delicious revelations to those who take the trouble and time to search and to experiment.

Alsace—Perplexing Identity and Rich Rewards

This heartbreakingly beautiful and historically fought-over region of France is home to some of the world's most dramatically distinctive, seductively aromatic, texturally alluring, and long-lived wines. The grape varieties themselves—not to mention the soils and microclimates in which they are grown and the stylistic inspirations of the growers—are so diverse that they permit synergistic pairings with virtually any cuisine on earth. The Vosges range draws off precipitation from westerly fronts, making Alsace one of the driest regions of France. Yet its many streams and snowcapped peaks supply an ample source of groundwater for the vines on its lower slopes, rendering this narrow strip between mountains and Rhine a wine-growing paradise. A single official appellation covers this entire region, and nearly all wines are labeled with the name of their grape variety.

A note on labeling: With the exception of a few growers who have introduced winery-internal coding or schematics to signify degree of dryness, one simply doesn't know (barring the sort of information we have supplied in this guide) whether a given Alsace wine will taste dry or slightly sweet. Another source of potential confusion is the proliferation of cuvées and bottlings at the typical Alsace address, each separately named, with the fruits of many individual parcels or pickings segregated. (Alsace grows nobly sweet late-harvest wines, too, but all of those far transcend the price limitations of this guide.)

Grapes

The ostensibly humble **Chasselas** and **Sylvaner** are less aromatically striking than most of the grapes of Alsace but in places—and especially from old vines—can render wines of distinctive character. Furthermore, these are generally inexpensive and thus feature significantly in this guide. **Pinot Blanc**, or "Pinot d'Alsace," in fact generally refers to a blend, most often of grapes of the low-acid **Auxerrois** and the true Pinot Blanc. Such sweetly perfumed yet generally dry-finishing blends are among the most common of Alsace's top values. **Riesling** is capable in Alsace of some of its most complex, long-lived expressions, yet it is also a source of many very affordable wines. The pungently herbal, resinous, citric **Muscat d'Alsace**; rich, subtly smoky, meaty **Pinot Gris**; and **Gewurztraminer**—with its aromas of rose petal, lychee, bacon fat, mint, black pepper, and brown spices, as well as its sumptuous texture and opulence—are all at their best in Alsace, if somewhat less often available at modest prices. **Pinot Noir**—the sole local black grape—is increasingly demonstrating its potential for excellence, and blends of multiple varieties represent a tradition in revival.

Vintage Smarts

Early indications are that 2008 will prove to be an outstanding vintage in Alsace. The 2005 and 2007 vintages have been very successful, while 2004 and 2006 were challenging, resulting in wines that must be selected with care.

Drinking Curves

Enjoy Pinot Blanc or Sylvaner within three to four years of its vintage. Alsace Riesling, Pinot Gris, Gewurztraminer, and Muscat all exhibit an uncanny ability to live long and evolve harmoniously in bottle, although within the price parameters of this guide, one cannot partake of the very best and most resilient wines that these grapes have to offer. As a safe rule, one should plan to enjoy within four to six years wines from these grapes that are recommended below.

The Savoie and the Jura—Mountains and Mysteries

Looking east across the basin of the Saône River from Burgundy's Côte d'Or, one sees the geological twin of that "Golden Slope," the mountains of the Jura. On a clear day, one can even make out Mont Blanc and the Savoie to the southeast. These mountains that parallel the Côte d'Or, the Mâcon, and Beaujolais at a distance of roughly fifty to eighty miles are home to diverse and remarkable vines, microclimates, and wine-growing traditions, most of them little appreciated even inside France, let alone abroad.

The Jura's classic wines will strike most tasters as among the most unusual and out-of-step with modern fashion in France, if not the world. So, if intrigue and mind-expansion are part of what motivates you, you absolutely must take at least a few sips and sniffs, even if it is in the end simply to wrinkle your nose—the surest sign of wonder! There are a few lovely, fresh-fruited wines from **Chardonnay** (a grape that may have originated there) and **Pinot Noir**—including outstanding-value sparkling cuvées—that one might compare with wines from elsewhere. But the most typical Jura wines combine sherry-like characteristics of oxidation and the pungent influence of microbial film permitted to grow on the surface of the wines in barrel. The appellation Côtes du Jura covers virtually the entire region like an umbrella, with three others—Arbois, Château Chalon, and l'Étoile—specific to certain groups of villages. The white grape **Savaignin** forms the basis for many of the region's most prestigious wines, and two unusual reds are of great importance as well: the pale but highly perfumed **Poulsard**, and the ruddier **Trousseau**.

The Savoie represents such a crazy quilt of vine varieties, sites, and styles—spread like beads spilled on an undulating carpet—as to render generalizations difficult. In its largest sector, from the **Jacquère** grape, the Savoie renders (under the appellations Abymes, Apremont, Arbin, and Chignin) wines that are among the world's foremost values in crisp, refreshing, delicate, low-alcohol whites, some grown in rubble deposited by a mega-avalanche in 1248 when Mont Granier collapsed, burying entire villages. Savoie reds grown nearby from Syrah's peppery, rustic ancestor **Mondeuse** range from simple and light to concentrated and tannic. A constellation of complex, pungent whites stems from the indigenous **Altesse** grape (a.k.a. **Roussette de Savoie**), of which those grown on the steep terraces of Jongieux and Marestel are noteworthy. Bugey—representing a multitude of villages to the north of the Rhône River—is best known for light red, sweet sparkling wines that are utterly infectious and distinctive. **Chignin Bergeron** (Roussanne) generally transcends the price limitations of the present guide.

Vintage Smarts and Drinking Curves

The Jacquère-based wines of the Savoie should generally be enjoyed in the youngest available vintage—within two years at latest—so vintage character should not be made a significant consideration in choosing them. Sparkling wines of the Savoie, including Bugey, should also be enjoyed as young as possible. Mondeuse reds can be held for four or more years—the 2005s are excellent now—and wines based on the Altesse grape (Roussette de Savoie) can have long life spans, although the oxidizing effects are an acquired taste. The fresh-style Chardonnay wines of the Jura should be enjoyed within 2–3 years of the vintage. The classic oxidized Jura wines, on the other hand, can safely be held for a minimum of six to eight years.

Top Wine Values of Alsace, the Savoie, and the Jura by Winery

LUCIEN ALBRECHT *(Alsace)*

Auxerrois Cuvée ♀ **$$** From older vines, this cuvée typically adds diverse tropical fruits and bittersweet zest to its citrus theme.

Pinot Blanc Réserve ♀ **$** Subtly creamy, easy-drinking, Auxerrois-dominated refresher brimming with luscious citrus and tinged with mineral nuances.

Riesling Réserve ♀ **$$** Citrus and red berry fruit augmented by floral perfume; tartly refreshing and generally just barely sweet.

BARMES-BUECHER *(Alsace)*

Pinot Auxerrois ♀ **$$** Biodynamic farming and early yet ripe harvesting yield irresistibly juicy refreshment with smoky, zesty, nutty accents.

LAURENT BARTH *(Alsace)*

Pinot d'Alsace ♀ **$$$** Ripe pit fruits, citrus, and herbs inform a juicy but honeyed, well-concentrated palate, with the barest suggestion of sweetness.

PAUL BLANCK (*Alsace*)

Pinot Auxerrois ♀ $$$ Loaded with ripe pit fruits, citrus, and sweet flowers, lusciously juicy yet creamy textured, this finishes with hints of honey and coffee.

PIERRE BONIFACE (*Savoie*)

Apremont Les Rocailles ♀ $ A floral, zesty, chalky Jacquère-based refresher betraying no underripeness even in rained-on vintages.

Apremont Les Rocailles Prestige ♀ $$ More mouth filling and minerally nuanced than Boniface's regular bottling, yet always refreshingly lip-smacking.

Rousette de Savoie Les Rocailles ♀ $$ Scents of buckwheat, lemon oil, white pepper, and flowers lead to a zesty and subtly oily palate.

DOMAINE BOTT-GEYL (*Alsace*)

Pinot d'Alsace ♀ $$ Including not only Auxerrois and Pinot Blanc but also 10–12% each of Pinot Gris and Pinot Noir, this synergistic Bott original is loaded with orchard and citrus fruits, flowers, and mineral notes.

Pinot Gris Les Elements ♀ $$$ Cut and refreshment more typical of Riesling, yet ample richness; bright mandarin and peach; saline, meaty, nutty undertones; and a barely detectable hint of sweetness.

Riesling Les Elements ♀ $$$ Peaches, flowers, and honey; a soothing texture; and savory, saline, pungent mineral suggestions.

PATRICK BOTTEX (*Savoie*)

Bugey-Cerdon La Cueille ♀ SD ♀ $$ A deep-pink libation that's sweet and sparkles, with scarcely more alcohol than the typical beer and an unmatchable conglomeration of red and black fruits irresistible to all but insufferable wine snobs.

ALBERT BOXLER (*Alsace*)

Sylvaner ♀ $$$ Typical of this estate's stylistic refinement: effusively floral, with crystalline orchard fruit character, lush but unlike many a Sylvaner shapely, not fat.

AGATHE BURSIN *(Alsace)*

Riesling ♀ **$$$** Black tea, sage, musk melon, citrus, and peach inform a Riesling that balances creaminess of texture and brightness.

Sylvaner ♀ **$$** A florally bittersweet, honeyed, smoky, creamy-textured, chalky, rich value from a young estate.

HUBERT CLAVELIN *(Jura)*

Crémant du Jura Brut–Comté Chardonnay Tête de Cuvée ♀ **$$** This outstanding-value, fine-grained "traditional method" sparkler offers fresh apple, wheat toast, lemon zest, gentian, and honey.

MARCEL DEISS *(Alsace)*

Pinot Blanc ♀ **$$$** Famed blend-favoring vintner Jean-Michel Deiss adds Pinot Gris and Pinot Noir to his Auxerrois and Pinot Blanc, rendering ravishing aromas and a silken-textured palate of pit fruits, spice, flowers, and citrus.

DIRLER-CADE *(Alsace)*

Pinot ♀ **$$** This distinctive, unorthodox 100% Pinot Noir—vinified white (with a faint copper shimmer)—is creamy yet gripping and loaded with pit fruits.

Sylvaner Vieilles Vignes ♀ **$$$** From venerable vineyards, this displays sage; citrus and nut oils; apples; a glycerin-rich, creamy palate; and finishing clarity rare for Sylvaner.

DOMAINE DUPASQUIER *(Savoie)*

Rousette de Savoie Altesse ♀ **$$$** A wine of refinement and aromatic mystery, mingling flowers, toasted nuts and buckwheat, and citrus zest, this finishes with saline savor and hints of crushed stone.

MICHEL FONNÉ *(Alsace)*

Muscat d'Alsace ♀ **$$** This offers a rare opportunity to savor the unique virtues of Alsace Muscat affordably: pungent resin, peppermint, sage, citrus zest, acacia, and coffee; lushness yet invigoration.

Pinot Blanc Vignoble de Bennwihr ♉ $ This amazingly inexpensive offering typically displays lovely aromas of sweet clover or apple blossom, pear, citrus zest, iodine, and brown spices, proving infectiously and unquenchably refreshing.

Pinot Gris Roemerberg Vieilles Vignes SD ♉ $$$ An opulent, oily-rich, soothingly lingering Pinot Gris from tiny berries: carnal, peachy, sometimes exhibiting rose petal and brown spice aromas.

Riesling Vignoble de Bennwihr ♉ $$ Ripe orchard fruits accented by cress, herbs, and citrus zest; lush ripeness yet delicacy; sometimes a hint of sweetness but also of mineral intrigue.

Riesling Rebgarten Vieilles Vignes ♉ $$$ Scents of pink grapefruit and honey; a lush, silken palate loaded with refreshing citrus; and a finishing balance of richness and vivacity characterize this virtually dry Riesling.

FRÉDÉRIC GIACHINO *(Savoie)*

Abymes Monfarina ♉ $$ Offering sensational quality-price rapport, this clear, invigorating, citrus- and pit fruit–filled Jacquère, tinged with salt, white pepper, chalk, and shrimp shell, leaves you panting for the next sip.

Roussette de Savoie Altesse ♉ $$ Lemon oil, marzipan, and kirsch inform this penetrating, piquant expression of Altesse.

DOMAINE GRESSER *(Alsace)*

Gewurztraminer Kritt ♉ $$$ Sweet pea, rose petal, spices, lime, and coconut inform this subtly creamy, succulent, dry yet alcoholically moderate Gewurztraminer that finishes quite refreshingly and with alkaline and stony hints.

Pinot Noir Brandhof ♇ $$$ A surprisingly affordable example of its class: refreshingly red fruited, subtly bitter, tart, saline, savory, and chalky.

HUGEL *(Alsace)*

Gentil ♉ $ Hugel's homage to traditional Alsace blends reflects its Gewurztraminer and Sylvaner base in smoked meat, herbs, and rose petal, as well as a plush texture. Riesling donates palate brightness.

Gewurztraminer ♀ **$$$** Boasting sap and strength for a generic bottling, as well as true dryness, this incredibly versatile wine typically offers smoked meat, coffee, mint, rose petal, celery seed, and black pepper.

Riesling ♀ **$$** Hugel's satin-textured yet refreshing basic Riesling typically displays lime, honey, a hint of petrol, nut oils, fruit pits, and a completely dry finish.

EMMANUEL HUILLON (Jura)

Arbois Pupillin Chardonnay ♀ **$$$** An Arbois (without added sulfur) that strikingly calls to mind chicken broth, oyster and clam juice, and ocean water; amazingly savory and salivation inducing.

DOMAINE DE L'IDYLLE (Savoie)

Arbin Mondeuse ♀ **$$** This makes a good introduction to Mondeuse, with mulberries, meat stock, and black pepper; sappy, bittersweet, subtly astringent, and versatile.

Roussette de Savoie Altesse ♀ **$$** Honeydew melon, pineapple, lavender, lemon zest, toasted nuts, and a hit of sherry- or Jura-like flor pungency and nutty piquancy inform a wine whose finish boasts considerable grip.

JOSMEYER (Alsace)

Pinot Blanc Mise du Printemps ♀ **$$$** Owner Jean Meyer's long-running themes of food friendliness, elegance, and Auxerrois are well displayed in this refreshing alliance of flowers, herbs, citrus zest, and luscious melon and orchard fruits.

ANDRÉ KIENTZLER (Alsace)

Chasselas ♀ **$$** Suggesting hay, straw, and flowers in the nose, this juicy and refreshing, subtly saline and chalky Chasselas displays rare distinction.

Riesling Réserve Particulière ♀ **$$$** Luscious and zesty citrus, tart black or red berries, pungent penetration, firmness, brightness, chew, salinity, and crushed stone anticipate the single-site Rieslings for which Kientzler is renowned.

MARC KREYDENWEISS *(Alsace)*

Pinot Blanc Kritt ♀ $$ Organic pioneer Kreydenweiss's blend of
Pinot Blanc and Auxerrois suggests pear cider and honeysuckle.
Rich, often strikingly creamy, it finishes lusciously but without a hint
of sweetness.

PAUL KUBLER *(Alsace)*

Pinot Gris K ♀ $$$ Peach and quince preserves with notes of lychee
and smoked meat inform this ripe, full-bodied, yet fully dry Pinot
Gris.

Riesling K ♀ $$$ This cuvée typically features luscious citrus, saline
minerality, and herbal pungency; runs in a refreshing and quite
delicate direction; and is well and truly dry.

KUENTZ-BAS *(Alsace)*

Auxerrois Collection ♀ $$ From the midrange at Kuentz-Bas, this
old-vines wine from chalky slopes offers citrus zest, red fruits, and
smoke, with caressing, creamy, yet insistently juicy palate persistence.

Riesling Collection ♀ $$$ Fruit incorporated from the estate's
grand cru holdings shows in intriguing mineral accents with a
mélange of melon, pit fruits, and citrus zest.

DOMAINE LABBÉ *(Savoie)*

Abymes ♀ $ Multiple bottlings each year preserve freshness in this
pear, clover, lime, and chalk–suffused, saline, CO_2-tinged, supremely
versatile (occasionally barely off-dry) Jacquère.

DOMAINE ALBERT MANN *(Alsace)*

Auxerrois Vieilles Vignes ♀ $$ Tangerine, honey, diverse flowers,
nut oils, and malt; marvelous balance of textural richness with an
uncommon vivacity for this grape: Here's a wine not to miss!

Crémant d'Alsace ♀♀ $$$ Based on the same blend as the Mann
Pinot Blanc (below), with more creaminess and more vivacity, this
effervescent essence of pit fruits, flowers, citrus, and mineral stuff is
absolutely irresistible and one of the most distinctly delicious and
affordable sparkling wine treasures in the world.

Gewurztraminer ⑤D 🍷 \$\$\$ Rose petals, orchard fruits, brown spices, and subtle smokiness are allied to honeyed richness, discreet sweetness, and refreshment one rarely encounters with this grape.

Pinot Blanc 🍷 \$\$ Offering extraordinary price-quality rapport, this smoke- and salt-tinged blend of Auxerrois and true Pinot Blanc, redolent of orange blossom, pit fruits, and citrus, is subtly creamy yet ravishingly juicy.

JEAN MASSON *(Savoie)*

Apremont Cuvée Nicolas 🍷 \$\$ One of numerous single-site bottlings from Masson, this typically shows lemon, grapefruit, brown spices, and raw almond; is waxy in texture and chalky; yet is juicy finishing.

Apremont Vieilles Vignes 🍷 \$\$\$ Distinguished by its heavier bottle and oversized, pale green label, this floral, citric, pit-fruited, and mineral wine nicknamed "du Siècle" by Masson will amaze you with its versatility at table.

Apremont Vieilles Vignes Traditionelle 🍷 \$\$ Loaded with floral essences and subtly citric and chalky, this simplest (gold-labeled) Masson bottling offers startling purity and infectious juiciness, lift, and invigoration (at 11.5% alcohol). One sip will hook you!

MEYER-FONNÉ *(Alsace)*

Gentil d'Alsace 🍷 \$ From an unorthodox blend of Muscat and Pinot Blanc with a bit of Riesling and Gewurztraminer, Meyer's Gentil is juicy, lush, subtly spicy, and herb and coffee tinged.

Pinot Blanc Vieilles Vignes 🍷 \$\$ This offers a delightful combination of creaminess and honeyed richness with refreshment, featuring citrus and ripe pit fruits tinged by herbs and smoke.

Riesling Vignobles de Katzenthal 🍷 \$\$\$ Muscat-like suggestions of sage, resin, orange blossom, and lemon zest lead to a smoothly textured and satisfyingly juicy, lush, and soothing palate.

FRÉDÉRIC MOCHEL *(Alsace)*

Pinot Gris 🍷 \$\$\$ An unusually juicy, succulent example of its variety, scented with ripe peach, hints of red berry, and wood smoke; displaying a faintly oily texture; and offering considerable interest of herbs and spices.

Riesling ♙ $$$ This shows the class of Mochel's grand cru site: sassily citric, pungently herbal, decidedly chalky, stony, and saline.

Sylvaner ♙ $$ Here is proof of how refreshing and downright intriguing this supposedly humble variety can be in the north of Alsace. Pungent lemon zest, pear skin, and herbs dominate.

DOMAINE DE MONTBOURGEAU *(Jura)*

Crémant du Jura Brut ♙ ♙ $$$ Here's another superb value sparkler from Jura Chardonnay: subtly nutty and floral, mineral, and refreshingly citric.

Étoile Cuvée Spéciale ♙ $$$ An outstanding example of classic oxidized-style Jura wine from pure Chardonnay left untouched in barrel for five years to become penetratingly, pungently nutty and citric, with hints of toast and caramel.

DOMAINE DE L'ORIEL–GÉRARD WEINZORN *(Alsace)*

L'Oriel ♙ $$ This blend of Riesling, Pinot Gris, Gewurztraminer, and Muscat boasts soothing richness, with pit fruits, citrus cream, nut oils, honey, rose petal, and smoked meats backed by discreet sweetness.

Riesling ♙ $$$ Full of ripe white peach and luscious citrus; depending on vintage perhaps laced with honey, white truffle, or narcissus. Even when oily, soft, and plush on the palate, this keeps its freshness.

ANDRÉ OSTERTAG *(Alsace)*

Sylvaner Vieilles Vignes ♙ $$ Elusively smoky, meaty, and chalky; exhibiting juicy, apple-y fruit, a doughy, waxy texture, and a succulent finish. This will turn cartwheels on your table!

FRANK PEILLOT *(Savoie)*

Roussette du Bugey Montagnieu Altesse ♙ $$$ A striking introduction to Altesse, this reveals green tea, quince, clover, linden flower, and herbs, mingling in a luscious, silken-textured, delicate, subtly bitter, fascinating, and food-friendly mélange.

ANDRÉ PFISTER *(Alsace)*

Pinot Blanc ♉ **$$** Smelling of ripe apple, almond, and flowers, young Melanie Pfister's Pinot Blanc saturates the palate with juicy apple and melon fruit tinged with citrus zest and honey.

Riesling Silberberg ♉ **$$$** Brimming with orchard fruits, citrus, flowers, and herbs, this typically balances nutty richness and ripe fruit with herbal pungency, tart citricity, and salty minerality, finishing with invigorating length.

ANDRÉ AND MICHEL QUENARD *(Savoie)*

Abymes ♉ **$$** This shows the floral, citric, subtly mineral, and low-alcohol refreshment that Jacquère grapes can offer in these chalky soils.

Chignin ♉ **$$** Like the Quenards' Abymes, a consistently refreshing, floral, and subtly mineral alpine wine par excellence.

DOMAINE RENARDAT-FÂCHE *(Savoie)*

Bugey-Cerdon ♉ 🆂🅳 ♉ **$$$** Deeply pink, berry-rich, sparkling, low-alcohol, and sweet, this is a treat except for wine snobs, who will be tormented!

JEAN RIJCKAERT *(Jura)*

Arbois En Paradis Vieilles Vignes Chardonnay ♉ **$$$** The absolute showstopper among Rijckaert's "low-end" cuvées offers uncanny richness with brightness, complexity, pungency, and length, featuring pear, flowers, nuts, citrus, mysterious carnality, and minerality.

Chardonnay ♉ **$$$** A stupendous value from Rijckaert's old-vine holdings, this grips tenaciously, displaying apple, pineapple, mandarin, salt, citrus, and persistently pungent herbal, floral, fungal, and mineral notes.

Côtes de Jura Les Sarres Chardonnay ♉ **$$$** Mingling scents and flavors of apple, lime, pineapple, and coconut with pungent nuttiness and a whiff of fino sherry–like flor, this opulently rich yet bright white will fascinate almost endlessly at table.

CHARLES SCHLERET *(Alsace)*

Pinot Blanc ♀ **$$$** Largely Auxerrois, this cuvée offers effusive scents and creamy, sherbet-like palate expressions of citrus fruits and sweetly herbal nuances in a soft but refreshing finish; a model of delicacy and infectious drinkability.

JEAN-PAUL SCHMITT *(Alsace)*

Pinot Gris ♀ **$$$** This surprises with its balance: low in residual sugar, yet under 14% alcohol. Full of ripe peach and citrus, it's almost Riesling-like in brightness, while preserving the smokiness, spiciness, and oily richness typical of Alsace Pinot Gris.

Riesling ♀ **$$$** Truly dry, ripe, and interesting in flavor, yet with only 12.5% alcohol, this sassy, bright, lean but refreshingly saline, citric, herbal, apricot-fruited Riesling performs well with all manner of cuisine.

SCHOFFIT *(Alsace)*

Chasselas Vieilles Vignes ♀ **$$** Tasting like no other wine from this grape, this wine is Pinot Gris–like in its soothing, glossy richness, with herbs, honey, spices, and smoked meats.

Pinot Blanc Auxerrois Vieilles Vignes SD ♀ **$$$** Generous with pit fruits, citrus zest, and herbs; opulent, creamy, with noticeable sweetness; this gains counterpoint from fusil, smoky, subtly bitter notes.

Riesling Harth Tradition SD ♀ **$$$** Offers abundant, sweetly aromatic herbs and luscious citrus; unusually creamy textured and effusive for a Riesling. This will segue into rather than cut against rich fare.

PIERRE SPARR *(Alsace)*

Pinot Gris Réserve SD ♀ **$$** This plush, honeyed, generously pit-fruited, slightly sweet, and subtly smoky entry is typical of the soft, sometimes slightly blurry style of Sparr's huge lineup.

MARC TEMPÉ *(Alsace)*

Riesling Zellenberg ♀ **$$$** Amazingly opulent, honeyed, and rich, this hauntingly nuanced Riesling is typical of the ways in which biodynamic vintner Marc Tempé follows his own syncopated beat.

ANDRÉ & MIREILLE TISSOT *(Jura)*

Arbois Selection ♀ **$$$** A perfect introduction to its genre, this brilliantly complements a wide range of cuisine with its piquant, bittersweet floral character; citrus zest; nutty, chalky, sherry-like notes; and a rich yet bright cast.

Crémant du Jura Brut ♀ ♀ **$$** This Pinot Noir–Chardonnay-based cuvée is among the world's best sparklers for the money. Like walking into a flowering greenhouse, the nose here leads to a tangy, chalky, creamy, finely effervescent palate and a lip-smacking yet thought-provoking finishing savor.

F. E. TRIMBACH *(Alsace)*

Gewurztraminer ♀ **$$$** Trimbach's classic Gewurztraminer offers a model of restraint and refreshment more growers should emulate: rich yet bracing, dry yet only 13.5% alcohol, featuring smoked meats, celery seed, sea breeze, rose petal, and sweet pea.

Pinot Gris Réserve ♀ **$$$** Creamy fullness yet juicy refreshment. Peaches, brown spices, smoked meat, musk, and hints of chalk mark a wine often not released for two or more years.

Riesling ♀ **$$** What Trimbach calls their "classic" Riesling is consistently food-friendly, bright and juicy, and firm and dry.

Riesling Réserve ♀ **$$$** From some top sites, this is loaded with citrus, pit fruits (and their pits), flowers, and herbs, combining richness with invigoration, clarity, and fascinating suggestions of minerality. It shows you why Trimbach's deep, dense, and yet higher-priced Riesling cuvées are Alsace benchmarks.

JEAN VULLIEN & FILS *(Savoie)*

Roussette de Savoie ♀ **$$$** A pungent nose of orange zest, buckwheat, nutmeg, and toasted hazelnut leads to a subtly oily yet juicy and refreshing palate featuring citrus zest, chalk, and lightly toasted nuts and grains.

DOMAINE WEINBACH *(Alsace)*

Sylvaner Réserve ♀ **$$$** A veritable greenhouse of subtly scented leafy things fills the nose; the mouth is caressed by juicy citrus, nut oils, and herbal-floral essences; and one is left by this wine from the

Fallers' famed estate with faint bittersweetness, luscious refreshment, and a wonderful sense of mineral mystery and elegance.

DOMAINE ZIND-HUMBRECHT *(Alsace)*

Gewurztraminer ♀ **$$$** From younger vines in top sites, this cuvée proves how richness and elegance can coexist. Dried herbs, celery root, rose petal sachet, sea breezes, and bacon fat typically inform a truly dry, full-bodied, but infectiously juicy and even mineral Gewurztraminer.

Pinot Gris ♀ **$$$** Sacrificing fruit from prestigious sites results in a smoky, spicy pungency and honeyed richness, as well as memorable nuances of mushrooms, nut oils, or musk.

Riesling ♀ **$$$** Assembled from early harvests in various sites to achieve a totally dry yet relatively low-alcohol result, this generic bottling from the most celebrated estate in Alsace is pungently herbal; succulently citric and pit fruited; resinous, fusil, nutty, and honeyed.

BORDEAUX WINE VALUES

by Robert M. Parker, Jr.

Thinking Outside the Prestigious Appellations

Bordeaux is the world's greatest wine region in terms of the large production of high-quality wines, their international renown, and their extraordinary aging potential. However, the wines that everyone cherishes, and those that are written about in wine publications as well as on the Internet, are primarily priced well beyond the $25 required for a wine to quality as a bargain selection. Bordeaux's historic prestige can be traced to the fact that it was the first major wine region in France to classify the top estates. In 1855, Bordeaux did it with their wines from the large Médoc area (they also included one wine from the Graves region south of Bordeaux). That five-tiered classification of first, second, third, fourth, and fifth growths has stood for more than 150 years with only one change, the elevation of Mouton-Rothschild from second growth to first growth in 1973. There were subsequent classifications in 1959 of the wines of Graves, and every ten years there is a classification of the wines of St.-Émilion. In essence, if you are shrewd enough to find the bargains of Bordeaux, you will essentially write off any wine in these classifications as they will be entirely too expensive to qualify as a bargain selection. And while many of the top châteaux make a second wine under a secondary label, those, too, often exceed $25 a bottle.

All of that being said, there is no doubt that there are terrific bargains available from Bordeaux given the high-quality winemaking as well as the fact that this is the epicenter of oenology, breakthrough technology, and viticultural practices that have worldwide impact. However, consumers need to learn about the bevy of lesser-known Bordeaux appellations. Forget St.-Estèphe, Pauillac, St.-Julien, Margaux, Pessac-Léognan, Pomerol, and St.-Émilion. As great as these wines can be, 99% of them will be priced over $25. The bargains will emerge from the lesser-known appellations that border the above-mentioned famous regions.

The world's richest consumers are obsessed with luxury names and prestigious appellations, but with a little knowledge, some outstanding bargains can be found, particularly in such top vintages as 2000, 2003, and 2005. What follows is a list of wines that, depending on the value of the dollar, can often be purchased for under $25.

Vintage Smarts

Keep in mind that 2005 wines will always come at a high premium. Certainly it is a top vintage, but when you consider the price of the same wines in 2004 or 2006, even though they may not be quite as complete, ripe, and pure as the 2005s, usually at half the price, they do represent a shrewder value. Of course, it all comes down to the consumer, but vintage variations in quality are reflected in dramatically different prices. 2004 and 2006 will always be less expensive than 2005, but 2005 will have produced, in most cases, the finest wines. The most challenging vintage in which to find good values in 2007, but 2008 (still in barrel, and not being released until 2010) offers surprising quality and should turn out to be greatly superior to 2007 and 2006, and just a notch below 2005.

Drinking Curves

By and large, most of these wines are meant to be drunk in their youth. However, even minor Bordeaux can last a surprisingly long time, in spite of its humble pedigree. I have had many of these estates' offerings last 8–10 years in top vintages. (That is only if they are stored in a cold environment.) In a good vintage (e.g., 2000, 2003, 2005), most of these cuvées hit their peak within 2–3 years, where they remain for another 3–4 years, and can actually hold on for another 5–6 after that. In some cases, these wines remain drinkable at age twenty, but that is not the point. These offerings are meant to be consumed in their youth. Less successful vintages (e.g., 2004, 2006, 2007) are best drunk in their first 3–4 years of life. This plays into the strength of bargain picks because most consumers are looking for immediate gratification, and these wines offer that.

Bordeaux's Top Wine Values by Winery

DOMAINE DE L'A (*Côtes de Castillon*)

🍷 $$$ Usually a blend of Merlot, Cabernet Franc, and Cabernet Sauvignon bottled unfined and unfiltered, these seriously endowed, opulent, and full-bodied wines drink beautifully for 10–12 years.

D'AGASSAC *(Haut-Médoc)*

🍷 **$$$** Elegant, with an almost Margaux-like nose of floral scents intermixed with red and black fruits, as well as hints of wood and damp earth, this wine is medium bodied, with good tannin, beautiful purity, and a heady finish. Drink it over its first 6–8 years.

D'AIGUILHE *(Côtes de Castillon)*

🍷 **$$$** A superb, full-bodied, layered, and super-concentrated claret, this silky blend of mostly Merlot and smaller percentages of Cabernet Franc can be enjoyed over its first 8–10 years.

D'AIGUILHE QUERRE *(Côtes de Castillon)*

🍷 **$$$** Full bodied with superb richness, a layered texture, a multidimensional mouth-feel, and a finish that lasts nearly 40 seconds, the best vintages of this wine can easily compete with some of the top crus. Consume over its first decade.

AMPELIA *(Côtes de Castillon)*

🍷 **$$$** Wine from Ampelia displays terrific fruit, medium body, and excellent acidity, precision, purity, and length. Usually even better after 1–2 years of cellaring, it drinks well for about a decade.

ARIA DU CHÂTEAU DE LA RIVIÈRE *(Fronsac)*

🍷 **$$$** The luxury cuvée from Château de la Rivière, primarily Merlot, this dense purple-hued, medium- to full-bodied, beautifully textured wine is best drunk over its first decade.

AU GRAND PARIS *(Bordeaux)*

🍷 **$** This fruity, dark-ruby-colored, medium-bodied, decent effort offers up hints of herbs as well as soft texture. While not terribly distinctive, it's not bad either.

D'AURILHAC *(Haut-Médoc)*

🍷 **$$$** This dense ruby/purple-colored wine is deep and medium to full bodied, with superb richness, silky but noticeable tannin, and a long finish. This relatively big wine has more in common with a classified growth than a cru bourgeois and should be drunk over 10–15 years.

BAD BOY *(Bordeaux)*

🍷 **$** This bargain-priced Bordeaux blend often hits a home run. Silky textured, medium bodied, pure, and delicious, it is best drunk over its first 3–4 years.

BEAULIEU COMTES DE TASTES *(Bordeaux Supérieur)*

🍷 **$$$** Usually made from a blend of half Merlot and the rest Cabernet Franc and Cabernet Sauvignon, this sensational wine exhibits excellent texture, medium body, and soft tannins and is a beauty to enjoy over 5–6 years.

BEL-AIR LA ROYÈRE *(Premières Côtes de Blaye)*

🍷 **$$** Attractive notes of sweet currant and strawberry fruit emerge from this lush, silky-textured, fruity wine. It will offer delicious drinking over its first 3–4 years.

BELLE-VUE *(Haut-Médoc)*

🍷 **$$$** This wine reveals more tannin than most, along with great fruit, medium body, and plenty of character. Give it a year or two of bottle age, and enjoy it over the following 7–8.

BERTINEAU ST.-VINCENT *(Lalande-de-Pomerol)*

🍷 **$$$** Typically made in a forward, fruity, delicious style, this wine generally boasts plenty of chocolate, berry fruit, and spice characteristics along with a luscious, hedonistic texture. It drinks nicely for 3–5 years.

BOLAIRE *(Bordeaux Supérieur)*

🍷 \$\$\$ An amazingly high percentage of Petit Verdot (39%) combined with Merlot and Cabernet Sauvignon results in one of the more distinctive wines of Bordeaux. Medium bodied with stunning depth, richness, and texture, it generally drinks well for 10 years.

BONNET *(Bordeaux)*

Blanc 🍷 \$ With gobs of fruit and a crisp, fresh style, this richly fruity, lively white wine is ideal for drinking over its first year.

Divinus 🍷 \$\$ The luxury cuvée from Bonnet, this wine, which is usually a blend of Merlot and Cabernet Sauvignon, is medium bodied and fruity with excellent depth and length.

Réserve 🍷 \$\$\$ The Réserve exhibits a subtle touch of herbs, spice, and cedar. Enjoy it over its first 3–4 years.

BORD'EAUX *(Bordeaux)*

🍷 \$ With a rare (for Bordeaux) screw-cap finish, this 100% Merlot fruit bomb offers plenty of chocolate, soft tannins, medium body, and excellent purity. It is even available in a 3–liter bag in a box, which should provide serious relief for financially stressed wine consumers. Consume it during its first 1–2 years.

BOUSCAT *(Bordeaux Supérieur)*

Cuvée Gargone 🍷 \$\$ While Bouscat's regular offering is often unimpressive, their Cuvée Gargone possesses serious concentration, beautiful density, a lovely texture, and a long, pure finish. It typically drinks well for 3–5 years.

BRANDA *(Puisseguin-St.-Émilion)*

🍷 \$\$ Readers looking for a fruity, medium-bodied, well-made, pure, smooth claret should check out this reliable performer from a St.-Émilion satellite appellation. It offers lovely drinking over 4–5 years.

BRISSON *(Côtes de Castillon)*

♟ $$$ Delicious up-front blackberry and currant fruit notes intertwined with licorice, spice, and a hint of wood smoke jump from the glass of this medium-bodied, richly fruity, well-balanced wine. It generally drinks well for 3–6 years.

BRONDEAU *(Bordeaux)*

♟ $$ This inexpensive, delicious cuvée possesses dense cherry and currant fruit, medium body, and good accessibility. Drink during its first 2–3 years.

CAMBON LA PELOUSE *(Haut-Médoc)*

♟ $$$ Possessing an exotic, flamboyant, fruity bouquet of black cherries, wood smoke, tobacco, and spice, this lush, round, and opulent red is ideal for drinking over its first 5–6 years.

CAP DE FAUGÈRES *(Côtes de Castillon)*

♟ $$$ Always one of the top Côtes de Castillons, Cap de Faugères is typically a weighty, deep, rich effort offering a flamboyant nose of black fruits, coffee, chocolate, and toasty oak. It generally keeps for a decade.

CHARMAIL *(Haut-Médoc)*

♟ $$$ An exquisite, sexy wine displaying sweet fruit; round, ripe tannins; an endearing opulence; and a long finish, this cuvée generally ages well for a decade.

LES CHARMES-GODARD *(Bordeaux)*

♟ $$ This richly fruity white reveals tropical fruit notes, good acidity, medium body, and lovely purity. It offers very nice drinking for 3–4 years.

CITRAN *(Haut-Médoc)*

♟ $$$ Loads of oak intermixed with plenty of black currant fruit, licorice, and incense jumps from the glass of this flashy, ostentatiously styled Bordeaux. Medium bodied and spicy, with plenty of body, fruit, and depth, Citran typically drinks well for a decade.

CLOS CHAUMONT (*Premières Côtes de Bordeaux*)

♀ $$$ Medium to full bodied with velvety tannins, lush fruit, and a layered mouth-feel with no hard edges, this sexy and seductive wine should be drunk over 4–5 years.

CLOS L'ÉGLISE (*Côtes de Castillon*)

♀ $$$ One of the least expensive wines produced by Gérard Perse, Clos l'Église (primarily Merlot and the rest Cabernet Sauvignon and Cabernet Franc) displays medium body, loads of fruit, and a soft, round mouth-feel and finish. It can be enjoyed during its first 5–6 years.

CLOS MARSALETTE (*Pessac-Léognan*)

♀ $$$ Offering a bouquet of roasted herbs, charcoal embers, and sweet cherries and currants, this elegant, light-on-its-feet wine can be enjoyed during its first 7–8 years.

CLOS PUY ARNAUD (*Côtes de Castillon*)

♀ $$$ Clos Puy Arnaud typically exhibits crushed rock/mineral characteristics along with hints of black cherries, intense fruit, and a beautiful mouth-feel. It can drink well for 7–8 years.

CONFIANCE DE GÉRARD DEPARDIEU
(*Premières Côtes de Blaye*)

♀ $$$ Actor Gérard Depardieu, along with Bernard Magrez, winemaker Jean Cordeau, and Michel Rolland, turns out something special as this fabulous cuvée competes with a second- or third-growth Médoc. Displaying notes of cedar wood, black currant, tobacco leaf, and spice box, it requires 1–2 years of bottle aging and can be drunk over the following 10–15.

LE CONSEILLER (*Bordeaux*)

♀ $$$ A sensational wine from a humble *terroir*, with fabulous smoky black raspberry, cassis, licorice, black truffle, and toast aromas, this concentrated wine should provide plenty of pleasure during its first 5–7 years.

COUFRAN (Haut-Médoc)

♟ $$$ Displaying notes of sweet cherries intermixed with hints of espresso roast and dried herbs, Coufran tends to be medium bodied with some noticeable tannin. It keeps for 10–15 years.

COURTEILLAC (Bordeaux Supérieur)

♟ $$ With medium body, sweet tannin, and lovely fruit, this wine is typically ideal for drinking in its first 5–6 years.

CROIX DE L'ESPÉRANCE (Lussac-St.-Émilion)

♟ $$$ The seriously structured and tannic Croix de l'Espérance often transcends its lowly appellation, with deep, concentrated flavors of black fruits, forest floor, roasted herbs, and licorice usually only found in a much more expensive wine. Made from 100% Merlot, this blockbuster often needs 2–3 years of cellaring, and most top vintages can keep for 12–15 years.

CROIX MOUTON (Bordeaux Supérieur)

♟ $$$ A super-Bordeaux from a humble vineyard, this blend of Merlot and Cabernet Sauvignon with dollops of Cabernet Franc, Petit Verdot, and Malbec is deep, supple, lush, and opulent. A terrific wine for its pedigree and price, it should be drunk in its first 4–5 years.

LA CROIX DE PERENNE (Premières Côtes de Blaye)

♟ $$$ In top vintages, this mini–Le Pin (a blend of primarily Merlot and a small quantity of Cabernet Franc) is superb. Voluptuous and silky textured with a stunning finish, it will drink beautifully over 7–8 years.

LA CROIX DE PEYROLIE DE GÉRARD DEPARDIEU
(Lussac-St.-Émilion)

♟ $$$ Terrific fruit on the attack follows through on the midpalate and finish of this dense, pure, textured, and multidimensional wine, which often requires 3–5 years of bottle age and can last for a decade thereafter.

DALEM *(Fronsac)*

🍷 $$$ Medium bodied and concentrated with well-integrated acidity and tannin, this beautiful Fronsac generally evolves nicely for a decade or more.

DAUGAY *(St.-Émilion)*

🍷 $$$ A straightforward yet enormously attractive, fruity effort, this medium-bodied wine should be drunk within 5–6 years following the vintage.

LA DAUPHINE *(Fronsac)*

🍷 $$$ With beautiful purity, symmetry, and power as well as elegance, this is a fresh, full, soft Fronsac with sensational concentration and depth. It will often keep for 10–15 years.

LA DOYENNE *(Premières Côtes de Bordeaux)*

🍷 $$ This unfined/unfiltered blend of about 80% Merlot and the rest Cabernet Sauvignon and Cabernet Franc exhibits a big, sweet nose of sandy, loamy soil, spice wood, damp earth, and copious quantities of cherries and currants. Hedonistic, lush, elegant, and pure, it can be enjoyed for 3–4 years following the vintage.

D'ESCURAC *(Médoc)*

🍷 $$ One of the finest cru bourgeois in the Médoc, this well-made effort generally offers notions of black olive, black currant, spice box, and cedar in its complex, classically styled bouquet. Medium bodied with excellent purity, richness, and power, sweet tannin, beautiful fruit, and admirable depth, it can last for a decade or more.

L'ESTANG *(Côtes de Castillon)*

🍷 $$ A tasty wine from this backwater appellation, L'Estang typically possesses a deep ruby color with a moderately intense bouquet of red and black fruits intermixed with earth, spice, and a bit of roasted herbs. Soft, silky, and medium bodied, this pure, well-balanced Côtes de Castillon can age for 5–6 years.

FAIZEAU *(Montagne-St.-Émilion)*

♟ $$$ In top vintages, this 100% Merlot from Montagne-St.-Émilion is full bodied, ripe, and seamless. It can drink well for a decade.

FERET-LAMBERT *(Bordeaux Supérieur)*

♟ $$ An excellent Bordeaux Supérieur with admirable purity, outstanding intensity, and a long finish with no hard edges, this medium-bodied wine should be consumed during its first 7–8 years.

FERRAND *(Pessac-Léognan)*

♟ $$$ A stylish, elegant wine with sweet, dusty red cherry and currant fruit interwoven with some burning embers, this wine is medium bodied, with silky tannins and excellent ripeness and purity. Drink it in its first 7–8 years.

FLEUR ST.-ANTOINE *(Bordeaux Supérieur)*

♟ $$ Often a sleeper of the vintage from a humble appellation, this medium-bodied wine possesses oodles of fruit, a lush texture, and a long, heady, pure finish. Drink it over its first 5–6 years.

FOUGAS MALDORER *(Côtes de Bourg)*

♟ $$$ When young, these wines usually have some tannin to shed, but a dense ruby color and big, sweet nose of chocolate-covered cherries are enticing. Medium bodied, structured, and surprisingly powerful, they last for 7–8 years.

FOUGÈRES LA FOLIE *(Pessac-Léognan)*

♟ $$$ This beautiful Pessac-Léognan exhibits soft tannins, a lush mouth-feel, and a pure finish, and can drink well for 5–6 years.

FUSSIGNAC *(Bordeaux)*

♟ $$ A richly fruity, round, supple, seductive offering, this Bordeaux Supérieur drinks well for 3–4 years.

MAISON GALHAUD *(Bordeaux)*

♈ **$$$** A beautiful generic Bordeaux offering plenty of cedar, black currants, and cherries as well as notions of licorice and earth. It can drink nicely for 3–4 years.

GIGAULT *(Premières Côtes de Blaye)*

♈ **$$$** A lush, seductive bouquet jumps from the glass of this medium-bodied wine. With heady glycerin, loads of fruit, beautiful purity, and no hard edges, it should be drunk in its first 3–4 years.

GIRONVILLE *(Haut-Médoc)*

♈ **$$** This wine possesses excellent texture, medium body, and a beautiful 20-second finish. Enjoy it over its first 5–6 years.

GRAND MOUËYS *(Premières Côtes de Bordeaux)*

♈ **$$** Always a reliable performer, Grand Mouëys produces a medium-bodied, richly fruity, attractive wine with black currant, licorice, roasted herb, and loamy soil characteristics. Drink it over its first 5–6 years.

GRAND ORMEAU *(Lalande-de-Pomerol)*

Regular cuvée ♈ **$$$** The open-knit, accessible regular cuvée from Grand Ormeau boasts an opulent, plush, concentrated mouth-feel. This beautifully textured, heady, round wine should be enjoyed over its first 7–8 years.

Cuvée Madeleine ♈ **$$$** The Cuvée Madeleine is similar to the regular cuvée but slightly more structured, earthy, and backward. It tends to benefit from an extra year of bottle aging and keeps for a decade.

LES GRANDS-MARÉCHAUX *(Premières Côtes de Blaye)*

♈ **$$** Medium to full bodied, velvety textured, sumptuous, and long, this sensational wine can drink well for 3–4 years. Moreover, there are usually 7,000 or more cases, so availability should be good.

LES GRANDS CHÊNES (Médoc)

♆ $$$ This superb 25-acre Médoc estate (owned by Bordeaux visionary Bernard Magrez) produces a blend of Merlot and Cabernet Sauvignon that is much better than its pedigree would suggest. It is a full-bodied, well-endowed, impressively constituted wine with sweet tannin as well as loads of character and personality. Enjoy it over its first 10–12 years.

LA GRAVIÈRE (Lalande-de-Pomerol)

♆ $$$ Soft, heady, lush black cherry fruit interwoven with chocolate and coffee bean notes is followed by a sweet, fleshy, mouth-filling, hedonistic wine. Drink this medium-bodied wine over its first 5–6 years.

GREE LAROQUE (Bordeaux Supérieur)

♆ $$$ This well-made, concentrated, medium-bodied lower-level Bordeaux exhibits excellent density along with pure tannins and a nose reminiscent of a good Graves (hints of wet stones, volcanic ash, sweet cherry, and cassis fruit). Enjoy this beauty over its first 4–5 years.

GUERRY (Côtes de Bourg)

♆ $$$ A flamboyant wine with copious sweet cherry, smoky chocolate-like flavors, full body, considerable opulence, and a long, silky finish. Drink it over its first 6–8 years.

GUIONNE (Côtes de Bourg)

♆ $$$ Powerful, rich, concentrated, but with silky tannins, superb concentration, and a pedigree and complexity that far exceed its modest appellation, this can be a knockout wine to drink in its first decade.

HAUT-BERTINERIE (Côtes de Blaye)

♆ $$$ Exhibiting plenty of citrus and fresh mineral-infused green apple and honeysuckle, this is a fruity wine, medium bodied, and best drunk within 2–3 years.

♥ $$$ Dominated by Merlot, the red wine is deliciously soft and fruity.

HAUT-BEYZAC *(Haut-Médoc)*

Haut-Médoc du Haut-Beyzac ♥ $$ Exhibiting attractive aromas of cedar, red currant, damp earth, and spice box, this medium-bodied, pure, soft wine should drink well for 4–5 years.

I Second ♥ $$$ This red offers blacker fruits as well as more depth and richness, medium to full body, and excellent ripeness, purity, and length. Consume it over its first 7–8 years.

HAUT-CANTELOUP *(Médoc)*

♥ $$ Pure and medium bodied with excellent fruit concentration and precision, this wine drinks well for 4–5 years.

HAUT-CARLES *(Fronsac)*

♥ $$$ Medium bodied, structured, and pure. Purchasers would be well advised to give this promising effort a few years of bottle aging and enjoy it over the following 12–15.

HAUT-COLOMBIER *(Côtes de Blaye)*

♥ $$ A richly fruity wine, silky textured, medium bodied, and very hedonistic. Drink it over its first 4–5 years.

HAUT-MAZERIS *(Canon Fronsac)*

♥ $$$ Admirable purity, depth, and texture are found in this medium-bodied, structured, tannic wine. Consume it over its first 10–15 years.

HAUT-MOULEYRE *(Bordeaux)*

♀ $$ Attractive notes of melon, citrus, and grapefruit emerge from the medium-bodied, fresh, dry, well-made white from this estate.

♥ $$ This estate's red, usually a blend of equal parts Merlot and Cabernet Sauvignon, is a serious wine, well endowed with cherry, black currant, and charcoal notes. On the palate it has very good body, purity, and length.

HORTEVIE *(St.-Julien)*

🍷 $$$ If St.-Julien produced a fruit bomb, this would be it. Impressively endowed with medium to full body and beautiful purity, this is fresh, tannic, and vibrant. It should drink well for 10–15 years or longer.

JAUGUE BLANC *(St.-Émilion)*

🍷 $$$ It's hard to find a value-priced wine from this appellation these days. This wine is medium bodied, fleshy, and quite silky. Drink it over its first 5–6 years.

LALANDE-BORIE *(St.-Julien)*

🍷 $$$ A graceful, charming, seductive St.-Julien possessing sweet cassis fruit intermixed with forest floor, spice box, and earth characteristics. This is a beauty to drink within its first decade.

LARRIVAUX *(Haut-Médoc)*

🍷 $$$ A classy Haut-Médoc, this wine displays medium body, excellent fruit intensity, an enticing texture, admirable purity, and a spicy, relatively velvety finish. Drink it over its first decade.

LAUBES *(Bordeaux)*

🍷 $$ A sexy blend of Merlot and Cabernet Sauvignon, this is a modern, pure, flashy style of wine. Drink it over its first 3–4 years.

DES LAURETS *(Puisseguin-St.-Émilion)*

🍷 $$ This wine exhibits plenty of sweet berry fruit, cedar, spice box, and licorice characteristics, medium body, silky tannins, and a beautiful mouth-feel. Consume it over its first 4–5 years.

LAUSSAC *(Côtes de Castillon)*

🍷 $$$ Laussac's offerings are loaded with spicy, lush, herb-tinged black fruit and velvety tannins. A medium-bodied wine, this is meant for consumption in its first 4–5 years.

LYONNET *(Lussac-St.-Émilion)*

♥ **$$** An attractive effort from a St.-Émilion satellite, this is a medium-bodied wine with light tannin that should drink well for 4–5 years.

MA VÉRITÉ DE GÉRARD DEPARDIEU *(Haut-Médoc)*

♥ **$$$** A structured, tannic, backward blend of mostly Merlot and Cabernet Sauvignon with the rest Cabernet France and Petit Verdot, this long, deep, concentrated, powerful Haut-Médoc benefits from 2–3 years of cellaring and keeps for 10–15 years.

MARSAU *(Côtes de Francs)*

♥ **$$** Dominated by Merlot, the fruity, soft Marsau is a hedonistic, charming effort meant to be drunk over its first 5–7 years.

MARTINAT-EPICUREA *(Côtes de Bourg)*

♥ **$$$** A blend of mostly Merlot and some Malbec, this lush, opulent, hedonistic wine should be enjoyed over its first 7–8 years.

MEJEAN *(Graves)*

♥ **$$$** Creamy textured, with real opulence, this gorgeous wine can be drunk early or cellared for 7–10 years.

MESSILE AUBERT *(Montagne-St.-Émilion)*

♥ **$$$** The layered mouth-feel and up-front personality of this deeply fruity Montagne-St.-Émilion will provide plenty of pleasure over its first 5–6 years.

MILLE-ROSES *(Haut-Médoc)*

♥ **$$$** A blend of Merlot and Cabernet Sauvignon, this round, generously endowed, soft Haut-Médoc can be drunk when released or kept for 5–6 years.

MONT PERAT *(Bordeaux)*

♥ **$$** This is a serious white, with rich, concentrated honeysuckle and melon notes and no evidence of wood in the aromas or flavors. The wine is nicely textured, fleshy, and best drunk over 3–4 years.

MOULIN HAUT LAROQUE *(Fronsac)*

♟ $$$ Superior concentration, medium to full body, beautiful integration of acidity and tannin, and a long finish result in an impressive Fronsac. Drink over 10–12 years from its release.

MOULIN ROUGE *(Médoc)*

♟ $$ This sexy, sensual, dark-ruby-hued Médoc is a blend of 60% Merlot and 40% Cabernet Sauvignon. Soft tannins, a velvety texture, and abundant fruit and spice result in an endearing wine that should provide enjoyment over the next 5–6 years.

MYLORD *(Bordeaux)*

♟ $ A charming petit Bordeaux with lovely currant and cherry fruit, some delicate spice, and a beautiful, silky texture, this pure, midweight wine is delicious and best drunk over its first 1–3 years.

PATACHE D'AUX *(Médoc)*

♟ $$ This Cabernet-dominated effort exhibits medium body, a pleasant spicy character, and plenty of fruit as well as length. Drink it within 5–10 years.

PELAN *(Côtes de Francs)*

♟ $$ This wine displays beautiful sweetness, a medium-bodied texture, outstanding purity, and a long, heady finish. Drink it over its first 5–6 years.

PERENNE *(Côtes de Blaye)*

♟ $$ This 100% Sauvignon Blanc exhibits a lovely bouquet of figs, grapefruit, and melons as well as a crisp, luscious finish. Drink it over its first 3–4 years.

PERRON LA FLEUR *(Lalande-de-Pomerol)*

♟ $$$ The medium-bodied, round, generously endowed Perron La Fleur offers scents of sweet cherries, ripe strawberries, subtle herbs, and coffee. It is best drunk over its first 5–6 years.

PEY LA TOUR *(Bordeaux Supérieur)*

🍷 **\$\$** The Pey La Tour exhibits aromatics of sweet cherry, black currant, subtle herbs, cedar, and spice box combined with a long, rich attack and midpalate, resulting in an impressive, supple-textured generic Bordeaux to drink over its first 2–3 years.

PEYFAURES *(Bordeaux Supérieur)*

Regular cuvée 🍷 **\$\$** The very good, reasonably priced, regular cuvée exhibits a pretty, dark ruby color along with sweet currant and herb notes. It is best consumed over its first several years.

Dame de Coeur 🍷 **\$\$\$** Peyfaures's luxury cuvée, the Dame de Coeur possesses more oak and extraction than the regular cuvée, but I am not convinced it is any better. More tannic, structured, and backward, it can improve with age, but that is always questionable with wines from such humble appellations.

LE PIN BEAUSOLEIL *(Bordeaux Supérieur)*

🍷 **\$\$\$** Le Pin Beausoleil is a surprisingly big, full-bodied, deep, concentrated wine. A remarkable effort for its humble appellation and price, it drinks well for 5–7 years.

PLAISANCE ALIX *(Premières Côtes de Bordeaux)*

🍷 **\$\$\$** This is a round, generous, opulent effort from a low-level pedigree that transcends its category by a considerable margin. Drink it over its first 5–6 years.

POTENSAC *(Médoc)*

🍷 **\$\$\$** A superb value, the Potensac has a classic bouquet of sweet red and black fruits, as well as gorgeous texture and purity. Medium bodied and concentrated, this wine behaves like a Médoc cru classé. Moreover, it ages very well for 10–15 years. Very impressive!

LA PRADE *(Côtes de Francs)*

🍷 **\$\$\$** This wine easily competes with the "big boys" of nearby St.-Émilion. It is an opulent, full-bodied, velvety-textured, seriously concentrated effort with no hard edges. Drink it over the next 5–7 years.

PUYGUERAUD *(Côtes de Francs)*

♟ $$$ This is a beautifully textured, dense-purple-colored effort. The bouquet offers up aromas of tobacco leaf, black currant, cherry, charcoal, and a hint of background wood. Drink it over its first 5–7 years of life.

RECLOS DE LA COURONNE *(Montagne-St.-Émilion)*

♟ $$ This medium-bodied, ripe wine exhibits attractive fruit as well as immediate drinkability. Consume it in its first 4–5 years.

RECOUGNE *(Bordeaux Supérieur)*

Regular cuvée ♟ $$ This medium-bodied, old-style Bordeaux is an attractive wine displaying classic smoky, cedary, forest-floor, and red as well as black currant characteristics.

Terra Recognita ♟ $ A second cuvée, the delicious Terra Recognita reveals a slightly less complex bouquet as well as sweet fruit, medium body, and a more straightforward flavor profile.

RICHELIEU *(Fronsac)*

♟ $$$ This opulent, beautifully textured wine is a blend of about two-thirds Merlot and one-third Cabernet Franc. The wine has a lush texture, silky tannins, and a medium- to full-bodied, long finish. Drink it over a decade or more.

ROQUETAILLADE *(Graves)*

♟ $$$ This delicious blend of mostly Sauvignon Blanc and about 10% Sémillon from an up-and-coming estate possesses loads of mineral and ripe melon-like characteristics, terrific fruit purity, medium body, and a surprisingly long, textured, dry finish. It drinks well for 4–6 years.

LA ROSE PERRIÈRE *(Lussac-St.-Émilion)*

♟ $$ Transcending its modest upbringing and appellation, this medium-bodied wine exhibits sweet cherry and strawberry fruit along with hints of road tar and high-quality *barriques*. Drink it over its first 3–4 years.

ROUILLAC *(Pessac-Léognan)*

♟ $$$ Readers looking for high-quality Pessac-Léognan at a bargain price should check out Rouillac, a château on the rise. This stylish, complex, medium-bodied wine has terrific fruit intensity, superb purity, and a long, lush, silky finish. Drink it over its first 7–8 years.

ST.-GENES *(Premières Côtes de Blaye)*

♟ $$ This ripe, heady, medium-bodied, silky-smooth blend of about three parts Merlot to one part Cabernet Franc is noteworthy. Consume it within 3–4 years.

STE.-COLOMBE *(Côtes de Castillon)*

♟ $$ Drink this richly fruity, soft and accessible wine over its first 4–5 years.

SERGANT *(Lalande-de-Pomerol)*

♟ $$$ This attractive Lalande-de-Pomerol is medium bodied, elegant, and cleanly made. It can be enjoyed over 3–4 years.

LA SERGUE *(Lalande-de-Pomerol)*

♟ $$$ This beautifully perfumed, medium- to full-bodied, concentrated, and silky-textured Lalande-de-Pomerol can offer abundant pleasure over 7–8 years.

SOLEIL *(Puisseguin-St.-Émilion)*

♟ $$$ Soleil's offering displays a fat, fleshy texture, decent acidity, and sweet tannin. Consume it over 5–6 years.

DOMAINE DES SONGES *(Bergerac)*

♟ $$ This crisp, light- to medium-bodied Bergerac exhibits good freshness, plenty of citrus, and a medium-bodied finish. Drink it over its first 2–3 years.

TAGE DE LESTAGES *(Montagne-St.-Émilion)*

♟ $$ Juicy ripe cherry and black currant fruit, some damp earth, roasted herbs, and spice, in addition to an opulent, medium- to full-bodied mouth-feel, make for a lusty wine. Drink it over its first 4–5 years.

THÉBOT *(Bordeaux)*

♟ **$$** A seductive, hedonistic blend of mostly Merlot and a dose of Cabernet Franc, the Thébot is meant to be drunk during its first several years. You can't ask for much more from a generic Bordeaux.

THIEULEY *(Bordeaux)*

Regular cuvée ♟ **$** The straightforward regular cuvée is a fruity, tasty, classic Bordeaux with no hard edges. It is best drunk during its first 3–4 years.

Regular cuvée ♀ **$** A honeyed grapefruit/citrus-filled, medium-bodied, tasty, up-front white meant to be drunk in its first 2–3 years.

Cuvée Francis Courselle ♀ **$$** Those looking for more oak should check out the Cuvée Francis Courselle, which shows a richer, slightly more textured style than the regular cuvée. It is not fresher or more lively, just a different rendition that should drink nicely for 2–3 years.

Héritage de Thieuley ♟ **$$** A newer cuvée, Héritage de Thieuley, is outstanding, a dense, rich, concentrated, and well-balanced effort.

Réserve Francis Courselle ♟ **$$$** The Réserve Francis Courselle can be oaky but reveals chocolate and berry fruit in its medium-bodied, ripe, attractive personality.

LE THIL COMTE CLARY *(Pessac-Léognan)*

♀ **$$** Readers looking for a white Bordeaux possessing notes of honeyed grapefruit, pineapple, and wet stones, an attractive texture, and good fruit will enjoy this effort. It should provide pleasure over 4–6 years.

TIRE PÉ LA CÔTE *(Bordeaux)*

♟ **$$** This reliable estate fashions an elegant, richly fruity, medium-bodied wine exhibiting a sweet nose of licorice, black currants, and forest floor, good purity, and a layered mouth-feel. Drink it over its first 5–6 years.

TOUR BLANCHE *(Médoc)*

♟ $$$ While pleasant, the Tour Blanche is not a star. Medium bodied, with good structure and plenty of muscle, it should be drunk within 5–6 years.

TOUR DE MIRAMBEAU *(Bordeaux)*

♟ $$$ Medium bodied, crisp, dry, and refreshing, but obviously designed for near-term consumption, this white is best drunk over the course of 1–2 years.

TOUR ST.-BONNET *(Médoc)*

♟ $$$ Reminiscent of a mini–Grand-Puy-Lacoste with its cassis fruit; attractive aromatics; lush, sweet, medium-bodied flavors; and inky ruby/purple color, the Tour St.-Bonnet sells for a fraction of the price of the Grand-Puy-Lacoste. Drink it over its first 5–7 years.

LES TOURS SEGUY *(Côtes de Bourg)*

♟ $ This medium-bodied red shows loads of black currant, cranberry, and cherry fruit, a hint of minerality, soft tannin, and adequate acidity. Drink it within 4–5 years.

TROIS CROIX *(Fronsac)*

♟ $$$ This fruity, surprisingly soft wine possesses excellent concentration and overall balance. Enjoy over 7–8 years.

VALMENGAUX *(Bordeaux)*

♟ $$ A consistent winner in nearly every vintage, this wine tastes as if it comes from a much more renowned *terroir*. There is not a hard edge to be found, so enjoy it over 4–5 years.

VERDIGNAN *(Haut-Médoc)*

♟ $$$ A consistently well-made cru bourgeois, this wine displays moderate tannin, medium body, and good length and ripeness. Drink it over its first 7–8 years.

DE VIAUD *(Lalande-de-Pomerol)*

🍷 **$$$** This classic, structured effort is medium bodied, with excellent density and light to moderate tannin. It should benefit from some bottle aging and drink well for 7–8 years.

LA VIEILLE CURE *(Fronsac)*

🍷 **$$$** Superb concentration, full-bodied power, wonderful symmetry, purity, texture, and a multidimensional mouth-feel are all found in this fabulous wine. Cellar for 1–2 years and drink over the following decade.

VIEUX CHÂTEAU PALON *(Montagnes-St.-Émilion)*

🍷 **$$$** This elegant, medium-bodied, well-made, pure wine should drink nicely for 5–6 years at the minimum.

VIEUX CLOS ST.-ÉMILION *(St.-Émilion)*

🍷 **$$$** Readers looking for a forward, velvety-textured, richly fruity St.-Émilion should check out this earthy, herbal, fruit-filled offering. Soft tannins suggest this hedonistic wine is best drunk over its first 7–8 years.

VILLARS *(Fronsac)*

🍷 **$$$** This attractive Fronsac possesses very good concentration, light tannin, and medium body. Consume it over 7–8 years.

VRAI CANON BOUCHE *(Canon Fronsac)*

🍷 **$$$** The full-bodied power and sensational concentration and purity of this wine are the result of serious efforts in the vineyard. The wine should age beautifully for 15 or more years.

BURGUNDY AND BEAUJOLAIS WINE VALUES

by David Schildknecht

Yes, There Are Still Values Left Here!

Burgundy has a reputation for complication, and that is understandable, if one focuses on the intricacies of vineyard classification that apply to some of the most expensive and hallowed acreage on earth or on the countless factors relevant to rendering top quality and the apparent proclivity for things to go wrong along the way. In certain respects, though, Burgundy is simple. For the most part, one is concerned with just two grapes—**Pinot Noir** for red and **Chardonnay** for white. Growers and commentators typically point out the differences in flavor that are said to reflect *terroir,* in other words soil and microclimate. But with one exception, the whole of Burgundy represents variation on a common theme: limestone and clay. Stylistically, too, most vintners and observers can agree on a common set of ideals for Burgundy wine, both red and white: clarity of flavor, striking perfume, a balance of caressing textural richness with vivacity and refreshment, and an imponderable measure of seductive mystery. Burgundy also has a reputation for high prices. But these should remain the ideals, even in its less expensive echelons and even if too much of what is produced in Burgundy fails to meet them regardless of price.

Subregions and Appellations

The perspective of value leads us to consider Burgundy in specific and limited ways. The so-called **Côte d'Or** or "golden slope"—divided into northern and southern halves, the Côte de Nuits and Côte de Beaune—runs from Burgundy's ancient capital, Dijon, south to around a dozen miles past the region's wine capital of Beaune, and is home to the majority of Burgundy's historically renowned Pinot Noir and Chardonnay wines. Its roster of famous communes (not to mention their lists of premier and grand cru vineyards) signifies high prices. But certain villages are still known for value, including (taken from north to south) Marsannay, Fixin, Pernand-Vergelles, Chorey-les-Beaune, and (for Chardonnay) St.-Romain. Furthermore, many top-flight Côte d'Or growers offer limited amounts of distinctive Chardonnay or Pinot Noir wines not entitled by their locations to labeling with a village name, but rather simply given the generic appellation Bourgogne. A large number of top Côte d'Or values, though, are cut from quite different cloth. Those labeled Bourgogne **Aligoté**—from Burgundy's second white grape—can be delightfully invigorating yet also richly textured, with complexity of the sort that calls forth floral and mineral vocabularies. The minority **Gamay** grape—when blended with Pinot—yields sometimes delightful and always relatively inexpensive wines of the appellation Passetoutgrains, or Passe-Tout-Grains.

South of the Côte d'Or commences a string of hillsides known collectively as the **Côte Chalonnaise**, whose village appellations—Bouzeron (solely for Aligoté), Givry, Mercurey, Rully, and Montagy (solely for Chardonnay)—do not enjoy the reputation of those to its north but are among the best sources of value in Burgundy. Here too, though, the values that will mostly concern us are labeled not with the village names but with the appellation Bourgogne (or Bourgogne Aligoté).

Continuing south, one enters the high, often rugged limestone hills and dramatically diverse exposures of the **Mâcon**, effectively the world capital (and quite possibly the cradle) of Chardonnay and arguably home to the world's greatest values from that grape, wines that combine richness with refreshment and boast considerable nuance. Most common are those labeled Mâcon-Village, with the names of particular villages permitted in certain instances (such as Mâcon-Viré or Mâcon-Vergisson). The more prestigious and typically more expensive appellations of St.-Véran, Pouilly-Fuissé, and Pouilly-Vinzelles will figure less often in the list of values that follows. Mâconnaise Estates and *négociants* such as Brett Brothers, Domaine des Deux Roches (Collovray and Terrier), Domaine de la Feuillarde, Château de la Greffière, Louis Jadot, and Verget all render notable Chardonnay values.

At the southern edge of the Mâcon commences **Beaujolais**—in which the **Gamay** grape and granite soils dominate—which terminates just north of the city of Lyon. Beaujolais's notoriety has worked against it recently. For more than four decades, America's shores were annually lapped by a frothy purple ocean of "Nouveau," and growers were happy to have a ready market for wine that could bring a cash return before most of France's vintners had even done their first racking. Sadly, much of this wine—and indeed much of what passed for Beaujolais—was crafted in a formulaic mold, resulting in tutti-frutti, banana bubble gum–scented, heady, sometimes headache-inducing beverages that had little to do with the region's true potential. As Beaujolais Nouveau has fallen from fashion, this region has fallen into profound economic crisis. But the seeds and sprouts of a revival are present, and a few maverick growers sell every bottle they can fill. Taste the more serious of these, and you'll understand why a century ago, the best wines of Fleurie, Moulin-à-Vent, Morgon, and others of what are today Beaujolais's crus went head-to-head in price and reputation with many a Pinot from the Côte d'Or. Expect considerable stylistic variation among wines of Beaujolais, but from all of the best addresses, expect outstanding value. The principle appellation is Beaujolais-Villages, although in the often chalky soils of the south, wines are labeled simply Beaujolais. Ten appellations (all but two named for individual villages) are designated as Beaujolais Crus, and virtually all of these fall within the price parameters set for this guide. Considerable amounts of Chardonnay are grown in Beaujolais, too, some of which is outstanding. In short, all of the best wines grown in Beaujolais offer sensational quality-price rapport. Look in particular for wines from such growers and *négociants* as Jean-Marc Burgaud, Nicole Chanrion, Pierre-Marie Chermette (Domaine du Vissoux), Domaine Cheysson, Michel Chignard, Clos de la Roilette, Georges Descombes, Bernard Diochon, Georges Duboeuf, Louis Jadot (incorporating Château des Jacques and Château des Lumières), Marcel Lapierre, Alain Michaud, Dominique Piron, Potel-Aviron, Domaine des Terres Dorées (Jean-Paul Brun), Jean-Paul Thévenet, Château Thivin, and Georges Viornery.

Halfway between Paris and the Côte d'Or—in short, well north and west of any of the rest of Burgundy and sitting on a band of fossil-laden white chalk called Kimmeridgian that runs through southern Champagne, the central and eastern Loire, and across the English Channel—is **Chablis** (sometimes known—together with its related vineyards—as the Auxerre or Yonne). Its best-known vinous manifestation is surely that wine whose world-famous name is so frequently usurped. True Chablis tastes like no other Chardonnay, including its cousins from farther south in Burgundy. Not primarily about fruits and berries, Chablis seems to demand animal and mineral vocabularies in an attempt to capture its elusive scents and flavors. The vineyards of Chablis are classified in four categories, but grand and premier cru vineyards need not concern us here due to their prices. The vast majority of wine and value in Chablis is officially appellation Chablis. A category known as Petit Chablis—for wines from lesser sites and soil—nevertheless includes some values well worth seeking out. Nor are wines with "Chablis" in their name the end of our subject. Surrounding areas—particularly vineyards near the small city of Auxerre, but also Chitry, Vézelay, and other villages—are home to a host of wine values. Most are labeled as Bourgogne; those from the Aligoté grape (just as in the rest of Burgundy) carry the appellation Bourgogne Aligoté. From Chablis and the rest of the Auxerre, look in particular for wines from the following growers and *négociants:* Jean-Marc Brocard, Domaine de la Cadette, Ghislain and Jean-Hugues Goisot, Roland Lavantureux, Alice and Olivier De Moor, Gilbert Picq et ses Fils, and Domaine Servin.

Vintage Smarts—White

Significant variations in quality and style by vintage must be expected in white Burgundy. The Côte d'Or and Côte Chalonnaise whites of 2005 and 2006 are richer and higher in alcohol, with the 2006s especially generous and more sensual than the 2005s, as well as especially successful in the realm of generic Bourgogne and in cooler, less-renowned villages. Wines of the 2008 and large 2007 crop tend more toward brightness and refreshment.

Vintages in the Mâcon share broad similarities with those to the north, but the differences can also be quite important. It is better at this point to favor the 2007s, as 2006 was much more challenging here. (By contrast, 2004—although the modestly priced wines from this vintage should by now have been drunk up—was at least as successful in the Mâcon, if not more so, than in the Côte d'Or.)

Vintages 2004, 2007, and 2008 are strong on the classic Chablis virtues of crispness and clarity and express characteristics that can only be described as "mineral," while the wines of 2005 and 2006 (two of the earliest harvests in Chablis history) tend toward more pronounced richness and higher alcohol yet at their best remain elegant, refined, and refreshing.

Vintage Smarts—Red

Even more so than with white Burgundy, significant variations in quality and style by vintage should be anticipated in red. There have been few vintages as outstanding for their balanced ripeness and complexity as 2005, a year (following a relatively weak 2004 vintage) in which minor appellations, including generic Bourgogne, excelled and have greater aging potential than normal. It is hard to generalize about 2006. Some Pinots suffer from alcoholic bloat combined with only modest ripeness of flavor and awkward tannins, but the more successful wines—even including some of generic appellation—often exhibit a combination of generous fruit, sensual texture, and delicacy that make them a delight. Wines from 2007 generally offer generosity and ripeness, if not depth, with the emphasis on fresh, at times tart fruit. Ripening is often more difficult in the Côte Chalonnaise, where for example 2006 is weaker than in the Côte d'Or.

The best of Beaujolais is on display in its wines of 2005, which have generous, ripe fruit, yet also real depth. Things were trickier in 2004, 2006, 2007, and 2008, but in each of these vintages, adept growers with vines in good locations were able to harvest clean, ripe fruit for highly expressive wines.

Drinking Curves—White

The reputation of premier and grand cru white Burgundies for aging in bottle has in recent years suffered a decline so steep that it almost seems like the work of malicious gremlins. Whatever the reasons for the premature aging of expensive white Burgundies, the less expensive examples recommended in this guide—whether from the Côte d'Or, Côte Chalonnaise, or the Mâcon—should, to be safe, be enjoyed within 2–3 years of vintage. While premier or grand cru Chablis can age wonderfully (when everything goes right!), Petit Chablis and generic Chablis ought generally to be drunk up within 3–4 years. (In excellent vintages, generic Chablis from top-flight growers may hold well or even develop interestingly for longer.)

Drinking Curves—Red

Only an exceptional few of the best red Burgundies of generic or village appellation recommended in this guide are capable of (let alone worth) cellaring for long. As a safe rule, one should plan to enjoy them within 3–4 years of vintage (those of the outstanding 2005 vintage being an exception). On the other hand, the widespread notion that Beaujolais wines must be drunk up as young as possible is a myth. Generic Beaujolais or Beaujolais-Villages is best enjoyed within 2–3 years of vintage—while its fruit is still vivid—but cru Beaujolais from top estates (particularly those whose concentration or structure has merited comment in the list of recommendations that make up most of this chapter) can be fascinating to follow for 3–5 years. Whether one prefers them in maturity is simply a matter of personal taste, influenced by the sorts of foods with which one chooses to serve them.

Burgundy's and Beaujolais's Top Wine Values by Winery

BERTRAND AMBROISE *(Côte d'Or)*

Bourgogne 🍷 **$$$** For a generic Burgundy, this is amazingly dark in color, loaded with raw black fruits and graphite, and saturates the palate with a formidable, bittersweet intensity of fruit, mineral, meat, and tannin.

HERVÉ AZO *(Chablis/Auxerre)*

Chablis 🍷 **$$$** This wine made at Brocard (see below) brims with citrus, and in ripe years tropical fruits; is tinged with chalk dust and subtly saline mineral suggestions; and typically finishes with impressive lift and length.

JULIEN BARRAUD *(Mâcon)*

Mâcon-Chaintré Les Pierres Polies 🍷 **$$$** The son of star vintners Daniel and Martine Barraud recently began crafting this wine of concentration, polish, clarity, and low-key richness.

JEAN-MARC BOILLOT *(Côte D'or and Côte Chalonnaise)*

Montagny ler Cru 🍷 **$$$** From purchased grapes, this showcases succulent orchard fruits, floral perfume, citrus zest, and nut oils. Even when creamy and plush, it doesn't lack verve.

DANIEL BOULAND *(Beaujolais)*

Morgon Vieilles Vignes 🍷 **$$$** This beauty offers ripe cassis and blackberry allied to raw meatiness, pungent herbs, wood smoke, and suggestions of ocean breeze, its vividly juicy black fruits mingled with something that seems to encrust your palate!

REGIS BOUVIER *(Côte d'Or)*

Fixin 🍷 **$$$** This rare bargain among Côte d'Or village wines delivers ripe black fruits with notes of wood smoke, salted beef stock, and iodine for an attractively lean, well-concentrated impression.

DOMAINE DES BRAVES (PAUL CINQUIN) *(Beaujolais)*

Régnié 🍷 **$$** A relatively light color presages this wine's caressing lightness of touch on the palate. Like a subtly salted blend of strawberry chiffon and nut paste, it's delightfully mouth filling and refreshing.

BRETT BROTHERS *(Mâcon)*

Mâcon-Cruzille 🍷 **$$$** From ancient vines, this extract-rich Mâcon displays impressive, meaty richness; palate-saturating intensity of citrus and orchard fruit; and subtly smoky, zesty, saline complexity.

Mâcon-Uchizy La Martine 🍷 **$$** This offers honey, mint, and lavender–tinged orchard and tropical fruits; creamy texture yet infectious juiciness and vivacity; and satisfying length.

JEAN-MARC BROCARD *(Chablis/Auxerre)*

Bourgogne Jurassique 🍷 **$$$** From what Brocard calls his *"trio géologique"* (reflective of three different soil types near Chablis), this refined, lip-smacking Chardonnay suggests lime, sweet pea, cucumber, chalk, and salt.

Bourgogne Kimmeridgien 🍷 **$$$** This delivers a hint of mothball on the nose, along with fresh cherry and lime. Distinctive chalkiness mingles with lusciously mouth-coating fruit and an impressively sappy cling.

Bourgogne Portlandien 🍷 **$$$** Here we have low-toned brothy richness, a satiny texture, and a dusty crushed-stone character that saturates the palate.

Saint-Bris 🍷 **$$$** This Sauvignon Blanc from the vast Brocard establishment is bright and refreshing, clean and penetrating, with pungent gooseberry, herb, citrus, and almost dusty crushed stone notes.

BUISSON-CHARLES *(Côte d'Or)*

Bourgogne Aligoté 🍷 **$$** A little-recognized master of Merusault vinifies humble Aligoté displaying pear distillate, lemon zest, and mint on the nose; a (for this grape) surprising degree of creaminess in the mouth; and a clear, juicy finish.

JEAN-MARC BURGAUD *(Beaujolais)*

Beaujolais-Villages Château de Thulon 🍷 **$** This offers textural presence and memorable concentration of ripe red fruits, rose hips, and deep, marrow-like meatiness, and like all Burgaud wines, it is improbably delicious and complex for its price.

Morgon Les Charmes 🍷 **$$** This fills the nose and mouth with ripe plums, cherries, and violets; offers exuberantly, vividly juicy fresh fruit generosity, silken texture, and fine-grained tannin; and finishes with genuine depth of black fruits, marrow, smoked meat, and saline minerality.

Morgon Côte de Py 🍷 **$$$** A nose of crushed stone; pungent, musky flowers; and fresh pomegranate and red raspberry leads to a correspondingly bright, tart, but ripe palate wreathed in flowers and a long finish at once cleansing, invigorating, intriguing, and enticing.

DOMAINE DE LA CADETTE *(Chablis/Auxerre)*

2006 Bourgogne Vézelay La Châtelaine 🍷 **$$$** Citrus, pit fruits, fruit pits, chicken stock, shrimp shell reduction, herbs, and flowers mingle in a subtly creamy yet irresistibly refreshing matrix. Few wines worldwide—much less in Burgundy—can offer you a rapport of quality and price comparable to this cuvée from a pioneer in outlying Vézelay, Jean Montanet.

JEAN CALOT *(Beaujolais)*

Morgon Vieilles Vignes 🍷 **$$$** Of Calot's several cuvées, this one characteristically offers copious ripe black fruits and peach threaded with smoky and gamy nuances and finishing with an alkaline mineral note.

NICOLE CHANRION *(Beaujolais)*

Côte de Brouilly 🍷 **$$$** Suggesting tart red raspberry, rhubarb, beef marrow, and ham hock, and finishing with sap and invigoration, here is an ideal refutation of the claim that wine from Beaujolais is simple.

CHANSON PÈRE & FILS *(Beaujolais)*

Fleurie 🍷 $$ Recent quality enhancements at Beaune-based Chanson extend to some excellent Beaujolais, such as this Fleurie with lingering purple plum, toasted pecan, soy, and wet stone flavors.

DOMAINE DE LA CHAPELLE *(Mâcon)*

Mâcon-Solutré-Pouilly 🍷 $$ Intense salinity, chalkiness, and bright citricity render this rather Chablis-like. Fruit skin tartness and toasted grain and nut bitterness add interest to an invigorating finish.

PIERRE-MARIE CHERMETTE (DOMAINE DU VISSOUX) *(Beaujolais)*

Beaujolais Pierre Chermette 🍷 $ The remarkable consistency and value of Chermette's low-sulfur wines begins with this refreshing, lightweight, yet concentrated essence of salt- and chalk-tinged tart cherries with their pits and flowers.

Beaujolais Vieilles Vignes Cuvée Traditionelle 🍷 $$ Surprisingly dark in color for a wine so light in body (at 11.5% alcohol), this is loaded with red and black fruits and flowers, accented with citrus-rind pungency and saline minerality, and displays a kinetic inner intensity that will leave your palate refreshed and invigorated.

Brouilly Pierreux 🍷 $$$ With mouthwatering black and blue fruits distinctly tinged by fruit pits, smoked meat, chalk, and a medicinal iodine note, this formidably concentrated wine never forgets its duty to refresh.

Fleurie Les Garants 🍷 $$$ This gripping yet mouthwatering Fleurie typically possesses distinctively fine-grained tannin amid palate-staining cassis, plum, bitter fruit pit, tactile cinnamon spice, salt, and stone.

Fleurie Poncié 🍷 $$$ Smelling intensely of fresh black raspberry and cassis, along with hints of wood smoke and salt spray, this is positively palate staining in its intense berry concentrate laced with saline, stone, iodine, and peat.

ROBERT CHEVILLON (*Côte d'Or*)

Bourgogne Passetoutgrains ♟ **$$$** Two-thirds from old Gamay vines and full of ripe, smoke- and brown spice–tinged cherry fruit and roasted meats, this is an affordable treat from one of the Côte d'Or's foremost growers.

DOMAINE CHEYSSON (*Beaujolais*)

Chiroubles ♟ **$$** This lip-smacking yet thought-provoking revelation of quality for its appellation features ripe fresh red raspberries accented by orange zest, white pepper, nut oils, and mineral notes.

MICHEL CHIGNARD (*Beaujolais*)

Fleurie Les Mories ♟ **$$$** This practically overflows with blueberry and black cherry, mingled with subtly bitter notes of black tea, cherry pit, peat, and tart fruit skin, and manages to be by turns soothing and invigorating.

DOMAINE DAVID CLARK (*Côte d'Or*)

Bourgogne Passetoutgrains ♟ **$$$** From ex–Formula One engineer Clark, a well-concentrated, finely tannic cuvée displaying lovely red fruits, subtle gaminess, and a bright, sappy finish.

CLOS DE LA ROILETTE (*Beaujolais*)

Fleurie ♟ **$$$** Proof that "profound Beaujolais" is no oxymoron: Alain Coudert's extraordinary-value ageworthy Fleurie suggests among other things ripe red fruits, leather, wood smoke, toasted nuts, raw beef, moss, and wet stones.

DOMAINE DU CLOS DU FIEF (*Beaujolais*)

Julienas ♟ **$$$** Michel Tête's Julienas displays positively kinetic intensity and an almost white wine–like vivacity and refreshment, with red raspberry, rhubarb, smoked meat, and mineral salts leading to an audaciously penetrating finish.

BRUNO COLIN (*Côte d'Or*)

Bourgogne ♟ **$$$** From one branch of a famous Chassagne-Montrachet clan, a Chardonnay balancing textural richness with clarity and refreshment.

PIERRE-YVES COLIN *(Côte d'Or)*

Bourgogne ♉ **$$$** Old vines in excellent places deliver lightly baked apple, marzipan, lily, and lemon cream flavors, with textural richness yet refreshment.

PHILIPPE COLLOTTE *(Côte d'Or)*

Marsannay Vieilles Vignes ♉ **$$** This rare, palate-saturating Côte d'Or value offers vividly juicy fresh black raspberry backed by honeysuckle, iodine, wet stone, soy, and clean red meat.

G. DESCOMBES *(Beaujolais)*

Morgon ♉ **$$$** Brimming with black fruits and threaded with decadently bittersweet floral perfume, this concentrated cru finishes with focus and lip-smacking brightness. Mossy animal and mineral depths emerge with time in bottle.

GÉRARD DESCOMBES (DOMAINE LES CÔTES DE LA ROCHE) *(Beaujolais)*

Juliénas ♉ **$$$** Redolent of ripe black raspberries—its sense of sweetness nicely checked by lightly bitter fruit skin astringency and an invigorating saline tang—this sappy, vigorous, persistent wine is a delight. (Gérard Descombes should not be confused with Georges—see above—who signs himself just "G.")

DOMAINE DES DEUX ROCHES (COLLOVRAY & TERRIER) *(Mâcon)*

Mâcon-Villages Plants du Carré ♉ **$$** From a dynamic duo (also responsible for the amazing-value Domaine Antugnac wines—see under "Languedoc"), a citric, honeyed, chalky, faintly oak-tinged, but persistently juicy Chardonnay.

Saint-Véran ♉ **$$$** Under the "Collovray & Terrier" label, this represents a richly textured but understated amalgam of melon, citrus, and mineral nuances.

BERNARD DIOCHON *(Beaujolais)*

Moulin-à-Vent ♉ **$$$** Liqueur-like cherry fruit and smoked meat characteristically inform this deeply rich and glycerin-filled wine, but with underlying structure, should one care to test its aging potential.

BENOÎT DROIN *(Chablis/Auxerre)*

Petit Chablis ♀ **$$$** From high up above the grand cru Les Clos, this pure, persistent wine displays ripe peach, fresh lime, and hints of crushed stone.

JOSEPH DROUHIN *(Côte d'Or, Chablis)*

Bourgogne Laforet ♀ **$$** Like other wines (below) from famous *négociant* Drouhin, this nuanced and persistent Pinot represents an ideal place to begin discovering the wiles of Burgundian Pinot Noir.

Bourgogne Véro ♀ **$$$** High-toned red cherry, raw red meat, mineral, and floral elements as well as silken texture point to the top-quality villages (and even a couple of premiers crus) from which this is sourced.

Chorey-les-Beaune ♀ **$$$** Consistently offering high-toned cherry-almond, brown spices, subtle fruit-pit bitterness, purity, and salinity, this is a delicate, penetrating, highly satisfying Pinot.

GEORGES DUBOEUF *(Beaujolais)*

Brouilly ♀ **$** The myriad Beaujolais bottlings of *négociant* Georges Duboeuf represent perennial values in the American marketplace, especially the so-called "flower label" cuvées, such as this consistently blue-fruited, lip-smacking Brouilly.

Brouilly Domaine de Grand Croix ♀ **$$** One of Duboeuf's many bottlings from individual estates, this saturates the palate impressively with tart black fruits, inner-mouth floral perfume, spices, and salts.

Chiroubles ♀ **$** Delicately caressing, seductively peony-scented, and full of ripe berries.

Fleurie ♀ **$$** Black fruit and wet stone laden, yet retaining an attractively lilting sense of delicacy.

Fleurie Clos des Quatre Vents ♀ **$$** A sappy, saline, tangy, palate-coating wine loaded with high-toned berry fruit.

Juliénas ♀ **$** Florally perfumed, loaded with berry fruit, accented with moss and black tea.

Juliénas Château des Capitans 🍷 **$$** Consistently well concentrated and redolent of ripe black fruits and smoked meat, with at times a bit of tannin to shed.

Morgon 🍷 **$$** This charms with scents and flavors of *frais des bois,* cherry, fennel, and at times green tea or cocoa powder, with saline, savory, carnal undertones informing its finish. The duty to refresh is never forgotten.

Morgon Domaine Jean Descombes 🍷 **$$** This extroverted wine is consistently imposing in richness, loaded with black fruits, and irresistibly luscious and bright, its animal undertones and hints of salt and wet stone adding finishing interest.

Moulin-à-Vent Domaine des Rosiers 🍷 **$$** Intensely black-fruited, invigoratingly tart, and saline, this frequently introduces herbal and roasted-meat notes as well as impressive textural presence and finishing grip.

Moulin-à-Vent Tour de Bief 🍷 **$$** This estate's bottling generally features a tart concentration of black fruits with suggestions of salted nuts.

VINCENT DUREUIL-JANTHIAL *(Côte Chalonnaise)*

Bourgogne 🍷 **$$$** This plush yet lively Chardonnay typically offers generous helpings of white peach, papaya, and pineapple, tinged with coconut, spice, and vanilla from the barrel.

Bourgogne Aligoté 🍷 **$$** This amazing value offers citrus, pineapple, sweet corn, herbs, nut oils, chicken stock richness, surprisingly creamy texture for Aligoté, and an invigorating finish of salts, chalk, and shrimp shell.

Bourgogne Passetoutgrains 🍷 **$$** Ripe and plump, with exceptionally pure raspberry and pomegranate fruit, refined tannins, and a generous finish, this offers amazing quality for a blend of Pinot and Gamay.

BENOIT ENTE *(Côte d'Or)*

Bourgogne Aligoté 🍷 **$$$** This smells of distilled cherry, lemon, and pistachio. Quite dense yet bright on the palate, it finishes delightfully and invigoratingly with cherry, citrus, and zesty, chalky pungency.

DOMAINE DE LA FEUILLARDE *(Mâcon)*

Saint-Véran Tradition ♀ $$ This cuvée offers genre-typical aromas of fresh apple, lemon, and chalk dust. In the mouth it evinces persistent brown spices, mineral salts, and zesty citrus.

Saint-Véran Vieilles Vignes ♀ $$$ From very old vines, this offers a rich, creamy-textured mouthful of musk melon, orchard fruits, almond, brown spices, and floral perfume, finishing with chalky, stony, saline mineral accents.

JEAN-PHILIPPE FICHET *(Côte d'Or)*

Bourgogne ♀ $$$ Peach, nut oils, and bittersweet floral notes in the nose lead to a palate exhibiting the Fichet-trademark alliance of creamy richness (but without an ounce of fat) with precision of fruit and mineral, and a ripe, bright acidity.

Bourgogne Aligoté ♀ $$ Offering toasted nuts and grain, palpable citrus zest pungency and chalky minerality, and genuinely intriguing carnal depth, this will prove compatible with bitter vegetables and offer a counterpoint to rich sauces.

JEAN FOURNIER *(Côte d'Or)*

Marsannay Cuvée St.-Urbain ♥ $$$ In this lovely introduction to Marsannay, pit fruits and meat stock are thought-provokingly laced with notes of fruit pit, salt, and stone, and the finish is always both intriguing and refreshing.

DOMAINE DES GERBEAUX *(Mâcon)*

Mâcon-Solutré Le Clos ♀ $$ Peach, floral, and vanilla aromas; a creamy palate richness with bitter notes of peach kernel; and a tactile sense of lees and chalk inform this wine of considerable richness and depth.

Pouilly-Vinzelles Les Longeays ♀ $$$ This displays toasty, smoky notes from the barrel; ripe apple-y fruit complemented by citrus zest and chalk; an especially creamy texture for a white Burgundy of its price; and an imposingly long finish incorporating a reprise of spicy, smoky barrel inflections.

VINCENT GIRARDIN *(Côte d'Or)*

Bourgogne Cuvée St.-Vincent 🍷 **$$$** From Vincent Girardin's vast collection, this mingles citrus, flowers, honey, spice, and chalky mineral suggestions in a rich yet refreshing whole.

GHISLAIN AND JEAN-HUGUES GOISOT *(Chablis/Auxerre)*

Bourgogne Aligoté 🍷 **$$** Chicken stock, lemongrass, cherries with their pits, basil, and lemons and tangerines with their pips are among the elements of this infectiously juicy, sleekly textured, and invigorating bundle of vinous energy and consistently extraordinary value.

Bourgogne Côtes d'Auxerre 🍷 **$$$** This bottling can typically exhibit browned butter, quince, yellow plum, acacia, lime, and ginger. Creamy yet zesty and refreshing, it offers convincing length with a distinctly chalky sense of minerality.

MICHEL GOUBARD *(Côte Chalonnaise)*

Bourgogne Montavril 🍷 **$$$** Full of high-toned, tart red fruits with surprisingly saline, meaty, anything-but-sweet undertones and flatteringly silken, this manages to be expansive despite its relatively light weight.

Bourgogne Mont Avril Fût de Chêne 🍷 **$$$** Goubard's top cuvée is subtly marked by its stay in barrel; the nose and flavors are slightly gamy and the texture subtly grainy, with salt-tinged, tart red or black fruits leading to an invigoratingly gripping finish.

CHÂTEAU DE LA GREFFIÈRE *(Mâcon)*

Mâcon–La Roche–Vineuse Sous le Bois 🍷 **$$** This characteristically offers a delightful nose of honeysuckle, fresh apple, and chalk dust. Refreshing, silken textured, yet delicate, it finishes with subtle notes of lees, chalk, and toasted nuts and grain.

Mâcon–La Roche–Vineuse Vieilles 🍷 **$$** Typically smelling of gardenia, papaya, honeysuckle, and nutmeg, satisfyingly lush and creamy, with notes of chalk and toasted nuts and grain, this finishes with lasting piquancy and salinity.

Saint-Véran ♀ **$$** This features savory, saline, nutty, and milled-grain aromas and flavors and is typically relatively light in weight yet nevertheless displays flattering creaminess of texture and a resolutely mineral finish.

LOUIS JADOT *(Côte d'Or, Mâcon, and Beaujolais)*

Beaujolais ♥ **$** From the chalky southern reaches of the Beaujolais region, this offers consistently tart red fruit character and a penetratingly bright, clean, and refreshing finish in which some tasters are sure to swear they detect crushed stone.

Beaujolais-Villages ♥ **$** For sheer ubiquity, this surpasses even Jadot's Mâcon-Villages. Brimming with black fruits tinged with citrus zest, bitter hints of fruit pit, and the tartness of berry skins, it offers a consistently clean, refreshing, and genuinely energetic display of Gamay-granite synergies.

Bourgogne ♀ **$$$** Scented with peach and often red berries, nicely balanced between creaminess of texture and freshness, this finishes with an invigorating, zesty kick.

Mâcon-Villages ♀ **$$** Few white wines from Burgundy are as familiar a sight in American shops and restaurants as this one, and it never fails to offer clear, apple-y fruit, subtle suggestions of flowers and minerals, and a satisfyingly juicy finish free of heat or bitterness.

(LOUIS JADOT) CHÂTEAU DES JACQUES, CHÂTEAU DES LUMIÈRES *(Beaujolais)*

Morgon ♥ **$$$** This wine's sheer brightness and dense concentration of red fruits and saline mineral dimension as well as the underlying, marrow-like sense of rich meat stock are all quite striking. Smoky, gamy nuances in the long, savory finish are typical for Morgon.

Moulin-à-Vent ♥ **$$$** This dense, structured blend from numerous sites displays bright raspberry and pomegranate fruit, deep marrow-like meatiness, and accents of cask and salt in its finish.

JACKY JANODET (DOMAINE DES FINE GRAVES) *(Beaujolais)*

Moulin-à-Vent ♥ **$$$** Ripe black cherry, charred meat, and cherry-pit bitterness typically inform the nose and fill the mouth in a firm, dense display, with abundant fruit and deep marrow-like meatiness.

MICHEL LAFARGE *(Côte d'Or)*

Aligoté Raisins Dorés ♉ $$$ Grapes from ancient vines permitted to ripen to a golden hue deliver tropical fruits, opulent texture, and in many years a positively honeyed finish, but always with a core of refreshment and chalkiness, even in vintages where it is ample and honeyed.

Bourgogne Aligoté ♉ $$ One of Lafarge's exceptional generic bottlings of red and white, none of which should be missed, this delivers bracing, shiver-inspiring refreshment, with the impression that it has been starched with minerals.

Bourgogne Passetoutgrains ♉ $$ This invigorating and versatile Pinot-Gamay blend displays bright, tart sour-cherry fruit, hints of game, and a finish of meat broth, wood smoke, cherry pit, and sharply focused fruit.

Bourgogne Passetoutgrains L'Exception ♉ $$$ From ancient vines, this is as bright and invigorating as its sibling but full of deep meatiness and dark berry fruit, augmented by a subtly oily texture.

JEAN-CLAUDE LAPALU *(Beaujolais)*

Beaujolais-Villages Vieilles Vignes ♉ $$ There is a density and intensity of ripe black fruits, a tactile sense of mineral extract, and a meaty, smoky depth here that you won't find anywhere else under this appellation.

MARCEL LAPIERRE *(Beaujolais)*

Morgon ♉ $$$ From a father figure of the "back-to-the-future Beaujolais," this fills the nose with high-toned distilled berry and herbal essences, sweetly pungent floral notes, forest floor, and game. Meaty, mineral complexities inform a consistently refreshing and thought-provoking finish.

LOUIS LATOUR *(Côte d'Or, Côte Chalonnaise, Chablis, Beaujolais)*

Montagny 1er Cru ♉ $$$ A long-running, high-production hit, this versatile Chardonnay delivers honeysuckle; pear; a luscious, polished, subtly creamy palate; and chalky, stony mineral finishing notes.

ROLAND LAVANTUREUX *(Chablis/Auxerre)*

Chablis 🍷 **$$$** This typically smells of gooseberry, lime, pear, and cherry, often faintly astringent as well as brightly juicy and invigorating even in ripe vintages.

DOMAINE DE LA MADONE *(Beaujolais)*

Beaujolais—Le Pérreon 🍷 **$$** This manages to consistently preserve freshness, purity, and vigor. Lightweight and soft in feel, it displays abundant bitter black fruits, pungent herbs, pepper, salt, and chalk.

FRÉDÉRIC MAGNIEN *(Côte d'Or)*

Bourgogne 🍷 **$$$** Cherry and vanilla mingle with gamy notes on the nose. In the mouth, this displays slightly rustic tannins but generous, sappy dark fruits and carnal and mineral dimensions that cling impressively.

MICHEL MAGNIEN *(Côte d'Or)*

Bourgogne Grand Ordinaire 🍷 **$$$** From the family estate of *négociant* Frédéric Magnien (see above), and from a site not even allowed to call itself plain Bourgogne, this is palate-staining Pinot, with abundant underlying tannins allied to lavishly ripe, sweet fruit and the spiciness of oak.

JEAN MANCIAT *(Mâcon)*

Mâcon-Charnay Franclieu 🍷 **$$$** An engaging nose of bittersweet flowers, lemon, and wet stone leads to a palate of impressive richness and palpable extract, finishing saline and chalky.

ALAIN MICHAUD *(Beaujolais)*

Brouilly 🍷 **$$** This bottling consistently brims with herb- and brown spice–tinged blueberries, finishing with invigorating hints of bitter fruit skin, tart fruit pits, salt, and wet stone.

Brouilly Prestige Vieilles Vignes 🍷 **$$$** With black fruits and pepper joining its herbal display, this has a distillate-like intensity, a lush mouth-feel, and a bright, penetrating, palate-staining, stone-paved finish.

FRANÇOIS MIKULSKI *(Côte d'Or)*

Bourgogne Aligoté ♀ **$$** From ancient vines in Meursault, this is brimming with ripe, pure pear nectar and grapefruit, polished and subtly creamy yet clean and refreshing on the palate. It offers chalky and invigoratingly bitter citrus-rind notes in its finish.

ALICE & OLIVIER DE MOOR *(Chablis/Auxerre)*

Bourgogne Aligoté ♀ **$$** Displaying a surprisingly doughy substantiality for its appellation, yet consistently bright and invigorating, this delivers scents and flavors of lemon pip, cherry, toasted almonds, chicken stock, and herbs.

Bourgogne Aligoté Vieilles Vignes ♀ **$$$** This old-vines bottling displays succulence, grip, and complexity, with distinctly floral, high-toned almond, lychee, apricot, and pineapple allied to an ineffable set of mineral nuance.

Bourgogne Chitry ♀ **$$$** This Chardonnay exhibits lovely, piquant lemon, toasted praline, tangerine zest, ginger, and cardamom in a surprisingly rich, mineral-broth-like matrix.

SYLVAIN PATAILLE *(Côte d'Or)*

Bourgogne Passetoutgrains ♥ **$$$** This irresistibly delicious Pinot-Gamay blend from ancient vines is full of black fruits and toasted nuts, soothing in texture yet invigoratingly bright.

R. & L. PAVELOT *(Côte d'Or)*

Pernand-Vergelesses ♀ **$$$** It's rare for a wine of this village to be offered for a price like that of this polished, refined, wood- and chalk-tinged Chardonnay.

PAUL PERNOT *(Côte d'Or)*

Bourgogne ♀ **$$$** The richness of pit and citrus fruits; the layering of savory, saline, and chalky mineral dimensions; the balance of luscious creaminess and bright refreshment; and the sheer length of this incredible value from vines in Puligny outclass most village-level white Côte d'Or Burgundies selling for three times as much.

HENRI PERRUSSET *(Mâcon)*

Mâcon-Farges Vieilles Vignes ♀ **$$$** This old-vines bottling consistently offers a deft balance of ripeness and textural allure with refreshment and invigoration.

GILBERT PICQ ET SES FILS *(Chablis/Auxerre)*

Chablis Vieilles Vignes ♀ **$$$** This displays luscious pit fruits and citrus backed by a crustacean-like savory, saline minerality, with hints of spice and lemon pip adding pungency to an invigorating finish.

DOMINIQUE PIRON *(Beaujolais)*

Fleurie ♟ **$$$** Offering smoked meat, ripe black raspberry, mocha, and a tactile pungency one is tempted to describe in mineral terms, this finishes with an unusually firm grip for a Beaujolais.

Morgon ♟ **$$$** This offers a complex aromatic mélange of black cherry, black tea, and hints of game and smoked meat, with pungent notes of herb and pepper in the finish.

Régnié ♟ **$$** Smelling of ripe strawberries and toasted nuts, this displays an alluring saline, savory cast rather than overt fruitiness and finishes with real verve.

CHÂTEAU DU PIZAY *(Beaujolais)*

Morgon ♀ **$** Sweetly scented with lightly cooked black raspberries, this astonishingly inexpensive Morgon offers a sappy and well-concentrated palate impression with hints of smoked meat and finishes with salt-tinged black fruits.

DANIEL POLLIER *(Mâcon)*

Mâcon-Villages ♀ **$$** This offers highly affordable excellence, with apple and cherry-blossom aromas, bright juicy citrus, nut oils, and an impressive cling of mineral nuances in its finish.

POTEL-AVIRON *(Beaujolais)*

Côte de Brouilly ♟ **$$** From a highly quality-conscious *négociant* who promotes organic farming and barrel aging, this is loaded with blueberry fruit and suffused with a graphite- or wet stone–like sense of minerality. It strikes an elegant balance between sheer juicy refreshment and serious complexity and grip.

Juliénas 🍷 $$ This serious cru displays fresh red raspberry, purple plum, brown spices, and smoked meat. Well concentrated and with a tart berry edge and invigorating freshness on the palate, it finishes with spice and tartness, saline, and stony mineral suggestions.

Morgon Château-Gaillard Vieilles Vignes 🍷 $$$ This displays floral perfume and deep, marrow-like, dark chocolate richness, along with clear, juicy, pepper- and spice-tinged berry fruit.

Morgon Côte du Py Vieilles Vignes 🍷 $$$ Black cherry, purple plum, coriander, and orange zest inform the nose of this tightly structured cru, and in the mouth tart and zesty fruit skin and saline mineral notes lend a sense of invigoration.

Moulin-à-Vent Vieilles Vignes 🍷 $$$ Impressively concentrated, almost thickly textured, and noticeably tannic, this cru is loaded with spiced black cherry and plum as well as possessed of a deep, clean meatiness.

MARION PRAL *(Beaujolais)*

Beaujolais Cuvée Terroir 🍷 $ This is cleansing and refreshing, loaded with sweetly ripe black and pit fruits; its tang and brightness of tart fruit skin and saline mineral notes lend invigoration.

JEAN RIJCKAERT *(Mâcon)*

Mâcon-Villages 🍷 $$ Rijckaert's goals of moderate alcohol, absence of obvious wood, purity, and clarity are consistently upheld here as well as in his numerous slightly more expensive cuvées.

JOËL ROCHETTE *(Beaujolais Villages)*

Beaujolais-Villages 🍷 $$ This upbeat Beaujolais offers a sweetly floral, snappy, pungent, slightly tart blackberry and brown spice experience guaranteed to leave your mouth refreshed and happy to take the next sip.

FRANCINE & OLIVIER SAVARY *(Chablis/Auxerre)*

Chablis Vieilles Vignes 🍷 $$$ More than a merely reliable exemplar of Chablis, this smells of cherries, Meyer lemons, and thyme, its lovely cherry and citrus fruit tinged with salt and chalk, and for all of its brightness and mineral cast, it boasts a glossy texture and pleasant fullness.

DOMAINE SERVIN *(Chablis/Auxerre)*

Chablis Cuvée Les Pargues ♀ **$$$** Unfiltered and late bottled, this cuvée from a distinctive site boasts apricot, cherry, and grapefruit mingled with subtly saline chicken stock and shrimp shell reduction, resulting in a depth and shimmering clarity of flavor astonishing for its price.

Petit Chablis ♀ **$$** Sweetly ripe aromas of peach, nut oils, and lily are followed by saline and brightly citric flavors and a bracing, palpably mineral citrus zest, herb, and peach-skin finish.

DOMAINE DES SOUCHONS *(Beaujolais)*

Morgon Cuvée Lys ♟ **$$$** Scented with purple plum, red raspberry, and violets, vividly fresh and bright, this mouth-filling cru finishes with the tangy tartness of fruit skin and a hint of smoky (some will say mineral) pungency.

DOMAINE DES TERRES DORÉES (JEAN-PAUL BRUN) *(Beaujolais)*

Beaujolais l'Ancien Vieilles Vignes ♟ **$$** This homage to "ancient" methods represents an incredible value. Vivid, tart, fresh black fruits; profuse flowers; and salty, chalky mineral notes lead to an invigorating and practically indelible finish.

Beaujolais Blanc Chardonnay ♀ **$$** A gorgeous bouquet of flowers with citrus, pit fruits, and saline, chalky notes; a positively chewy and substantial palate; and a refreshing, lilting, savory, saline, scallop-like finish. This is among the finest Chardonnay values on the planet.

Beaujolais Rosé d'Folie ♀ **$$** This irresistibly luscious wine of an obscure genre is redolent of fresh raspberries and strawberries tinged with salt and chalk.

JEAN-PAUL THÉVENET *(Beaujolais)*

Morgon ♟ **$$** Cherry distillate, orange zest, wood smoke, toasted nuts, black tea, and cherry pit lend bittersweetness to this wine's expansive, lush, yet refreshing finish palate.

DOMAINE THIBERT PÈRE ET FILS *(Mâcon)*

Mâcon-Fuissé ♀ $$ Smelling of lime, subtly bitter fruit pits, sage, and meat stock, and well concentrated on the palate, this offers a fine combination of substantiality with brightness and lift.

Saint-Véran ♀ $$$ This downright aggressive Chardonnay smells of white peach, lemon, sage, and black pepper. Bright, well concentrated, and pungent, it grips with citrus, pepper, and chalky-stony mineral suggestions.

CHÂTEAU THIVIN *(Beaujolais)*

Côte de Brouilly ♥ $$$ Saline, smoked meat, juniper berry, and tart black fruit flavors tend to dominate in this aromatically nuanced, understated Beaujolais whose finish of brightness and mineral savor sometimes displays a lashing of tannin.

VERGET *(Mâcon, Côte D'or, Chablis/Auxerre)*

Bourgogne Grand Élevage ♀ $$$ Treated to a longer stay in barrels than the "regular" Verget Bourgogne, this is typically opulent, honeyed, and subtly creamy, but never heavy.

Bourgogne Terroir de Côte d'Or ♀ $$ This boasts luscious pit and tropical fruits, toasted nuts, and often red berry notes, a soft texture, juicy refreshment, and considerable length.

Mâcon-Bussières Les Terreaux ♀ $$$ Evoking lemon and musk melon, this wine's often exotically ripe side is wedded to refreshing citrus, and it finishes with invigorating hints of lemon zest and salt.

Mâcon-Bussières Vieilles Vignes de Monbrison ♀ $$$ This Chardonnay from a parcel of ancient vines characteristically achieves a remarkable balance between richness, stuffing, and refreshment; exotic fruit, and chalky, saline minerality; and nutty piquancy and citricity.

Mâcon-Bussières Vieilles Vignes du Clos ♀ $$$ This tends toward melon and tropical fruit ripeness with accents of chalk and salts. A wine of formidable concentration and length.

Mâcon-Vergisson La Roche ♀ $$$ Characteristically smelling of ripe apricot, buddleia, lemon, and chalk dust, and expansive, often quite rich, yet always refreshing, this partially barrel-fermented Chardonnay offers considerable nuance and complexity.

Mâcon-Villages ♀ **$$** A tribute to *négociant* Jean-Marie Guffens's skill in pulling surprising character and concentration from a simple appellation, this is brimming with orchard fruits and flowers, often surprisingly creamy and expansive, yet always generously refreshing and mineral tinged.

M. J. VINCENT *(Beaujolais and Mâcon)*

Julienas Domaine Le Cotoyon ♀ **$$$** From the proprietors of Château Fuissé, this typically displays bright black cherry and blackberry fruit, a dense palate for Beaujolais, and a blazingly bright, tart, saline, chalk-textured finish.

Pouilly-Fuissé Proprieté Marie-Antoinette Vincent ♀ **$$$** Melon, apple, and grapefruit mingle on the nose and palate of a Chardonnay that combines polished texture, honeyed richness, bright citricity, and chalky, stony nuances.

GEORGES VIONERY *(Beaujolais)*

Brouilly ♀ **$$** This typically proffers profuse black and blue fruits, displays a lush palate cut by hints of fruit skin bitterness and wet stone, and finishes with exemplary persistence.

Côte de Brouilly ♀ **$$** Here is an intense aroma of fresh blueberries, often backed by an almost liqueur-like richness on the palate, with graphite, toasted nut, chalk, and stone undertones joining in an intensely savory, dynamic, positively lip-smacking finish.

CAVE DE VIRÉ *(Mâcon)*

Viré-Clessé Les Acacias ♀ **$$** This cuvée from the Viré co-op displays fresh apple, flowers, and a hint of honey in the nose; a soft, soothing, subtly creamy yet still refreshing palate; and a finish of apple and lemon cream dusted with nutmeg and drizzled with honey.

Viré-Clessé Les Charlottes ♀ **$$** Treated to a small contingent of new barrels, this displays underlying firmness despite flattering creaminess suggestions of chalky minerality and invigorating notes of fruit skin, citrus, and herbs.

LANGUEDOC AND ROUSSILLON
WINE VALUES

by David Schildknecht

Great Bargains and Great Ambitions

What brought to prominence, beginning in the mid-1980s, two of France's oldest wine-growing regions—but ones whose fortunes seemed to have suffered a steady decline since the Middle Ages—was qualitative innovation and the search for bargains, each reinforcing the other. The Languedoc and Roussillon—which together form the great Mediterranean arc of wine-growing west and south of the Rhône—are still caught between a market niche and image as sources of inexpensive wine on the one hand, and a slowly emerging recognition on the other that these regions are home to some of the world's most profoundly exciting libations. The name "Roussillon" was until recently known to wine lovers—if at all—through the often-used conjunction "Languedoc-Roussillon." Nevertheless, there are good climatic and cultural reasons—not to mention the preference of the growers—for treating separately the fewer than one hundred thousand variously classified acres tucked up against the Spanish border and overlooking the Mediterranean and the highest peaks of the Pyrenees. Furthermore, Roussillon is arguably the most exciting—perhaps last—wine-growing frontier of France, now overrun by newcomers from all over France and abroad, lured by the smell of vinous black gold.

The Languedoc and Roussillon are blessed with sunshine but frequently cursed with drought. This sensitivity has wide repercussions, especially in the choice of vines, sites, and soils capable of mitigating heat and permitting vine roots to go deep. Elevation, proximity to the Mediterranean, north- or east-facing slopes, and old vines are a few such mitigating factors. Quality-conscious hand-harvesters (who are in the minority) must be prepared to pick with careful timing and selectivity to achieve wines that retain vivacity and taste genuinely ripe, not just high in potential alcohol. Much of the Languedoc is trapped in a downward spiral of ever-higher yields (abetted by lax laws and special pleading) chasing ever-lower prices (to the point of fomenting grower riots). Those who cannot break free of this cycle are farming on borrowed time. The shakeout taking place in these regions is grim, but savvy consumers the world over are its beneficiaries. Meanwhile, more and more truly exciting wines are emerging from the Languedoc from growers who practice rigorous selectivity of fruit and farm exceptional locations. It is, in short, the best of times and worst of times for this vast region and its growers.

Some parts of the Languedoc are still as uncharted by France's wine laws as they are off the beaten track of the world's wine lovers. Increasingly, though, the long arm of the law has already reached out—arguably too eager to introduce hierarchy and rules—and the results can be bewildering. New official appellations have been created at a rapid pace, and the larger of these act as umbrellas for often disparate terrains and microclimates. In order not to add further confusion, the introduction that follows will offer only a fairly brisk summary of the most important Languedoc and Roussillon subregions. Many of the most interesting wines lack the name of any official appellation, less often because of where they are grown than because so many growers sensibly choose to utilize the grape varieties and the percentages of these that they deem best, rather than following what often seem arbitrary or even ill-conceived regulations. Such wines are generally labeled as *vins de pays,* sometimes merely as *vins de table.* The territories covered by these numerous *vins de pays* are generally too large for their names to offer any clue to style, *terroir,* or microclimate. In our abbreviated tour below, few of them will be mentioned, and in the individual wine entries that make up the bulk of this chapter, only names of full-fledged *appellations contrôlées* will appear as part of a wine's description.

Grapes

The same three red wine grapes are of greatest importance here as in the Southern Rhône, namely **Grenache, Syrah**, and **Mourvèdre**, and to a lesser extent **Carignan** (more prominent here than in the Rhône) and **Cinsault**, the latter two generally head-pruned (bush) vines that do not respond well to machine harvest but are arguably perfectly adapted to the rigors of these climes and capable of qualities far beyond their lowly reputations. Counoise also features interestingly in a few vineyards and wines, and on rare occasions Tempranillo or Malbec. Cabernet(s) and Merlot are widely planted, but except in the extreme west of the Languedoc, they are confined largely to straightforward and inexpensive single-variety bottlings. In a few cool sectors, Pinot Noir has potential.

White wines represent an experimental, at times downright disorderly side of Languedoc and Roussillon viticulture. There are some great successes, especially in Roussillon, but these are still the exceptions. And the combinations and permutations of grape varieties are enormously diverse. Many of these are based on the trio of the most prominent Rhône white grapes: **Marsanne, Roussanne**, and **Viognier**. The traditional varieties **Grenache Blanc, Bourboulenc, Muscat, Rolle** (a.k.a. Vermentino), and **Clairette** also figure throughout this vast area, and in Roussillon in particular exciting whites feature the **Grenache Gris** and **Macabeo**. **Picpoul** even has its own appellation for tangy, saline, dry whites grown near the seacoast. Considerable acreage of Sauvignon and Chardonnay persists—the latter important in the Limoux sector of the western Languedoc (where Mauzac, a.k.a. Blanquette, is the traditional local grape)—but most of this ends up in simple "varietal" bottlings, to compete (if it can) in the vast international sea of such wines.

Subregions of the Languedoc and Roussillon

Officially, the Languedoc begins at the edge of the Rhône River's southern terminus, where pebbly landscapes east and south of Nîmes resemble Châteauneuf-du-Pape and utilize largely the same red and white grapes. **Costières de Nîmes** (which has bounced back and forth—legally speaking—between the regions of Rhône and Languedoc) is home to some of the most amazing red wine values on earth.

Created nearly a quarter century ago, the now vast **Coteaux du Languedoc** is an umbrella appellation, straddling three French *départements* and a vast range of soils and microclimates, and—at least in principle—covering a significant percentage of the Languedoc's finest wines (although many, as previously noted, are bottled without the imprimatur of *appellation contrôlée*). In some coastal areas, sweet wines from the Muscat were traditionally favored and are still enshrined in numerous appellations. Nowadays, though, production of dry reds is building this sector's reputation, with impressive results issuing from a number of villages that are permitted to append their names to "Coteaux du Languedoc." One subappellation, Grès de Montpellier—southwest of Metropolitan Montpellièr—incorporates the town of St.-Pargoire, where several of the most profound and expensive Syrah-based wines of the Languedoc are grown. Another,

Pic St.-Loup—north of Montpellier—has become the poster child of the Coteaux du Languedoc by succeeding (with blends of Grenache, Syrah, and Mourvedre) in creating a quality image and prices to match the dramatic rocky promontory for which this breezy sector is named. The **Terrasses du Larzac** subappellation west of Montpellier is also home to several of the most profound wines of the Languedoc, from villages (some permitted to append their names to "Coteaux du Languedoc") such as Aniane, Jonquières, Montpeyroux, and St.-Saturnin. South of there, and approaching the city of Béziers, comes a cluster of important wine towns running along the right bank of the little Hérault river, among others Pézenas, Nizas, Caux, and Gabian. (The adjacent area known as "Vin de Pays Côtes de Thongue" is home to some excellent wine values and interesting viticultural experiments as well.) Along the coast halfway between Montpellier and Béziers, the subappellation of **Picpoul de Pinet** renders saline, light, and refreshing wine values completely unlike any other wines in the Languedoc. South of Béziers and immediately east of Narbonne along the coast lies butte-like La Clape, a former island and home to several impressive growers of powerfully ripe reds.

A broad, mountainous expanse of vineyards northwest of Béziers—largely on stony, schist-based soils—characterizes the contiguous appellations of **Faugères** and **St.-Chinian** (in whose southwestern sector the soils change to chalk-clay). Many wines of these appellations feature impressive performances by Mourvèdre and Syrah, with Grenache and Carignan in supporting roles, and certain villages are becoming recognized as centers of excellence. Heading west from St.-Chinian and paralleling the river Aude into the interior of France, one comes to the expansive appellation of **Minervois**, including a range of especially favorable microclimates with *appellation contrôlée* Minervois La Livinière. Imposingly rich, ripe wines represent the ideal in this part of the Languedoc. West of Minervois, around the ancient city and modern tourist destination of Carcassonne (including the appellation of Cabardès), blends between the red Rhône grapes and the Merlot and Cabernets of Bordeaux predominate. And south along the Aude—in far cooler vineyards than elsewhere in the Languedoc—production is devoted largely to sparkling wine (notably appellation Limoux) and to still Chardonnay and Pinot Noir. Minervois, with its 10,000 acres of vines, is a large appellation. But it is dwarfed by **Corbières**, which incorporates three times the acreage, on the other side of the Aube, extending into the mountains as far south as the Roussillon frontier.

This vast area is known for a lot of inexpensive and often rustic reds, the richest of which can offer good value. But there are pockets—and vintners—generating genuinely exciting wines, particularly in the southern Corbières, which segues into one of the oldest appellations in the South of France, **Fitou**, split into discrete coastal and inland sectors. The traditionally dominant grape there is Carignan, although Grenache, Mourvèdre, and Syrah are increasingly important.

Tucked up against the perpetually snowy Pyrenees and the Spanish border, Roussillon is northern Catalonia, a region once dominated by another monarch and tongue than those of France or the Languedoc. Its geological complexity of schist, gneiss, granite, and limestone and its microclimates are distinct, although in the north it borders Fitou and Corbières. The most prevalent appellations are **Côtes du Roussillon-Villages** and **Côtes du Roussillon**. But the requirement of three different grapes for red wines of the former (when in practice many of the best wines rely solely on the superb synergy of Carignan and Grenache); the absence of Grenache Gris (the basis for some of this region's most exciting whites) from the list of grapes approved for either appellation; and the sense of place conveyed by the *vin de pays* designation "Côtes Catalanes," which is the default for much of this region, all conspire to encourage many growers to deviate from the rules of appellation. Among the important wine villages in the north of Roussillon, along the Agly River, are Vingrau, Tautavel, and **Maury**, the last of which has its own appellation for fortified Grenache. Sweet fortified Muscats here (and in the immediately adjacent Languedoc) trade as appellation **Muscat de Rivesaltes**. Latour de France, Montner, Bélesta, and high-elevation Calc are among the centers of exciting new talent (and a few veterans). The subappellation **Côtes du Roussillon Les Aspres** has recently been created for wines in the south, and along a brief but torturously twisting and dramatically terraced strip of coastline, as well as for several miles inland, run the interlocking and long-established appellations of **Collioure** (for dry wines, the reds dominated by Grenache, Syrah, and Mourvèdre) and **Banyuls** (for Grenache-based, fortified sweet wines), which have benefited from the recent renaissance of Roussillon as a whole.

Vintage Smarts

Given the enormous variations in microclimate, soil, grape varieties, and viticultural approaches, it is exceedingly difficult to generalize about vintage character in the vast Languedoc and in Roussillon, or even many times within their subregions and appellations. In general, 2007 has resulted in an especially exciting crop of wines that combine ripeness and richness with lift and energy. Conditions in 2006 were less felicitous, but adept growers in most regions have succeeded quite well. The 2004 and drought-plagued 2005 vintages were challenging, too, but there are many outstanding wines in both instances.

Drinking Curves

Most whites of the Languedoc are best enjoyed within a year of two of harvest, although some Grenache Gris–based whites from Roussillon are proving to have significant aging potential. With Languedoc or Roussillon reds, the variation in potential is enormous. A safe rule of thumb is to enjoy most of the least expensive reds within 2–3 years of harvest, recognizing that the better wines can have up to a decade or more of aging potential, and in fact many wineries don't even release their top bottlings for several years. This is a part of the world in which viticulture and winemaking styles are rapidly evolving, and part of the fun in following their progress is to see how many wines from recent vintages may surprise us with their cellar potential.

Languedoc's and Roussillon's Top Wine Values by Winery

DOMAINE AIMÉ (*Minervois*)

Minervois ♟ $$ This blend of Carignan, Syrah, and Grenache features plum paste, beetroot, and bittersweet notes of dark chocolate and resinous herbs, with a surprising impression of density and grip, ripeness without superficial sweetness, and clear, juicy finishing fruit.

DOMAINE DES AIRES HAUTES (*Minervois*)

Malbec ♟ $ The Chabbert brothers consistently craft wines of extraordinary value, including this dark purple Malbec, an exotic from the Aires Hautes arsenal featuring pure, deep scents and flavors of ripe black fruit. Bracingly tart and pungently peppery, it offers amazing refreshment.

Minervois Les Combelles ♟ $ This is ripe cherry and herb scented, soft and generous, and characteristically finishes with sappy persistence, if occasionally slight heat.

Minervois La Livinières 🍷 $$ This cuvée typically offers vanilla- and brown spice–tinged ripe red and black fruits and is richly satisfying while eschewing superficial sweetness; it finishes with animal and mineral nuances.

Sauvignon Blanc 🍷 $ This Sauvignon, typically brimming with ripe melon, pineapple, grapefruit, and herbs, offers both stuffing and refreshment.

MAS AMIEL *(Maury, Côtes du Roussillon-Villages)*

Côtes du Roussillon Le Plaisir 🍷 $$$ This Grenache-based cuvée (some vintages of which have been bottled as *vin de pays*) typically displays aromas and flavors of strawberry and blackberry, its pure fruit allied to a subtly creamy texture and augmented by brown spices, herbs, soy, white pepper, and crushed stone.

Côtes du Roussillon-Villages Notre Terre 🍷 $$$ A blend of Grenache with Mourvèdre, Syrah, and a bit of Carignan, this features fruit preserves, smoky black tea, game, pepper, rosemary, and chocolate. Creamy, and with a meaty core, its fruit-filled finish includes saline savor, hints of smoke, and crushed stone.

Maury 10 Ans d'Age Ⓢ 🍷 $$$ This tawny, cask-matured, fortified Grenache offers aromas of dried cherries, cocoa powder, distilled raspberry, and pungent hints of resin and molasses. Tart cherry-skin character and bright acids keep its sweetness from dominating, and it finishes with a surprising abundance of primary black fruit character.

Maury Vintage Ⓢ 🍷 $$$ Black raspberry and black cherry preserves are laced with candied lemon zest, white pepper, bitter chocolate, and brown spices in this fortified Grenache that retains a lovely sense of vibrancy and brightness, never acting cloying and finishing with panache. It's great with chocolate, but experiment!

Muscat de Rivesaltes Ⓢ 🍷 $$$ Confectionary in sweetness and lushly creamy in texture, but with refreshing vivacity and pungency. Sage, candied lemon and grapefruit rind, and orange blossom are key notes in this striking wine, which you should sample even if you think you don't like sweet.

LE CLOS DE L'ANHEL *(Corbières)*

Corbières Les Terrassettes ♟ **$$** This is alive with bright, high-toned blackberry, purple plum, and black cherry, laced with sage, rosemary, and black pepper, and finishes with real grip.

DOMAINE ANTUGNAC *(Aude)*

Chardonnay ♟ **$** This Aude Valley wine from the proprietors of Domaine des Deux Roches (see under "Burgundy") is redolent of fresh apple, honey, and pungent, shrubby herbs. Delicate yet mouth-filling and briskly refreshing, it offers uncanny mineral suggestion of wet stone, chalk, and salt.

Pinot Noir ♟ **$$** This is a thoroughly satisfying, barrel-rendered representation of the classic Pinot virtues, astonishingly high in quality for its price. Ripe but tartly refreshing red fruits mingle with intriguing meatiness. A bright yet caressingly textured and uplifting palate impression segues into a savory, saline finish.

DOMAINE D'AUPILHAC *(Coteaux du Languedoc Montpeyroux)*

Coteaux du Languedoc Montpeyroux ♟ **$$$** Sylvain Fadat's principle bottling can be counted on to deliver ripe black fruits along with textural richness, deep meatiness, and mineral complexity.

Lou Maset ♟ **$$** Full of fresh raspberry and cherry fruit tinged with white pepper and herbs, anything this lacks in complexity it makes up for in sheer lip-smacking generosity.

MAS D'AUZIÈRES *(Coteaux du Languedoc)*

Coteaux du Languedoc Les Éclats ♟ **$$$** Grown near Pic St.-Loup on "shards" of limestone for which it is named, this juicy, elegant, charming "second wine" balances textural creaminess and vivacity, featuring smoke-tinged ripe black fruits, herbs, and rich meat stock.

DOMAINE BAPTISTE-BOUTES *(Minervois)*

Minervois ♟ **$** This consistently offers generous, very ripe black fruits laced with licorice, pepper, shrubby herbs, and vanilla, displaying considerable depth, a caressing texture, and a lip-smacking finish.

MAS DE LA BARBEN *(Coteaux du Languedoc)*

Coteaux du Languedoc La Danseuse ♀ $$$ This tank-raised Grenache-Syrah blend's imposing, persistent sweetness of red fruit preserves is accompanied by meaty, herbal, and smoky black tea–like inflections.

DOMAINE LA BASTIDE *(Corbières)*

Syrah ♀ $ A surprisingly mouth-filling Syrah from young vines full of red raspberry and tart cherry, this finishes with carnal, herbal, and chocolate notes. (For another wine from the same producer, see also "Guilhem Durand" below.)

DOMAINE DE BAUBIAC *(Coteaux du Languedoc)*

Coteaux du Languedoc ♀ $$ This offers sweet black fruits along with a plush texture and a combination of bay, licorice, roasted meats, and salt that reflects its high percentage of Mourvèdre.

MAS DE BAYLE *(Coteaux du Languedoc)*

Coteaux du Languedoc Cuvée Tradition ♀ $ A relatively lightweight Languedoc red with exuberant, ripe red raspberry; beef marrow; and fragrant herbal aromas and flavors, with a luscious, lip-smacking sheer juiciness and a long spice- and herb-tinged finish.

DOMAINE BEGUDE *(Limoux)*

Limoux Chardonnay ♀ $$ Utterly beguiling. Full of flowers, citrus, orchard fruits, and almond, this offers some lushness of texture while remaining bright and refreshing, and displays a shimmering sense of minerality that would almost be worthy of a Chablis costing three times the price.

DOMAINE BERTRAND-BERGÉ *(Fitou)*

Fitou Cuvée Ancestrale ♀ $$ This cuvée offers consistently extraordinary quality-price rapport. Memorably high-toned and ripe, it brims with infectiously juicy ripe black fruits mingled with licorice, chocolate, brown spices, roasted meat, and mineral inflections.

Fitou Origines 🍷 $ Features black cherry, roasted meats, fennel, soy, and rosemary; juicy and unusually refreshing for a Languedoc red. This really stains the palate.

DOMAINE DE BILA-HAUT (M. CHAPOUTIER)
(Côtes du Roussillon-Villages)

Occultum Lapidem 🍷 $$$ Featuring a similar Grenache-Shiraz-Carignan blend to Chapoutier's basic bottling (above), this offers textural finesse and length while preserving the essential synergy of ripe black fruits, herbal essences, and ineffable "mineral dust."

Les Vignes de Bila-Haut 🍷 $$ This least expensive Bila-Haut blend is already an extraordinary value. Concentrated, refined, and refreshing, this displays herbal pungency; stony, saline mineral suggestions; and seamless bright black fruit.

DOMAINE DE BLANES *(Côtes du Roussillon)*

Le Clot 🍷 $$ This Syrah-dominated cuvée offers sweet aromas of cherry distillate and black raspberry jam; a fresh, mouth-filling impression free of superficial sweetness; and a satisfying, intensely black-fruited finish tinged with brown spices and smoky, toasted nuttiness.

Muscat Sec 🍷 $$ Uncompromisingly dry and brisk, this uncannily versatile wine displays dramatically intense aromas of pine tar, candied orange peel, and apricot, and packs a long, resinous, zesty finish.

BORIE LA VITARELLE *(St.-Chinian)*

St.-Chinian Les Terres Blanches 🍷 $$ Syrah with a bit of Grenache, this captures generous black raspberry and plum as well as notes of chocolate and Provençal herbs on a silken-textured palate, with subtly chalky, meaty undertones.

MAS DES BRUNES *(Côtes de Thongue)*

Cuvée des Cigales 🍷 $$ A blend of Syrah and Grenache, this smells of esterous distilled cherry and smoky, pungent crushed stone. Finely fruited and textured, it is amply mouth filling and long.

DOMAINE CABIRAU *(Côtes du Roussillon-Villages)*

Grenache Serge & Nicolas 🍷 $$ What this wine from importer Dan Kravitz's property in Maury might lack in complexity, it makes up for in sheer mouth-filling generosity of fruit and a lip-smacking finish.

CHÂTEAU CABRIAC *(Corbières)*

Corbières Marquise de Puivert 🍷 $$ Resinous herbs, licorice, and shrubs typically mingle with tart berry fruits and nut oils, leading to a satisfying, sappy, clinging finish of considerable refinement and brightness for its appellation.

MAS CAL DEMOURA *(Coteaux du Languedoc Terrasses du Larzac)*

Coteaux du Languedoc l'Infidèle 🍷 $$$ This estate's principal red, with intriguing suggestions of local herbs and shrubs, ripe yet understated black fruits, deep meatiness, notes that can only be called mineral, and a soothing texture.

L'Etincelle 🍷 $$ A juicy, satisfying plush, wholly unorthodox blend of Chenin Blanc, Grenache Blanc, Muscat, and Roussanne, this features white peach, quince, acacia, melon, cress, and white pepper.

CHÂTEAU DE CALADROY *(Côtes du Roussillon-Villages)*

Côtes du Roussillon-Villages Les Schistes 🍷 $$ A tank-rendered Grenache-Carignan-Syrah blend, this displays a high-toned distilled plum and blackberry preserve aroma, a glycerin-rich and smoothly satisfying palate to which fennel and crushed stone add complexity, and a lingering finish.

CALVET-THUNEVIN *(Côtes du Roussillon-Villages)*

Constance 🍷 $$ This amazing value from a star partnership offers sweet and alluring aromas of crème de cassis and black raspberry jam, leading to a palate of liqueur-like richness, dark chocolate, exotic spices, coconut, and coffee as well as wet stone and pencil lead. (Note that because of trademark issues, wines will be labeled "Thunevin-Calvet" from 2009.)

DOMAINE CAMP GALHAN (*Costières de Nîmes*)

Amanlie ♀ $$ This Viognier-Roussillon blend offers pungent cress, lemon zest, and white pepper along with ripe peach. While satisfyingly rich, it preserves refinement and refreshment.

Les Grès ♀ $$$ Black cherry, plum, sandalwood, game, rosemary, wood smoke, and stone inform this invigorating blend, with a fascinating counterpoint of plush, soothing texture and brightness of fruit.

Les Perassières ♀ $ This lush and clinging yet wonderfully juicy and freshly fruited blend features sandalwood, smoked meats, plum, blackberry, licorice, and rosemary.

Sauvignon Blanc ♀ $ Citrus, herbs, and flowers inform a juicy, generously pure-fruited match for Sauvignons costing twice the price.

MAS CARLOT (*Costières de Nîmes*)

Costières de Nîmes Les Enfants Terribles ♀ $$ This incredible value Mourvèdre-Syrah unforgettably juxtaposes sweet plum and blueberry preserves with classic blood-in-a-bottle raw-meat Mourvèdre character. Thyme, rosemary, cocoa powder, and vanilla add interest, and the brightness of the fruit keeps the flamboyant richness from becoming cloying.

Grenache-Syrah Cuvée Tradition ♀ $ Gamy, pungently smoky, with a satisfying, slightly grainy texture and a rush of salts, bitter herbs, and cooked black currant in the finish.

Marsanne-Roussanne ♀ $ A stimulating meld of peach fuzz, flowers, herbs, and honey, with a caressing and subtly oily feel and a lingering, engagingly juicy, bittersweet finish.

DOMAINE LA CASENOVE (*Côtes du Roussillon*)

La Colomina ♀ $$ This rich and intense blend of Carignan, Grenache, and Syrah mingles toasted pecan, cocoa powder, black tea, ginger, herbs, and smoked meats, finishing with invigorating saltiness and remarkable grip.

MAS CHAMPART (*St.-Chinian*)

St.-Chinian Causse de Bousquet ♟ **$$$** Among the Languedoc's most poised and sophisticated wines for its price, this bright, tenacious cuvée typically features lusciously ripe, fresh black fruits, highly aromatic herbs, smoked or roasted meats, and shrimp shell reduction.

CHAMPS DES SOEURS (*Fitou*)

Fitou Bel Amant ♟ **$$** Smelling of blackberry and beef blood, this fills the mouth with meat juices and tart but ripe black fruits and brings iodine and wet stone mineral character to bear on a long, subtle finish.

M. CHAPOUTIER (DOMAINE DE BILA-HAUT)
(See under BILA-HAUT, above.)

MAS DE CHIMÈRES (*Coteaux du Languedoc*)

Coteaux du Languedoc ♟ **$$** This Syrah-based blend displays considerable complexity and subtlety, with distilled cherries, licorice, sage, black pepper, and bitter chocolate. Salty, smoky nuances add next-sip enticement to the finish.

PIERRE CLAVEL (*Coteaux du Languedoc*)

Cascaille ♟ **$** This distinctively delicious white blend displays pear nectar, citrus, pungent herb, and salt spray.

Coteaux du Languedoc La Copa Santa ♟ **$$$** This barrel-fermented, Syrah-dominated blend consistently offers palate-saturating richness of black fruits and chocolate tinged with smoke, salt, and hints of resin.

Coteaux du Languedoc Les Garrigues ♟ **$$** With a nose full of its namesake—that scrubby, shrubby, resinous mélange of Provençal herbs and underbrush—along with black cherry and cassis, this is infectiously juicy on the palate, subtly tinged with salt and truffle, and quite creamy in texture; it finishes brightly with pure cassis, cherry, and herb.

Le Mas ♗ $ This juicy, fresh-fruited, and relatively light blend of Grenache, Carignan, Syrah, and Cinsault focuses on fresh red fruits augmented by smoked meat, resinous herbs, and orange zest. It finishes with ample refreshment and chalky, bitter hints.

CLOS BELLEVUE (FRANCIS LACOSTE) *(Muscat de Lunel)*

Muscat de Lunel Ⓢ ♗ $$ Labeled without vintage, this displays honey and orange blossom in the nose, leading to a rich, sweet, yet still elegant palate saturated with honey, nougat, chocolate, and orange rind.

DOMAINE DU CLOS DES FÉES *(Côtes du Roussillon-Villages)*

Côtes du Roussillon Les Sorcières ♗ $$$ The estate's intro-level red—largely Carignan and Grenache—displays black cherry preserves, mint, flowers, black pepper, toasted walnut, and soy. The jam-like dark fruits in its finish carry an almost tactile sense of wet stone and graphite.

Vieilles Vignes Blanc ♗ $$$ Star vintner Hervé Bizeul's Grenache-based white is a true original. Positively dripping with honey and heady, haunting floral perfume, a hint of sweetness enhances its aroma and its creamy, polished texture.

CLOS MARIE *(Coteaux du Languedoc Pic St.-Loup)*

Coteaux du Languedoc Cuvée Manon ♗ $$$ This lower-priced wine from a Languedoc star combines a range of indigenous and Rhône white grapes for a wine of honeyed richness yet vivacity, loaded with flowers, citrus, and distinct mineral suggestions.

Coteaux du Languedoc Pic St.-Loup l'Olivette ♗ $$$ This blend beautifully illustrates the combination of depth of ripe black fruits; mineral, animal, and herbal nuance; and lip-smacking vivacity and tenacity that are at the heart of Clos Marie's reputation.

CLOT DE L'OUM *(Côtes du Roussillon-Villages)*

Côtes du Roussillon-Villages Compagnie des Papillons ♗ $$$ From old Carignan and Grenache vines, this infectiously juicy red offers bittersweet cassis, wet stone, licorice, lead pencil, game, and alluring floral elements, finishing with salt, stone, and graphite.

COL DE LAIROLE (CAVE DE ROQUEBRUNN) *(St.-Chinian)*

Coteaux du Languedoc 🍷 $ An amazingly inexpensive, sappy, rustic, slightly gamy, black-fruited, medium-bodied red, with smoky, resinous, and toasted nut overtones.

COL DES VENTS (COOPÉRATIVE DE CASTELMAURE) *(Corbières)*

Col des Vents Corbières 🍷 $ Aromas of ripe black cherry and mulberry with hints of thyme and rosemary lead to a juicy, satisfying black fruit– and herb–filled palate incorporating suggestions of game and crushed stone.

MAS CONSCIENCE *(Coteaux du Languedoc Terrasses du Larzac)*

Le Cas 🍷 $$$ This rich yet juicy, bracing and downright elegant Carignan displays vivid blackberry preserves, maple syrup, fennel, licorice, dark chocolate, and toasted nuts.

CÔTE MONTPEZAT *(Coteaux du Languedoc)*

Prestige Cabernet Sauvignon–Syrah 🍷 $$ Ripe cassis, roasted meats, herbs, and black tea combine with toasty vanilla and resin notes from the barrel for a richly textured and surprisingly dense chalk-tinged mouthful.

COUME DEL MAS *(Collioure and Banyuls)*

Collioure Schistes 🍷 $$$ From old, terraced Grenache vines, this displays the liqueur-like, full-throttle (alcohol-be-damned), and richly black-fruited style that is a hallmark of their estate, yet retains clarity and primary juiciness.

Folio 🍷 $$$ This fascinating blend of Grenache Blanc and Gris with Vermentino smells of fennel, resin, fresh lime, and sea spray. Full and lush yet insistently bright and invigorating, it finishes with herbal, citric, saline, and iodine notes.

CHÂTEAU COUPE ROSES *(Minervois)*

Minervois La Bastide ♟ **$** Redolent of sage, marjoram, resin, tar, juniper, and black raspberry, this Grenache-based blend is bright yet soft in texture, finishing with lip-smacking salinity and pungently herbal invigoration.

Minervois Cuvée Vignals ♟ **$$** This predominantly Grenache-Syrah blend offers the impressively clinging meatiness of marrow and pan-drippings aroma, together with plum, bay leaf, fennel, and marjoram.

DOMAINE DU COURBISSAC *(Minervois)*

Eos ♟ **$** This low-sulfur old-vine Carignan-based blend from Alsace's Marc Tempé overflows with ripe black fruits, tinged with smoky mineral and musky floral pungency. Alluring in texture, it finishes with sap and verve.

Minervois ♟ **$$** This fabulous value offers infectiously juicy, incredibly luscious black fruits; fascinatingly (at times decadently) floral, animal, herbal, spice, and mineral nuances; a polished, silken palate; and a finish guaranteed to stretch from ear to ear.

CHÂTEAU CREYSSELS *(Picpoul de Pinet)*

Picpoul ♀ **$** An infectiously juicy palate brimming with pit and citrus fruits and tinged with fennel and salt will send you back sip after sip for this high-class, all-season "refrigerator white."

JEAN-LOUIS DENOIS *(Limoux)*

Chardonnay Brut Blanc de Blancs ♀ **$$** It will be hard to find a sparkling wine easier to guzzle or harder to forget for this price. Citrus, berries, flowers, and pit fruits all vie for aromatic attention; textural richness unites with bracing refreshment; saline, chalky minerality, a fine mousse, and a refined finish seal the deal.

DOMAINE DEPEYRE *(Côtes du Roussillon-Villages)*

Côtes du Roussillon-Villages ♟ **$$$** This high-Syrah blend boasts a gorgeous aroma of cassis, blueberry, black tea, toasted pralines, and sandalwood; a rich, ripe palate revealing savory, meaty depth; and remarkable buoyancy and liveliness.

MAS DE LA DEVEZE *(Côtes du Roussillon-Villages)*

Côtes du Roussillon Villages 66 🍷 **$$$** This irresistible, amazing-value Grenache-Carignan-based blend named for the number of the French *département* Pyrénées-Orientales offers chocolate-covered black fruits, black tea, and toasted nuts, with stone and smoke nuances adding interest to a rich yet dynamic finish.

DOMAINE DONJON *(Minervois)*

Minervois Grande Tradition 🍷 **$** This Grenache-based blend offers a pungently smoky and satisfying ripe amalgam of crushed stone, charred wood, blackberry, and cassis. Polished in feel, with medicinal-herbal bitterness, it offers surprising lift and impressive cling.

Minervois Prestige 🍷 **$$** This barrel-aged Syrah-Grenache is like a black-fruited elixir mingled with chocolate, resinous herbs, walnut oil, and beef stock. It finishes with sap and stamina.

Minervois Rosé 🍷 **$** Brimming with red fruits and melon; tinged with herbs, salt, and pepper; and silken in texture, this is so lusciously fruit juice–like you'll swear it contains a hint of residual sugar, but it's bone dry.

GUILHEM DURAND *(Corbières)*

Syrah 🍷 **$** Full of ripe red fruits, tart rhubarb, pepper, herbs, and brown spices; rich in texture; and sappy and lip-smacking in finish, this puts to shame 95% of the far too many inexpensive Syrahs on the market. (For another Syrah from Durand, see under DOMAINE LA BASTIDE, above.)

ERMITAGE DU PIC ST.-LOUP
(Coteaux du Languedoc Pic St.-Loup)

Coteaux du Languedoc Pic St.-Loup 🍷 **$$** Smelling of game, sage, cassis foliage, and black fruits, this offers good palate concentration and finishes with sappy, tarry, resinous, tartly berried brightness.

Coteaux du Languedoc Pic St.-Loup Cuvée Sainte Agnès 🍷 **$$$** This Syrah-based blend offers fresh black raspberry and cassis, bitter chocolate, sage, thyme, and mint, saturating the palate and finishing with excellent intensity if at times a trace of heat.

Coteaux du Languedoc Pic St.-Loup Cuvée Sainte Agnès
♀ $$$ This blend of six white grapes offers lovely ripe peach, fig, honey, rosemary, nut oils, and hedge flowers; a glossy palate of surprising refreshment and elegance; and a well-concentrated finish.

ÉTANG DES COLOMBES *(Corbières)*

Corbières Bois des Dames ♀ $$$ Generous barrel-aged Carignan, Syrah, and Grenache offer a sweet mélange of jam-like black fruits, brown spices, and wood smoke.

Corbières Tradition ♀ $ Smoke wreathed and herb tinged, sweetly ripe black fruits saturate the palate. This eschews the clunky earthiness, gaminess, and excessive fat that too often come with the territory of Corbières.

Corbières Vieilles Vignes Bicentenaire ♀ $$ In theory an upgrade from the Tradition bottling (above) but not always better, this offers generous mouthfuls of deep ripe black fruits, humus, and salted beef stock, with generally refined tannins.

Viognier ♀ $$ Lushly textured, this plays ripe, acacia-tinged peach off pungent cress and white pepper, refreshing the palate and free of the excessive oiliness or bitterness so common with this grape.

CHÂTEAU L'EUZIÈRE *(Coteaux du Languedoc Pic St.-Loup)*

Coteaux du Languedoc Pic St.-Loup Almandin ♀ $$$ Delivering copious mulberries or blackberries, lavender, rosemary, and ocean breeze, and displaying rich beef stock–like underlying meatiness, this is invigoratingly bright and distinctively profound for the price.

DOMAINE FAURMARIE *(Coteaux du Languedoc Grès de Montpellier)*

Coteaux du Languedoc Grès de Montpellier l'Écrit Vin ♀ $$$ This delivers an impressive combination of ripe black fruits with beef blood, plums, and bay leaf, reflecting its high percentage of Mourvèdre. Juicy and intense, it finishes with notes of tar, resin, black tea, and a salty tang.

Coteaux du Languedoc Grès de Montpellier Les Mathilles 🍷 $$
Smelling of blueberries and smoked meats, and remarkably rich for
its price, it offers an impressive, low-toned finish of bittersweet black
and blue fruits with an undertone of wet stones.

CHÂTEAU FONT-MARS *(Picpoul de Pinet)*

Coteaux du Languedoc Picpoul de Pinet 🍷 $ Smelling and tasting
of candied lime, honeydew, and something approaching brown-
spiced, pickled watermelon rind, this juicy, outrageously exuberant,
and exotic Picpoul will grace any table and stump any wine geek.

LA FONT DE L'OLIVIER *(Côtes de Thongue)*

Carignan Vieilles Vignes 🍷 $ Featuring ripe mulberry and
blackberry, smoky toasted walnut, and alluring brown spices, this
pungent, sappy, mouth-filling essence of an unjustly unloved grape
deserves respect.

CHÂTEAU FONTANÈS

(See under LES TRAVERSES DE FONTANÈS, below.)

DOMAINE DE FONTENELLES *(Corbières)*

Corbières Cuvée Notre Dame 🍷 $$ This Syrah-Mourvedre-
Carignan blend displays plum paste, roasted meats, and brown
spices, lavishing the palate with sappy fruit and substantial meaty
depth, and finishing with lip-smacking satisfaction.

DOMAINE DE FONTSAINTE *(Corbières)*

Corbières 🍷 $ Comprised largely of Carignan, this offers candied
black cherry, resinous herbs, and game; a glossy texture; lots of floral
and sweet berry inner-mouth perfume; and underlying meat and
stone.

Corbières Réserve La Demoiselle 🍷 $$ From a centenarian stand
of Carignan, this densely packed, smoothly textured wine mingles
sweet, esterous ripeness, bitter fruit-skin pungency, chalky mineral
nuances, shrubby herbs, and meat stock.

DOMAINE FOULAQUIER *(Coteaux du Languedoc Pic St.-Loup)*

Coteaux du Languedoc Pic St.-Loup l'Orphée 🍷 **$$** Loaded with ripe cherry, plum, perfumed flowers, and brown spices, underlain by roasting meat, resin, herbs, and salt, this offers authoritative density and a tenacious finish, demonstrating why Foulaquier's are among the most exciting wines and incredible values in the Languedoc.

Coteaux du Languedoc Pic St.-Loup Le Rollier 🍷 **$$$** From old-vine Grenache and Syrah, this offers sweet, esterous distilled strawberry and plum, Provençal herbs, resin, chalk, and practically sizzling spices, with an impressively sappy cling.

Coteaux du Languedoc Pic St.-Loup Les Tonillières 🍷 **$$$** This Grenache-based blend characteristically offers treble, pure, penetrating berry fruits; floral perfume; pungent herbs; a silken texture; and myriad, fascinating mineral nuances.

DOMAINE LA GALINIÈRE *(Minervois)*

Domaine La Galinière Cabernet Sauvignon 🍷 **$** Amazingly—given the spotty results with this grape in the Languedoc—this is ripe, polished, and refreshing, emphasizing cassis, cherry, green peppercorns, and leafy herbs.

Domaine La Galinière Merlot 🍷 **$** Offering consistently lovely bittersweet fruit, herbs, and pepper, and a juicy, sappy, clean and soft-textured palate, this wine, with its genuinely ripe and quite vivacious finish, is a great choice if one insists on Merlot.

DOMAINE GARDIÈS *(Côtes du Roussillon-Villages)*

Côtes du Roussillon Mas Las Cabes Rouge 🍷 **$$** Red raspberry, cherry, mocha, vanilla, toasted pecan, marjoram, and cedar inform this Syrah-dominated blend, with smokiness and salinity adding invigoration to its finish.

Côtes du Roussillon-Villages Les Millères 🍷 **$$$** This four-way blend smells of lightly cooked red raspberry, grenadine, walnut husk, juniper, and subtly integrated vanilla and spice. Vividly sappy tart red fruit, resin, tar, cardamom, and pepper coat the palate and linger invigoratingly.

Mas Las Cabes Blanc ♀ $$ Dominated by the orange blossom, mint, and apricot of Muscat, into which is blended a little Grenache Blanc and Maccabeu, which supply depth and richness, this is irresistibly juicy, with intriguing saline, savory, and smoky accents.

DOMAINE GAUBY *(Côtes du Roussillon-Villages)*

Côtes du Roussillon Blanc Les Calcinaires ♀ $$$ This silken-textured, luscious blend of Muscat, Chardonnay, Macabeo, and Grenache Gris from Roussillon pioneer and master vintner Gérard Gauby evokes orange blossom, pineapple, lime, mint, and Persian melon, tinged with white pepper and chalk.

Côtes du Roussillon-Villages Les Calcinaires ♟ $$$ Juicy yet firm textured, this red blend offers concentrated bittersweet black and blue fruits; licorice; smoky, saline, chalky, woodsy, and meaty complexity; and a lip-smacking, intensely wet stone finish.

GAUJAL ST.-BON *(Picpoul de Pinet)*

Coteaux du Languedoc Picpoul de Pinet ♀ $ Talk about sensational value: this gets the most out of the Picpoul. Bracing notes of orange zest, white pepper, and ocean salinity on a snappy palate, lead to an irresistibly refreshing finish.

DOMAINE GAUTIER *(Fitou)*

Fitou ♟ $$ Gamy, slightly funky notes mingle with dried berries, smoked meat, pungent herbs, and toasted nuts in this sturdy, slightly rustic, mouth-filling, and strong-finishing Fitou.

DOMAINE DU GRAND ARC *(Corbières)*

Corbières Cuvée des Quarante ♟ $$ This Carignan-heavy blend offers a plush palate of rich black fruits, interesting spiciness, licorice, chocolate, and suggestions of roasted meats. It finishes clear, bright, and juicy.

Corbières Nature d'Orée ♟ $ This features blackberry, black tea, and black cherry (with an emphasis on the cyanic bitterness of the pits). Truly palate-staining and bright, it offers black-fruited, lip-smacking persistence.

Corbières Réserve Grand Arc 🍷 $ Smelling of blackberry, licorice, and wood smoke, this tastes of blackberry preserves and tiny, bittersweet licorice candies and finishes with staining intensity, if some rusticity of tannin.

DOMAINE DU GRAND CRÈS *(Corbières)*

Corbières Blanc 🍷 $$$ This consistently striking Roussanne-Viognier blend offers melon, flowers, pear, pungent cress, salt, and chalk in a lush, silken-textured, yet refreshing and dynamic medley.

Corbières Majeure 🍷 $$$ This Syrah-based cuvée offers alluring scents of rose hip, cherry, and purple plum, with a well-concentrated, sappy, fresh, not in the least heavy palate and intriguing mineral persistence.

CHÂTEAU GRANDE CASSAGNE *(Costières de Nîmes)*

Costières de Nîmes Hippolyte 🍷 $$ From the Dardé brothers' best Syrah, with a smidgen of Mourvèdre, this suggests blueberry preserves laced with rosemary and marjoram. A gamy meatiness emerges on the sumptuous, full palate.

Costières de Nîmes Rosé 🍷 $ With a wealth of herbs, black pepper, tart cherry, subtle notes of raw meat, and savory, saline mineral suggestions, this versatile rosé boasts a finish that practically won't quit.

LA GRANGE DE QUATRE SOUS *(St.-Chinian)*

Les Serrottes 🍷 $$$ An unorthodox blend mingles Malbec and a bit of Cabernet Franc into Syrah for a rich yet restrained display of black cherry and roasted meat, accented by white pepper, cardamon, and crushed stone.

GRANGE DES ROUQUETTE *(Costières de Nîmes)*

GSM 🍷 $ This Grenache-Syrah-Mourvèdre blend offers considerable richness for its price. A nose of ripe blackberries, herbs, black pepper, and game leads to a juicy, expansive palate and a salt, smoke, and herb–tinged, faintly bitter finish.

DOMAINE DES GRECAUX *(Coteaux du Languedoc Montpeyroux)*

Coteaux du Languedoc Montpeyroux Terra Solis 🍷 $$$ This Grenache-dominated blend offers gorgeous ripe black fruits suffused with a dusty, smoky note often associated with schist soils. Persistently piquant, pungent penetration leaves the palate not just stained but refreshed.

MAS DE GUIOT *(Costières de Nîmes)*

Costières de Nîmes Numa 🍷 $$$ Showcasing old-vine Syrah, this offers roasted and smoked meats, leather, brown spices, Provençal herbs, stewed purple plum, rhubarb, and blackberry, with a glossy texture and faint woodiness.

CHÂTEAU HAUT FABRÈGUES *(Faugères)*

Faugères Cuvée Tradition 🍷 $ Offering the fruit intensity of kirsch or *prunelle* distillate, along with smoky, toasty nuttiness, this sappy, very ripe blend gives way to a touch of rusticity, but for the price one can hardly complain.

HECHT & BANNIER *(Various Regions)*

Côtes du Roussillon-Villages 🍷 $$$ If you don't claim to smell crushed stone or pungent scrub here, then you never will (not in a glass, anyway). Black fruits, mocha, and brown spices inform a creamy palate. Iodine and toasted-nut bitterness add a counterpoint to a remarkably sappy, juicy, vigorous finish.

Minervois 🍷 $$$ A Syrah-Grenache-Carignan blend that mingles sappy black fruit, resinous herbs, bitter chocolate, and a smoky, meaty pan dripping–like essence, displaying a lovely counterpoint of creamy texture to bright fruit freshness that typifies the exceptional values of this new specialist *négociant*.

Saint-Chinian 🍷 $$$ This Syrah-Grenache-Mourvèdre blend demonstrates the heights to which its appellation can aspire. Smoke, stone, and nut oils inflect a luscious, smoothly textured palate full of blue and black fruits and meat stock, with hints of fruit-pit bitterness and minerals adding interest to a tenacious finish.

DOMAINE HEGARTY-CHAMANS (*Minervois*)

Minervois No. 2 🍷 **$$$** Grenache based and Syrah laced, this offers black and blue fruits of amazing sheer richness and opulence and striking purity, yet freshness as well as mineral, animal, and herbal nuances. (Note: The cuvée-numbering system here is in the process of changing, but all of the estate's wines are recommended.)

Minervois No. 3 🍷 **$$** This bright, versatile blend featuring Carignan and Syrah offers generous black fruits, mint chocolate, black tea, licorice, resinous herbs, and a hint of game.

DOMAINE DE L'HORTUS (*Coteaux du Languedoc Pic St.-Loup*)

Bergerie de l'Hortus Classique Blanc 🍷 **$$** A blend of Roussanne Chardonnay, Sauvignon, and Viognier, this l'Hortus "second wine" offers faintly bitter herbal and floral nuances over a base of apple, peach, almond, and citrus, finishing with a lick of salt.

Bergerie de l'Hortus Coteaux du Languedoc Pic Saint-Loup 🍷 **$$** This cuvée dominated by Syrah with Grenache and Mourvèdre nicely showcases Pic St.-Loup pioneer Jean Orliac's handiwork. Black cherry, pepper, nut oils, violet, and herbal scrub inform a bright, mineral-tinged palate.

LES JAMELLES (*Various Regions*)

Chardonnay 🍷 **$** Refreshing apple-fruit with alkaline, wet stone, brown spice, and toasty notes; offers real personality when compared with most Chardonnays selling for remotely close to the price of this one from Limoux. Les Jamelles Pinot Noir sometimes excels, too.

Merlot 🍷 **$** Les Jamelles' Merlot delivers where so many other inexpensive wines from this grape fail, offering black cherry, dark chocolate, cinnamon, tomato foliage, humus, and decadent floral notes with a smooth texture and juicy persistence.

CHÂTEAU JOUCLARY (*Cabardès*)

Cabardès Tradition 🍷 **$$** This smooth-textured testimony to the potential synergy of Rhône and Bordeaux grapes in the western Languedoc mingles floral, nut-oil, herbal, and roasted-meat elements with restrained but ripe dark fruits.

DOMAINE LACROIX-VANEL *(Coteaux du Languedoc)*

Coteaux du Languedoc Fine Amor 🍷 **$$$** The idealistic Vanel's typically satin-textured and luscious blend varies but favors Grenache, offering alluring floral, herbal, tea-like, animal, and mineral shadings to its ripe black fruits.

DOMAINE LAFAGE *(Côtes du Roussillon)*

Côte d'Est 🍷 **$** This irresistibly bright, juicy blend of Grenache Blanc, Chardonnay, and a splash of Muscat features flowers, fennel, sage, toasted nuts, and salted citrus.

Côte Grenache 🍷 **$** Strawberry preserves and cocoa powder; pungent resinous herbs, smoke, and white pepper; and an infectiously juicy and subtly creamy palate make this incredible value impossible to put down.

Côte Sud 🍷 **$** Plum paste, cherry, iodine, chocolate, lavender, licorice, singed meat, salts, and iodine inform a wine with a finish so long it seems impossible when one sees the price!

Côtes du Roussillon Cuvée Lea 🍷 **$$** This silken-textured, subtly salty, and deeply blue-fruited Syrah-Grenache-Carignan finishes long on vivid fruit skin, licorice, marjoram, iodine, and sea salt.

Cuvée Centenaire 🍷 **$** A blend of old-vine Grenache Blanc and Gris with a little Macabeo, this displays musky flowers and grapefruit rind, holding one's interest with a counterpoint of vivacious citricity, silken richness, and faintly oily texture.

Novellum Chardonnay 🍷 **$** From Lafage's vast expanse of acreage and cuvées, this consistently delivers a profusion of juicy, fresh fruit with creamy texture and intriguing minerality, and puts to shame 90% of Chardonnays twice as expensive.

DOMAINE LANCYRE *(Coteaux du Languedoc Pic St.-Loup)*

Coteaux du Languedoc Pic St.-Loup Vieilles Vignes 🍷 **$$$** This deep, sappy, seamless Syrah-Grenache is typically loaded with plum, black cherry, and grenadine and tinged with pungent, resinous herbs, wood smoke, crushed stone, and iodine.

Coteaux du Languedoc Rosé ♀ **$$** Simply one of the finest pinks on the planet, with enough grip to reach out of the glass and throttle you were you to be overheard disrespecting rosé! Tart red fruits, pungent herbs, smoked meat, and minerals make for thinking as well as reflexively drinking.

Roussanne ♀ **$$** This offers strikingly penetrating floral, herbal, musk, and citrus zest aromas; a firm, bright palate full of peach fuzz; and a multifaceted fan of a finish.

CHÂTEAU LASCAUX *(Coteaux du Languedoc Pic St.-Loup)*

Coteaux du Languedoc ♀ **$$** Generous with red fruits, smoked meat, soy, and pungent herbs, this finishes with a salty-meaty savor, if occasionally some rusticity of tannin.

FAMILLE LIGNÈRES *(Corbières)*

Cabanon de Pascal ♀ **$$** This effusive Grenache-based cuvée is full of ripe strawberry and raspberry garnished with high-toned herbs and citrus zest.

MAS LUMEN *(Coteaux du Languedoc)*

Coteaux du Languedoc Prélude ♀ **$$$** This gorgeous cuvée displays abundant black and blue fruits laced with licorice, flowers, oriental spices, diverse herbs, roasted meats, mineral salts, and saddle leather, finishing with terrific cling.

MAXIME MAGNON *(Corbières, Fitou)*

Corbières Campagnes ♀ **$$$** With a floral and fresh black-fruited perfume and a combination of lift and refreshment with palate saturation and polished texture, this Carignan from old vines finishes with an amazing nutty, mineral, and herbal complexity.

Corbières Rozeta ♀ **$$$** Suffused with tart red and black raspberry, brine-like salinity, and smoked meat, this palpably extract-rich, mouth-coating, yet elegant low-sulfur cuvée is among the most distinctively delicious and refreshing wines of the Languedoc.

CHÂTEAU MARIS *(Minervois)*

Syrah La Touge ♀ **$$$** Maris achieves a stunning degree of sheer ripeness without the wines becoming cloying or their typically 15–16% alcohol betraying itself as heat or roughness. This opulent and seamless cuvée offers black and blue fruits, chocolate, soy, cracked black pepper, espresso, and smoked meat.

DOMAINE MASSAMIER LA MIGNARDE *(Minervois)*

Carignan Expression ♀ **$$$** This dense yet infectiously juicy barrel-fermented Carignan features walnut oil, dark chocolate, resin, and sweetly ripe black fruits tinged with salt and chalk.

Cuvée des Oliviers ♀ **$** Sauvignon Blanc this ripe and juicy—featuring mint, lemon, flowers, and hints of peach and melon—is not easy in the Languedoc, and at this price, it's incredible!

Minervois Cuvée Aubin ♀ **$$** This Grenache-dominated cuvée fills the mouth with salt- and pepper-dusted ripe black fruits, heady floral perfume, scrubby herbs, and meat juices.

Tenement de Garouilhas ♀ **$$$** This wooded blend of Syrah, Carignan, and Grenache offers a flamboyant amalgam of cooked fruits, toasted nuts, spices, coconut, toasted almond, roasted meats, and chocolate that one wants to attack with a spoon!

CHÂTEAU DE MATTES-SABRAN *(Corbières)*

Corbières Clos du Redon ♀ **$$** This Syrah typically features black pepper–laced cherry liqueur on an outrageously rich palate, its suggestion of sweetness tempered by underlying red meat, pungent sage, and the faint, quite pleasant bitterness of cherry stones.

Corbières Dionysos ♀ **$$** Black cherry, cardamom, and toasted pralines on the nose lead to an impressively rich yet effusively juicy palate with satisfying notes of beef stock and chocolate mingling with ripe black fruits.

Corbières Le Viala ♀ **$** Stewed rhubarb and spiced black fruits on a rich—almost heavy—palate make this a winter-weight wine.

LAURENT MIQUEL (St.-Chinian)

Viognier ♙ $ This offers classic peach and acacia aromas and a lush, silken, richly fruited palate, and manages to avoid being blowsy, excessively oily, or bitter, as are too many inexpensive wines from this grape.

CHÂTEAU MORGUES DU GRÈS (*Costières de Nîmes*)

Costières de Nîmes Capitelles des Mourgues ♙ $$$ This implacably dense yet fine-grained, palate-staining Syrah-Grenache offers expansive black currant, black pepper, licorice, resin, chocolate, and roasted meat.

Costières de Nîmes Les Galets Doré ♙ $ Grenache Blanc with a bit of Roussanne, this offers striking perfume of honeysuckle, narcissus, peach, musk melon, and white pepper, leading to a succulent, subtly oily, and exceedingly bright finish.

Costières de Nîmes Les Galets Rosé ♙ $ This Syrah-based pink seems to have hoarded fresh, tart red raspberries and herbs with abandon and delivers them in a lip-smacking, refreshing, glossy, light (despite 13.5% alcohol) package. Suggestions of salt, stone, and roasted meat add complexity.

Costières de Nîmes Les Galets Rouge ♙ $ This juicy, forthright, palate-staining cuvée of Syrah, Grenache, Mourvèdre, and Carignan features cassis and blackberry tinged with bitter chocolate and pungent Provençal herbs.

Costières de Nîmes Terre d'Argence ♙ $$ From old-vine Syrah and Grenache, this features persistent purple plum, licorice, juniper, and sage on an impressively dense and fine-grained palate.

Terre d'Argence ♙ $$ A blend of Viognier and Roussanne heavily perfumed with peach, apricot, lily, and acacia, and offering a correspondingly opulent, even weighty palate impression, with hints of cress and white pepper in the finish.

MOURREL AZURAT *(Fitou)*

Fitou Mourrel Azurat ♀ $ From the talented team of Massamier la Mignarde (see above), this offers amazing value. Ripe plum, pungent herbs, leather, and saline and stony mineral notes make for complexity on the cheap!

MAS MUDIGLIZA *(Côtes du Roussillon)*

Côtes du Roussillon Carminé ♀ $$ This silken, slightly oily Grenache from a young estate displays outstanding depth, subtlety, and refinement redolent of black raspberry, dark chocolate, roasted meats, rosemary, lavender, and sweet-smoky machine oil.

CHÂTEAU DE NAGES *(Costières de Nîmes)*

Costières de Nîmes Cuvée Joseph Torres ♀ $$$ This superbly concentrated and rich anise- and black pepper–tinged Syrah blend illustrates how to make a flashy, sweetly fruited, very ripe, barrel-aged wine while preserving balance, clarity, and polish.

Costières de Nîmes Reserve ♀ $ Liqueur-like in its red berry essence, with black tea and herbal overtones, this luscious and positively palate-saturating Grenache-based blend finishes infectiously with sweetly ripe fruit.

CHÂTEAU DE LA NÉGLY *(Coteaux du Languedoc la Clape)*

Coteaux du Languedoc La Clape La Brise Marine ♀ $$ A cuvée of Bourbelanc, Roussanne, and Marsanne, this exudes ripe honeydew melon, mint, Provençal herbs, and honey, finishing with an invigorating, offsetting herbal and fruit-rind pungency and bite.

Coteaux du Languedoc La Clape La Côte ♀ $$ Château de la Négly is responsible for some of the Languedoc's richest wines, and this dense, powerful entry-level blend displays salted plum paste, black cherry liqueur, resinous herbs, and smoky, charred game.

LA NOBLE (*Carcassonne*)

La Noble Chardonnay 🍷 $ This Chardonnay from the Aube represents a consistently amazing value. Fresh green apple, thyme, clover, and salted almond inform a bright, juicy palate with a surprising sense of textural richness.

CHÂTEAU D'OR ET DE GUEULES (*Costières de Nîmes*)

Costières de Nîmes Rouge Sélect 🍷 $$ This dense, superripe, silken-textured, phenomenally fine value brings smoky, gamy, pungently herbal cherry-pit and crushed-stone complexity to its sweet fruit preserve matrix.

CHÂTEAU D'OUPIA (*Minervois*)

Minervois Tradition 🍷 $$$ This Carignan-dominated blend delivers juicy, bittersweet black cherry fruit, chocolate, and chopped liver, generously coating the palate yet finishing with next-sip-inviting freshness as well as herbal and mineral interest.

L'OUSTAL BLANC (*Minervois*)

Naïck 🍷 $$ Typical for the l'Oustal team, this Carignan-based blend (for legal reasons, labeled with an arabic numeral rather than vintage date) is flamboyant, almost over-the-top, and improbably rich for its price, featuring liqueur-like cassis, prune, white raisin, black tea, cinnamon, and nutmeg.

DOMAINE PECH REDON (*Coteaux du Languedoc la Clape*)

Coteaux du Languedoc La Clape Les Cades 🍷 $$ This bracingly tart, finely tannic, high-Carignan cuvée offers black raspberry with black pepper, toasted walnut, and herbs.

Coteaux du Languedoc La Clape L'Épervier 🍷 $$$ This extravagantly ripe yet beautifully delineated Grenache-Syrah-Carignan blend features chalk-tinged, kirsch-macerated dried cherries and crème de cassis underlain by fine tannins.

YANNICK PELLETIER *(St.-Chinian)*

Saint-Chinian l'Oiselet ♗ **$$$** With generous cherry and black raspberry fruit tinged by brown spices and pungent smokiness of a sort often associated with schist soils, this offers a juicy, bittersweet intensity and fine-grained tannins.

PEÑA *(Côtes du Roussillon-Villages)*

Cuvée de Peña ♗ **$** The wines of this small co-op are nearly impossible to beat for value, and this Syrah-Carignan-Grenache displays resinous, smoky aromatic pungency; ripe purple plum and blackberry; and a lip-smacking if slightly chewy finish.

Cuvée de Peña Rosé ♗ **$** This pink blend of Grenache and Syrah brims with strawberries, cherries, herbs, almonds, and stones and offers sappy, juicy, lip-smacking palate saturation and length.

Viognier Ninet de Peña ♗ **$** Full of acacia, peach, pear, and tropical fruits; juicy and lush on the palate with invigorating saltiness and a faintly peppery nip, this lingers with wafting florality.

DOMAINE DE LA PETITE CASSAGNE *(Costières de Nîmes)*

Costières de Nîmes ♗ **$$** This amazingly rich, savory, superbly balanced sensational value is stuffed with black cherries, roasted chestnuts, marjoram, and dark chocolate, with carnal and peat-like undertones.

PLAN DE L'OM *(Coteaux du Languedoc)*

Coteaux du Languedoc Miejour ♗ **$$$** Primarily Grenache and Syrah, this typically features understated strawberry and white pepper, lavender, and marjoram, finishing juicily with a peppery bite and faintly bitter fruit-skin edge.

Coteaux du Languedoc Paysage ♗ **$$** While not the last word in complexity, this offers deep, richly clinging, faintly bitter black fruits, resin, and brown spices.

DOMAINE DES PERRIÈRES (MARC KREYDENWEISS)
(Costières de Nîmes)

Costières de Nîmes ♟ $$ Showcasing the potential of old Carignan vines (along with Syrah and Grenache), this delivers carnal, herbal, and mineral nuance in a package of imposing richness.

CAVE DE POMEROLS *(Picpoul de Pinet)*

Picpoul de Pinet Hugues Beaulieu ♟ $ Smelling of clover, lemon, and ocean breeze, this lilting refresher delivers juicy salt- and chalk-tinged citrus, making for an ideal "refrigerator white."

DOMAINE DU POUJOL *(Coteaux du Languedoc)*

Coteaux du Languedoc Podio Alto ♟ $$$ Mingling plum and cherry with the faint bitterness of their pits, violet, leather, and herbs, this offers juicy satisfaction with animal and mineral inflections.

Coteaux du Languedoc Rosé ♟ $$ Fresh red raspberries, bacon, and freshly cracked black pepper inform this infectiously bright, juicy, yet quite lush rosé.

DOMAINE DE POULVALREL *(Costières de Nîmes)*

Costières de Nîmes ♟ $$ This soothing, delectable Syrah-Grenache delivers ripe plums, cassis, black raspberry, pungent herbs, cocoa powder, sweet spices, black pepper, and clean meatiness.

Costières de Nîmes Les Perrottes ♟ $$$ This impressively dense and fine-grained Syrah-Grenache offers cassis, chocolate, mint, and smoked meat, with an alkaline, slightly vegetal suggestion of seaweed.

PUECH AURIOL *(Coteaux du Languedoc)*

Ad Hoc ♟ $ Aromas of ripe cassis, blueberry, sandalwood, iodine, toasted nuts, and roasted meats lead to an equally diverse set of flavors and a saline, subtly bitter, black-fruited finish.

Puech Auriol ♟ $$ This highly concentrated, Carignan-based blend displays juicy and refreshing black and blue fruits mingled with pungent herbs and toasted nuts, with iodine, cherry pit, and chalk adding to its finish.

DOMAINE PUIG PARAHY (*Côtes du Roussillon*)

Côtes du Roussillon Le Fort Saint-Pierre ♟ **$$** This cuvée features salted purple plum, black fruits, chocolate, and raw meat, its juicy primary fruitiness and refined tannins as well as its carnality no doubt due in part to very old vines and its share of Mourvèdre.

Côtes du Roussillon Georges ♟ **$** Full of irresistibly ripe and invigoratingly fresh black fruits tinged with dark chocolate and nut oils, this satin-textured yet refreshing red offers a lovely view of southern Roussillon.

DOMAINE PUYDEVAL (*Carcassonne*)

Puydeval ♟ **$** A soft, satisfyingly mouth-filling, unusual blend of Cabernet Franc with some Syrah and Merlot features mulberry, walnut oil, beetroot, fennel, and a hint of bitter fruit pit.

CHÂTEAU DE RIEUX (*Minervois*)

Minervois ♟ **$$** Lovely, deep black cherry mingled with dried mushrooms, thyme, marjoram, and roasted meats inform this admirably refined, juicy blend.

CHÂTEAU RIGAUD (*Faugères*)

Faugères ♟ **$** A new project guided by Claude Gros, Château Rigaud's Syrah-Grenache–based Faugères displays smoke-wreathed black fruit aromas and a satin-textured, deeply rich palate. Its inaugural 2007 vintage represents a mind-boggling value apt to evolve interestingly in bottle for several years.

DOMAINE RIMBERT (*St.-Chinian*)

Le Chant de Marjolaine ♟ **$$$** From old Carignan vines, this consistently displays bittersweet black fruits, beetroot, and herbs, tinged with pungent smoke and crushed stone. Its flavors always benefit from taking on some air.

St.-Chinian Les Travers de Marceau ♟ **$$** This blend typically features dried cherries and smoky, crushed-stone pungency in the nose, along with roasted meat, shrubby herbs, and salty, stony finishing notes that manage not to obscure the fruit.

LE ROC DES ANGES *(Côtes du Roussillon-Villages)*

Côtes du Roussillon-Villages Segna de Cor 🍷 **$$$** The estate's second wine, this consistently offers dark berry fruit, game, resinous herbs, toasted nuts, and stony, saline mineral nuances.

DOMAINE SAINT ANTONIN *(Faugères)*

Faugères Magnoux 🍷 **$$$** This Syrah-heavy blend smells of plum, bittersweet black cherry, and meat stock lavished with thyme and rosemary, all of which inform a savory, rich palate of polished texture, salty minerality, and clean meatiness.

Faugères Tradition 🍷 **$$** Among the most amazing wine values of the Languedoc, this typically explodes from the glass with fresh black raspberry, smoke, bracing salinity, and stone dust, striking a wonderful palate balance of bright black fruit, savory meatiness, and stony, salty notes.

CHÂTEAU SAINT-GERMAIN *(Coteaux du Languedoc)*

Coteaux du Languedoc 🍷 **$** This offers a fascinating, esterous nose of candied cherry, brown spices, and orange liqueur. Plump and juicy on the palate, in some years it can be slightly dried out by its alcohol.

DOMAINE ST.-MARTIN DE LA GARRIGUE
(Coteaux du Languedoc Grès de Montpellier)

Coteaux du Languedoc Blanc 🍷 **$$** This subtly creamy blend of five whites features honey and flowers with resin and herbs—in short, it's like a walk through its namesake *garrigue*—along with juicy apricot, lemon zest, resin, and brown spices.

Coteaux du Languedoc Bronzinelle 🍷 **$$** Smelling of roasted game, black cherries, soy, and dark chocolate, this mouth-filling and strikingly saline cuvée coats the tongue with abundant, fine tannins and finishes with notes of cocoa and brown spices.

Coteaux du Languedoc Rosé 🍷 **$** Succulent and subtly oily, this exuberant pink tastes of salt-tinged watermelon, underlain by a marrow-like meatiness.

Coteaux du Languedoc Tradition 🍷 **$** This amazingly inexpensive blend of Carignan and Syrah offers black raspberry, rosemary, salt, and wet stone, leading to a bright, infectiously juicy finish.

Picpoul de Pinet ♀ $ Smelling of resin, grapefruit rind, and clove, this fills the mouth with refreshment (the first duty of this appellation) and clings with excellent persistence of chalk and salt.

CHÂTEAU SAINT ROCH *(Maury, Côtes du Roussillon-Villages)*

Côtes du Roussillon Chimères ♀ $$ Another phenomenal value from the irrepressible Jean-Marc Lafage (see above), this rich yet elegant blend from Maury displays creamy black fruits, lily, cocoa powder, white pepper, nut paste, and whiffs of smoke.

DOMAINE SARDA-MALET *(Côtes du Roussillon)*

Côtes du Roussillon Le Sarda ♀ $$ Black tea, black cherry, floral perfume, herbs, brown spices, toasted nuts, and vanilla are among the typical themes of this lush and refreshing value.

DOMAINE LA SAUVAGEONNE *(Coteaux du Languedoc)*

Coteaux du Languedoc Pica Broca ♀ $$ Primarily Grenache and Syrah, this typically displays a nose of cooked black raspberry and bitter chocolate, backed by bacon or beef blood. Palate-filling, sultry, invigorating, and persistent, it finishes with a smoky pungency often associated with such schist sites.

Coteaux du Languedoc Les Ruffes ♀ $ This energetic cuvée consistently smells of black raspberry, lavender, and black pepper, flooding the palate with a smooth-textured amalgam of juicy sweet raspberry fruit, licorice, lavender, smoked meat, and pepper.

DOMAINE DES SOULANES *(Côtes du Roussillon-Villages)*

Côtes du Roussillon-Villages Sarrat del Mas ♀ $$$ This offers very ripe black fruits accented with toasted walnuts, pralines, and pungent crushed stone; a creamy texture; and a subtly sweet, nutty finish.

Cuvée Jean Pull ♀ $$ Typically loaded with black fruits and displaying undertones of stone, salt, and roasted meat, this manages to be both lush and lively.

DOMAINE TABATAU *(St.-Chinian)*

Saint-Chinian Lo Tabataire ♀ $$$ Typically featuring plum, blackberry, singed meat, smoky black tea, bay leaf, and black pepper, this displays refined tannins and impressive finishing intensity.

DOMAINE DES TERRES FALMET *(St.-Chinian)*

Carignan 🍷 $ This needs air to open up, revealing lovely scents and flavors of blackberry and blueberry, nut oils, and aromatic woods, and finishing with satisfyingly juicy persistence.

Saint-Chinian l'Ivresses des Cimes 🍷 $$ Brimming with black currant, chocolate, and black cherry, and tinged with baking spices, this can be slightly grainy in texture yet delightfully elegant and effortless in its outpouring of finishing fruit.

THUNEVIN-CALVET (See CALVET-THUNEVIN, **above.**)

LA TOUR BOISÉE *(Minervois)*

Minervois 🍷 $ From Grenache, Carignan, and Cinsault, this estate's basic bottling typically smells and tastes of fresh black fruits, sometimes with hints of birch beer, roasted meats, or toasted nuts, and finishes with appealing juiciness and an invigorating hint of salinity.

Minervois Blanc 🍷 $ A blend of Marsanne with a bit of Macabeo and an efficacious dollop of Muscat, this smells of melon, sage, apricot, and orange blossom; offers juicy, herb-tinged melon fruit and a subtly waxy feel on the palate; and finishes with herb, citrus zest, and a hint of honey.

Minervois Cuvée Marielle et Frédérique 🍷 $$ This cuvée adds Syrah and Mourvèdre to the mix, capturing (without oak) rich, pure, sweet black fruits along with herbal, mineral, and animal nuances. Give it time to open up in the air!

DOMAINE DE LA TOUR PENEDESSES
(Coteaux du Languedoc)

Coteaux du Languedoc Cuvée Antique 🍷 $$ One of the consistent best among this estate's bewilderingly long list of cuvées, this brims with cherry and blackberry liqueur laced with brown spices, soy, cocoa powder, and resin, finishing full throttle, seamlessly sweet, and impressively rich.

Coteaux du Languedoc les Volcans ♟ $$$ Known until 2007 and in a slightly different blend as Montée Volcanique, this spicy, black-fruited cuvée is voluminous, liqueur-like, and as eruptive as its name suggests, although roughness and heat occasionally creep into its finish.

DOMAINE DE LA TOUR VIEILLE *(Collioure and Banyuls)*

Collioure La Pinède ♟ $$$ This plush yet bright Grenache-Carignan blend typically offers generous black raspberry and bittersweet cherry with iodine, cherry pit, pepper, toasted nuts, chocolate, and salted beef.

Collioure Puig Ambeille ♟ $$$ This palate-coating Grenache-Carignan-Mourvèdre offers a profusion of flowers and black-fruit aromas backed by meaty intensity, with hints of herbs, vanilla, resin, and wet stone.

Collioure Puig Oriole ♟ $$$ Deep meatiness, loads of ripe black fruit, overtones of lavender and resin, salty, iodine-like mineral notes, and brown spices all lend complexity to this bright, elegant, formidably long, amazing value.

LES TRAVERSES DE FONTANES
(Coteaux du Languedoc Pic St.-Loup)

Cabernet Sauvignon ♟ $$ Neither the prominent prunes and dried cherries nor this wine's saline finish are particularly Cabernet specific, but the same could be said of legions of far less tasty and far more expensive warm-weather Cabernets.

JEAN-LOUIS TRIBOULEY *(Côtes du Roussillon-Villages)*

Les Bacs Vieilles Vignes ♟ $$$ Simply among the world's most extraordinary values, this creamy, palpably dense, yet elegant Grenache-Carignan from Maury offers improbably rich black raspberry jam, chocolate, tar, nut paste, brown spices, and crushed stone.

CHÂTEAU DE VALCOMBE *(Costières de Nîmes)*

Costières de Nîmes Syrah-Grenache Tradition ♟ $ Black currant, rosemary, dark chocolate, and roasted meats inform this slightly warm and cooked-fruit red of impressive sheer intensity and cling.

VILLA SYMPOSIA *(Coteaux du Languedoc)*

Coteaux du Languedoc l'Equilibre 🍷 $$$ One of the most polished and complex Languedoc wines available for its price; strikingly sweetly fruited, soothing, and sumptuous, with mineral, animal, and herbal complexity and a savory, nuanced finish.

CHÂTEAU VIRGILE *(Costières de Nîmes)*

Costières de Nîmes 🍷 $ Copious black cherry and raspberry, bittersweet licorice and juniper, and cocoa powder inform this tannic yet audaciously ripe concentrate.

WALDEN *(Côtes du Roussillon)*

Côtes du Roussillon 🍷 $$ Hervé Bizeul's soft-textured homage to Thoreau and calling card for the Agly Valley's old vines offers lovely dark fruits, smoked meat, roasted nut, and saline and crushed-stone mineral suggestions.

LOIRE VALLEY WINE VALUES

by David Schildknecht

Bargain Garden of France

The valley of the Loire River is the bargain garden of France. For more than half of its 700 miles, slopes within 20 miles of the river's shores team with vines, some indigenous, most introduced down the centuries from all over the rest of France. From few if any other places on earth can one still harvest such affordable yet distinctively delicious wines; the stylistic range is so vast that it would bewilder if it did not bewitch us. The Loire's wines generally offer forthright, generous vinous personalities and food compatibility, while frequently harboring a depth that reflects their historically and geologically layered origins. Even top crus from this region's leaders—including those of global wine-growing champions—remain remarkably modest in price. And there is an abundance of young talent, both homegrown and drawn from afar to this beautiful region with its outstanding, still-affordable vine acreage.

In an area this vast, not only are many localities inherently less conducive to interesting wine than others, but there are copious quantities of lackluster or flawed wines from each of the Loire's more than 60 appellations. In that respect, American consumers have an advantage over their French counterparts in the enormous range of quality Loire growers whose wines have been winnowed out for representation by dozens of specialty French wine importers.

Not only the grapes and styles of the Loire are diverse; so too are its appellations and overlapping regional designations. A sketch must suffice, with the relevant grapes taken in the context of their districts of production. For ease in locating wines of a given grape or region, the producers whose wines are recommended and briefly described in the body of this chapter have also been listed below by their principal wine types.

Regions and Grapes

A huge expanse of vineyards near the mouth of the Loire at Nantes is dominated by white, bone-dry, light wines, largely belonging to one of four subappellations of **Muscadet**. (The grape is Melon de Bourgogne but is frequently referred to as Muscadet.) No other group of wines this inexpensive is so distinctively delicious, potentially complex, or food-friendly. Few other dry wines of the world taste satisfying and ripe at less than 12% alcohol, are so refreshing, or stimulate the appetite like Muscadet. Think of it as the naked wine. Without alcohol, residual sugar, oak, body, or obvious fruit aromas, it had better be naturally well built and blemish free if it is going to entice us without benefit of clothing or makeup.

Stick to the following growers and you will be rewarded (although, make a mistake and you won't be out a lot of dough): Serge Batard, Domaine de Beauregard, Château de la Bourdinière, Claude Branger, André-Michel Bregeon, Château de Chasseloir, Château de la Chesnaire, Eric Chevalier (Domaine de l'Aujardière), Gilbert Chon, Château du Cleray, Domaine de la Chauvinière, Michel Delhommeau, Domaine des Dorices, Domaine de l'Écu (Guy Bossard), Château de la Fessardière, Domaine Gilarderie, Domaine Gras-Moutons, Jacques Guindon, Domaine Herbauges, Joseph Landron—Domaine de la Louvetrie, Domaine Luneau-Papin, Domaine de la Pépière (Mark Ollivier), Domaine de la Quilla, and Château de la Ragotière.

Farther upstream, from around the city of Angers to the neighborhood of Saumur, are vineyards that (like those of Muscadet) follow roughly 75 miles of shoreline, many stretching 20 or more miles to the south. Here, the overwhelmingly dominant white grape is **Chenin Blanc**, vinified dry or nobly sweet. In addition to wines of the umbrella appellations **Anjou** and **Saumur**, this region incorporates the dry wines of **Savennières** and nobly sweet wines of the **Coteaux du Layon**. (Since very few of these sweet wines fall within the parameters set for this guide, their subappellations will not concern us.) Chenin Blancs grown in these regions are among the world's potentially most profound and ageworthy wines, managing a trick virtually unique to this grape and place: being voluminous and palpably dense while offering lively, mouthwatering acidity.

Sources of white wine value in Anjou and Saumur (and whose wines are profiled in the body of this chapter) include: Domaine des Baumards, Domaine Cady, Domaine du Closel, Château d'Epiré, Domaine aux Moines, René and Agnès Mosse, Domaine Richou, Château Soucherie, and Château de Villeneuve.

The central Loire—officially and collectively known as **Touraine**—is also home to a wealth of outstanding wines from Chenin Blanc, in dry, off-dry, and nobly sweet versions. Best known among these is **Vouvray**, but neighboring **Montlouis** boasts great wines, too, and along a tiny tributary to the north, the **Coteaux du Loir** (with no "e") and its cru **Jasnières** is the site of one of the Loire's several amazing revivals of vines in once prestigious locations. While the top wines of Vouvray and Montlouis transcend the parameters of this guide, the rest of these Chenin-based wines are among the world's amazing wine values. Selection is paramount, though, because underripe or over-cropped Chenin can be unappealingly bitter, and this grape is by no means entirely amenable to the machine picking that for economic reasons now dominates the Loire. Sources of value include: Domaine Allias, Domaine des Aubuisières, Domaine de Bellivière, Domaine Brazilier, Domaine Le Briseau, Didier and Catherine Champalou, Domaine de la Charrière (Joël Gigou), Laurent Chatenay, Regis Cruchet, Domaine Deletang, Julien Fouet, Pascal Janvier, Domaine Les Loges de la Folie, Alexandre Monmousseau, Vincent Raimbault, Bénédict de Rycke, Rochers des Violettes, and Domaine de la Taille aux Loups (Jacky Blot).

Chenin Blanc's red cousin **Pineau d'Aunis** has recently, in a few select hands (particularly in the Coteaux du Loir), demonstrated that it can render serious and highly distinctive red wines. But the principal red grape of Angers and Saumur is **Cabernet Franc**. The Loire's three great red wine appellations are **Saumur-Champigny, Bourgueil,** and **Chinon**. Depending on soil, site, and stylistic intent, these wines can range from refreshingly simple and ideal for serving chilled, to rich, complex, and profound. Collectively, these reds have a mixed reputation, because if underripe (as they too often are) they can be weedy and vegetal. At its best though, Loire Cabernet Franc delivers a sweet, ethereal, floral perfume, a silken texture, a piquant nuttiness and spice, and a combination of black fruit richness with refreshment that is matchless.

Check out the following for the real deal: Yannick Amirault, Bernard Baudry, Château de la Bonnelière, Catherine and Pierre Breton, Domaine de la Butte (Jacky Blot), Domaine de la Chanteleuserie, Château Coulaine, Château Gaillard, Charles Joguet, Frédéric Mabileau, Manoir de la Tête Rouge, Domaine de Noiré, Domaine de Pallus, Domaine de la Perrière, Philippe Pichard (Domaine de la Chapelle), Jean-Marie Raffault, La Source du Ruault, Château de Vaugaudry, and Château de Villeneuve.

The vast Central Loire harbors a legion of bargains made neither from Chenin Blanc nor from pure Cabernet Franc. East of the city of Tours, a majority of wines are simply labeled "Touraine," the whites usually **Sauvignon Blanc** and the reds usually blends, featuring in addition to Cabernet Franc and Pineau d'Aunis **Gamay**, **Malbec** (here called "Côt"), and **Pinot Noir**. A few individual appellations are also gaining well-deserved recognition, most notably **Cheverny** (where, curiously, the whites must have Chardonnay blended into their dominant Sauvignon Blanc). The handful of really successful Touraine Sauvignons are more delicious and interesting than at least 75% of what's grown in nearby and prestigious Sancerre and Pouilly-Fumé but cost half as much, and they can easily compete on a world stage as well. Touraine red blends may not be as well known but many are charmers.

Look for outstanding values in white or red Touraine from: Pascal Bellier, Mikäel Bouges, François Cazin (Le Petit Chambord), Clos Roche Blanche, Clos du Tue-Boeuf, Domaine des Corbillières, Domaine de la Garrelière, Domaine des Huards, Henry Marrionet (Domaine de la Charmoise), Jean-François Merieau, Jacky Preys, Thierry Puzelat, Château de la Presle, Vincent Richard, and Domaine du Salvard.

The eastern arc of the Loire is Sauvignon Blanc territory, incorporating the famous neighboring appellations of **Sancerre** and **Pouilly-Fumé.** As well known as these two are, many of their wines offer outstanding value. A little inland from the river and abutting Sancerre lies the appellation of **Menetou-Salon**, and two outposts farther west—**Reuilly** and **Quincy**—offer wines less expensive but at times superb. Pinot Noir is the minority partner throughout this part of the Loire, often vinified as delectable rosé, sometimes as a light red, and occasionally as a red of serious pretensions. A background of high yields and widespread machine harvesting drags down the quality of many Sauvignons from the eastern Loire, because even more than Chenin Blanc, Sauvignon Blanc takes wicked vengeance if overcropped or underripened, displaying a hard edge and aggressive scents of green pepper, asparagus, grass clippings, boxwood, or cat pee. The contrast with the best wines from this grape and region could not be greater!

Start looking for Sauvignons from these producers: Michel Bailly, Francis Blanchet, Gérard Boulay, Michel Brock, Alain Cailbourdin, Jacques Carroy, Celestin-Blondeau, Daniel Chotard, Serge Dageneau, Domaine Fouassier, Fournier Père & Fils, Philippe Gilbert, Bertrand Graillot, Domaine Jamain, Claude Lafond, Baron de Ladoucette, Domaine Mardon, Thierry Merlin-Cherrier, Regis Minet, Gérard & Pierre Morin, Henry Natter, André Neveu, Henry Pellé Philippe Portier,

Hippolyte Reverdy, Jean Reverdy, Pascal & Nicolas Reverdy, Mathias Roblin, Jean-Max Roger, Jean-Claude Roux, Hervé Seguin, F. Tinel-Blondelet, La Tour Saint-Martin, and Domaine des Vieux Pruniers.

Vintage Smarts

Frosts and other factors combined to render the 2007 and 2008 crops exceedingly short for Muscadet, but quality is relatively good. For Sauvignon Blanc, 2007 and 2008 present a relatively high-acid profile, and achieving full ripeness was a challenge, in contrast with the unusually soft 2005s or the decidedly mixed but occasionally exotically ripe 2006s. Chenin Blanc succeeded admirably in 2005, whereas 2004 and 2006 ranged from rained-on and disappointing in Vouvray and Montlouis to excellent (even in as nearby a subregion as the Coteaux du Loir). The 2007 and 2008 vintages, too, presented considerable challenges, but there are plenty of successes. (The special challenges presented to production of nobly sweet wine need not concern us in the present context, as nearly all such wines transcend the price limitations set for this guide.) 2005 was a superb vintage for Loire Cabernet Franc and reds in general, whose like was not remotely approached in the two subsequent vintages, from which one must simply choose more carefully—but then, that's the point of this guide!

Drinking Curves

Contrary to received "wisdom," well-made Muscadet wines can typically be worth enjoying for up to 3 years. With few exceptions (and most of those more expensive), Loire Sauvignons, too, are best enjoyed within 3 years of their vintage. Whites from Chenin Blanc, by contrast, can often evolve fascinatingly for far longer; indeed, the best Loire Chenins are among the world's longest-lived wines. From within the value sector, a good rule of thumb would be to drink Chenins (whether dry or off-dry) within 5 years, although those with residual sugar generally age longer and more gracefully. Rosés and fruity styles of red should be enjoyed within 18 months, but the more serious Bourgueils, Chinons, and Saumur-Champignys—which includes even some of those that are value priced—can be worth holding on to for at least 4–6 years. In virtually every instance, though, young Loire wines have a vivid fruit or (especially in the cases of Muscadet) a subtly yeasty, effervescent immediacy that is most intense when they are new. For that reason, many people will find themselves preferring to drink these wines as young as possible to enhance precisely those virtues.

The Loire's Top Wine Values by Winery

DOMAINE ALLIAS *(Vouvray)*

Vouvray Demi Sec [SD] ♀ $$ Typically offering quince, citrus, green tea, flowers, and diverse mineral allusions, this is discreetly sweet, silken textured, and richly mouth filling, yet has bright citricity and is memorably tenacious.

YANNICK AMIRAULT *(Bourgueil)*

Bourgueil La Coudraye ♀ $$$ Of Amirault's numerous different lots this smells of fresh blackberries, blueberries, and machine oil. Richly fruited and vibrantly juicy on the palate, it incorporates lovely inner-mouth floral notes and hints of salt and sage, leading to a rather brisk, pure-fruited finish free of any superficial sweetness.

DOMAINE DES AUBUISIÈRES *(Vouvray)*

Vouvray Brut Méthode Traditionelle ♀ $$ This food-friendly bubbly tweaks the nose with lemon oil, salt spray, and pungent flowers. Chalky, saline, and alkaline on the palate, and with moderately fine *mousse,* it clings impressively with hints of honey and bittersweet citrus oil.

Vouvray Cuvée Silex ♀ $$ This candidate for the greatest wine value on the planet smells scintillatingly floral, sweetly herbal, and full of citrus and orchard fruits. Utterly transparent in the mouth, with billowing floral perfume and salt-stone minerality, it refreshes mind and palate with the utmost subtlety and eloquent complexity.

Vouvray Demi-Sec Cuvée Les Girardières [SD] ♀ $$ This off-dry cuvée is redolent of orchard fruits and herbal-floral distillate, with suggestions of quince preserve and almond paste often adding a patisserie note. Lusciously fruity, subtly sweet, honeyed, and creamy, it finishes with soothing richness yet buoyancy.

MICHEL BAILLY *(Pouilly-Fumé)*

Pouilly-Fumé Les Loges ♀ $$ This particularly pure, understated Pouilly-Fumé is free of any bitterness, persistently refreshing, and features myriad herbal, floral, and mineral nuances.

SERGE BATARD *(Muscadet)*

Muscadet Côtes de Grandlieu Les Hautes Noëlles 🍷 $ Smelling of fresh lime, sea spray, chalk dust, and milled wheat, this satin-textured Muscadet is loaded with luscious, Chenin-like quince fruit and flowers, as well as diverse suggestions of minerality.

BERNARD BAUDRY *(Chinon)*

Chinon Les Granges 🍷 $$$ Generously black-fruited, briny, subtly meaty, piquantly nutty, and possessed of fine-grained, savory tannins, this is a great introduction to Chinon from a master vintner.

DOMAINE DES BAUMARD *(Savennières)*

Savennières 🍷 $$$ Aromas of snuffed candlewick, quince, flowers, musk, and sea spray are among the fascinating and alluring elements of this dense and texturally rich yet bright and refreshing introduction to Savennières.

DOMAINE DE BEAUREGARD *(Muscadet)*

Muscadet de Sevre et Maine sur Lie 🍷 $ With subtle melon, peach, and chalk-dust aromas, this is surprisingly lush for Muscadet yet doesn't lack cut or refreshment.

PASCAL BELLIER *(Cheverny)*

Cheverny 🍷 $ Pear, nut oils, caraway, mint, white pepper, musky floral perfume, and mineral salts inform this delightfully refreshing, vivacious, impressively tenacious Sauvignon.

DOMAINE DE BELLIVIÈRE *(Coteaux du Loir)*

Coteaux du Loir l'Effraie 🍷 $$$ Flowers, quince, peach, nut oils, spices, and myriad mineral notes vie for attention in this superb, glossy-textured, rich yet dynamic Chenin from the Loir's premier pioneers.

Coteaux du Loir Le Rouge Gorge 🍷 $$$ This wine from Pineau d'Aunis features sour cherry, roses, almond, herbal elixir, pungent pepper, and spice. Bright and invigorating, yet subtly creamy, it boasts explosive finishing potential.

FRANCIS BLANCHET *(Pouilly-Fumé)*

Pouilly-Fumé Calcite ♀ **$$** Bracing, invigorating, almost stingingly pungent, this excellent introduction to its appellation typically features citrus, herbs, passion fruit, and gooseberry.

Pouilly-Fumé Vieilles Vignes ♀ **$$$** This bright, firm cuvée from old vines in pebbly chalk typically displays citrus zest and herbal pungency with saline and crushed-stone finishing suggestions.

Pouilly-Fumé Silice ♀ **$$$** From flint-rich soils, this infectiously juicy, subtly smoky, and palate-seducing Sauvignon typically features currant, gooseberry, high-toned herbs, and flowers (honeysuckle, lily, or iris).

CHÂTEAU DE LA BONNELIÈRE *(Chinon, Touraine)*

Chinon ♀ **$$** The Château's principal bottling, this is impressively dense, with aromas of blackberry, mulberry, toasted walnut, and mint. It coats the palate broadly with fine tannin and a nippy cling of ginger and pepper.

Chinon Rive Gauche ♀ **$** This brims with tart but ripe cherry and blackberry, tinged with baking spices and toasted nuts. Succulent and sappy on the palate, it finishes with bright black fruits and pungent spice and pepper.

MIKÄEL BOUGES *(Touraine)*

Touraine Côt [Malbec] Les Côtes Hauts ♀ **$** Stunningly dark purple, this bursts from the glass with bright black raspberry fruit, then proceeds to shock you with its seemingly tannin-less behavior, white wine refreshment, and invigorating salinity.

Touraine Sauvignon La Pente de Chavigny ♀ **$** Redolent of resinous herbs, caraway, and citrus zest, this brims with luscious honeydew melon and tart gooseberry, finishing with an invigoratingly salty tang.

GÉRARD BOULAY *(Sancerre)*

Sancerre ♀ **$$$** Herbal, floral, citric, and displaying orchard, black, or tropical fruits, Boulay's juicy, mouth-filling, vivacious Sancerre typically offers real textural nuance as well.

CHÂTEAU DE LA BOURDINIÈRE *(Muscadet)*

Muscadet de Sèvre et Maine sur Lie ♀ $ Citrus and orchard fruits dominate this juicy, refreshing, straightforward, and inexpensive example of its genre.

CLAUDE BRANGER *(Muscadet)*

Muscadet de Sèvre et Maine sur Lie Les Gras Moutons ♀ $$ A wine of mind-boggling complexity for its price: Delicate and juicy yet at the same time expansive and mouth filling, it stains the palate with citrus, iodine, broth-like herb, and Chablis-like meat stock.

DOMAINE BRAZILIER *(Coteaux du Vendômois)*

Coteaux du Vendômois Tradition ♀ $$ This intriguing and refreshing blend of Cabernet Franc, Pineau d'Aunis, and Pinot Noir from an obscure Touraine appellation features toasted pecans, fresh blackberries, raw beef, ripe tomatoes, and cherry-pit bitterness.

ANDRÉ-MICHEL BRÉGEON *(Muscadet)*

Muscadet de Sèvre et Maine sur Lie ♀ $ A subtle interplay of raw almond, citrus, flowers, and pit fruits; a cool, clear, refreshing fruit personality; and a suffusion of salt and oyster-shell mineral character add up to a wine of refinement and nuance.

CATHÉRINE & PIERRE BRETON *(Bourgueil)*

Bourgueil Galichets ♥ $$$ Faintly bitter fresh black and blue fruits typically mingle with subtle brown spices, and a firm but juicy palate impression is underlain by suggestions of chalk or wet stone.

Bourgueil Trinch! ♥ $$$ As its name—to be called out when clinking together glasses—suggests, this refreshes young, with cassis and blackberry fruit, hints of dark chocolate, and invigorating salinity and tartness.

DOMAINE LE BRISEAU *(Coteaux du Loir)*

La Pangée ♥ $ This flagrantly red-fruited blend of Pineau d'Aunis and Gamay is infectiously juicy and close to the fresh grape.

MICHEL BROCK (*Sancerre*)

Sancerre Le Coteau ♀ $$$ Abundant citrus, orchard fruits, and herbs offer satisfyingly sappy intensity and vivacious freshness.

DOMAINE DE LA BUTTE (*Bourgueil*)

Bourgueil Le Pied de la Butte ♀ $$$ This simplest cuvée from Jacky Blot (see under Domaine de la Taille aux Loups) smells of fresh blackberry, mulberry, and a hint of game, and offers creaminess along with clarity and brightness.

DOMAINE CADY (*Coteaux du Layon*)

Coteaux du Layon ⑤ ♀ $$$ This tank-raised introduction to nobly sweet Chenin offers spiced orchard fruit preserves and honey in a soothing and delicate combination, finishing with deftly balanced sweetness and mineral hints.

ALAIN CAILBOURDIN (*Pouilly-Fumé*)

Pouilly-Fumé Cuvée de Boisfleury ♀ $$$ Featuring currant, mint, catnip, and floral perfume, this is long on citrus, herbs, and saline and crushed-stone mineral suggestions.

JACQUES CARROY (*Pouilly-Fumé*)

Pouilly-Fumé ♀ $$ Blazingly bright, fresh, and pungent in its citrus and herb intensity, this really grips with fascinating suggestions of salt and stone, for a real "aha!" experience of Pouilly-Fumé.

FRANÇOIS CAZIN (LE PETIT CHAMBORD) (*Cheverny*)

Cheverny ♀ $$ Quite possibly the world's finest Sauvignon value, this typically exudes lemon, tarragon, white peach, and nut oils, and occasionally hints of gooseberry or red fruits; combines luscious ripeness with refreshing brightness; and delivers thought-provoking mineral nuances as well.

CÉLESTIN-BLONDEAU *(Sancerre)*

Sancerre Cuvée des Moulins Bales ♀ $$$ Sweetly scented and invigorating in its meld of peppermint, flowers, pear, quince, lime zest, and cress, this bright, elegant Sancerre seems suffused with chalky, stony dust.

DIDIER & CATHERINE CHAMPALOU *(Vouvray)*

Vouvray ♀ $$ With barely noticeable sweetness backing ripe orchard fruits, citrus, herbal essences, and brown spices, this typically polished and creamy, yet ethereally delicate and mineral-nuanced, Chenin makes a perfect introduction to Vouvray.

Vouvray Cuvée des Fondraux 🆂🅳 ♀ $$ This slightly sweet, barrel-matured Vouvray typically offers a ravishing amalgam of talcum, quince, honey, high-toned herbs, beeswax, and acacia; a creamy, satiny feel; and uncanny finishing lift.

DOMAINE DE LA CHANTELEUSERIE *(Bourgueil)*

Bourgueil Cuvée Alouettes ♟ $$ Smelling of toasted pralines and blackberries, with fine-grained tannins and an unstoppable flow of fruit, this finishes from ear to ear, tinged with bitter herbs, black chocolate, soy, and iodine.

Bourgueil Cuvée Vieilles Vignes ♟ $$ Firm but juicy and bright on the palate and with fine-grained tannins, this mouthful of blackberry, plums, and toasted nuts finishes with sap, energy, and tenacity.

DOMAINE DE LA CHARRIÈRE *(Coteaux du Loir)*

Jasnières Clos du Paradis ♀ $$$ A fascinating interplay of apple, quince, lemon, and peach with sea-breeze-like suggestions of salt informs this Chenin with a faintly oily texture and a lithe and penetrating finish.

Jasnières Clos St.-Jacques ♀ $$$ This palate-coating Chenin from old vines offers alkaline, almost oceanic, mysterious depths of aroma and flavor; high-toned, nutty pungency; and a mouthwatering impression of ripe quince.

CHÂTEAU DE CHASSELOIR COMTE LELOUP DE CHASSELOIR *(Muscadet)*

Château de Chasseloir Comte Leloup de Chasseloir Muscadet de Sèvre et Maine sur Lie Cuvée des Ceps Centenaires ♗ **$$** This Muscadet from ancient vines with the impossibly long name represents one of the most remarkable wine values on the planet. Chalk dust, white truffle, herbs, and Chablis-like chicken stock are among the flavors that often inform its characteristically lean, bright, focused, subtly bitter, and implacably mineral personality.

LAURENT CHATENAY *(Montlouis)*

Montlouis Sec Les Maisonettes ♗ **$$$** This offers abundant flowers and orchard fruit (peony, peach) allied to a distinctively saline suggestion that helps counteract a faint bitterness seemingly born of sheer extract.

DOMAINE DE LA CHAUVINIÈRE *(Muscadet)*

Muscadet de Sèvre et Main sur Lie ♗ **$** This rich, rather Chenin-like Muscadet offers abundant citrus, flowers, and herbs, and a satisfyingly long finish dripping with ripe fruit.

DOMAINE DES CHESNAIES *(Bourgueil)*

Bourgueil Rosé ♗ **$$** Suggesting mulberry, black currant, fresh spinach, and nut oils, this juicy, delicate, and refreshing rosé finishes with stimulating hints of fruit skin and toasted-nut bitterness.

Bourgueil Vieilles Vignes ♙ **$$** These old vines deliver real depth as well as impressive sheer cling, tinging this wine's copious blackberry fruit with nutmeg, green tea, iodine, and fresh spinach.

CHÂTEAU DE LA CHESNAIRE *(Muscadet)*

Château de la Chesnaire Muscadet de Sèvre et Maine sur Lie ♗ **$** An inexpensive member of the large Chereau-Carré family of Muscadet, this is infectiously juicy, with luscious pit and citrus fruits mingled with flowers, herbs, and a suggestion of sea breeze.

ERIC CHEVALIER (DOMAINE DE L'AUJARDIÈRE)
(Muscadet)

Fié Gris ♀ $$$ From ancient vines of the distinctive Fié Gris variant of Sauvignon (though grown in Muscadet), this offers chalk-tinged, luscious, and refreshing pineapple, mint, grapefruit, gooseberry, and white peach.

GILBERT CHON *(Muscadet)*

Château de la Salominière Muscadet de Sèvre et Maine sur Lie ♀ $ This beguiles with such intriguing elements as apricot blossom, grapefruit, quince, and at times bitter black fruits, offering a vibrant, juicy, tingling mouthful of refreshingly tart fruit skin and chalk.

Clos de la Chapelle Muscadet de Sèvre et Maine sur Lie ♀ $ Flowers and fresh lime skate onto the palate with terrific precision, cut, and clarity, inscribing invigorating mineral grooves in a matrix of lime and peach.

DANIEL CHOTARD *(Sancerre)*

Sancerre ♀ $$$ Smelling of lemon, sea breeze, and subtle herbs and flowers, this carries its intriguing floral perfume onto a citric, clear, subtly saline, chalky, peaty palate presence that leaves you invigorated.

CHÂTEAU DU CLERAY (SAUVION) *(Muscadet)*

Muscadet de Sèvre et Maine sur Lie Cardinal Richard ♀ $$ Representing a special selection among Sauvion's numerous bottlings, this surprisingly rich, broad Muscadet features fresh citrus and pit fruits, hints of honey, and suggestions of chalk and iodine.

Muscadet de Sèvre et Maine sur Lie Réserve Haute Culture ♀ $$ Another Muscadet of relatively full body and richness, loaded with peachy fruit, along with salinity and a wealth of flowers and foliage, that puts one in mind of walking into a greenhouse.

CLOS ROCHE BLANCHE *(Touraine)*

Touraine Cabernet 🍷 **$$** Featuring fresh mulberry, blackberry, leather, and tobacco, and suffused with iodine-rich lobster-shell minerality, this fascinating, organically grown wine never forsakes its duty to quench thirst.

Touraine Gamay 🍷 **$$** Generous with fresh strawberry and cherry that behave as though they have been macerated on black tea and cherry stones, this wine's faint bitterness is a perfect foil for its sheer generosity of fruit, and its silken texture and juicy, subtly nutty finish encourage the next sip.

CLOS DU TUE-BOEUF *(Touraine, Cheverny)*

Cheverny Frileuse 🍷 **$$** Here we have citrus, melon, toasted caraway, and roasted peanuts. Mouthwatering and invigorating citricity and salinity engender a fascinating tension with textural creaminess.

Cheverny Rouillon 🍷 **$$** This firm but juicy blend of Pinot Noir and Gamay highlights sour cherry and plum tinged with wood smoke, peat, cinnamon spice, and wet stone.

Touraine Sauvignon 🍷 **$$** This low-sulfur wine smells of lime, caraway, parsnip, and a hint of honey. Lush and dense for its appellation, it loads the palate with nuts, caraway, subtly caramelized parsnip or celeriac, and citrus zest.

DOMAINE DU CLOSEL *(Savennières)*

Savennières La Jalousie 🍷 **$$$** This unusually generous take on its appellation combines juicy citrus and orchard fruit with textural richness and plenty of herbal and mineral (saline, chalky, oyster-shell) complexity.

DOMAINE DES CORBILLÈRES *(Touraine)*

Touraine Cabernet 🍷 **$** The Barbou family's surprisingly creamy yet invigoratingly juicy Cabernet is only a bit less remarkable than their Sauvignon, featuring toasted praline, lightly cooked blackberries, cherry pits, machine oil, and licorice.

Touraine Sauvignon ♀ $ From pioneers in the genre, this rich yet refreshing Sauvignon represents an astonishingly consistent value. Intensely mouthwatering, this wine typically bursts with pure, ripe honeydew melon or white peach, accented by fresh lime and orange, cress, passion fruit, pennyroyal, and toasted caraway and nuts.

CHÂTEAU DU COULAINE *(Chinon)*

Chinon ♀ $$ This typically offers tart blackberry, toasted nuts, and brown spices, beetroot and subtly bitter floral and coffee accents, and a salinity that helps enliven its refreshing finish.

RÉGIS CRUCHET *(Vouvray)*

Vouvray Demi-Sec SD ♀ $$$ Generous floral perfume, spiced orchard fruit, lanolin, and a bittersweet citrus oil character combine on a polished palate that successfully integrates quite high residual sugar.

SERGE DAGUENEAU *(Pouilly-Fumé)*

Pouilly-Fumé Les Pentes ♀ $$$ This rich yet spine-tingling cuvée offers gorgeous aromas of ripe honeydew melon, pear, lime, and herbal distillates, leading to a juicy mouthful of melons and orchard fruits, typically tinged with sage, pear pip, roasted coffee, citrus zest, and toasted caraway.

DOMAINE DÉLETANG *(Montlouis)*

Montlouis Demi-Sec Les Batisse SD ♀ $$$ Among Déletang's numerous cuvées, this abounds in luscious citrus, sweetly aromatic herbs, and a bracing sense of gooseberry tartness playing against confectionary notes of nougat and fruit preserves.

MICHEL DELHOMMEAU *(Muscadet)*

Muscadet de Sèvre et Maine sur Lie Cuvée Harmonie ♀ $ Scented with pear, quince, and lime—almost as if a bit of Chenin had been blended in—this rich yet refreshing cuvée boasts real depth of nut-oil richness, orchard fruit, and saline, savory minerality.

Muscadet de Sèvre et Maine sur Lie Cuvée Saint Vincent ♀ $
Cool, refreshing, soothing citrus dominates this Muscadet, with hints
of pear, salt, and chalk. Its infectiously juicy finish adds the faint but
invigorating tart bitterness of pear skin and citrus zest.

DOMAINE DES DORICES *(Muscadet)*

Muscadet de Sèvre et Maine sur Lie Cuvée Choisie ♀ $ Smelling
of lime fruit and chalk with hints of honey and smoke, and reflecting
its old-vines material in its chalky density, this refresher offers lip-
smacking concentrations of lime, salt, and crushed stone.

Muscadet de Sèvre et Maine sur Lie Grande Garde ♀ $$ This
literally great-keeping cuvée and utterly amazing value—usually
released only after 2 years in bottle—displays a fantastic aromatic
mélange of diverse flowers (often gentian or clover), sweet herbal
essences, brine, and wet-stone mineral elements.

Muscadet de Sèvre et Maine sur Lie Hermine d'Or ♀ $
Gooseberry, white currant, nettle, lime peel, and herbs inform a
polished, subtly creamy yet brightly refreshing palate of superb purity
and strikingly saline, chalky, stony length.

DOMAINE DE L'ÉCU *(Muscadet)*

Muscadet de Sèvre et Maine sur Lie Expression de Gneiss ♀ $$
This characteristically most juicy and refreshing of Bossard's cuvées
is nonetheless dominated even in the nose by elusively mineral scents
and finishes with invigorating salinity as well as an herbal bite.

Muscadet de Sèvre et Maine sur Lie Expression de Granite ♀ $$
Few wines of this price are so fascinatingly delicious as Guy Bossard's
trio of Muscadet from three soils. The infectiously juicy, satin-
textured Granite is scented with fresh lime, fennel, tangerine zest,
and flowers, almost honeyed yet refreshing, and tinged with iodine,
oyster shell, and citrus zest.

Muscadet de Sèvre et Maine sur Lie Expression d'Orthogneiss
♀ $$ This cuvée smells intriguingly of roasted, salted peanuts; citrus
zest; and pungently musky flowers. Salt, chalk, and peanuts seem to
infuse a refreshing mouthful of citrus and chicken stock.

CHÂTEAU D'ÉPIRE *(Savennières)*

Savennières ♀ **$$** Pronouncedly mineral even in its aromas, suggesting oyster shell and sea breeze, along with quince, lime, and buddleia, this palpably thick yet bright Savennières is like a mineral soup with clinging, crystalline residue.

Savennières Cuvée Speciale ♀ **$$$** Riper and more opulent than the corresponding basic Savennières (above), this displays exotic floral notes and in some years a discreet hint of sweetness.

CHÂTEAU DE LA FESSARDIÈRE *(Muscadet)*

Muscadet ♀ **$** Grown outside of Muscadet's better-known subregions, this bursts with fresh lime and flowers and is subtly creamy yet refreshing, with finishing suggestions of wet stone.

DOMAINE FOUASSIER *(Sancerre)*

Sancerre Les Grands Goux ♀ **$$$** Any of the six Fouassier cuvées can generally be recommended, but this one smells especially bracingly of salted citrus and herbs, and while tending toward softness, it is satisfyingly juicy.

Sancerre Les Romains ♀ **$$$** This cuvée from flint soil is invigoratingly pungent and mouthwatering, satiny in texture, and features white currants, floral perfume, grapefruit, pineapple, and herbs.

JULIEN FOUET *(Saumur)*

Saumur ♀ **$$** This sensational value sports aromas of fresh lime, yellow plum, and musky, narcissus-like floral perfume; is positively galvanizing in its brightness; and floods every recess of your palate with lime, grapefruit, yellow plum, white peach, and salty, chalky, savory shrimp-shell mineral matter.

FOURNIER PÈRE & FILS *(Sancerre, Pouilly-Fumé)*

Pouilly-Fumé Les Caillots ♀ **$$$** While not terribly complex, this is formidably substantial, bright, and bracing, with pineapple, pungent herbs, nut oils, and a hint of smoke.

Sancerre Les Belles Vignes ♀ $$$ This features citrus, mint, gooseberry, and cassis, a silken texture and palpable sense of extract, and a clean and refreshing finish.

Sauvignon ♀ $$ An enticing amalgam of citrus, pit fruits, and herbs informs a creamy-textured yet luscious, refreshing, seemingly mineral-tinged palate.

CHÂTEAU GAILLARD *(Saumur)*

Saumur ♀ $$ From old, biodynamically farmed vines, this features black fruits, beetroot, toasted nuts, and wood smoke on a palate of fine intensity and brightness, leading to a savory, lip-smacking finish.

DOMAINE DE LA GARRELIÈRE *(Touraine)*

Touraine Cendrillon ♀ $$$ From the estate's best Sauvignon, blended with a bit of barrel-fermented Chardonnay and (generally) Chenin, this displays floral and herbal top notes followed by nut oils and mouthwatering citrus.

Touraine Sauvignon ♀ $$ Playing above its class, this typically displays luscious citrus wreathed in flowers, mint, and chalk dust. Unexpectedly lush, luscious, and dense for its grape and region, it finishes with expansive richness yet refreshment and fascinating mineral interest.

DOMAINE GILARDERIE *(Muscadet)*

Domaine Gilarderie Muscadet de Sèvre et Maine sur Lie ♀ $ With lovely purity of orchard fruits tinged with herbs and chalk, this offers a palate-saturating, almost Chablis-like mineral experience and a long, lip-smacking finish.

PHILIPPE GILBERT *(Menetou-Salon)*

Menetou-Salon ♀ $$$ Subtle but beguiling scents of flowers, lemon zest, honey, herbs, and chalk dust prepare the way for a surprisingly rich and positively silken yet persistently juicy and invigorating mouthful of citrus, flowers, and herbs.

BERTRAND GRAILLOT *(Coteaux du Giennois)*

Coteaux du Giennois ♀ $ From an obscure sector north of Pouilly-Fumé, this intriguing bargain Sauvignon is densely chalky and features citrus, caraway, pineapple, and passion fruit.

DOMAINE GRAS-MOUTONS *(Muscadet)*

Domaine Gras-Moutons Muscadet de Sèvre et Maine sur Lie ♀ $ This old-vines cuvée typically displays a diverse bouquet of flowers, herbs, melons, and citrus zest; saturates the palate with juicy fruit and diverse mineral nuances; and finishes refreshingly yet almost sweetly ripe, with a delta of mineral mass.

JACQUES GUINDON *(Muscadet)*

Coteaux d'Ancenis ♀ $ This Gamay rosé is a lovely floral, tart-berried, and briskly dry treat each summer after its release.

Muscadet Coteaux de la Loire sur Lie Prestige ♀ $ Loaded with quince, apple, pear, sometimes black fruits, beeswax, diverse herbs, juniper, salt, chalk, and wet stones, this consistently delights and fascinates.

DOMAINE HERBAUGES *(Muscadet)*

Muscadet Côtes de Grandlieu Château de Lorière ♀ $ Offering lime, pineapple, pear, and a greenhouse-like amalgam of shrubbery and flowers, this is softer than the Choblets' "Classic" bottling but finishes with juicy generosity and a lick of salt.

Muscadet Côtes de Grandlieu Classic ♀ $ Amid Jerome and Luc Choblet's array of bottlings, this is luscious, bright, full of rich, crustacean mineral suggestions, and guaranteed to get your juices flowing and your thoughts turning to the next meal.

Muscadet Côtes de Grandlieu Clos de la Fine ♀ $ This lush yet refreshing Muscadet offers a distinctive and subtly creamy combination of citrus, pit fruits, yeast, grain (a bit wheat beer–like), jasmine, almond, salt, and chalk.

Muscadet Côtes de Grandlieu Clos de la Sénaigerie ♀ $ This saline, stone-licking, pungently nutty Muscadet offers remarkable succulence and sheer cling.

DOMAINE DES HUARDS *(Cheverny)*

Cheverny ♀ $ Displaying appellation-typical caraway, lime, mint, and sea breeze in the nose, and a polished and subtly waxy palate, this finishes with low-toned nuttiness, toasted caraway, and faintly bitter herbs.

Cour-Cheverny François ler ♀ $$ From ancient Romorantin vines, this displays intriguing notes of musk, peat, citrus zest, and alkaline minerality. Uncompromisingly dry, it finishes with lip-smacking citricity and salinity.

DOMAINE JAMAIN *(Reuilly)*

Reuilly Pierre Plates ♀ $$ Pungently penetrating herb and citrus zest are allied to luscious bush and orchard fruits and invigorating saline and chalky mineral suggestions in an extraordinary value Sauvignon that will conduct you in a dance of delight.

PASCAL JANVIER *(Coteaux du Loir)*

Jasnières ♀ $$$ This profoundly delicious and implausibly affordable Chenin is pure, cool-fruited, refined, and refreshing, showering you in flowers, orchard fruits, citrus, salt, and crushed stone, finishing with lip-smacking penetration and potency.

Jasnières Cuvée du Silex ♀ $$$ This silken-textured Chenin from Janvier's top site shimmers alluringly in multiple senses, with ripe quince, narcissus, pear, lychee, and fresh lemon playing against salt, stone, oyster shell, and downright ineffable mineral notes.

CHARLES JOGUET *(Chinon)*

Chinon Cuvée de la Cure ♀ $$$ With hints of herbal pungency and charred meat to accompany its juicy black-fruit concentration, this typically displays more tannin than the Joguet Petites Roches bottling.

Chinon les Petites Roches ♀ $$ Fresh blackberry and mulberry; a well-focused, finely tannic, invigoratingly tart palate impression; and lip-smacking juiciness characterize this simply delicious Cabernet Franc.

BARON PATRICK DE LADOUCETTE *(Pouilly-Fumé)*

Sauvignon Blanc ♀ $$ From a producer of expensive and renowned Pouilly-Fumé and Sancerre, this introductory-level Sauvignon Blanc smells of Thai basil, cress, and lime, and fills the mouth with juicy citrus, pit fruits, and distinct suggestions of crushed stone.

CLAUDE LAFOND *(Reuilly)*

Reuilly Clos Fussay ♀ $$ Unusually soft and generous for its appellation, yet not lacking for pungency or refreshing juiciness, this finishes with invigorating, mouth-cleansing notes of herbs, chalk, and fruit skin.

JOSEPH LANDRON *(Muscadet)*

Domaine de la Louvetrie Muscadet de Sèvre et Maine le Fief du Breil ♀ $$ The nose is plunged into a veritable greenhouse of floral and foliage aromas. Quite creamy in the mouth, with ripe pear and quince as well as persistent floral, herbal, and meat-stock accents, this grips with salt, chalk, iodine, and tart fruit skin.

Domaine de la Louvetrie Muscadet de Sèvre et Maine sur Lie Cuvée Domaine ♀ $ Each of Jo Landron's many cuvées makes its distinctive statement. This one from younger vines on light soil offers saline meat and herb stock with an invigorating lashing of salt and citrus.

Domaine de la Louvetrie Muscadet de Sèvre et Maine sur Lie Hermine d'Or ♀ $ From old vines, this palate-staining and surprisingly doughy cuvée mingles squash, pumpkin, peach, flowers, iodine, meat stock, and pungent lime zest.

Muscadet de Sèvre et Maine Clos de la Carizière ♀ $ This vivacious Muscadet from a former quarry displays a saline, dusty nose; lemon, melon, summer squash, and meat stock; and sappy, lip-smacking persistence with myriad mineral nuances.

Muscadet de Sèvre et Maine Haute Tradition ♀ $$$ This barrel-fermented cuvée displays a fascinating meld of mineral, yeast, and fruit. Fruit-skin bitterness and subtle resinous wood notes are nicely integrated in a rounded palate, leading to a sedate, low-toned finish.

DOMAINE LES LOGES DE LA FOLIE *(Montlouis)*

Montlouis Demi-Sec [SD] 🍷 $$$ Redolent of honey, lavender, quince, and chalk dust, lush but juicy and refreshing, this coats the palate with quince paste and vanilla cream, complemented by toasted nuts, bitter chocolate, and quinine.

Montlouis Méthode Traditionelle Brut 🍷 $$ This versatile sparkling wine value is loaded with luscious quince, vanilla, flowers, and suggestions of cherry cream soda, yet finishes dry.

DOMAINE LUNEAU-PAPIN *(Muscadet)*

Muscadet de Sèvre et Maine sur Lie Clos des Allées Vieilles Vignes 🍷 $$ Luneau-Papin's Muscadets are among the world's greatest white wine values. This smells of apple blossom, apple seed, lemon, and honey; is lusciously full of fruit and surprisingly plush in texture for Muscadet; and finishes with real density and nut-oil richness yet supreme refreshment.

Muscadet de Sèvre et Maine sur Lie Clos des Noëlles 🍷 $$$ Originating in old, low-yield vines, this rich, plush, yet refreshing and thought-provoking late-released cuvée delivers kaleidoscopic and deep aromas and flavors of nut oils, chalk and stones, orchard fruits, and flowers.

Muscadet de Sèvre et Maine sur Lie L d'Or 🍷 $$$ Almost shockingly rich wine for its appellation, this quince-, flower-, and sea breeze–scented Muscadet offers a superbly mouth-coating concentration of quince, honey, herbs, chalk dust, wet stone, and salt.

FRÉDÉRIC MABILEAU *(St.-Nicolas-de-Bourgueil)*

Saint-Nicolas-de-Bourgueil Les Rouillères 🍷 $$ Smelling of mulberry with hints of shrubbery, this plumbs some of the nutty depths and saline, chalky, smoky, peppery mineral inflections of which Cabernet Franc is capable in these soils.

MANOIR DE LA TÊTE ROUGE *(Saumur)*

Saumur Bagatelle ♇ $$ Blueberries with green herbs, nutmeg, and walnuts waft from the glass. In the mouth this is delightfully luscious, pure, and polished, with finely integrated tannins and a hint of chalk in the finish.

DOMAINE MARDON *(Quincy)*

Quincy Cuvée Très Vieilles Vignes ♇ $$ Quite lush and refined by appellation standards, this delivers pungent sage and citrus rind, salt-tinged melon, and black currant.

HENRY MARRIONET (DOMAINE DE LA CHARMOISE) *(Touraine)*

Touraine Sauvignon ♇ $$ Scents of melon, yellow plum, lime, parsnip, and caraway lead to a lush palate full of distilled pit fruits, chalk, salt, toasted caraway, and herbs, finishing with faintly toasty, zesty bitterness.

JEAN-FRANÇOIS MÉRIEAU *(Touraine)*

Touraine Côt Les Cent Visages ♇ $$ This Malbec offers a nose of black currant and blackberry with smoky toasted-nut adjuncts. It brightly saturates the palate with black pepper, tart blackberry skin, toasted nuts, and raw beef.

Touraine Sauvignon Les Arpents des Vaudons ♇ $ Smelling of mint, dill, lime, and caraway, with a notably rich texture for its genre yet refreshing citricity and chalky, saline mineral notes, this comes off rather like a Touraine margarita.

THIERRY MERLIN-CHERRIER *(Sancerre)*

Sancerre ♇ $$$ This manages to be lush yet delicate; to display enormous richness yet clarity and cut; and to penetrate and cling with vivid citrus, herb, white pepper, chalk, and mineral salts.

RÉGIS MINET *(Pouilly-Fumé)*

Pouilly-Fumé Vieilles Vignes ♀ $$$ Flint-inflected aromas of gooseberry, currant, nettle, and green tea in the bouquet lead to a persistent, substantial, but bright, refreshing palate with gooseberry, salt, chalk, toasted caraway, and orchard fruits.

DOMAINE AUX MOINES *(Savennières)*

Savennières—Roche aux Moines ♀ $$$ Rarely is wine from a legendary source of greatness this affordable! Expect haunting floral notes, quince, nut oils, crushed stone, citrus oils, bitter herbs, occasionally truffle, and white pepper in a bell-clear call-and-response of fruit and severe minerality that can put you into a trance.

ALEXANDRE MONMOUSSEAU *(Vouvray)*

Vouvray Clos Le Vigneau ♀ $$ From a member of the well-known merchant family Monmousseau, this single-vineyard wine offers quince, melon, narcissus, and herbs. Tending toward softness, it is generously juicy and barely off-dry.

GÉRARD & PIERRE MORIN *(Sancerre)*

Sancerre Vieilles Vignes ♀ $$$ This cuvée specific to the U.S. market offers mint-like high-toned herbs, citrus, and orchard fruits in a typically faintly oily, mouth-coating, persistently luscious and refreshing classic of its appellation.

RENÉ & AGNÈS MOSSE *(Anjou)*

Anjou ♀ $$ This low-sulfur cuvée typically smells of lees, lanolin, citrus and tropical fruit, and lightly smoky notes from the barrel. Creamy and slippery on the palate, it glides off gently but with abundant lingering nutty richness.

HENRY NATTER *(Sancerre)*

Sancerre ♀ $$$ Luscious citrus, pit fruits, flowers, caraway, toasted nuts, and diverse herbs inform this often subtly creamy, generous Sancerre that finishes with licks of salt and chalk.

ANDRÉ NEVEU *(Sancerre)*

Sancerre Le Grand Fricambault ♀ $$$ Marginally the least expensive of several Neveu cuvées, this typically offers a slightly prickly, invigoratingly bright amalgam of gooseberry, red currant, and nettle, finishing with invigorating lip-smacking salinity.

DOMAINE DE NOIRE *(Various Regions)*

Chinon Rosé ♀ $$ Even Jean-Max Manceau's pink wine can occasionally well exceed 14% alcohol yet be no less infectiously juicy for it. Indeed, this typically brims with berries, blossoms, and herbs, representing a triumph of its genre.

Chinon Soif de Tendresse ♥ $$ This recently inaugurated cuvée preaches the gospel of ripe, juicy, black-fruited Cabernet Franc to the uninitiated and converted alike, taking a slight chill nicely and finishing with piquant notes of black walnut and herbs.

Chinon Cuvée Élegance ♥ $$$ This cuvée preserves snappy, bright black fruit, here allied to invigorating salinity, piquant toasted nuttiness, and suggestions of roasted-meat character.

DOMAINE DE PALLUS *(Chinon)*

Chinon Les Pensées de Pallus ♥ $$$ Full of subtly tart red and black fruits and toasted nuts, and possessed of a deep, marrowy, meaty sweetness, this Cabernet is elegant, low-key, clear, juicy, subtly smoky, and spicy.

HENRY PELLÉ *(Menetou-Salon)*

Menetou-Salon ♀ $$ Pellé's basic cuvée offers a bracing and zesty, if at times rather lean and firm, introduction to the appellation.

DOMAINE DE LA PÉPIÈRE (MARC OLLIVIER)
(Muscadet)

Muscadet de Sèvre et Maine sur Lie ♀ $ Among Ollivier's several distinctively delicious cuvées, this smells of fresh apple and almond with subtle floral overtones. Surprisingly silken in texture but fresh and lively on the palate, it clings impressively with suggestions of nut oils and tart-skinned orchard fruits.

Muscadet de Sèvre et Maine sur Lie Clos des Briords ♀ **$$** From ancient vines, this boasts orchard fruits, nuts, herbs, and flowers allied to salt, chalk, and stone, finishing with amazing grip but no hardness or austerity.

Muscadet de Sèvre et Maine sur Lie Cuvée Eden ♀ **$$** This relatively new cuvée offers considerable richness of fruit, alluring florality, zesty citricity, and oyster-shell and wet-stone mineral character.

DOMAINE DE LA PERRIÈRE *(Chinon)*

Chinon Vieilles Vignes ♀ **$$$** This simply delicious Chinon offers lightly cooked or candied blackberry and cassis that saturate the palate.

PHILIPPE PICHARD (DOMAINE DE LA CHAPELLE) *(Chinon)*

Chinon Les Trois Quartiers ♀ **$$** Dominated by fresh, juicy black cherry, faintly bitter cherry pit, and toasted nuts, this cuvée finishes with tannins overridden by thirst-quenching fruit.

PHILIPPE PORTIER *(Quincy)*

Quincy ♀ **$$** This typically smells of fresh herbs and passion fruit, often combining a slight creaminess with refreshing brightness and loading the palate with citrus, apple, wet stone, and herbs.

CHÂTEAU DE LA PRESLE *(Touraine)*

Touraine Gamay ♀ **$** Proof that the humble Gamay can offer delights beyond its familiar confines of Beaujolais, with fresh mulberry, plums, and toasted hickory, a slippery-silky texture, and a piquantly nutty finish.

Touraine Sauvignon ♀ **$** This tasty and ridiculously inexpensive wine leads with lemon, peppermint, and gooseberry; throws a wicked right hook of jaw-dropping pungency; then administers a dose of smelling salts to bring you 'round.

JACKY PREYS *(Touraine)*

Fié Gris ♀ $$ From ancient vines of a progenitor of Sauvignon, this tenacious, creamy, yet refreshing wine features pungent herbs, resin, citrus zest, toasted nuts, caraway, herbs, salt, melon, kumquat, and pineapple.

THIERRY PUZELAT *(Touraine)*

Touraine Pineau d'Aunis ♀ $$$ Smelling sweetly of cherry and cinnamon, infectiously juicy, deeply fruited (almost liqueur-like), and loaded with alluring brown spices, sweet inner-mouth floral perfume, and well-integrated, tea-like bitterness, this makes a compelling case for seriously delightful "minor" Loire reds.

DOMAINE DE LA QUILLA *(Muscadet)*

Muscadet de Sèvre et Maine sur Lie ♀ $ Expect fresh citricity, pungent mineral suggestions, and a juicy mouthful often fuller in alcoholic body than is typical for this appellation.

JEAN-MARIE RAFFAULT *(Chinon)*

Chinon ♀ $$ This quite silken-textured basic bottling is loaded with black fruits, tinged by vanilla, chocolate, and the bitterness of cherry pits.

Chinon Clos d'Isoré ♀ $$$ This offers a richly textured, formidably concentrated and complex medley of black cherry, blueberry, herbs, flowers, and raw beef, tinged with iodine and cherry pit and underlain with chalk and wet stones.

Chinon Les Galuches ♀ $$$ Black fruits here mingle with beef broth, iodine, and bitter cherry stones. Juicy, bright, and faintly saline, this persists with ripe yet invigoratingly tart fruit.

CHÂTEAU DE LA RAGOTIÈRE *(Muscadet)*

Muscadet de Sèvre et Maine sur Lie ♀ $ Ragotière's black-labeled Muscadet offers abundant citrus, pit fruits, nuts, and salty, chalky mineral allusions, and is satisfyingly juicy and versatile but does not lack a "serious" side.

VINCENT RAIMBAULT *(Vouvray)*

Vouvray ♀ **$$** This bottling is finished with scarcely detectable residual sugar. Smelling of quince, citrus zest, nutmeg, and apple, it offers a lovely counterpoint of richness of fruit and silkiness with refreshment.

Vouvray Sec ♀ **$$** Quince, vanilla, herbal distillates, nut oils, and brine all typically inform this invigorating, persistently juicy, and by turns saline and stony Chenin Blanc.

HIPPOLYTE REVERDY *(Sancerre)*

Sancerre ♀ **$$$** Pear, lime, honeydew melon, perfumed flowers, oregano, and white pepper inform this lusciously juicy Sauvignon. The brightly citric, invigoratingly saline finish here can send shivers down your back.

JEAN REVERDY *(Sancerre)*

Sancerre La Reine Blanche ♀ **$$$** This admirably concentrated, brisk, and refreshing Sauvignon typically combines gooseberry, white grapefruit, and diverse herbs with cut, clarity, and a smoky, Pouilly-Fumé-like pungency.

PASCAL & NICOLAS REVERDY *(Sancerre)*

Sancerre Cuvée Les Coûtes ♀ **$$$** High-tension, at times youthfully austere, but always penetrating and invigorating, this rendition of Sancerre full of citric and herbal pungency might not be the easiest introduction to its appellation but should not be missed!

VINCENT RICHARD *(Touraine)*

Touraine Sauvignon ♀ **$** Typically smelling of fresh lemon and orange mingled with dill, mint, and cress, this can display an unexpected sense of creaminess to accompany its rich nut-oil notes but finishes refreshing and saline.

DOMAINE RICHOU *(Anjou)*

Anjou Sec Chauvigné ♀ **$$** With alluring floral perfume, bright citrus, red-berry nuances, and diverse mineral expressions, this bright, compact, refreshing Chenin finishes with an invigorating hint of bitterness.

Coteaux de l'Aubance La Grande Selection SD ♀ **$$$** Nobly rich but moderate in price, this offers layers of creamy fruit laced with flowers on a palate with well-buffered, subtle sweetness.

MATTHIAS ROBLIN *(Sancerre)*

Sancerre ♀ **$$$** This texturally alluring Sancerre from relatively clay-rich soils features citrus, herbs, green tea, and a whiff of petrol.

ROCHERS DES VIOLETTES *(Montlouis)*

Montlouis Demi-Sec SD ♀ **$$$** This subtly sweet Chenin is gorgeously perfumed with citrus, vanilla, and flowers (apple blossom and basswood). Generously juicy, with hints of crushed stone and honey, it manages to be both invigorating and soothingly smooth.

Montlouis Sec Cuvée Touche Mitane ♀ **$$$** This offers lime, blueberry distillate, flowers, herbs, quince, and Chablis-like chicken stock, tinged with iodine, chalk dust, and an exotic hint of blueberry. Clear and pure, pungent and invigorating, dense yet buoyant, it saturates the palate and leaves you intrigued and refreshed.

JEAN-MAX ROGER *(Sancerre, Menetou-Salon)*

Menetou-Salon Moroguès Le Petit Côte ♀ **$$$** Scented with mint and green tea, this user-friendly Sauvignon typically offers a gentle but clear and juicy palate impression and finishes with subtle herbal and mineral notes.

Sancerre Les Caillottes ♀ **$$$** Featuring pungent herbs, currants, melons, and orchard fruits, this Sancerre is luscious and juicy, at times almost a bit loose, but appealingly ripe, soothing, and still refreshing.

JEAN-CLAUDE ROUX *(Quincy)*

Quincy ♀ $$$ Musk melon, ripe pear, and musky floral scents waft decadently from the glass. An oily texture adds to the allure of this elegant Sauvignon and superb value that retains mineral interest and refreshment.

BENEDICTE DE RYCKE *(Coteaux du Loir)*

Coteaux du Loir Tradition ♀ $$$ With a nose of lemon peel, quinine, and flowers, this cuvée displays a tactile sense of citrus rind and chalk dust in the mouth and a substantial, mouth-filling personality, with a juicy, saline finish.

DOMAINE SAINT NICOLAS *(Fièfs Vendéens)*

Fiès Vendéens Jacques ♥ $$$ With a view of the Atlantic, this barrel-aged Pinot Noir and its aromas of raw meat, sour cherry, cherry pit, and iodine pour on ripe, tartly refreshing fruit tinged with chalk and iodine.

DOMAINE DU SALVARD *(Cheverny)*

Cheverny ♀ $ This frequent U.S. ambassador for its appellation is brisk and juicy, yet often quite succulent, with satisfying deep salt, caraway, and chalk-inflected citrus, orchard fruit, and root vegetables.

HERVÉ SÉGUIN *(Pouilly-Fumé)*

Pouilly-Fumé ♀ $$$ Generous helpings of white peach, cassis, flowers, and pungent herbs mingle in an intense concentrated, silken-textured, lush, and luscious palate and seem to flow transparently over a shimmering bed of stones.

CHÂTEAU SOUCHERIE *(Anjou)*

Coteaux du Layon Ⓢ ♀ $$$ This gorgeous and remarkably bargain-priced, nobly sweet Chenin Blanc from Pierre-Yves Tijou and his sons features quince and pear preserves, lily and gardenia, honey and white chocolate, mint, and citrus zest, preserving delicacy and sheer lip-smacking drinkability.

LA SOURCE DU RUAULT *(Saumur-Champigny)*

Saumur Champigny ♥ $$ This Cabernet boasts pure, ripe, bright blackberry fruit with sage oil and ginger pungency; carob; brown spices; and saline, chalky mineral expressions that will truly leave you licking (the residue from) your lips.

DOMAINE DE LA TAILLE AUX LOUPS *(Montlouis, Vouvray)*

Montlouis Sec Les Dix Arpents ♀ $$$ The least expensive of Jacky Blot's barrel-matured Chenins offers lovely flowers, citrus, melons, and orchard fruits. With lift and elegance, this soars to a finish subtly tinged with citrus-zest bitterness and stony, salty minerality.

Vouvray Sec Les Caburoches ♀ $$$ Smelling of apple blossom and musk melon, this offers a pure mouthful of ripe, delicately chalk-tinged melon and orchard fruits and finishes with a faintly alkaline bitterness and suggestion of crushed stone.

F. TINEL-BLONDELET *(Pouilly-Fumé)*

Pouilly-Fumé L'Arret Buffatte ♀ $$$ This displays pungent herbs, pepper, and citrus in an open, elegant, and juicy style of admirable clarity, cut, and brightness.

Pouilly-Fumé Genetin ♀ $$$ Ripe orchard fruits, sweetly aromatic herbs, and crushed stone play major roles in this generous example of its appellation.

LA TOUR SAINT-MARTIN *(Menetou-Salon)*

Menetou-Salon Morogues ♀ $$ Redolent of citrus zest, passion fruit, faintly bitter herbs, melon, and at times gooseberry, this nearly always exhibits a nice sense of textural lushness to complement its bright acidity.

CHÂTEAU DE VAUGAUDRY *(Chinon)*

Chinon ♥ $$ Mint, bell pepper, and salt-tinged bright blackberry are backed by fine-grained tannin, with an abundance of black fruits retaining the upper hand in the finish.

Chinon Rosé ♀ $$ Tart but ripe blackberry, peony, toasted nuts, and saline and alkaline mineral notes offer a whirl of flavor in this bright, thirst-quenching, yet softly textured tribute to its genre.

DOMAINE DES VIEUX PRUNIERS *(Sancerre)*

Sancerre ♀ $$$ Featuring green herbs, citrus, and a Chablis-like chicken-stock character, this refined, subtle, and satisfying Sancerre more than merits its unusually modest price.

CHÂTEAU DE VILLENEUVE *(Saumur and Saumur-Champigny)*

Saumur ♀ $$ A classic exhibition of Chenin Blanc density with vivacity, this seems starched with chalk dust as well as loaded with quince, beeswax, citrus rind, and flowers.

Saumur-Champigny ♥ $$$ Expect this to brim with ripe blackberry and mulberry, nut oils, pungently smoky, spicy Latakia tobacco, and smoked meat, offering a lovely counterpoint of creamy texture and bright fresh fruit.

PROVENCE WINE VALUES

by David Schildknecht

Pretty Not Just in Pink

More than three-quarters of the wine produced in Provence is rosé, and most of that is drunk within the region, both by natives and by the tourists who flock there. Their uncritical comportment in fact goes far toward explaining the existence of an ocean of pink plonk. But it would be not merely a shame but a mistake for American wine lovers to ignore Provence, first off precisely on account of its rosés, the small upper echelon of which are the most interesting as well as delicious pinks on the planet, but also because of a range of distinctively delicious and affordable reds (and a few whites).

Ask a denizen of the Luberon or southern Rhône what part of France he or she inhabits, and chances are you will be told "Provence." In this loose usage, Provence encompasses most of Mediterranean France and much of the Rhône Valley. As an official French wine region, however, Provence begins on the left bank of the Rhône shortly above its Mediterranean delta and extends east to the Italian border and north to the edge of the Alps: large enough, surely, without adding to it! Only a few official appellations of Provence (most of whose wines are too expensive to merit inclusion here) apply to individual villages or small groups of villages. The vast majority fall under one of several umbrella appellations, the most widespread of which is Côtes de Provence.

Grapes

The ubiquitous dry rosé wines of this region feature the grapes familiar from the southern Rhône, heavily weighted toward the **Cinsault** and **Grenache** that are in fact favored for pink wines throughout Mediterranean France. To these are sometimes added small amounts of local Provençal variety **Tibouren**. The evolution of red wines in Provence during the late twentieth century has revealed wonderful synergies between grapes familiar from the southern Rhône— **Grenache, Syrah, Mourvèdre, Carignan**—and **Cabernet Sauvignon,** and several Provence appellations reflect this. Provençal whites, too, share grape varieties with the southern Rhône—notably **Grenache Blanc, Marsanne, Roussanne,** and **Viognier**—however, more prominent roles are assigned to **Clairette** and **Vermentino** (a.k.a. Rolle), and grapes from southwestern France have pitched camp here too: **Sauvignon Blanc, Ugni Blanc,** and occasionally **Sémillon.** Since the vineyards of Provence cover such a vast area and extend from the coast to the foothills of the Alps, the range of styles and favored blends varies considerably. Among red wines, Cabernet, Syrah, and certain variants of Grenache dominate in the higher elevations, while Grenache and Mourvèdre favor the coast. Provençal wines express their exposure to sunshine in ripe flavors and levels of alcohol generally over 13.5%, but they are almost never heavy.

And of Course . . . Don't Forget Corsica!

American wine lovers unfamiliar with the often strikingly delicious and complex wines of Corsica should introduce themselves, if possible, although it must be admitted that relatively few Corsican wines are as yet well distributed in the U.S. Wine is grown around practically the entire perimeter of this island, the best-known growing areas being at its extreme northern and southern tips. The dominant white grape is **Vermentino**, augmented by **Muscat** and **Ugni Blanc**, whereas the reds feature—in addition to **Carignan, Grenache,** and **Syrah**—several indigenous grapes, notably **Nielluccio, Sciaccarellu,** and **Carcagiolu.** It can safely be said that this cast of vine characters, together with the unique microclimates and fiercely proud local populace, make for a range of wines whose like will not be found elsewhere on earth, bold and at times almost savage in a way that seems to reflect the rocky, scrubby landscape. Look out particularly for those of Clos Teddi, Domaine Granjolo, Domaine Leccia, and Domaine Maistracci.

Vintage Smarts

Given the enormous variations in microclimate, soil, grape varieties, and viticultural approaches, it is virtually impossible to generalize about vintage character in Provence and Corsica. The generally high quality of vintage 2007 deserves special mention, however.

Drinking Curves

Most rosé wines of Provence are best enjoyed within a year of bottling, but the very finest (a few of which are still available stateside for $25 or less) can be worth holding 2–3 years. Among reds, it is impossible to generalize, but in the $25 and under range, one will generally be buying wines best enjoyed within 3–6 years of vintage.

Provence's and Corsica's Top Wine Values by Winery

CHÂTEAU DES ANNIBALS *(Coteaux Varois)*

Coteaux Varois Rosé Suivez-Moi Jeune Homme ♀ $$ This Cinsault-Grenache blend's lovely pale color presages the wine's delicacy, refinement, and white wine–like personality. Peach, lemon, resinous herbs, and pungent flowers in the nose usher in a refreshing, generous, yet lightweight palate and a finish in which peach fuzz, herbal oils, and chalk add tactile invigoration.

DOMAINE LA BLAQUE *(Coteaux de Pierrevert)*

Viognier ♀ $$ A refreshingly delicate and juicy rendition of a sadly much-abused variety; redolent of acacia, white peach, and white pepper, with a clean, chalky finish.

Coteaux de Pierrevert Rosé ♀ $ From Grenache and Cinsault with smidgeons of Syrah and Vermentino, this rosé from the aptly named Alpes-de-Haute-Provence is always lushly fruited—suggesting ripe watermelon—and infectiously juicy.

Coteaux de Pierrevert ♟ $ The sensational-value, mouth-filling, intro-level La Blaque red vividly recalls (expensive!) Cornas from the Rhône in its combination of ripe black cherry and raw beef liver tinged with brown spices, augmented by tea, cocoa powder, iodine, and savory shrimp-shell reduction.

CLOS TEDDI *(Corsica [Patrimonio])*

Patrimonio Tradition ♀ $$$ From inaccessibly rugged, stony, dry northern terrain, Marie-Brigitte Poli's oily-rich in texture yet invigoratingly bright white (from Vermentino) offers a fascinating interplay of citrus, wild herbs, wood smoke, and crushed stone.

Patrimonio Tradition ♟ $$$ A memorably intense blend, from its pungent aroma of dried herbs and bittersweet floral notes to the essence of herbs, beef marrow, and sheer stony minerality that positively encamp on the palate.

MAS DE LA DAME *(Les Baux de Provence)*

Les Baux de Provence La Gourmande 🍷 **$$** From the jagged Alpilles mountains immortalized by van Gogh comes this juicy, fruit-filled, intro-level blend of Grenache and Syrah garnished with herbs and black pepper.

DOMAINE DU DRAGON *(Côtes de Provence)*

Côtes de Provence Rosé 🍷 **$$** Featuring melon, pear, and tart red raspberry tinged with herbs, this exuberantly fruity, soft, and white wine–like rosé offers simple but generous satisfaction.

Côtes de Provence Hautes Vignes 🍷 **$** This sensational value— a variable blend of Mourvèdre, Cabernet Sauvignon, Syrah, and Grenache—typically evinces ripe plums, raspberry, roasted meats, bitter herbs, and saline savor; offers amazingly rich texture for a tank-raised red; and finishes with real grip.

Côtes de Provence Cuvée Saint-Michel 🍷 **$$** Matured one year in barrel, this lush, polished blend (generally of Syrah and Cabernet, with Grenache and Mourvèdre) features blackberry, cassis, prune, fennel, parsnip, and roasted meats.

MAS DE GOURGONNIER *(Les Baux de Provence)*

Les Baux de Provence 🍷 **$$** The Mas de Gourgonnier red cuvée blended for the U.S. differs significantly in varietal makeup each vintage, but ripe black fruits, game, and vividly evocative Provençal herbs are always present.

DOMAINE DE GRANJOLO *(Corsica [Porto Vecchio])*

Porto Vecchio 🍷 **$$** This glossy yet refreshing Vermentino grown practically on beach sand at the southern tip of Corsica mingles cress, brown spices, apricot, citrus rind, and melon, and finishes positively tenaciously.

DOMAINE LECCIA *(Corsica [Patrimonio])*

Y.L. 🍷 $$$ With only Yves Leccia's initials scrawled across the label by way of identification, this sappy, concentrated blend features red raspberry and strawberry preserves mingled with rose petals, black tea, and fennel pollen, and clings with fascinating fossil and marine nuances.

DOMAINE MAISTRACCI *(Corsica [Corse Calvi])*

Corse Calvi e Prove 🍷 $$$ This concentrated and palate-searching blend of Grenache, Nielluccio, and a bit of Syrah offers an alluring amalgam of prunes, dates, chocolate, rose hips, wild fennel, rosemary, and pungent suggestions of ocean breeze and sweat.

CHÂTEAU DU ROUËT *(Côtes de Provence)*

Côtes de Provence Rosé Cuvée Esterelle 🍷 $$ From among no fewer than five rosé cuvées at Rouët, this typically mingles melon, blackberry, rhubarb, herbs, and pepper in an aromatic and succulent mélange with tactile finishing pungency.

Côtes de Provence Rosé Cuvée Réservée 🍷 $$ This is meatier, more savory, and more concentrated but less refreshing than the Esterelle. Strawberries, herbs, and saline with carnal undertones fill the palate and inform an impressively concentrated finish.

CHÂTEAU DE ROQUEFORT *(Côtes de Provence)*

Côtes de Provence Rosé Corail 🍷 $$ This innovative and talented vintner blends some Clairette and Vermentino into his "Rhône" reds for a juicy and mouth-filling yet light and invigorating rosé that mingles red raspberry, herbs, salt, and chalk.

TRIENNES *(Coteaux d'Aix-en-Provence)*

Les Aureliens Rouge 🍷 $$$ A project of Burgundy's famous Seysses family (Domaine Dujac), this Cabernet-Syrah blend is notable for its polish and refinement as well as its generosity of red fruit, roasted meat, and herbs.

CHÂTEAU LES VALENTINES *(Côtes de Provence)*

Côtes de Provence Rosé ♟ **\$\$\$** This dry, meaty, herb- and mineral-tinged rosé is far from an afterthought or a by-product of red wine production. Here, pink is taken seriously, which by no means renders the results less delightful!

FRANCE'S SOUTHWEST WINE VALUES

by David Schildknecht

The term "southwest of France"—at least when it comes to wine—is pretty much shorthand for "everything in this quarter of France that's not Bordeaux." Such a vast diversity of places and grapes is thereby incorporated that we can only briefly pause to mention some of those that most often result in distinctively delicious wines of moderate price.

Just upstream along the Dordogne River from Bordeaux are the communes and wines of **Bergerac** and **Monbazillac**, where Sémillon and Sauvignon Blanc dominate in dry and nobly sweet wines, the latter far less expensive than those of Sauternes and in some instances world-class. A host of obscure and indigenous grapes inform wines north of Toulouse in the **Duras, Marmandais, Fronton,** and **Gaillac.** Also north of Toulouse, on either shore of the river Lot, is **Cahors,** traditionally featuring the Malbec (known locally as "Auxerre") and offering numerous reds worthy of value hunters' attention. West toward the Atlantic coast (and surrounding the Armagnac brandy region) lie vast tracts whose inexpensive whites from Ugni Blanc, Colombard, Gros Manseng, Sauvignon Blanc, and Chardonnay are bottled as **Côtes de Gascogne.** South of here lies Madiran, the potential ferocity and tannic intensity of whose local Tannat grape can to some extent be measured by the practice of softening it through the addition of no less formidable varieties than Cabernet Sauvignon and Cabernet Franc. The same applies to the Basque-country reds of Irouléguy farther south. Whites (of appellation Pacherenc du Vic Bilh) from Madiran's neighborhood feature the Gros Manseng and Petit Manseng (occasionally also Arrufiat), which are also the basis for the musky, carnal, mysteriously complex dry and late-harvested sweet wines of Jurançon in the Pyrenean foothills to the south.

Vintage Smarts
Given the enormous variations in microclimate, soil, grape varieties, viticultural approaches, and styles, it is simply impossible within the confines of this guide to generalize about vintage character in France's vast Southwest.

Drinking Curves

Many of Southwest France's red wines are quite robust and worth following for 6 or more years in bottle. The whites—with the exception of sweet wines—are nearly always meant to be drunk young, and those of the popular Côtes de Gascogne as young as possible, and certainly within one year.

Southwest France's Top Wine Values by Winery

DOMAINE ARRETXEA *(Irouléguy)*

Irouléguy 🍷 **$$$** This firm but fine-grained, mouth-coating blend of Tannat and two Cabernets features black fruits, iodine, sealing wax, pungent herbs, grilled red meats, and tar.

CHÂTEAU D'AYDIE (LAPLACE) *(Madiran)*

Château d'Aydie Madiran 🍷 **$$$** This Tannat-based red offers rich, robust, bitter, stony mineral-saturated black fruit.

CHÂTEAU BARRÉJAT *(Pacherenc, Madiran)*

Pacherenc du Vic Bilh 🍷 **$** Aromas of chrysanthemum, narcissus, and citrus oils lead to an oily-textured palate intriguingly laced with musky, bittersweet floral essences.

Madiran 🍷 **$$** Blackberry, kirsch, nut oil, and buddleia inform this ripe, user-friendly, unusually supple Madiran.

DOMAINE BELLEGARDE *(Jurançon)*

Jurançon Cuvée La Pierre Blanche 🍷 **$$** This Petit Manseng–based white evokes narcissus, peppermint, white pepper, and orange, lemon zest, musk, toasted sunflower seeds; and wood smoke rises from the glass. The first sip grips with oily texture and penetrating pungency, after which the wine won't let go!

DOMAINE LA BERANGERAIE *(Cahors)*

Cahors Cuvée Maurin 🍷 **$$** This tank-raised Malbec displays juicy cassis and elderberry backed by fine-grained tannins and an expansive finish tinged with humus, black pepper, and iodine.

DOMAINE BORDENAVE *(Jurançon)*

Jurançon Sec Souvenirs d'Enfance 🍷 **$$** This oily-rich yet bright introduction to the mysterious and too-little-known Jurançon incorporates lemon oil, musk, and black pepper, finishing long, savory, saline, zesty, and peppery.

Jurançon Moelleux Harmonie **[S]** 🍷 **$$$** Decadent and exotic in aroma, mingling musk, orange blossom, and mushrooms, this is creamy and oily, its orange liqueur and nut paste complimented by high residual sugar.

DOMAINE CASSAGNOLES *(Côtes de Gascogne)*

Côtes de Gascogne 🍷 **$** This multigrape blend smells faintly grassy as well as distinctively saline, and a bracing, invigorating palate presence follows suit. Fresh lime, salt, sage, and pepper make for a pleasingly pungent finish.

Côtes de Gascogne Sauvignon 🍷 **$** This offers grassy, saline, and fresh lime aromas and flavors but displays more sap and generosity than the corresponding blend, with honeydew melon and mint making for a refreshing and aromatically alluring refrigerator white.

DOMAINE CAUHAPÉ *(Jurançon)*

Jurançon Chante des Vignes 🍷 **$$$** This 100% Gros Manseng from the region's best-known estate features pineapple fruit accented by hints of honey, musk, and brown spices; a subtly oily palate; and subtle tartness balancing honeyed richness.

CHÂTEAU LA COLOMBIÈRE *(Fronton)*

Fronton Cuvée Coste Rouge 🍷 **$$$** This pungent, tannic Négrette offers intense aromas of Szechuan peppercorns, fennel, and toasted nuts, leading to a mouthful of black fruits and herbal concentrates shot through with pepper and smoke.

CLOS LA COUTALE *(Cahors)*

Cahors 🍷 **$$** This satin-textured, palpably dense, yet bright-finishing blend of Malbec with a bit of Merlot saturates the palate with white pepper– and cardamom-dusted dark stewed fruits, nut oils, black walnut, braised fennel, and dark chocolate.

DOMAINE ETXEGARAYA *(Irouléguy)*

Irouléguy 🍷 **$$$** A blackish, chewy blend of Tannat, Cabernet Franc, and Malbec, this smells of ripe mulberries and blackberries mingled with sage, boxwood, and smoky, toasted nuts, leaving a dark stain of salted, smoke-tinged, bitter black fruit.

Irouléguy Lehengoa 🍷 **$$$** This ominously dark and smoky Tannat from ancient vines offers an implosive and persistent concentration of bitter black fruits allied to salts, chalk, wet stone, red licorice, and toasted nuts.

CHÂTEAU FLOTIS *(Fronton)*

Fronton Carré Violet 🍷 **$** This Négrette-based blend displays cooked black fruits mingled with toasted nuts, game, and smoked meats, leading to a finish of impressive sheer grip.

DOMAINE GENOUILLAC *(Gaillac Burgale)*

Gaillac Burgale 🍷 **$$** This opaque and satisfyingly grainy-textured blend of Syrah with the local Duras and Fer Servadou evokes ripe purple plums, black licorice, lavender, toasted nuts, and smoked meat.

GRANDE MAISON *(Bergerac, Monbazillac)*

Bergerac Sec Sophie 🍷 **$$** Displaying melon, lime, and fig variations on Sauvignon and Sémillon, this offers richness and polish rare for its appellation and price.

Monbazillac Cuvée des Anges ⑤ 🍷 **$$$** Here is the true character of noble rot at an unbelievable price. Toasted brioche, musk, white truffle, gardenia, honey, and candied citrus rind waft from the glass and inform a rich, creamy, and expansive yet—amazingly— practically levitating elixir.

CHÂTEAU HAUT MONPLAISIR *(Cahors)*

Cahors 🍷 **$$** This 100% Malbec basic bottling full of ripe black raspberry, mulberry tinged with cardamom, white pepper, and peat finishes with refreshingly invigorating salinity, smoky pungency, and bite.

Cahors Prestige ♀ $$$ Notes of cedar, brown spices, and sawdust signal the presence of wood, although this fine-grained wine's fundamental devotion to concentrated salt-, spice-, and pepper–tinged ripe black fruits is never in doubt.

DOMAINE LA HITAIRE *(Côtes de Gascogne)*

Côtes de Gascogne Les Tours ♀ $ Among many Gascogne wines from branches of the Grassa family, this blend evokes musk melon and herbs on an oily-textured palate cut by a juicy note of fresh lemon.

DOMAINE DE MÉNARD *(Côtes de Gascogne)*

Côtes de Gascogne Colombard-Sauvignon ♀ $ This offers a lot of character for an inexpensive Gascogne white, bracing and infectiously refreshing, with emphasis on lime, melon, gooseberry, and herbs.

CHÂTEAU MONTESIER *(Bergerac)*

Bergerac La Tour de Montesier ♀ $ Smelling of fresh lime, mint, honey, and orange zest, this incredible value invigorates and brightens the palate, finishing with satisfying juiciness and subtly bitter notes of citrus oil.

Bergerac Montesier La Tour ♀ $$ This more ambitious, barrel-aged, Sauvignon-dominated cuvée features lemon zest, caraway, toasted grain, and nuts, spices, and herbs in an imposingly rich, subtly oily, yet persistently invigorating performance.

MOUTHES LE BILHAN *(Côtes de Duras)*

Côtes de Duras La Pie Colette ♀ $$ This Merlot features smoke-tinged ripe cassis and blackberry of unexpected exuberance and refreshment, finishing fascinatingly with added suggestions of black olives, toasted nuts, and brine.

PRODUCTEURS PLAIMONT *(Côte St.-Mont, Côtes de Gascogne, Madiran, Pacherenc)*

Pacherenc du Vic Bilh ⬜SD⬜ 🍷 $$ The subtly oily, musky, floral, and elusive charms of the Gros Maneseng make for a fascinating and versatile off-dry libation.

Madiran 1907 🍷 $$ Named for the date the Madiran appellation was expanded to its present size, this Tannat-Cabernet blend preserves freshness and tames the tannins, resulting in an easy introduction to its genre.

DOMAINE DE POUY *(Côtes de Gascogne Blanc)*

Domaine de Pouy Côtes de Gascogne 🍷 $ This ubiquitous, refreshing, yet subtly oily blend of Ugni Blanc and Colombard from Yves Grassa typically displays a quite heady pungency of lime and tangerine zest, brown spices, salt-tinged gooseberry, and peat.

DOMAINE DE RIEUX *(Côtes de Gascogne)*

Domaine de Rieux Côtes de Gascogne 🍷 $ This refreshing Ugni-Colombard blend from Grassa displays a Muscat-like nose of orange blossom, honey, and herbs, with anisette, gooseberry, and citrus oils on the palate. Few are the refrigerators that would not benefit from a bottle of it at all times.

DOMAINE SARRABELLE *(Gaillac)*

Gaillac Saint-André 🍷 $$ This well-concentrated, fine-grained example of the indigenous Fer Servadou grape offers tart yet luscious, ginger-, sage-, and oak-tinged red fruits, along with bloody beefiness.

DOMAINE DU TARIQUET *(Côtes de Gascogne)*

Sauvignon Blanc 🍷 $ From Yves Grassa, this smells of apricot, musk, and passion fruit. Its attractive ripeness is enhanced by subtle oiliness, and a bitter hint of apricot kernel attends the finish.

Chardonnay—Sauvignon Domaine Coté Tarriquet 🍷 $ Apple, ripe honeydew melon, lime, and black currant dominate this distinctly delicious and unorthodox blend whose lightness is accompanied by a subtle creaminess as well as a discreet hint of sweetness that nicely underscores the fruit.

TOUR DES GENDRES *(Bergerac)*

Bergerac Classique 🍷 $$ Bergerac and organic pioneer Luc de Conti render this sappy, gripping, and refreshing yet texturally rich example of unadorned, pure Sémillon and Sauvignon tinged with citrus zest and resinous herbs.

RHÔNE VALLEY WINE VALUES

by Robert M. Parker, Jr.

If the dollar hadn't collapsed over the last several years, some of the northern Rhônes such as St.-Joseph and Crozes-Hermitage would still be priced at $25 and under. One day, if history repeats itself, the dollar will rebound, and these wines will offer better value than they do today. Those are the two major appellations of the north, where the best bargains are, simply because the vineyard areas are much larger and the wines do not have the prestige or rarity that one finds in the very expensive wines of Hermitage, Côte Rôtie, Condrieu, and Cornas. However, there are some northern Rhône producers who make Côtes du Rhône just outside of the more prestigious appellations, and these can often be found for $25 and under.

The treasure trove of values that has existed for decades and continues to be one of the great sources for frugal consumers is the Côtes du Rhône and Côtes du Rhône-Villages appellations in the southern Rhône. With over 100,000 acres in vines and innumerable *terroirs* and microclimates, with much of the quality controlled by large cooperatives, quality ranges from insipid and sterile to very good to excellent. Readers need to focus on the estate-bottled level, where some terrific overachievers make beautiful wines that sell for a song. Also, several cooperatives, with custom cuvées culled by specialist American importers, turn out some gorgeous wines. Virtually 95% or more of all the Côtes du Rhônes are red wines, but there is some white and rosé produced. Moreover, the appeal of the Côtes du Rhônes and the Côtes du Rhône-Villages is enhanced by the fact that so many good vintages have emerged after the washout of 2002 and a torridly hot and irregular 2003.

Vintage Smarts and Drinking Curves

2004 is a good year, 2005 an excellent one; 2006 is at least very good, and for the southern Rhônes, 2007 is the greatest vintage in the last 30 years! For the most part, these wines are all meant to be drunk in their exuberant youthfulness, although some of the red wines from very good domaines in the Côtes du Rhône and Côtes du Rhône-Villages can last for up to a decade or more.

Other southern Rhône appellations that sometimes come in at $25 and under are Vacqueyras, occasionally Gigondas, Rasteau, Lirac, and of course the rosés of Tavel. Forget Châteauneuf-du-Pape. As great as its wines can be, they are no longer under $25. Moreover, most Vacqueyras, Gigondas, or the sweeter Beaumes-de-Venise are also going to be too expensive to qualify as best buys, but some can be found.

Lastly, for whites and rosés, both 2007 and 2008 are the vintages of choice, and the 2007 reds are the pick of the litter. The 2006s are very good, the 2005s excellent, and the 2004s good. Anything older than that needs to be approached with caution.

The Rhône Valley's Top Wine Values by Winery

DOMAINE ALARY *(Cairanne)*

Côtes du Rhône Font d'Estevans 🍷 $$$ Deep and rich with blacker fruits, this is a heady, succulent red.

Côtes du Rhône Font d'Estevans 🍷 $$$ Made from Alary's oldest vines; Chablis-like aromatics are followed by a medium-bodied, fresh, lively wine.

Côtes du Rhône La Gerbaude 🍷 $ A richly fruity, medium-bodied, elegant, complex red.

Vin de Pays Roussanne La Grange Daniel 🍷 $ Made from 100% Roussanne, this white exhibits good acidity, crisp rose-petal and floral notes, medium body, and a fresh, fruity finish with no evidence of oak.

DOMAINE DE L'AMAUVE *(Séguret)*

Côtes du Rhône-Villages Séguret Réserve 🍷 $$$ This pure, medium-bodied Côtes du Rhône–Villages displays a supple, silky-textured personality.

CHÂTEAU LES AMOUREUSES *(Côtes du Rhône)*

Côtes du Rhône La Barbare 🍷 $$$ This is a sensational Côtes du Rhône that has more in common with top-notch Châteauneuf-du-Pape than most Côtes du Rhônes. It is full bodied, pure, and deep.

Côtes du Rhône Les Charmes 🍷 $$$ Plenty of lively, peppery roasted herbs and sweet berry fruit, medium to full body, and beautiful purity in an up-front style.

Côtes du Rhône Cuvée Spéciale 🍷 $$$ This very pure, elegant Côtes du Rhônes is spicy and medium to full bodied.

DOMAINE D'ANDÉZON *(Côtes du Rhône)*

Côtes du Rhône 🍷 $ Possesses a lovely texture, crisp acids, medium to full body, and a long, smooth finish.

Côtes du Rhône–Villages La Granacha Signargues 🍷 $$$ A superb, full-bodied red with terrific precision, definition, and concentration.

DOMAINE LES APHILLANTHES *(Côtes du Rhône)*

Côtes du Rhône 🍷 $$ A straightforward bistro/brasserie-style red.

Côtes du Rhône Cairanne L'Ancestrale du Puits 🍷 $$$ Cairannes can be earthy and almost Burgundy-like in their tannin structure, but the Côtes du Rhône Cairanne L'Ancestrale du Puits exhibits plenty of cherry fruit intermixed with pepper and spice.

Côtes du Rhône Les Cros 🍷 $$$ This wine is deep and has the inkiest color and a chewy, espresso-roast, blackberry nose, but not the complexity and Provençal personality of the other wines from this estate.

Côtes du Rhône–Villages Les Galets 🍷 $$$ The brilliant Les Galets is complex, medium to full bodied, and has no hard edges.

DOMAINE D'ARBOUSSET *(Côtes du Rhône)*

Côtes du Rhône 🍷 $$ This solid, straightforward Côtes du Rhône is a silky, sensual wine best drunk over its first several years.

MAISON ARNOUX & FILS *(Vacqueyras)*

Vacqueyras Seigneur de Lauris 🍷 $$$ The powerful, concentrated, impressively endowed Vacqueyras Seigneur de Lauris is a deep, tannic, structured, dense red with gorgeous levels of sweet black cherry and blackberry fruit.

Vacqueyras Vieux Clocher 🍷 $$$ Possesses very good acidity as well as plenty of earth, licorice, black cherry, and plum-like fruit, and attractive sweet tannins.

BARGEMONE *(Coteaux d'Aix-en-Provence)*

Coteaux d'Aix-en-Provence 🍷 $ This has long been one of France's most delicious rosés. Drink it within its first 6–9 months of release.

Coteaux d'Aix-en-Provence 🍷 $ The Coteaux d'Aix-en-Provence white exhibits crisp white fruit and citrus notes, fresh acidity, light to medium body, and a good finish.

Coteaux d'Aix-en-Provence Cuvée Marina 🍷 $$ A new cuvée for this estate, the Cuvée Marina is a bit fuller than the Coteaux d'Aix-en-Provence and includes slightly more Syrah in the blend.

Coteaux d'Aix-en-Provence Cuvée Marina 🍷 $$ This Cuvée Marina red displays a touch of oak along with good stuffing, attractive berry fruit, a hint of wet stones, and a spicy finish.

Coteaux d'Aix-en-Provence Cuvée Marina 🍷 $$ The Cuvée Marina white offers up aromas of lemon blossoms, quince, licorice, and white currants in an attractive, light- to medium-bodied style.

DOMAINE BASTIDE DU CLAUX *(Côtes du Luberon)*

Malacare Côtes du Luberon 🍷 $$ This medium- to full-bodied, strikingly Pinot Noir–like cuvée shows the potential for complexity as well as freshness from the Côtes du Luberon.

LA BASTIDE ST.-DOMINIQUE *(Côtes du Rhône)*

Côtes du Rhône Jules Rochelonne 🍷 $$$ This is serious Côtes du Rhône, sexy, round, and medium to full bodied.

Côtes du Rhône–Villages 🍷 $$ The Côtes du Rhône–Villages is soft, round, and attractive.

DOMAINE DE LA BASTIDONNE *(Côtes du Ventoux)*

Les Coutilles Côtes du Ventoux 🍷 $$ The Les Coutilles displays moderate tannins, a hint of wood, and plenty of black cherry and currant notes intermixed with some Provençal herbs.

Les Puits Neufs Côtes du Ventoux 🍷 $$$ A real star, this sumptuous wine is medium to full bodied and silky smooth.

DOMAINE BEAU MISTRAL *(Rasteau)*

Côtes du Rhône-Villages St.-Martin 🍷 $$$ A brilliant effort composed of 45% old-vine Grenache and the rest old-vine Syrah along with a dollop of Mourvèdre, this is a peppery, earthy, dense, purple-colored, full-bodied, heady wine that captures the beautiful fragrance of the top reds from the southern Rhône and Provence.

Côtes du Rhône-Villages Rasteau 🍷 $$$ The Rasteau is rich and fruity with decent acidity as well as ripe tannin.

Côtes du Rhône-Villages Rasteau Cuvée Florinaelle 🍷 $$$ Compared to the "regular" Rasteau, the Rasteau Cuvée Florianaelle is similarly styled but fuller bodied with more richness, depth, structure, and tannin. It can benefit from 2–3 years of cellaring but can drink well for 12–15.

CHÂTEAU BEAUCASTEL *(Rhône Valley)*

Beaucastel Côtes du Rhône Coudoulet 🍷 $$$ Expansive, broadly flavored, and full bodied with no hard edges, its gorgeous fruit purity and long, spicy, heady finish make this wine almost the bottled essence of Provence.

Beaucastel Côtes du Rhône Coudoulet 🍷 $$$ This white can be outstanding. Dry, medium bodied, with good acidity, wonderful freshness, and obviously no oak whatsoever, it is a tasty, food-friendly wine.

Perrin et Fils Côtes du Rhône 🍷 $ The Perrin et Fils Côtes du Rhône is lovely, supple textured, and finishes round and generously.

Perrin et Fils Côtes du Rhône Réserve 🍷 $ This wine has excellent freshness, an invigorating, rich midpalate, and good acidity and spice in the finish.

Perrin et Fils Côtes du Rhône Réserve 🍷 $ This white possesses nice nectarine, apricot, and honeysuckle notes in a medium-bodied, dry, fruity style.

Perrin et Fils Côtes du Rhône-Villages ♗ $ An elegant, medium-bodied wine with superb aromatics and good depth, flesh, and length.

Perrin et Fils Côtes du Rhône-Villages Vinsobres Les Cornuds ♗ $$ With the beautiful freshness and liveliness that comes from higher-elevation and cooler-climate vineyards in the northern part of the southern Rhône, this wine is medium bodied, pure, elegant, and very Burgundy-like.

DOMAINE DES BERNARDINS *(Côtes du Rhône-Villages)*

Côtes du Rhône-Villages Beaumes-de-Venise ♗ $$ This wine exhibits elegance, good depth, and sweet black raspberry, pepper, earth, and spice characteristics, along with impressive freshness and laser-like clarity.

Doré des Bernardins Dry Muscat VdP ♗ $ This totally dry Muscat is a gorgeously flowery, peachy, dry, crisp, fresh, delicious effort that is bursting with personality. Enjoy it during its first year.

DOMAINE BOISSON *(Cairanne)*

Domaine Boisson Côtes du Rhône ♗ $$ Finished with a screw cap (a rarity in France), this is a delicious, sexy Provençal fruit bomb, medium to full bodied, lush, and fruity.

Domaine Boisson Côtes du Rhône-Villages Cairanne ♗ $$$ The outstanding Côtes du Rhône-Villages Cairanne is dense and chewy as well as elegant, pure, and flavorful.

Domaine Boisson Côtes du Rhône-Villages Cairanne l'Exigence ♗ $$$ A fruit-dominated wine possessing remarkable complexity, superb balance, and flawless harmony among all of its elements.

Domaine Boisson Côtes du Rhône-Villages Cairanne Clos de la Brussière Massif d'Uchaux ♗ $$$ The abundant fruit of this red admirably counterbalances its structure. It is deep, chewy, full bodied, superpure, and gorgeously textured.

Alain Boisson Côtes du Rhône-Villages Cairanne Cros de Romet ♗ $$$ This wine combines extravagant levels of fruit with compelling earthiness and spice. The result is a wine with incredibly complex, explosive aromatics and stunning fruit and richness, all presented in a full-bodied, flawlessly constructed style.

DOMAINE BRAMADOU *(Roaix)*

Roaix Côtes du Rhône-Villages 🍷 $$ Made in a medium-bodied, pure, elegant style that has no hard edges and just screeches Provence, this surprisingly soft, deep-ruby wine is meant for near-term consumption in a bistro setting.

ANDRÉ BRUNEL *(Côtes du Rhône)*

Côtes du Rhône Sommelongue Massif Duchaux 🍷 $$ This mostly Grenache cuvée exhibits excellent depth, with sweet black cherry notes intermixed with pepper and *garrigue* in a distinctive Provençal style.

DOMAINE DE LA BRUNÉLY *(Vacqueyras)*

Vacqueyras 🍷 $$$ This charming, fruity, elegant red possesses a nearly Pinot Noir–like style, but its classic Provençal character assures that it is from the southern Rhône.

DOMAINE DU CAILLOU *(Côtes du Rhône)*

Côtes du Rhône Bouquet des Garrigues 🍷 $$$ This wine tastes like the essence of Provence, spicy and peppery, with notes of lavender, roasted herbs, and plenty of sweet kirsch notes and black fruits.

PHILIPPE CAMBIE *(Côtes du Rhône)*

Côtes du Rhône Calendal 🍷 $$$ Beautiful ripeness, medium to full body, and superb purity characterize this lovely Côtes du Rhône.

DOMAINE CHAMFORT *(Vacqueyras)*

Vacqueyras 🍷 $$$ A superb offering, this wine exhibits full-bodied, powerful flavors of blueberries, blackberries, and earth. It is deep and chewy with noticeable but sweet tannin and a heady, spicy finish.

CHAPOUTIER *(Rhône Valley)*

Coteaux de Tricastin La Ciboise 🍷 $ The bistro-styled La Ciboise is a fruit-driven wine, light and ideal for uncritical quaffing or a simple picnic. It is mostly Grenache.

Coteaux de Tricastin Château des Establiers ♟ **$$** Chapoutier's excellent Château des Establiers comes from an area best known for superb black truffles. The wine has terrific fruit and is ripe, medium bodied, and filled with personality and character.

Côtes du Rhône Belleruche ♟ **$** Delicious, in a straightforward, fruity style with good body and seductive aromatics.

Côtes du Rhône Belleruche ♟ **$** This deliciously fruity, clean, medium-bodied wine bursts at the seams with personality and character. It is food-friendly and best drunk over its first several years.

Crozes Hermitage Les Meysonnières ♟ **$$** One of the better bargains in the Chapoutier portfolio. It boasts a sweet, blackberry, *herbes de Provence,* cassis-scented nose, crisp acidity, sweet, ripe berry flavors, medium body, and a soft finish.

Crozes Hermitage La Petite Ruche ♟ **$$** Loaded with fruit, this wine reveals a charming nose, ripe, mineral/orange–like flavors, excellent purity, and a crisp, dry finish. It can drink well for several years.

Gigondas ♟ **$$$** From totally destemmed fruit dominated by Grenache, this wine has good minerality and some spring flowers as well as earthiness.

Les Granges de Mirabel ♟ **$** This comes from volcanic soils and is an inexpensive Viognier that could easily pass for a Condrieu in a blind tasting.

Rasteau ♟ **$$$** Scorched earth, chocolate-covered cherries, pepper, and spice are all present in this attractive wine.

St.-Joseph Deschants ♟ **$$$** The regular cuvée of St.-Joseph, Les Deschants has personality, zesty acidity, and rather cool-climate red fruits with a stony minerality beneath them. It is delicious, with more substance than one expects of a *négociant* blend.

St.-Joseph Deschants ♟ **$$** This elegant and fresh white exhibits wonderful orange and nectarine notes with some honeyed citrus in a dry, fruity, medium-bodied style.

G.A.E.C. CHARVIN *(Côtes du Rhône)*

Côtes du Rhône Le Poutet 🍷 $$ A noteworthy choice for bargain hunters, this red exhibits plenty of kirsch liqueur, excellent ripeness, medium body, no hard edges, and loads of Provençal personality and soul.

Vin de Pays à Côté 🍷 $ Charvin's newest offering, a blend of 50% Grenache and 50% Merlot, is his comical takeoff on the movie *Sideways*. À Côté (French for "sideways") is surprisingly good, with very attractive, plump, gamy black cherry and chocolatey fruit intermixed with some cedar and sweet cherries.

CHAVE *(négociant label)* *(Côtes du Rhône)*

Côtes du Rhône Mon Coeur 🍷 $$$ A sensational wine offering superb purity, texture, and richness.

AUGUSTE CLAPE *(Rhône Valley)*

Côtes du Rhône 🍷 $$ A Syrah made just outside Cornas, this wine exhibits plenty of scorched-earth and black-fruit characteristics in its medium-bodied, pure, natural personality.

St.-Péray 🍷 $$ The Marsanne-dominated St.-Péray offers attractive notes of white currants, citrus oil, and a stony liqueur character that combine to give it an undeniable Chablis-like personality.

Vin des Amis Vin de Table (nonvintage) 🍷 $ Bargain hunters should always check out Clape's declassified Syrah called Vin des Amis. This nonvintage wine does not possess the complexity of Clape's top Cornas offerings, but it reveals more than a casual similarity to those wines.

CLOS CHANTEDUC *(Côtes du Rhône)*

Yves Gras of Domaine Santa Duc makes this wine for the brilliant restaurant critic and food writer Patricia Wells.

Côtes du Rhône 🍷 $$ Exhibiting classic characteristics of *garrigue*, fresh ground pepper, kirsch, licorice, and spice, this complex wine smells like the essence of an open-air market in Provence.

DOMAINE LA COLLIÈRE *(Rasteau)*

Côtes du Rhône 🍷 $$ A noteworthy red revealing full-bodied opulence and a layered, lush, succulent mouth-feel.

Côtes du Rhône Cuvée Oubliée 🍷 $$$ Dense, rich, and succulent, this wine boasts extraordinary intensity and full-bodied power.

Côtes du Rhône-Villages Rasteau 🍷 $$$ The excellent Côtes du Rhône-Villages Rasteau is a full-bodied, powerfully concentrated, meaty, expansive, substantial wine.

DOMAINES DES COTEAUX DES TRAVERS *(Rhône Valley)*

Cairanne 🍷 $$$ The surprisingly juicy, fruit-forward style of this wine moves away from the almost overt earthiness and spiciness of most wines from this appellation. This is a modern-style Cairanne, seductive, rich, fleshy, and surprisingly deep and long.

Rasteau 🍷 $$$ The basic cuvée of Rasteau boasts terrific fruit intensity, with notes of licorice and black cherries as well as hints of white chocolate and earth.

Rasteau Cuvée Prestige 🍷 $$$ Clearly dominated by its Grenache, this red has great fruit, full body, and a sumptuous texture, but can also exhibit higher acids and austere, firm, masculine tannins.

DOMAINE COURBIS *(St.-Joseph)*

St.-Joseph 🍷 $$$ The St.-Joseph from Domaine Courbis exhibits ripe cherry and strawberry fruit, light tannin, and an elegant personality. This is a rich, stylish example of the appellation.

DOMAINE LE COUROULU *(Vacqueyras)*

Vacqueyras Cuvée Classique 🍷 $$$ An undeniable bargain for a top-notch southern Rhône, this wine possesses incredible purity and richness as well as mouth-coating flavor intensity. It is medium to full bodied, fleshy, and pure.

CROS DE LA MÛRE *(Côtes du Rhône)*

Côtes du Rhône 🍷 $$ A sensational Côtes du Rhône, with a sweet, jammy, fruit-dominated palate, a big bouquet, silky tannins, and lush concentration.

DELAS FRÈRES *(Rhône Valley)*

Côtes du Rhône St.-Esprit 🍷 $ A blacker-style Côtes du Rhône with plenty of blueberry, blackberry, tar, and chocolatey notes in a medium- to full-bodied, ripe, deliciously fruity, and pure style.

Côtes du Ventoux 🍷 $ Mostly Grenache with small quantities of Syrah and Carignan, this bistro-style red is a front-end-loaded, fruity wine that is seductive and sensual.

Vacqueyras Domaine des Gênets 🍷 $$$ A blend of equal parts Syrah and Grenache, an unusual combination for Vacqueyras, this full-bodied effort oozes with blackberry and cassis fruit as well as lavender and *garrigue* in the background.

DOMAINE DES ESCARAVAILLES *(Rasteau, Roaix, and Cairanne)*

Les Antimagnes Côtes du Rhône 🍷 $ A heck of a bargain, this is a classic Côtes du Rhône in a medium-bodied, supple-textured, delicious style.

Cairanne Le Ventabren 🍷 $$$ Medium bodied in a slightly fresher, more Burgundian style than the Les Antimagnes.

Rasteau Heritage 🍷 $$$ An absolute blockbuster, with an almost Rayas-like kirsch/raspberry component, this wine displays terrific purity, medium to full body, and great length and ripeness.

Rasteau La Ponce 🍷 $$$ Full-bodied power and intensity characterize this wine, a blend of Grenache and Syrah from the high-elevation vineyards of Rasteau.

Roaix Les Hautes Granges 🍷 $$$ A real backward Côtes du Rhône-Villages, this is a beautiful wine with loads of lavender intertwined with cassis and forest floor. It is sumptuous and very Provençal (not always the case with Syrah from the south).

DOMAINE DE L'ESPIGOUETTE *(Vacqueyras)*

Vacqueyras 🍷 $$$ This Vacqueyras is impressively endowed and juicy, offering plenty of character and Provençal typicity as well as medium to full body.

DOMAINE DE FERRAND *(Côtes du Rhône)*

Côtes du Rhône Vieilles Vignes 🍷 $$$ Ferrand's Côtes du Rhône have much in common characteristically with the Châteauneuf-du-Papes. They are not quite as dense or as potentially long-lived, but they reveal complex notes of incense, seaweed, and salty ocean breezes intermixed with blacker fruits, roasted herbs, and meat juices.

FERRATON *(Crozes-Hermitage)*

Côtes du Rhône Samorens 🍷 $ Made mostly from Grenache Blanc, this wine displays plenty of citrus and hints of white peach in a tasty, medium-bodied, fresh, lively style.

Crozes-Hermitage La Matinière 🍷 $$$ Pure charm and finesse, this wine reveals pretty strawberry and cherry fruit intermixed with roasted herbs and earth.

Crozes-Hermitage La Matinière 🍷 $$$ A fruity, full-bodied wine that can drink nicely for 2–4 years, possibly longer.

DOMAINE FONDRECHE *(Côtes du Ventoux)*

Côtes du Ventoux Éclat 🍷 $$ This super wine is a blend of Roussanne, Grenache, Bourboulenc, and Clairette. With crisp acidity, it is evidence of the fabulous progression of quality that has taken place in the Côtes du Ventoux, still a treasure trove for value.

Côtes du Ventoux Fayard 🍷 $$ A blend of Carignan, Mourvèdre, Syrah, and a big dollop of Grenache, this is a very satisfying, pretty wine that you can never tire of drinking.

Côtes du Ventoux Nadal 🍷 $$$ A blend of mostly old-vine Grenache (vines planted in 1936) and old-vine Syrah, and the rest Mourvèdre, this red is full bodied, fleshy, and rich.

Mas Fondreche Côtes du Ventoux O'Sud 🍷 $$ This straightforward picnic-style wine has loads of crunchy raspberry and cherry fruit and some herbs, pepper, and spice, but an easygoing personality.

LA FONT DE PAPIER *(Vacqueyras)*

Vacqueyras 🍷 $$$ This Vacqueyras can be a dense, tannic, powerful effort to drink over a decade in strong vintages. In less successful years, it can be straightforward and one-dimensional and provide pleasurable drinking over several years.

DOMAINE DU FONTENILLE *(Provence)*

Côtes du Luberon 🍷 $ A superaromatic wine, this cuvée exhibits loads of pepper, earth, black cherry, and dusty, loamy soil notes. The wine's fruit, earthiness, and spiciness are classic characteristics of Provence. Seriously endowed and medium to full bodied, with excellent purity as well as depth, it should drink well for 2–3 years.

DOMAINE FONT SARADE *(Vacqueyras)*

Vacqueyras Cuvée Classique 🍷 $$$ The medium- to full-bodied and supple-textured Vacqueyras Cuvée Classique is a delicious, pure, well-balanced red.

Vacqueyras Cuvée Prestige 🍷 $$$ The controversial Vacqueyras Cuvée Prestige is aged in new oak and is certainly concentrated and well made, but it is somewhat atypical. The oak will integrate to a certain extent, but this is not your grandmother's Vacqueyras.

DOMAINE LA FOURMONE *(Vacqueyras)*

Vacqueyras Trésor du Poète 🍷 $$$ Primarily Grenache with a touch of Syrah, this delicious wine is medium to full bodied, luscious, fresh, and pure.

CUVÉE DES GALETS *(Côtes du Rhône)*

Côtes du Rhône Terre du Mistral 🍷 $ A terrific Côtes du Rhône that sells for a song, this wine possesses sweetness as well as loads of pepper, lavender, *garrigue*, kirsch, and licorice.

Vin de Pays de Gard 🍷 $ Revealing plenty of Grenache characteristics in its sweet cherry–, pepper–, and spice–scented nose, this good bistro-style red exhibits luscious fruit in its medium-bodied, easygoing style.

DOMAINE LA GARRIGUE *(Côtes du Rhône)*

Côtes du Rhône Cuvée Romaine 🍷 $$ A custom cuvée for importer Eric Solomon made from 60- to 90-year-old vines, this is all that a Côtes du Rhône should be. Full bodied and rich, this wine is luscious and heady. It is a remarkable wine, but readers who purchase it should be sure it has the Eric Solomon strip label since the same wine, bottled much later, is sold in other markets. In my opinion, those wines have lost a lot of their freshness.

Vacqueyras 🍷 $$$ The Vacqueyras (mostly Grenache and a bit of Mourvèdre), also a special bottling for Eric Solomon, is deep, full bodied, and intense, with beautiful purity, a layered mouth-feel, and a heady finish.

JEAN-MICHEL GÉRIN *(Rhône Valley)*

Syrah Vin de Pays 🍷 $ A red meant for easygoing drinking at a French bistro or brasserie.

Viognier Vin de Pays 🍷 $ The Viognier from Gerin is pleasant but not nearly as good as the one from his neighbor Michel Ogier.

ÉTIENNE GONNET DE FONT DU VENT *(Côtes du Rhône)*

Côtes du Rhône Confidentia 🍷 $$$ The Confidentia is a big, rich, inky Côtes du Rhône with sweet tannin, low acidity, and copious quantities of blackberry and charcoal-infused fruit with a hint of lavender.

Côtes du Rhône Notre Passion 🍷 $ The Notre Passion shows full body and loads of strawberry and black cherry fruit in a sexy, plush, concentrated, round, and generous style.

Côtes du Rhône Les Promesses 🍷 $ A blend of Grenache, Syrah, and Mourvèdre, the Les Promesses is a more elegant, lighter, and more superficial wine than its stablemates.

DOMAINE GRAMENON *(Côtes du Rhône)*

Côtes du Rhône 🍷 $$ A 100% Grenache wine with a Burgundy-like, smoky, animal, Pinot Noir–scented nose, as well as gobs of black-cherry fruit, an expansive, soft texture, superb purity, and a refreshing, deliciously fruity, velvety mouth-feel.

Côtes du Rhône Ceps Centenaires La Mémé 🍷 $$$ Produced from 100-plus-year-old Grenache vines, this is a lovely medium- to full-bodied, fruit-driven effort.

Côtes du Rhône A. Pascal 🍷 $$$ The A. Pascal is a leaner, more austere style of wine, but there is plenty of depth to it.

Côtes du Rhône Sierra du Sud 🍷 $$$ A natural, artisanal wine, offering a deep color and plenty of kirsch notes.

DOMAINE LES GRANDS BOIS *(Côtes du Rhône)*

Côtes du Rhône Trois Soeurs 🍷 $ A big, full-bodied, opulent Côtes du Rhône.

Côtes du Rhône-Villages Cairanne Cuvée Maximilien 🍷 $$ This big wine exhibits fabulous intensity and texture as well as a full-bodied mouth-feel, but no hard edges (despite the fact that approximately one-third of the wine is made from Mourvèdre). It exhibits terrific fruit as well as noble sweetness and *sucrosité* (the wine is totally dry).

Côtes du Rhône-Villages Cuvée Philippine 🍷 $$ This gorgeous expression of the southern Rhône Valley is pure, dense, and flamboyant. It saturates the palate but has no hard edges.

Côtes du Rhône-Villages Rasteau Cuvée Marc 🍷 $$$ Extremely full bodied, muscular, and dense, but neither hard nor astringent, this is a superconcentrated, beautifully pure wine possessing tremendous focus and vibrancy.

DOMAINE GRAND NICOLET *(Rasteau)*

Côtes du Rhône 🍷 $$ A heck of a wine that sells for a song, with its notes of raspberry, cherry, and earth, this deep ruby/purple-tinged wine oozes Provence.

Rasteau Vieilles Vignes 🍷 $$$ This wine exhibits the dense purple color and chewy, sweet floral fruit of old-vine Grenache, with wonderful texture and an almost inky richness as well as tremendous intensity and length. If this wine were from Châteauneuf-du-Pape, it would probably sell for two or three times the price. It is a brilliant wine that doesn't usually hit its peak until 2–3 years after release.

Rasteau Les Esqueyrons 🍷 $$$ Essentially the equivalent of a single-vineyard Rasteau, Grenache gets top billing in this wine, which is very rich, with fabulous intensity, purity, and depth.

DOMAINE GRAND VENEUR *(Côtes du Rhône)*

Domaine Grand Veneur Côtes du Rhône-Villages Les Champauvins 🍷 $$ Always a winner, this classic example of southern France is a pure wine in a medium- to full-bodied, ripe, lovely style.

Grand Veneur (Alain Jaume) Côtes du Rhône Réserve 🍷 $$ The medium-bodied Côtes du Rhône Réserve shows sweet kirsch fruit, an endearing texture, and no hardness.

Grand Veneur (Alain Jaume) Côtes du Ventoux Les Gélinottes 🍷 $ This is a classic French *vin de plaisir*. Soft, lovely, not complex, but with medium body and loads of fruit, this is a pretty example of a wine meant for drinking, not introspection.

Grand Veneur (Alain Jaume) Lirac Clos de Sixte 🍷 $$$ More tannin, minerality, and structure are found in the Lirac Clos de Sixte than in the other offerings from Alain Jaume.

Grand Veneur (Alain Jaume) Vacqueyras Grande Classique 🍷 $$$ Attractive, lush, and a very good wine from this underrated appellation.

GUIGAL *(Rhône Valley)*

Côtes du Rhône 🍷 $ Guigal's red Côtes du Rhône has become a staple of much everyday drinking. Full-bodied, dense, chewy, and ripe, it is a surprisingly big mouthful of juicy, velvety-textured wine.

Côtes du Rhône 🍷 $ This dry, very spicy, and savory Côtes du Rhône rosé is always a winner.

Côtes du Rhône 🍷 $ This is an amazing wine, revealing terrific honeysuckle notes intermixed with some white peach and tangerine skin in a medium-bodied, crisp, fruit-driven style with excellent acidity and depth.

DOMAINE DE LA JANASSE *(Côtes du Rhône)*

Côtes du Rhône 🍷 $$ Excellent texture, medium body, soft tannins, and low acidity make for quite a luscious style of wine.

Côtes du Rhône 🍷 $$ A high-class dry white that comes across like a mineral-laced Chablis from the north, this wine is medium bodied and delicious.

Côtes du Rhône Les Garrigues 🍷 $$$ With fabulous purity, superb texture, and an amazingly long finish, this is a blockbuster Côtes du Rhône at a great price.

Côtes du Rhône-Villages Terre d'Argile 🍷 $$ One of the more brilliant inexpensive wines of the southern Rhône is Janasse's Côtes du Rhône-Villages Terre d'Argile, which essentially means "clay soils." The wine is deep and medium to full bodied.

Vin de Pays Terre de Bussière 🍷 $$ Ripe and medium bodied with excellent acidity and freshness, this wine is not complex, but it is solid and mouth filling.

Viognier Vin de Pays 🍷 $$ A brilliant wine that could pass for a Condrieu but at a much lower price point, this superb, medium-bodied wine is a terrific *vin de pays* and underpriced.

DOMAINE LAFOND *(Côtes du Rhône)*

Côtes du Rhône Roc-Épine 🍷 $ An early-bottled bistro style of wine that is fruity and soft.

Lirac La Ferme Romaine 🍷 $$ Shows notes of lavender and other wild Provençal herbs, with plenty of pepper and oodles of black-cherry fruit in a medium-bodied, pleasure-built style.

Lirac Roc-Épine 🍷 $$ Cut from the same cloth as the Côtes du Rhône Roc-Épine (above), but with more body, fruit, and concentration.

Tavel Roc-Épine 🍷 $$ The superb Tavel Roc-Épine is dry, full-bodied, and slightly austere with superb purity as well as stunning intensity. This beauty should be enjoyed over its first 6–9 months.

PATRICK LESEC SELECTIONS *(Rhône Valley)*

Costières de Nîmes Gilbelle 🍷 $$ The Costières de Nîmes Gilbelle is a *vin de plaisir*—soft, fruity, round, and very savory, very Provençal.

Costières de Nîmes Vieilles Vignes ♟ $$ Deep and rich with no hardness or rusticity, Lesec's Costières de Nîmes Vieilles Vignes can be enjoyed over a decade.

Côtes du Rhône Bouquet ♟ $ This terrific offering shows a nice roasted-herb, scorched-earth, and chocolatey character, impressive ripeness, medium to full body, and a long finish.

Côtes du Rhône Cuvée Richette ♟ $$ A rather solid, dark ruby wine, somewhat monolithic compared to the other cuvées, but well made.

Côtes du Rhône-Villages Beaumes-de-Venise ♟ $$ The Côtes du Rhône-Villages Beaumes-de-Venise is medium bodied with a Provençal-like personality.

Côtes du Rhône-Villages Rasteau Vieilles Vignes ♟ $$$ This can be a powerful, meaty, rustic, and unevolved effort, with full body and some tannins that need resolution. It usually benefits from a few years of aging.

Côtes du Rhône-Villages Rubis ♟ $$ A classic bistro red from Provence, this medium-bodied wine is richly fruity and just out-and-out delicious.

Petite Crau ♟ $ This is what the French call a *vin de table*, but it is also a wine of pleasure. Dense ruby/purple, chunky, fleshy, it has surprising personality and soul for a wine in this price range.

Vacqueyras Vieilles Vignes ♟ $$$ This classic Vacqueyras Vieilles Vignes is an elegant, noble, deep wine that can age nicely for 7–8 years.

LA MAGEANCE *(Côtes du Rhône)*

Visan ♟ $$ A blend of 80% Grenache and 20% Syrah aged in tank and old wood *foudres*, this delicious unfined and unfiltered offering displays a deep ruby/purple color along with plenty of earthy, peppery, blackberry, and cherry fruit, full body, an endearing texture, and a seamless integration of alcohol, acidity, and tannin. It will drink well for 4–5 years following the vintage.

Visan Vieilles Vignes ♟ $$ Composed of 90% Grenache (60-year-old vines) and 10% Syrah (35-year-old vines), this cuvée exhibits sweet black cherry and black currant intertwined with notions of licorice, roasted herbs, and earth. It is a seriously endowed, supple, medium- to full-bodied, pure, impressively textured, long wine.

CHÂTEAU DE MANISSY *(Rhône Valley)*

Côtes du Rhône-Villages Lirac 🍷 \$\$ Beautiful elegance, ripeness, and freshness along with abundant amounts of sweet berry fruit, roasted herbs, pepper, and earth are found in this round, fresh, lively Lirac.

Côtes du Rhône-Villages Tavel 🍷 \$\$ Primarily Grenache with Clairette, Syrah, and Cinsault in the blend, this is a serious, bone-dry rosé revealing a slight austerity as well as copious quantities of fresh strawberry and cherry intermixed with notions of spring flowers and earth. It is big-boned, masculine, and slightly tannic.

MAISON DU MIDI *(Côtes du Rhône)*

Côtes du Rhône-Villages Plan de Dieu 🍷 \$\$\$ A dense, seriously packed and stacked wine, this is a full-bodied, rich, exciting, full-throttle Côtes du Rhône-Villages.

Côtes du Rhône-Villages Rasteau 🍷 \$\$\$ The exceptional Côtes du Rhône-Villages Rasteau is full bodied, muscular, and heady.

DOMAINE DE MARCOUX *(Châteauneuf-du-Pape)*

Côtes du Rhône 🍷 \$\$ The less expensive group of Marcoux wines includes this very good pleasure wine, the Côtes du Rhône, which is elegant and medium bodied.

Domaine La Lorentine Lirac 🍷 \$\$ The Armenier family's newest purchase in Lirac, the Domaine La Lorentine exhibits a deep, rich, savory character.

MARTINELLE *(Côtes du Ventoux)*

Côtes du Ventoux 🍷 \$\$\$ A well-made, attractively priced wine, ideal for bistro/brasserie drinking. With sweet, crunchy strawberry and cherry fruit along with hints of seaweed and underbrush, it has charm and early accessibility.

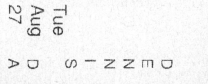

MAS DE BOISLAUZON *(Côtes du Rhône)*

Côtes du Rhône-Villages 🍷 $$ Consistently well-made, this wine exhibits nice loamy soil notes intermixed with some pepper, black currant, and cherry.

MAS DES BRESSADES *(Costières de Nîmes)*

Costières de Nîmes Cuvée Excellence 🍷 $ Made from 100% barrel-aged Syrah, the Costières de Nîmes Cuvée Excellence can display some less pleasant characteristics, including high tannin and an austere personality; however, its front-end aromatics tend to be attractive.

Vin de Pays Gard Cabernet Sauvignon/Syrah 🍷 $$ This wine is all charm and fruit. The acidity gives freshness, liveliness, and delineation to the wine's character. There is plenty of sweet black cherry and black currant fruit in this medium-bodied, straightforward wine.

Vin de Pays Gard Roussanne/Viognier 🍷 $$ The Roussanne component of the Vin de Pays Gard Roussanne/Viognier (equal parts of each) spends some time in new oak, and the result is an attractive bouquet of lemon oil, lychee nuts, and poached tropical fruits offered in a medium-bodied, exuberant, flamboyant style.

MAS DE GUIOT *(Costières de Nîmes)*

Costières de Nîmes Alex 🍷 $$ Named after the importer's son, the Costières de Nîmes Alex is the biggest wine of this portfolio, possessing excellent purity and depth as well as a nicely layered mouth-feel.

Costières de Nîmes Numa 🍷 $$ An ambitious, seriously endowed Costières de Nîmes, made from 100% Syrah aged in *barrique*.

Vin de Pays Cabernet Sauvignon/Syrah 🍷 $ The lighter-style VdP Cabernet Sauvignon/Syrah reveals plenty of soft fruit, no structural issues, and no problems with its sweet tannins.

Vin de Pays Grenache/Syrah 🍷 $ This wine is simple, solid, and pleasant, but one dimensional.

Vin de Pays Gard Syrah/Grenache 🍷 $ A blend of nearly equal parts Grenache and Syrah, the Vin de Pays Gard Syrah/Grenache (which is marketed as the Cuvée Tradition in countries other than the U.S.) is crunchy, fresh, and lively, with excellent purity, zesty acidity, and a long, heady finish.

MAS CARLOT   *(Costières de Nîmes)*

Clairette de Bellegarde 🍷 $ A superb example of Clairette, this wine will not keep for more than a year or so, but if drunk over its first 12 months, it will offer beautiful white citrus and honeyed pear characteristics as well as lively, vibrant acidity and freshness. It is an amazing "little" wine.

Costières de Nîmes Les Enfants Terribles 🍷 $ This wine offers oodles of fruit along with superb purity and freshness and a medium-bodied, savory, luscious personality.

Vin de Pays d'Oc Cabernet Sauvignon/Syrah 🍷 $$ A *barrique*-aged, Bordeaux-like effort, this possesses Cabernet's cassis character along with hints of mint, incense, and cedar, and could easily be mistaken for a Médoc cru bourgeois. It is ripe, with terrific fruit as well as impressive purity and length.

Vin de Pays d'Oc Marsanne/Roussanne 🍷 $ This crisp white exhibits notes of rose petals and tropical fruits, excellent texture and ripeness, and fresh acids.

Vin de Pays d'Oc Syrah/Grenache 🍷 $ Even though this wine is from Costières de Nîmes, because they've put the varietals on the label, Mas Carlot is forced to call it a *vin de pays*. With elegant berry fruit, good ripeness, and medium body, it is an ideal match for bistro/brasserie cuisine.

CHÂTEAU MAS NEUF   *(Costières de Nîmes)*

Costières de Nîmes Tradition 🍷 $ This medium-bodied wine is a straightforward, bistro-style red with notes of Provençal herbs, cherries, strawberries, and licorice.

Costières de Nîmes Tradition 🍷 $ A fresh, medium-bodied, elegant wine best drunk over its first 6–9 months.

Costières de Nîmes Tradition La Mourvache 🍷 $$$ An intriguing blend of equal parts Mourvèdre and Grenache, the La Mourvache is impressive. This spicy, rich, medium-bodied wine has sweet tannin and a long finish.

DOMAINE LA MILLIÈRE *(Côtes du Rhône)*

Côtes du Rhônes-Villages Vieilles Vignes 🍷 $$ This fine estate offers a very tasty, inexpensive Côtes du Rhône-Villages. It can be slightly austere and lean but still very good, tasting almost like a premier cru from Burgundy's Côte de Beaune.

LA MONARDIÈRE *(Vacqueyras)*

Vacqueyras Les 2 Monardes 🍷 $$$ This tasty, elegant effort exhibits a classic Provençal *garrigue* note interwoven with kirsch and spice-box aromas in its modestly intense bouquet and possesses impressive levels of fruit, good acidity, and sweet tannin.

CHÂTEAU DE MONTMIRAIL *(Vacqueyras)*

Vacqueyras Cuvée des Deux Frères 🍷 $$$ The medium- to full-bodied Vacqueyras Cuvée des Deux Frères is a hedonistic, silky-textured, fruit-driven effort.

Vacqueyras Cuvée de l'Ermite 🍷 $$$ A lush, heady, and seductive red.

DOMAINE DE LA MORDORÉE *(Côtes du Rhône)*

Côtes du Rhône 🍷 $$ This wine has good tannins, fresh acidity, and medium-bodied, pure, fresh, vibrant flavors that last on the palate.

Côtes du Rhône 🍷 $$ Almost as good as the Tavel from this estate (below) and a lot less expensive is their Côtes du Rhône Rosé. Fresh, medium- to full-bodied, and wonderfully deep and long, this terrific rosé should be drunk within its first year of release.

Côtes du Rhône Dame Rousse 🍷 $ This wine has a lot of muscle and density for a Côtes du Rhône and is best drunk over 4–5 years, although it can last up to a decade.

Lirac Dame Rousse 🍷 $$ Spicy, medium to full bodied, structured, but rich, full, and very impressive.

Tavel ♆ $$$ Another superb rosé from southern France, offering plenty of kirsch and spice characteristics, exuberant fruit, medium to full body, and an authoritative finish. This serious effort is befitting this appellation famous for one wine—rosé. Enjoy it over its first 6–9 months.

DOMAINE DE MOURCHON *(Séguret)*

Côtes du Rhône-Villages Séguret Tradition ♆ $$$ The Côtes du Rhônes from this estate are gorgeously made, pure, rich, beautifully textured, savory, and everything a wine in Provence should be. The value here, the Côtes du Rhône-Villages Séguret Tradition, is a brilliant wine, with plenty of blue and black fruits and moderately high tannins but a sweet and savory mouth-feel. This is a seriously endowed Côtes du Rhône.

MOURGUES DU GRÈS *(Costières de Nîmes)*

Costières de Nîmes Capitelles des Mourgues ♆ $$$ The Capitelles des Mourgues, usually the top cuvée from this estate, exhibits a full-bodied, earthy richness.

Costières de Nîmes Les Galets Dorés ♆ $ A crisp, aromatic effort with a fruity palate, a dry, fresh personality, and good acidity, this crowd-pleaser can be enjoyed with an assortment of cuisines.

Costières de Nîmes Les Galets Rouge ♆ $ Full bodied and oozing with fruit and glycerin, good acidity, freshness, and focus, this is a lovely red to consume over its first 2–4 years.

Costières de Nîmes Terre d'Argence ♆ $$ A very reliable wine that consistently tastes like the bottled essence of sunny Provence, this wine is peppery and spicy, with a boatload of ripe cherry fruit and silky tannins.

Costières de Nîmes Terre d'Argence Blanc ♆ $$ The very good Terre d'Argence blanc is surprisingly restrained compared to the Galets Dorés, in a medium-bodied, dry, refreshing style.

CHÂTEAU DE NAGES *(Costières de Nîmes)*

Costières de Nîmes Joseph Torres ♆ $$$ A plump, fleshy, full-bodied, silky-textured, delicious wine.

DOMAINE L'OLIVIER *(Côtes du Rhône)*

Côtes du Rhône-Villages 🍷 \$\$ The Grenache-dominated Côtes du Rhône-Villages is a deep, medium-bodied, and lusciously fruity effort.

Côtes du Rhône-Villages l'Orée du Bois 🍷 \$\$\$ A blacker, more modern-style wine that lacks the complexity of its sibling. However, it is generously endowed, juicy, and rich.

DOMAINE DE L'ORATOIRE ST.-MARTIN *(Cairanne)*

Côtes du Rhône-Villages Cairanne Cuvée Prestige 🍷 \$\$\$ This classic Provençal red from the southern Rhône displays excellent sweetness, full body, a rich palate, and outstanding purity as well as length.

Côtes du Rhône-Villages Cairanne Haut-Coustias 🍷 \$\$\$ With good fruit, full-bodied power, and admirable thickness as well as glycerin, this wine is deep, long, rich, and full bodied.

Côtes du Rhône-Villages Cairanne Réserve des Seigneurs 🍷 \$\$\$ A terrific wine that speaks loudly about the brilliance of the two brothers who run this estate, Frédéric and François Alary. This wine has admirable texture, purity, length, and full-bodied power.

CHÂTEAU PARADIS *(Coteaux d'Aix-en-Provence)*

Terre des Anges 🍷 \$ A custom cuvée from the brilliant oenologist Philippe Cambie, this interesting blend of Cabernet Sauvignon, Grenache, and Sauvignon Blanc offers wonderful freshness and dry, crisp flavors along with copious quantities of melon, citrus, strawberry, and berry fruit.

Tradition 🍷 \$ A blend of 55% Cabernet Sauvignon, 35% Grenache, and 10% Syrah, this custom cuvée exhibits a dense purple color with full-bodied crème de cassis, licorice, tobacco leaf, and spice-box notes, sweet tannin, fresh acids, and a terrific texture as well as length.

DOMAINE DU PÉGAÜ *(Côtes du Rhône)*

Domaine du Pégaü Plan Pégaü (nonvintage) 🍷 \$ A fine *vin de table*. Spicy, deep, and richly fruity, it can drink nicely for 2–3 years.

Domaine du Pégaü Pegovino/Plume Bleue VdP d'Oc 🍷 **$$** The Pegovino/Plume Bleue VdP d'Oc is sold under either the name Pegovino or Plume Bleue, depending on where the bottles end up. A classic Provençal wine offering roasted herb, new saddle leather, black cherry, currant, and loamy soil characteristics, it is a tasty, earthy effort with loads of personality.

Féraud-Brunel Côtes du Rhône-Villages 🍷 **$$** Under the Féraud-Brunel moniker, this brilliant Côtes du Rhône-Villages is a full-bodied, luscious red.

Féraud-Brunel Côtes du Rhône-Villages Rasteau 🍷 **$$$** An outstanding offering that exhibits plenty of tannin but enough fruit to balance out the wine's structure.

Sélection Laurence Féraud Côtes du Rhône-Villages Séguret Les Pialons 🍷 **$$$** A terrific wine from this village, with loads of fruit, pepper, and spice as well as good Provençal typicity.

CHÂTEAU PESQUIE (*Côtes du Ventoux*)

Côtes du Ventoux Quintessence Rouge 🍷 **$$$** Pesquie's top cuvée, the Quintessence, is a classic cool-climate Syrah from southern France. The higher elevation gives the wine great acidity as well as an extraordinary bouquet of acacia flowers, crème de cassis, blackberries, tar, licorice, and spice. Deep, full bodied, and layered, this is a gorgeous offering.

Côtes du Ventoux Les Terrasses Rouge 🍷 **$** The unfined and unfiltered Les Terrasses Rouge is a custom cuvée made for American importer Eric Solomon. Deep and full-bodied with velvety tannins, good acidity, and a long finish, this is a heck of a wine to drink over its first 4–5 years.

LE PLAN VERMEERSCH (*Côtes du Rhône*)

Côtes du Rhône Classic Red 🍷 **$** Composed of primarily Grenache and a small amount of Carignan, this wine possesses copious aromas of ground black pepper, black cherries, currants, and leafy, sandy, earthy notes.

Côtes du Rhône Classic White 🍷 **$** A crisp, lemon- and apple-scented wine displaying a hint of white currant as well as zesty acidity, this fresh, lively wine is best drunk in its first year.

Coteaux du Tricistan GT-V ♀ $$$ The GT-V (100% Viognier) from the Coteaux du Tricistan reveals a surprisingly stylish, elegant bouquet of white peaches and underripe apricots, good acidity, and excellent freshness.

DOMAINE DE POULVAREL (*Costières de Nîmes*)

Costières de Nîmes rouge ♀ $$ This richly textured offering tastes more like a northern Rhône, with its Syrah component dominating both the aromatics and flavors. It offers blackberry, licorice, and tar notes along with terrific fruit and medium to full body.

Costières de Nîmes rosé ♀ $ A delicate, stylish, subtle blend of 90% Grenache and 10% Syrah, this light- to medium-bodied rosé offers surprising minerality and freshness as well as a nuanced but discreet style.

Costières de Nîmes Les Perrottes ♀ $$ An unfiltered blend of 70% Syrah and 30% Grenache that spends time in both tank and small barrels, this is a strikingly cerebral wine with lots of floral and black and blue fruit nuances. It is medium- to full-bodied with good structure, and the wood influence provides a more backward, ageworthy style. It should drink well for a decade.

DOMAINE DE LA PRÉSIDENTE (*Cairanne*)

Cairanne Galifay ♀ $$$ This wine possesses some earthy tannins but excellent ripeness, medium body, and the potential to age for up to a decade.

Cairanne Grands Classiques ♀ $$$ The Cairanne Grands Classiques is ripe, long, and moves stylistically in the direction of the Galifay. It is medium bodied and very Provençal.

Cairanne Partides ♀ $$$ The most elegant and Burgundian of this group, medium bodied, crisp, refreshing.

Côtes du Rhône Velours Rouge ♀ $$ A remarkable Côtes du Rhône showing full body and no doubt a good dosage of Syrah given the blackberry and tar notes, but plenty of personality, soul, and Provençal typicity.

Côtes du Rhône-Villages Grands Classiques ♀ $$ Quite a tasty, full-throttle Côtes du Rhône that can drink nicely for 7–8 years.

CHÂTEAU RAYAS (*Côtes du Rhône*)

La Pialade Côtes du Rhône ♟ $$$ This lightweight red is a soft, bistro-style wine showing plum and cherry notes but little depth or complexity.

DOMAINE LA RÉMÉJEANNE (*Côtes du Rhône*)

Côtes du Rhône Les Arbousiers ♟ $$$ A dead ringer for a high-class Pinot Noir, at one-fifth the price. Elegant berry fruit, forest floor, and peppery characteristics lead to a wine with loads of kirsch, sweet tannin, and fresh acidity.

Côtes du Rhône Les Chevrefeuilles ♟ $$ This wine, revealing terrific density for a Côtes du Rhône, is round, deep, and seamlessly constructed.

Côtes du Rhône Terre de Lune ♟ $$ The rich Côtes du Rhône Terre de Lune reveals a surprisingly complex nose of acacia flowers, blackberries, chocolate, and lavender.

Côtes du Rhône-Villages Les Églantiers ♟ $$$ This wine reveals flowery cassis notes (probably due to Syrah in the blend), medium body, and more tannin than its siblings.

Côtes du Rhône-Villages Les Genevrières ♟ $$$ A fruit-driven, gorgeously plump wine with fresh acidity, loads of strawberries and cherries, and a spicy finish revealing a touch of pepper.

DOMAINE DE LA RENJARDE (*Massif d'Uchaux*)

Côtes du Rhône-Villages Massif d'Uchaux ♟ $$ This medium-bodied, elegant red is best consumed over its first several years.

Côtes du Rhône-Villages Massif d'Uchaux Réserve du Cassagne ♟ $$ Renjarde's top cuvée, the Côtes du Rhône-Villages Massif d'Uchaux Réserve du Cassagne is a medium-bodied, peppery, and spicy, delicious wine.

CHÂTEAU DES ROQUES (*Vacqueyras*)

Vacqueyras ♟ $$$ The components of this wine all come from Vacqueyras's limestone soils. It is a fruity, medium-bodied effort.

DOMAINE ROGER SABON ET FILS *(Côtes du Rhône)*

Côtes du Rhône 🍷 $ Sabon's inexpensive Côtes du Rhône can be a sleeper selection for shrewd bargain-hunting consumers. This is a lush, richly fruity, endearing style of wine that is ideal for bistros and brasseries.

CHÂTEAU SAINT COSME *(Côtes du Rhône)*

Côtes du Rhône 🍷 $ In some vintages, this Côtes du Rhône is made from 100% Syrah that is actually declassified wine from the estate vineyards in Gigondas blended with wine bought from Vinsobres and Rasteau. It is usually not terribly complex but mouth filling, very supple textured, and corpulent.

Côtes du Rhône 🍷 $ An amazing wine, medium bodied, fresh, lively, and an exceptional bargain in dry white southern Rhône wines.

Côtes du Rhône Les Deux Albions 🍷 $$ About half Syrah, with Grenache, Mourvèdre, and Carignan also in the blend. The very talented Gigondas proprietor Louis Barruol also blends in 10% of the white grape Clairette to give an almost Guigal Côte Rôtie La Mouline–like floral complexity to the black fruit character. This is a fat, fleshy, delicious wine.

Côtes du Rhône Le Poste 🍷 $$ Made from 100% Clairette, this remarkable wine is rich and medium to full bodied, with great finesse, complexity, and delicacy. Clairette doesn't have a reputation for holding up with bottle age, so drink it within its first several years.

Côtes du Ventoux Domaine de le Crillon 🍷 $$ 100% Grenache made in a Burgundian style, this wine is young, elegant, and not as weighty and exuberant as the other cuvées from this estate, but attractive.

Little James Basket Press Vin de Table (nonvintage) 🍷 $$ This sexy, ripe wine dominated by Grenache is an amazing value, with oodles of black cherry fruit in a thick, glycerin-emboldened style. It is full bodied, lush, and ideal for drinking in its first several years of life.

DOMAINE SAINT-DAMIEN (*Gigondas*)

Côtes du Rhône ♟ $$ The straight Côtes du Rhône is easygoing, medium bodied, and nicely made.

Côtes du Rhône Le Bouveau ♟ $$ Medium to full bodied with silky tannins, the Côtes du Rhône Le Bouveau provides a hedonistic mouthful of red wine.

Côtes du Rhône Vieilles Vignes ♟ $$$ This could easily pass for an outstanding Châteauneuf-du-Pape. Deep and full bodied with terrific texture, stunning richness, and a long finish, this is a brilliant Côtes du Rhône.

DOMAINE SAINT GAYAN (*Côtes du Rhône*)

Côtes du Rhône ♟ $$ Offering sweet kirsch intermixed with underbrush, pepper, and figs, this is an elegant, medium-bodied, fleshy wine.

SAINT JEAN DU BARROUX L'OLIGOCÈNE
(*Côtes du Ventoux*)

Côtes du Ventoux ♟ $$$ Made using a combination of organic and biodynamic farming methods in the vineyard; the result is a gorgeous blend of mostly Grenache, some Syrah, and the rest Carignan and Cinsault, with a bouquet that is reminiscent of a great Côte Rôtie. In the mouth, the wine is soft, velvety, medium to full bodied, pure, elegant, and exotic.

SANTA DUC SÉLECTIONS (*Côtes du Rhône*)

Côtes du Rhône Les Quatres Terres ♟ $$$ From four different villages, this wine is decent rather than exciting.

Roaix Les Crottes ♟ $$ The real gem from this portfolio is from the backwater, virtually unknown Côtes du Rhône-Villages of Roaix. The Roaix Les Crottes is a beauty and all that a delicious Provençal Côtes du Rhône should be. It apparently comes from very old vines, especially the Grenache, and is an amazing wine that sells for a song.

Sablet Le Fournas ♀ **$$** The Chablis-like Sablet Le Fournas is fresh and has loads of mineral and white citrus as well as a hint of quince. It is a delicious dry white.

Les Plans Vin de Pays ♀ **$** A good brasserie red in its simplicity and purity, with punchy strawberry and cherry fruit complemented by pepper and lavender (*vin de gourmand,* as the French say).

CHÂTEAU DE SÉGRIES (*Côtes du Rhône*)

Côtes du Rhône ♀ **$** This medium-bodied Côtes du Rhône is a classic wine primarily from Grenache.

Côtes du Rhône Clos de l'Hermitage ♀ **$$$** The blockbuster Clos de l'Hermitage is a full-bodied, muscular, dense wine.

Lirac ♀ **$$** Superb, rich in black fruit, very Provençal, and medium bodied.

Tavel ♀ **$$** The gorgeous strawberry/kirsch–laden Tavel is full and very expressive. A total hedonistic turn-on, this wine can drink splendidly well for 10–12 months.

CHÂTEAU SIGNAC (*Chusclan*)

Côtes du Rhône-Villages Chusclan Combe d'Enfer ♀ **$$** Medium bodied, nicely structured, well balanced, and pure.

Côtes du Rhône-Villages Chusclan Terra Amata ♀ **$$$** Medium to full bodied with luscious fruit, sweet tannin, and a long, expansive finish.

DOMAINE DE LA SOLITUDE (*Côtes du Rhône*)

Côtes du Rhône ♀ **$** Peppery *garrigue* notes dominate this medium-bodied, pleasant, bistro-styled Côtes du Rhône.

DOMAINE LA SOUMADE (*Côtes du Rhône*)

Cabernet Sauvignon Vin de Pays ♀ **$$** Deep and medium to full bodied, this Cabernet Sauvignon VdP lacks the complexity found in Bordeaux-based Cabernets, but it is mouth filling and chunky.

Merlot Vin de Pays ♀ **$$** The Merlot VdP offers soft tannins in a medium-bodied, straightforward, fleshy style with loads of texture as well as a plump mouth-feel.

Côtes du Rhône Les Violettes 🍷 $$$ The biggest sleeper in this portfolio is often the Côtes du Rhône Les Violettes, which can be like a mini Guigal La Mouline, with an exotic, fragrant bouquet of roses, lychee nuts, honeysuckle, cassis, and sweet cherries. This fat, fleshy, deep, hedonistic effort has much more complexity than one might suspect.

TARDIEU-LAURENT *(Rhône Valley)*

Côtes du Luberon Bastide 🍷 $$ An elegant, straightforward wine without much complexity, but a pleasant brasserie-style red.

Côtes du Rhône 🍷 $$ Another bistro-style red, made mostly from Grenache, with good acidity, a dark ruby color, and superficial strawberry and black cherry fruit.

Côtes du Rhône Guy Louis 🍷 $$$ A blend of mostly Grenache with some Syrah, this wine is rich, full bodied, and gorgeously plump and opulent.

Côtes du Rhône-Villages Les Becs Fins 🍷 $$$ This wine shows delicious black currant and blackberry in a medium-bodied, soft, round, generous style.

CHÂTEAU DES TOURS *(Côtes du Rhône)*

Côtes du Rhône 🍷 $$ This brilliant Côtes du Rhône is a medium- to full-bodied wine with stunning richness, an expansive mouth-feel, and seductive, silky tannins. The finest examples of this cuvée can drink well for a decade.

Côtes du Rhône 🍷 $$ This outstanding white Côtes du Rhône, made from 100% Grenache Blanc, exhibits superb density and richness along with a complex bouquet and a full-bodied mouth-feel.

Vin de Pays 🍷 $$ Deliciously fruity and soft, this *vin de pays* is a terrific bargain.

Vin de Pays 🍷 $$ The white Vin de Pays (mostly Clairette) displays attractive notes of white citrus, underripe bananas, and a hint of flowers in a medium-bodied, deliciously fruity style.

DOMAINE DU TUNNEL (STÉPHANE ROBERT) *(St.-Péray)*

St.-Péray ♟ $$$ 100% Roussanne, this flashy, stylish white possesses fabulous richness and comes across like a top-notch grand cru white Burgundy with surprisingly good acidity, impressive minerality, and huge floral and tropical fruit notes.

PIERRE USSEGLIO *(Côtes du Rhône)*

Panorama Vin de Table (nonvintage) ♟ $ Nearly all Merlot and the rest some southern Rhône varietals, this wine is fruity and ideal for drinking over its first couple of years.

Côtes du Rhône ♟ $ This excellent Côtes du Rhône is an attractive, plush wine that can drink nicely over 3–4 years.

GEORGES VERNAY *(Condrieu)*

Viognier Vin de Pays Le Pied de Samson ♟ $ This is a delicious, straightforward, up-front Viognier with plenty of apricot, honey, and peach notes. It has medium body and lacks the minerality and complexity of the estate's Condrieus, but it is well made and ideal for drinking in its first year of release.

CHÂTEAU VESSIÈRE *(Costières de Nîmes)*

Costières de Nîmes Red ♟ $ This 70% Syrah–30% Grenache blend exhibits a dense ruby color and sweet berry fruit notes intertwined with hints of licorice, earth, and pepper. It is a perfect bistro or brasserie red to drink during its first 1–2 years.

Costières de Nîmes Rosé ♟ $ A lively combination of 75% Syrah and 25% Grenache, this rosé offers abundant kirsch and framboise notes in its dry, crisp, pure personality.

Costières de Nîmes White ♟ $ Composed of 85% Roussanne and 15% Grenache, this medium-bodied white wine offers plenty of floral, honeyed citrus, and melon notes as well as a hint of underripe peaches. It is obviously aged completely in tank given its freshness and the absence of any hint of wood.

J. VIDAL-FLEURY *(Ampuis)*

Côtes du Rhône Le Pigeonnier ♟ $$ Deep and full bodied, this is a sumptuous style of Côtes du Rhône to drink over 3–4 years.

Côtes du Rhône (Viognier) ♀ $$ Vidal-Fleury's Côtes du Rhône (Viognier) is a beauty. Crisp and medium bodied in a richly fruity style, this is a heck of a Viognier at a very good price.

Côtes du Rhône-Villages ♀ $ The Côtes du Rhône-Villages exhibits classic Provençal characteristics, medium body, and admirable fruit, dried herbs, and spice notes.

Côtes du Ventoux ♀ $ A delicious bistro red offering heady alcohol, loads of sweet cassis and cherry fruit, and a fleshy finish.

Crozes-Hermitage (red) ♀ $$$ The red Crozes-Hermitage is light, medium bodied, and pleasant but unexciting.

Crozes-Hermitage (white) ♀ $$$ This white Crozes-Hermitage (100% Marsanne) is fresh and lively but straightforward and simple.

St.-Joseph ♀ $$$ Cleanly made, straightforward, foursquare, and fruity.

DOMAINE DE LA VIEILLE JULIENNE
(Châteauneuf-du-Pape)

Côtes du Rhône ♀ $$$ An interesting white wine made from a blend of Clairette, Grenache Blanc, Marsanne, Viognier, and Bourboulenc, this wine is crisp, elegant, and fruity.

Côtes du Rhône Lieu-Dit Clavin ♀ $$ This wine can be outstanding. Tasting more like a serious Châteauneuf-du-Pape than a Côtes du Rhône, it is medium to full bodied with silky tannin and a plump, lush mouth-feel. It can usually drink well for 5–7 years, and sometimes as long as a decade.

Vin de Pays ♀ $ Vieille Julienne's Vin de Pays is a straightforward, surprisingly big wine, with loads of fruit, tannin, and purity. While not complex, it is a mouth-staining, -filling red.

DOMAINE DE VIEUX TÉLÉGRAPHE *(Côtes du Ventoux)*

Le Pigoulet de Brunier ♀ $ Shrewd consumers seeking good value can always count on Le Pigoulet de Brunier, which comes mostly from the Côtes de Ventoux. It is a fruity, medium-bodied, bistro-style red meant for immediate consumption.

VIGNERONS DE CARACTÈRE *(Vacqueyras)*

Vacqueyras Chemin des Rouvières 🍷 **$$** As with all of these wines, the style of this red is one of fruity, good quality and immediate appeal.

Vacqueyras Cuvée Seigneur de Fontimple 🍷 **$$** A blend of mostly Grenache and the rest Syrah and Mourvèdre, this wine has loads of cherry fruit, some acidity, and plenty of charm.

Vacqueyras Domaine des Bastides d'Éole 🍷 **$$** Like its siblings, this wine is fruit laden, lush, and best drunk in its first 3–5 years.

Vacqueyras Domaine Bessons Dupré 🍷 **$$** A fruity, well-made Vacqueyras.

Vacqueyras Les Bois du Ménestrel 🍷 **$$** Commercially styled but pleasant in a straightforward, one-dimensional manner with good softness.

Vacqueyras Domaine de la Curnière 🍷 **$$** My favorites from this estate include the Domaine de la Curnière.

Vacqueyras les Hauts de Castellas 🍷 **$$** The delicious Les Hauts de Castellas is soft, ripe, and medium to full bodied.

Vacqueyras Domaine les Mas du Bouquet 🍷 **$$** One of my favorites from this portfolio, the Domaine les Mas du Bouquet is sumptuous.

Vacqueyras Domaine la Pertiane 🍷 **$$** Another fruity, commercially styled, pleasant red.

Vacqueyras Domaine de la Soleïade 🍷 **$$** Light, medium bodied, and pleasant.

Vacqueyras Marquis de Fonséguille 🍷 **$$** Another straightforward and simple red.

Vacqueyras Vallon des Sources 🍷 **$$** In some vintages, this has been my favorite from this estate; it is richly fruity with superb intensity, beautiful ripeness, medium to full body, and silky tannins.

GERMANY

GERMAN WINE VALUES

by David Schildknecht

In Riesling's Realm

Germany's international vinous reputation has been made by Riesling, a grape that not only stands behind some of the most deliciously diverse, complex, and ageworthy wines in the world, but also reflects its vintage and place of origin (down to the vineyard) with a clarity that few if any other grapes can rival. For the purposes of this guide to value, we confine ourselves to those German regions that are known for Riesling, since it is from this grape that most of the German wines with outstanding quality-price rapport originate, and it is wines from Riesling (always labeled as such) that make up the overwhelming majority of fine German wine sold in the U.S.

The majority of German Riesling sold in the U.S. is not dry (*trocken*) by the standards of Germany's wine law. American consumers have every good gustatory reason for rejecting a prejudice among German consumers to treat "*trocken*" on a wine's label as an imprimatur of quality (regardless of how tart, astringent, or unbalanced the contents of some bottles may be). The key quality criterion is *balance.* Riesling in Germany is singularly capable of generating harmoniously balanced (or, at least, exhilaratingly tension-filled) wines with as little as 7% alcohol and as much as 14%; with only a few grams of residual sugar or with a hundred or more. Nowhere else in the world, in fact, does a single grape variety generate such stylistic diversity. Expect almost any German Riesling labeled *trocken* to taste well and truly—perhaps adamantly, occasionally even (though not among the wines recommended here!) excessively—dry. Wines labeled *halbtrocken* will for all practical purposes taste dry as well. (The term *feinherb*—used increasingly on labels—is similar but too elastic to pin down, not to mention impossible to translate.) In the absence of the words "*trocken*" or "*halbtrocken*" on the label, the degree of sweetness in the bottle may and will vary considerably. But the best display an uncanny aptitude for balancing (even burying) residual sugar, and the notion that such off-dry wines are inherently less food-friendly is simply another prejudice, one that adventurous wine lovers will quickly disprove to themselves.

A further layer of terminology foisted by Germany's laws on its wines is their so-called Prädikat. Wines to whose grape must no sugar was added before fermentation are entitled to append one of the following predicates to the word "Riesling": "Kabinett," "Spätlese," "Auslese," "Beerenauslese," or "Trockenbeerenauslese" (and, with added conditions—notably freezing of grapes on the vine—the predicate "Eiswein" applies). These gradients refer solely to minimum levels of sugar at harvest (not in the finished wine—a Kabinett, Spätlese, or Auslese can range from bone-dry to sweet). Acidity, extract, the evolution of the grapes' skins—in short, factors that actually determine flavor—don't count in assigning Prädikat. What's more, adding some sugar before fermentation is not taboo and can sometimes be beneficial. So do not treat Prädikat in general—or any given predicate—as a quality imprimatur.

In practice, each grower decides for him- or herself what will count as Kabinett, Spätlese, or Auslese, although in general a Kabinett is the lightest-weight, Spätlese is richer and riper tasting (and, if sweet, then generally sweeter than the corresponding Kabinett), and Auslese is very ripe, often shading into noble sweetness. (Grapes of Beerenauslese-must weight or higher are destined to remain nobly sweet, and worthy exemplars exceed by a factor of three or more the price ceiling for this guide.) Growers have become sufficiently disenchanted with the legal framework that nowadays many sell even their best wines without any *Prädikat* on the label. Alcohol level can be a more useful guide to style, by permitting one to infer something about body and—in wines below 11%—the probability of at least slight sweetness.

Within the price range covered by this guide, we shall generally be concerned with wines either lacking Prädikat or else labeled Kabinett (and, less often, Spätlese). A boon to value seekers is that Kabinett Rieslings' position as the lowest rung on the Prädikat ladder, as well as their relative lightness, feeds a perception that keeps down the price. A generic estate Riesling Qualitätswein (or ObA, i.e., wine without Prädikat) often constitutes whatever batch, blend, or even single-harvest wine a grower elected to sell as his or her introductory-level offering. And almost without exception, even the most prestigious estates—those who don't know how to make less-than-excellent Riesling—sell such vinous calling cards at amazingly reasonable prices. In consequence, nearly all of the top names among Germany's growers are represented by at least one wine in this guide. In addition to their incredible versatility at table, top-flight German Rieslings offer consumers unprecedented value and confidence on account of their sheer stamina, whether locked up in a cellar for years or open in the refrigerator for days.

Grapes

While Riesling steals the German limelight, an extended cast of characters enlivens the scene even within the Riesling-growing regions that concern us in the present guide. This includes the entire Pinot family: Pinot Noir, Pinot Blanc, Pinot Gris, and occasionally even Chardonnay. The grape-crossing Scheurebe—especially in the Pfalz—produces memorably delicious and outrageously aromatic wines redolent of sage, pink grapefruit, and black currant. Rieslaner, occasionally met with in the Pfalz, represents another rare success from the wide world of German crossings. Muskateller is worth noting, along with Gewürztraminer (although it's much less common here than in neighboring Alsace, where it's spelled without umlaut). Long considered Germany's workhorse but uninteresting, Silvaner is reclaiming attention due its more serious exemplars. The less said the better, though, about the grape whose acreage is second to that of Riesling. Müller-Thurgau (a.k.a. Rivaner) scarcely ever produces a German wine of note, nor does it usually advertise its presence on the label. Always be suspicious of any German wine that does not indicate its grape of origin, as that is usually a sign that its identity would with good reason be taken as anything but a recommendation!

Regions

The major German Riesling-growing regions are linked together like a chain. The **Mittelrhein**—running south from the outskirts of Germany's former capital, Bonn—segues into the **Rheingau**, a region largely defined by the south-facing slopes along its right bank where the Rhine briefly runs east to west, while the opposite shore (and a considerable distance inland) constitutes **Rheinhessen**. Rheinhessen segues south into the **Pfalz** (its vineyards now separated by miles of broad plain from the Rhine), which in turn segues into Alsace as it reaches the French frontier. A relatively warm German growing area—from among those that concern us in this book—the Pfalz harbors the highest percentage of interesting wines from non-Riesling grape varieties. The river **Nahe**—nearly all of whose middle and lower reaches feature vineyards—runs into the Rhine near the western edge of the Rheingau. Germany's share of the long, twisting **Mosel**, with its improbably steep slate slopes, runs from the Luxembourg frontier to join the Rhine at Koblenz (in the northern sector of the Mittelrhein). The last few miles of the river **Saar** before it flows into the Mosel just upstream from Germany's Roman capital of Trier constitute a distinctive and important Riesling-growing region, as do the few miles of the tiny **Ruwer** just before it reaches the Mosel immediately downstream from Trier. (Since 2008, the law recognizes only the overarching term "Mosel" for what used to officially be "Mosel-Saar-Ruwer.")

In general, Rieslings display higher acidity and a more delicate frame in the Mosel, Saar, Ruwer, and Nahe growing regions, with those of the Nahe and Mittelrhein sometimes referred to as transitional between the styles of Mosel and Rhine. No matter what the region—but especially in wines of the characteristically rocky and relatively cool growing regions just mentioned—it is almost impossible to get far in trying to capture their character in words without feeling compelled to resort to mineral vocabulary. Wines of the Rheingau enjoy an ancient reputation as aristocrats, both in the sense of high regard and slight aloofness, especially in youth. Rieslings from Rheinhessen or the Pfalz are generally fuller bodied and somewhat lower in acidity than those of cooler regions, but there will be many exceptions depending on vintage, vineyard, and vintner.

Vintage Smarts

Both 2008 and 2007 represent what many German growers consider a return to "normalcy" after an unprecedented string of high-ripeness vintages that began in 1988. In these two most recent harvests, delicate Kabinett Rieslings and mouthwatering, seemingly mineral-saturated basic bottlings were again possible in ample quantities after several years of scarcity, thus rendering them outstandingly suitable vintages for value hunters. The 2006 vintage was highly variable, most memorably marked by nobly sweet wines from the Mosel (whose prices, however, put them largely beyond the scope of this guide) and by many terrific successes on the Nahe. The 2005 vintage is uniformly good to excellent, with the Mosel, Saar, Ruwer, and Nahe particularly favored. Those who like a bit more cut and acidity to their Riesling will like not only the 2008 and 2007 vintages, but also 2004, whose wines boast excellent concentration and virtually electric energy across all growing regions, albeit at the price of a Sauvignon-like dominance of citrus and herb pungency that will appeal more to some wine lovers than it does to others.

Given not only the longevity of German Rieslings from top-notch growers and sites—even of those in lower price echelons—but also their relative resistance to the vicissitudes of storage, here is one category where value-conscious wine lovers should not hesitate to sample wines found in the marketplace from older vintages. It is best to avoid 2000s, problematic from birth and now past their prime. But 2001 (especially on the middle Mosel) is an outstanding vintage, and 2002s from all over Riesling-growing Germany are charming, intriguing, and still irresistibly refreshing—indeed, many of them (like many 1998s) seem to be coming out of a shell into which they had crept for a few years. As elsewhere in Western Europe, searing heat and drought in 2003 produced atypical wines unprecedented in richness and body yet not always well balanced or refreshing.

Drinking Curves

As a rule of thumb, German Rieslings without Prädikat should be enjoyed within 6–8 years of harvest—the dry (*trocken*) versions a bit sooner—although there is no reason to avoid relishing any of them young when their primary fruit is most intense. Single-vineyard Kabinett or Spätlese bottlings can generally be counted on for 5–7 years if *trocken,* and a decade or more if they have a balancing residual sugar. In instances of high residual sugar, the wines will begin to taste drier after 6–8 years. Exceptions to these general rules seem to occur most often in ripe but relatively low-acid vintages that often blossom and wilt early, as was the case with 1999 and will probably prove true for most 2003s and 2006s.

Germany's Top Wine Values by Winery

ANSGAR-CLÜSSERATH *(Mosel)*

Trittenheimer Apotheke Riesling Kabinett [SD] ⚲ **\$\$\$** This delicate wine from young Eva Clüsserath characteristically offers pungent floral, fruit, and mineral characteristics that need time in the air or in bottle to show best.

C. H. BERRES *(Mosel)*

Ürziger—Würzgarten Riesling Kabinett 〔SD〕 ♉ **$$$** From another of the Mosel's major new talents; delicate, luscious, red berry and citrus filled.

VON BEULWITZ *(Ruwer)*

Kaseler Nies'chen Riesling Kabinett 〔SD〕 ♉ **$$$** A classic, red-berry-rich, spicy, floral, subtly sweet Ruwer Riesling from hotelier-restaurateur-vintner Herbert Weis.

VON BUHL *(Pfalz)*

Deidesheimer Keiselberg Riesling Kabinett trocken ♉ **$$** This well-balanced dry Riesling is typically loaded with melon and pit fruits; firm and quite full bodied, yet consistently refreshing; and possessed of salty, stony, alkaline, or chalky finishing notes.

Deidesheimer Leinhöhle Riesling Kabinett halbtrocken ♉ **$$** Citrus, sweet corn, aromatic herbs, and lip-smacking salinity are key notes in this lusciously refreshing wine boasting an uncanny balance of density and clarity, lightness, and lift. The sole *halbtrocken* left on von Buhl's list, it consistently represents one of the world's most versatile, irresistible, and complex Riesling values.

Riesling Kabinett Armand 〔SD〕 ♉ **$$** A blend across vineyards for those who crave overt yet balanced sweetness, this is full of sappy pit fruits, often tinged with musk, brown spices, and wood smoke.

DR. BÜRKLIN-WOLF *(Pfalz)*

Riesling trocken ♉ **$$** Well-concentrated and multifaceted (emphasizing pit fruits, herbs, and minerals), this basic Riesling happily reflects its prestigious producer's characteristic meticulousness and fine sources.

CLEMENS BUSCH *(Mosel)*

Riesling Kabinett trocken ♉ **$$$** From a top site along the impossibly curvaceous and steep lower Mosel, this generic bottling possesses impressive stuffing, subtle creaminess, and richness (typically at 12–13% alcohol), yet grace, refinement, and minerality as well.

A. CHRISTMANN *(Pfalz)*

Riesling trocken ♀ **\$\$\$** Sourced from outstanding sites, this generic Riesling exhibits pithy concentration, firm acidity, and thought-provoking nuance typical for the entire range at this prestigious estate.

JOH. JOS. CHRISTOFFEL *(Mosel)*

Erdener Treppchen Riesling Kabinett SD ♀ **\$\$\$** Veteran Christoffel (in collaboration with the Mönchhof's Robert Eymael—see below) renders Riesling that marries opulence and polish with transparency of flavor, here favoring smoke-tinged tangerine and sassafras.

Ürziger Würzgarten Riesling Kabinett SD ♀ **\$\$\$** This can't be beat for a classic rendition of a great site—featuring strawberry and kiwi fruit—from a great grower, its richness of texture, and a flavor uncannily married to virtual weightlessness.

CLÜSSERATH-WEILER *(Mosel)*

Trittenheimer Apotheke Riesling Alte Reben ♀ **\$\$\$** Relatively full bodied (12% alcohol is typical at this estate) but refreshingly bright and fascinatingly nuanced, this makes an impressive case for genuinely dry Mosel Riesling.

DR. CRUSIUS *(Nahe)*

Crusius trocken ♀ **\$\$** This soft, ingratiating cuvée of Auxerrois, Silvaner, Riesling, and Müller-Thurgau preserves the generosity, elegance, and nuance rightly associated with the Nahe.

Traiser Riesling SD ♀ **\$\$\$** Reliably sappy and fruit filled, with judicious sweetness, this generous Riesling is perfect for solo sipping.

KURT DARTING *(Pfalz)*

Riesling Kabinett SD ♀ **\$\$** Darting vinifies for purity and in-your-face fruit, bottling a wealth of wines that run counter to local fashion in their unabashed sweetness, as this generic Kabinett deliciously demonstrates.

DR. DEINHARD *(Pfalz)*

Ruppertsberger Reiterpfad Riesling Kabinett 🔲 ⏛ **$$** Off-dry and dry versions alike of this wine are full of the peachy fruit and earthy pungency typical of this village.

SCHLOSSGUT DIEL *(Nahe)*

Dorsheimer Riesling trocken ⏛ **$$$** This entry-level Riesling from a prestigious grower offers the pure, polished, juicy satisfaction of melons, citrus, red berries, and herbs, with an uncanny balance of stuffing and elegance.

HERMANN DÖNNHOFF *(Nahe)*

Riesling ⏛ **$$$** Combining stuffing with vivacity and clarity, and ripe fruit with elusive suggestions of things mineral, this generic Riesling offers a vivid window onto a great region and a celebrated vintner.

EMRICH-SCHÖNLEBER *(Nahe)*

Riesling Lenz ⏛ **$$$** This mouthwatering red berry–, citrus–, and flower-filled Riesling with its subtle hint at sweetness offers an abundance of nuance that will keep you coming back to the glass and shaking your head in wonder at what it delivers for the price.

Riesling trocken ⏛ **$$** Combining floral, citric, pit-fruited, and subtly smoky notes, and striking an uncanny balance between stuffing and refreshing lightness (at around 11.5% alcohol), this amazing value reflects without compromise both artisanship and superb, steep holdings.

ROBERT EYMAEL (MÖNCHHOF) *(Mosel)*

Erdener Treppchen Riesling Spätlese Mosel Slate 🔲 ⏛ **$$$** Mosel Slate—with its fist-axe-like rock on the label—represents one of the Mosel's most amazing values, delivering Chartreuse-like herbal essences along with ripe citrus and rich tropical fruits.

Ürziger Würzgarten Riesling Kabinett 🔲 ⏛ **$$** This combines creaminess and unapologetic sweetness with delicacy and refreshment.

FUHRMANN-EYMAEL (WEINGUT PFEFFINGEN) *(Pfalz)*

Riesling Kabinett Pfeffo ♀ **$$$** A pungently spicy, smoky, versatile, off-dry offering.

GIEŞ-DÜPPEL *(Pfalz)*

Bundsandstein Riesling trocken ♀ **$$$** Volker Gies's expressive, meticulously crafted, and underpriced array of wines from superb southern Pfalz slopes showcases the dramatic differences associated with three sorts of soil, here a sleek, pithy Riesling from sandstone, with subtle saline, fruit-pit, and alluringly floral notes.

Muschelkalk Riesling trocken ♀ **$$$** This dry Riesling combines creaminess with clarity and refreshment and offers flavors of ripe pit fruits with a downright mysterious set of mineral allusions.

Rotliegendes Riesling trocken ♀ **$$$** Pungent, smoky, and seemingly stamped by the red, slate-like rock on which it is grown as well as by the herbs underfoot, this vigorous, dry Riesling does not lack for refinement.

GRANS-FASSIAN *(Mosel)*

Trittenheimer Apotheke Riesling Kabinett ⓢⒹ ♀ **$$** A spunky, unabashedly sweet, tropical-fruit-filled Riesling.

MAXIMIN GRÜNHAUS (VON SCHUBERT) *(Ruwer)*

Maximin Grünhäuser Abstberg Riesling ⓢⒹ ♀ **$$$** When not dry, Grünhaus's basic bottlings are still not very sweet. Here, rich peachy fruit is accentuated and a lingering succulence enhanced by the bit of residual sugar.

Maximin Grünhäuser Abstberg Riesling trocken ♀ **$$$** This famous estate with its monopoly on three contiguous hillside sites characteristically fields from their top site (even at the low end of their price spectrum) a long-keeping, subtly mineral, and pit-fruited dry wine.

Maximin Grünhäuser Herrenberg Riesling ⓢⒹ ♀ **$$$** The hint of sweetness here typically brings out an element of brown spices, enhances the wine's lip-smacking primary juiciness, and sets up a fascinating counterpoint with its herbal and mineral elements.

Maximin Grünhäuser Herrenberg Riesling trocken ♀ $$$ An estate long priding itself on the quality of its wines without Prädikat here turns in a pungently herbal, smoky, crushed-stone-inflected Riesling of enormous versatility.

GUNDERLOCH *(Rheinhessen)*

Gunderloch Riesling trocken ♀ $$ This generic Riesling (from top-rated sites) consistently delivers a substantial yet vivacious mouthful of smoked meat, citrus, and stone. Is there a more reliably outstanding bargain in dry Riesling anywhere in the world?

Riesling Kabinett Jean Baptiste SD ♀ $$ This subtly off-dry, peach- and tangerine-scented staple of the Gunderloch lineup typically features a delightful counterpoint of creaminess with lightness and vivacity.

FRITZ HAAG *(Mosel)*

Riesling SD ♀ $$$ This juicy, sappy, pristine, richly fruited, well-stuffed, yet vivacious and elegant off-dry Riesling leaves no doubt in your mouth about the quality of its producer or the vineyards in which it grew.

Riesling trocken ♀ $$$ There is no more prestigious Mosel estate than this one, yet they still bottle a modestly priced generic Riesling that shares the craftsmanship and the dynamic interplay of fruit and stone of their entire line.

WILLI HAAG *(Mosel)*

Brauneberger Juffer Riesling Kabinett SD ♀ $$ One regularly encounters here an impeccably pure, juicily refreshing, and inexpensive treat. (Note that in most years there are multiple bottlings under this name. The penultimate digits of the wine's long official registration number identify the particular lot.)

REINHOLD HAART *(Mosel)*

Riesling Haart to Heart ♀ $$ The foremost farmer of the famed Piesporter Goldtröpchen vineyard bottles this affordable, versatile, virtually dry, rich yet refreshing melon, tropical fruit, and nut-oil–filled Riesling.

VON HÖVEL *(Saar)*

Oberemmeler Hütte Riesling Kabinett ⑤ 𝖄 $$$ Distinctively delicious and ridiculously underpriced, this wine from a superb Hövel *monopole* offers abundant flowers, pit fruits, spices, and mineral tang.

Riesling Balduin von Hövel ⑤ᴰ 𝖄 $$ Eberhard von Kunow's high-volume, reliably fruit-filled and invigorating generic Riesling is hard to beat for its price.

Scharzhofberger Riesling Kabinett ⑤ 𝖄 $$$ Typically creamy in texture and unabashedly sweet, the von Hövel Riesling Kabinetts nevertheless are consistently possessed of a lift, delicacy, and sheer refreshment that must be experienced to be believed.

HEXAMER *(Nahe)*

Meddersheimer Rheingrafenberg Riesling Quarzit ⑤ᴰ 𝖄 $$$ As astonishing on paper as in the glass, this features levels of both residual sugar and acidity that taken alone would prove irritatingly extreme, yet taken together make for electric invigoration.

JOHANNISHOF (H. H. ESER) *(Rheingau)*

Johannisberger Hölle Riesling Kabinett trocken 𝖄 $$$ Rich in texture yet slightly austere and overtly stony in personality, this (for a Kabinett) relatively full-bodied dry Riesling proves highly versatile at table.

Johannisberger Riesling Kabinett G ⑤ᴰ 𝖄 $$$ While relatively few Rheingau Kabinetts are bottled nowadays with significant residual sugar, those of the Johannishof vividly demonstrate the extra measure of expressiveness that entails. ("G" stands for the site, Goldatzel.)

Johannisberger Riesling Kabinett S ⑤ᴰ 𝖄 $$$ From the Schwarzenstein vineyard above the renowned Schloss Johannisberg, this versatile Riesling is full of fruit, stone, and spice.

JUSTEN (MEULENHOF) *(Mosel)*

Erdener Treppchen Riesling Kabinett ⑤ᴰ 𝖄 $$ More than one lot of engaging and archetypical off-dry Mosel Riesling is frequently bottled under this name from a given vintage.

KARLSMÜHLE (PETER GEIBEN) *(Ruwer)*

Kaseler Nies'chen Riesling Kabinett [SD] ♀ **$$$** On no account (least of all prejudice against "sweet" wine, which is hardly the adjective this wine will bring to mind) should Geiben's classic Rieslings from steep, red-slate Ruwer slopes be missed.

Lorenzhöfer Mäuerchen Riesling Kabinett [SD] ♀ **$$$** Succulent and subtly sweet, and brimming with smoke-wreathed, spice-tinged red berries, this epitomizes the distinctive virtues of off-dry Ruwer Riesling.

KELLER *(Rheinhessen)*

Grüner Silvaner trocken ♀ **$$** This perfectly embodies the recent renaissance of the traditional, long-downtrodden Silvaner. Full of herbal and mineral character, refreshing yet with body, it displays uncanny versatility at table.

Riesling Kabinett Limestone [S] ♀ **$$** Typically exuding honey, lemon, pear, and brown spices, this under–8% alcohol, unabashedly sweet Kabinett is intense yet nearly weightless.

Riesling trocken ♀ **$$** From a "pre-harvest" of ripe bunches undertaken to lighten the vines' load, this generic Riesling from a star vintner is full of pit fruits, quite substantial, and consistently delivers juicy, piquant refreshment.

KERPEN *(Mosel)*

Graacher Himmelreich Riesling Kabinett feinherb ♀ **$$$** Offering pit fruits and nut oils, flattering creaminess (a feature of most Rieslings at this estate), and stuffing without weight, this will prove fascinating and versatile in a wide range of contexts.

Wehlener Sonnenuhr Riesling Kabinett [SD] ♀ **$$$** In effect Kerpen's flagship wine, this features flowers, vanilla, apple, nut oils, and wet stone in a delectably delicate, subtly sweet testimony to the top-class vineyard in which it grows.

AUGUST KESSELER *(Rheingau)*

Estate Riesling 🆂🅳 ♀ $$$ Kesseler's estate-bottled generic Riesling (recognizable for its script "August Kesseler") originates in Rüdesheim vineyards of impeccable credentials. Peaches, vanilla, and brown spices typically inform this creamy yet refreshing delight.

Rheingau ♀ $$ Talk about generic: this wine labeled without further embellishment unites Riesling and Silvaner grown on sheer slate slopes around Lorch for a versatile, dry, remarkable value, subtly creamy, poised, juicy, and delicate, featuring pear, herbs, and nut oils.

Riesling Kabinett trocken ♀ $$$ This piquant, zesty, sappy, often downright sassy but always adamantly dry wine originates in Lorch's steep slate slopes.

Riesling R 🆂🅳 ♀ $$ This bottling, instantly recognizable for a letter "R" that nearly fills its label, represents Kesseler's selectively sourced yet high-volume secret weapon in the war against high Rheingau prices. Noticeably sweet and often downright honeyed and exotic, it nonetheless always remains juicy and refreshing.

REICHSGRAF VON KESSELSTATT *(Mosel, Saar, and Ruwer)*

Graacher Riesling trocken ♀ $$$ Pithy, nutty, and stony, this bottling represents lesser lots from a renowned site owned exclusively by Kesselstatt and offers real grip and smoky, wet-stone mineral notes that come to life at table.

Kaseler Riesling trocken ♀ $$$ This saline, citric, tartly red-berry-flavored Ruwer Riesling is typically spare yet lip-smacking in refreshment and impressively versatile.

Ockfener Bockstein Riesling Kabinett 🆂🅳 ♀ $$$ Relatively sweet yet impeccably balanced, this displays effusive orange blossom and tropical fruit characteristic of the best wines from the famous Bockstein vineyard.

Wiltinger Gottesfuss Riesling Kabinett feinherb ♀ $$$ A nutty, zesty, pit-fruited, fruit-pit-tinged, and mineral-inflected Riesling from one of the top sites on the Saar.

Wiltinger Riesling trocken ♀ $$$ Sourced from top-notch Saar sites, this typically offers a fascinating mélange of pit fruits, nuts, herbs, and salt.

R. & B. KNEBEL *(Mosel)*

Riesling Trocken von den Terrassen ♀ **$$$** This blend from four diverse sites consistently delivers impressive complexity for its price. Oily in texture, it can ascend to 13.5% or more alcohol, so bear that in mind in pairing it with food.

KOEHLER-RUPPRECHT *(Pfalz)*

Kallstadter Steinacker Riesling Kabinett halbtrocken ♀ **$$$** This vigorous, virtually dry wine stuffed with tangy pit fruits, ginger spice, and smoke illustrates the highly distinctive style of master vintner Bernd Philippi.

KRÜGER-RUMPF *(Nahe)*

Riesling Kabinett SD ♀ **$$** Given a sprawling collection of Krüger-Rumpf wines that includes numerous single-vineyard Riesling Kabinetts, it's best simply to state that any one of them ensures a veritable riot of fruits and flowers in the glass.

PETER-JAKOB KÜHN *(Rheingau)*

Oestricher Lenchen Riesling Kabinett SD ♀ **$$$** This offers strikingly floral aromas; combines stuffing and caressing texture with clarity, refreshment, and delicacy; and achieves an uncanny balance of residual sugar and acidity that will make sweetness the farthest thing from your mind as you enjoy putting it through its paces at table or savoring it solo.

Oestricher Riesling trocken ♀ **$$** This wine of an iconoclast maintains a lovely balance between stuffing and silkiness of texture on the one hand, and clarity, refreshment, and elegance on the other.

Riesling trocken Quarzit ♀ **$$$** One taste will almost surely suffice to explain why this adamantly dry, consistently sappy, bright, and energetic wine is named for a mineral.

JOSEF LEITZ *(Rheingau)*

Riesling Dragonstone SD ♀ **$$** There is no better example of the electric intensity or the uncanny balance between taut, invigorating acidity and a high level of residual sugar of which German Riesling is capable than this wine named for Rüdesheim's Drachenstein vineyard. Zesty lime, peach, pink grapefruit, red currant, and brown spices are among the flavors delivered with simultaneous penetration and delicacy.

Riesling Eins Zwei Drei ♀ **$$** The latest wine in Leitz's ambitious portfolio of extraordinary value Rieslings targeted at the U.S. market weighs in at a mere 12% alcohol and is crisp, sappy, satin textured, piquantly smoky, stony, salty, and full of ripe pit fruits.

Rüdesheimer Klosterlay Riesling Kabinett SD ♀ **$$** Typically at a mere 10% alcohol, and largely hiding its high residual sugar, this lavishes the palate with peaches, cherries, vanilla and lemon cream, flowers, and brown spices.

Rüdesheimer Magdalenenkreuz Riesling Spätlese S ♀ **$$$** The richest-tasting (though still delicate) Riesling among Leitz's value-priced wines, this is a veritable fruit fest with a polished, subtly oily feel and overt sweetness.

SCHLOSS LIESER *(Mosel)*

Riesling SD ♀ **$$** Apple, melon, and herbal essences mingle on a juicy and clear yet surprisingly rich palate, leading to a finish typically tinged by brown spices, toasted nuts, and wet stone.

Riesling Kabinett S ♀ **$$$** Often marked by yeastiness in their youth, the Lieser wines of Thomas Haag are typically delicate and high in residual sweetness, yet even this generic Kabinett seems positively saturated with floral and pit-fruit essences and crushed stone.

LINGENFELDER *(Pfalz)*

Bird Riesling ♀ **$** Part of a bargain-priced lineup that relies on purchased grapes, this versatile Riesling displays the sappy, saline tang typical of the Pfalz.

CARL LOEWEN *(Mosel)*

Leiwener Klostergarten Riesling Kabinett SD ♀ **$$$** Tending toward flavors of roasted pumpkin and squash—impressions enhanced by a waxy texture—this finishes with discreet sweetness, refreshing salinity, lift, and elegance.

DR. LOOSEN (*Mosel*)

Bernkasteler Lay Riesling Kabinett 🆂🅳 ♀ **$$$** Loosen presents price-conscious consumers with a near embarrassment of affordable riches, including off-dry Kabinetts each distinctively of their site, such as this dark cherry– and spice-filled Lay.

Erdener Treppchen Riesling Kabinett 🆂🅳 ♀ **$$$** Sassafras, licorice, tangerine, spice, and smoke characterize this epitome of the Treppchen vineyard.

Graacher Himmelreich Kabinett feinherb ♀ **$$$** Virtually dry, brightly citric, piquant, intensely mineral, and extremely versatile.

Riesling Blue Slate ♀ **$$** A dry Riesling of considerable flavor, depth, and sense of stuffing (at 12.5% alcohol) allied to elegance and refreshment.

Riesling Dr. L. 🆂🅳 ♀ **$** This consistently refreshing, focused, generously fruited, and discreetly sweet wine from purchased grapes is a superb visitor's card for Dr. Loosen and Mosel Riesling as a whole.

Ürziger Würzgarten Kabinett 🆂🅳 ♀ **$$$** With its key notes of strawberry and kiwi fruit, this manages to be at once lush and delicate.

Wehlener Sonnenuhr Kabinett 🆂🅳 ♀ **$$$** Displaying the vanilla cream and fresh apple signatures of its site, this follows its fellow Loosen Kabinett bottlings in allying richness more typical of wines labeled "Spätlese" with delicacy and lift.

ALFRED MERKELBACH (*Mosel*)

Erdener Treppchen Riesling Spätlese 🆂 ♀ **$$$** Orange, tangerine, pungent herbs, and a suggestion of smoke hover about this unabashedly sweet yet invigorating and thirst-quenching Spätlese.

Kinheimer Rosenberg Riesling Kabinett 🆂🅳 ♀ **$$** The Merkelbach brothers—who ship most of their production to the U.S.—are an astonishing source of value, including this pear- and apple-filled, gossamer, entry-level wine.

Kinheimer Rosenberg Riesling Spätlese ⑤ 🍷 $$$ While often less dramatically distinctive than Merkelbach's Treppchen or Würzgarten, this is archetypal orchard-fruit-filled and slate-kissed Mosel Riesling.

Ürziger Würzgarten Riesling Auslese ⑤ 🍷 $$$ Strawberry preserves, citrus marmalade, honey, and spice mark this rarity: namely, a classic Mosel Auslese for little more than the price of most top-notch Kabinetts.

Ürziger Würzgarten Riesling Kabinett ⑤⑰ 🍷 $$ Fresh strawberry, citrus, and subtle notes one can only describe as mineral make this incredibly refreshing and impossible to put down.

Ürziger Würzgarten Riesling Spätlese ⑤ 🍷 $$$ This red-berried Riesling's combination of richness and delicacy seems to defy gravity. (Note that different bottlings from the same site by Merkelbach are often distinguished from one another solely by a cask number.)

MESSMER *(Pfalz)*

Muskateller Kabinett 🍷 $$$ A rare affordable introduction to a delightfully distinctive and incredibly versatile genre, with herbal, citrus-zest pungency and a salty tang, backed by just barely registered sweetness.

Riesling Kabinett Muschelkalk 🍷 $$$ This Riesling named for its chalk soil delivers a versatile, satisfyingly pithy, pit-fruit-filled mouthful of Pfalz hospitality.

Riesling Kabinett trocken Schiefer 🍷 $$$ A glossy-textured and richly flavored yet, by dry Pfalz wine standards, bright and delicate Riesling from a rare-for-this-region slate site.

THEO MINGES *(Pfalz)*

Flemlinger Bischofskreuz Riesling Kabinett ⑤⑰ 🍷 $$$ Full of flowers, fruit, spices, and mineral inflections, this subtly sweet Kabinett bears an unusual and more than superficial resemblance to a Mosel Riesling.

Gleisweiler Hölle Riesling Kabinett trocken 🍷 $$$ This typically brims with fresh melon and orchard fruits, laced with tart notes of fruit skin, zesty citrus rind, pungent herbs, and tactile suggestions of what one struggles to describe as other than mineral.

Riesling halbtrocken ♀ $$ While this tastes virtually dry, its low residual sugar brings out pit-fruit and spice notes less evident in the corresponding *trocken* liter bottling.

Riesling trocken ♀ $$ Sold in liter bottles, this offers a sappy, citric, saline, smoky mouthful of earthy Pfalz virtues.

MARKUS MOLITOR *(Mosel, Saar)*

Bernkastler Badstube Riesling Kabinett [SD] ♀ $$$ Creamy richness and opulence added to Bernkastel-typical black fruits makes for an unusually sumptuous Mosel Riesling. (If you see a Molitor Spätlese you can afford, don't hesitate either!)

Riesling Kabinett feinherbt ♀ $$ Among the many astonishing values in Molitor's long lineup are both dry and (in this instance) virtually dry generic bottlings with a soothing texture and high fat content most wine lovers do not associate with the Mosel.

Wehlener Sonnenuhr Riesling Kabinett [SD] ♀ $$$ Even more than other wines in the sprawling Molitor portfolio, those from Wehlener Sonnenuhr reinforce its creamy, rich, and for Mosel relatively low-acid style.

Zeltinger Sonnenuhr Riesling Kabinett [SD] ♀ $$$ A broad, plush, yet low-alcohol take on one of the Mosel's great sites, filled with nut-oil and pit-fruit richness.

GEORG MOSBACHER *(Pfalz)*

Riesling Kabinett trocken ♀ $$ Stuffed with down-to-earth, pithy Pfalz virtues, this generic bottling is guaranteed to prove highly versatile.

VON OTHEGRAVEN *(Saar)*

Wiltinger Kupp Riesling Kabinett feinberb ♀ $$$ A wine combining considerable stuffing with elegance and alcoholic lightness, and tasting virtually dry, this offers a window onto the amazing food-friendliness of a great many dry and near-dry Saar Rieslings.

FRED PRINZ *(Rheingau)*

Hallgartner Jungfer Riesling Kabinett ⑤ℙ 🍷 $$$ Redolent of flowers, red berries, and citrus, this boasts finesse and judicious and impeccably balanced sweetness.

Riesling trocken 🍷 $$ This ultra-affordable bottling from purchased grapes reflects Prinz's consistently high standards, offering considerable nuance of flowers and salty, chalky minerality.

RATZENBERGER *(Mittelrhein)*

Riesling Kabinett trocken 🍷 $$ Far from the only consistently astonishing Ratzenberger value, this offers a broth-like "stone soup" with citrus and winter vegetables; a bit like a top-notch Chablis cru—at one-third the price.

Steeger St. Jost Kabinett halbtrocken 🍷 $$$ Amazingly versatile, this offers an interplay of profuse flowers, herbs, citrus, and minerals; refreshment and palate-saturating intensity allied to textural creaminess and delicacy; plus impeccable balance.

MAX. FERD. RICHTER *(Mosel)*

Graacher Domprobst Riesling Kabinett feinherb 🍷 $$$ The nutty depth inherent in this site and the rich yet slightly grainy Richter style perfectly complement each other.

Graacher Himmelreich Riesling Kabinett ⑤ℙ 🍷 $$$ This wine's abundant citrus, flowers, and suggestions of salt and stone reflect a single parcel high above the town of Bernkastel.

Mühlheimer Sonnenlay Riesling Kabinett feinherb 🍷 $$$ Richter's Rieslings make up in generosity and value for anything they might occasionally lack in refinement in their youth, and those from less well-known sites like this are especially worth sampling.

Veldenzer Elisenberg Riesling Kabinett ⑤ℙ 🍷 $$$ This wine from a cool side valley of the Mosel characteristically features tart black fruits and luscious, sweet-scented citrus such as pink grapefruit and blood orange.

Wehlener Sonnenuhr Riesling Kabinett ⑤ℙ 🍷 $$$ Typically an unusually bright and overtly stony expression of this great "sundial" site.

SCHLOSS SAARSTEIN *(Saar)*

Pinot Blanc ♀ $$$ Apple-y, nutty, refreshing, and wet stone tinged—enough to make you wonder why more Mosel or Saar vintners don't plant this grape.

Schloss Saarstein Riesling ♀ $$ This crisp, seemingly mineral-starched, and virtually dry Riesling is inexpensive and abundant thanks to an arrangement to assemble and bottle it off-premises.

SCHÄFER-FRÖHLICH *(Nahe)*

Riesling ♀ $$ This virtually dry estate Riesling represents a consistently extraordinary value, offering a kaleidoscopic interplay of fruits, flowers, minerals, and spice, alluring creaminess of texture with penetration and invigoration, and lip-smacking refreshment.

SCHMITT-WAGNER *(Mosel)*

Longuicher Maximiner Herrenberg Riesling Kabinett SD ♀ $$ A subtly sweet, red berry, citrus, and crushed stone–laced Riesling from ancient vines in a once famous site.

SELBACH-OSTER *(Mosel)*

Riesling Kabinett SD ♀ $$$ Selbach's sappy, citric generic Kabinett offers a handsome and affordable introduction to Mosel Riesling.

Zeltinger Himmelreich Riesling Kabinett halbtrocken ♀ $$$ This versatile, refreshing, and dry-tasting Riesling seems to have been starched with crushed slate stone and mineral salts, and combines a tactile sense of stuffing with elegance and refinement.

Zeltinger Schlossberg Riesling Kabinett SD ♀ $$$ Like most of the superb values from Selbach, this dramatically reflects its site, here in charred, smoky notes and an amazing concentration of pit fruits, citrus, and sheer stone given its light alcoholic weight.

SPREITZER *(Rheingau)*

Oestricher Doosberg Riesling Kabinett SD ♀ $$$ Displaying a conservatory's and orchard's worth of flowers, greenery, and fruits, this is Mosel-like in its delicacy, refinement, refreshment, and deftly balanced sweetness.

Oestricher Lenchen Riesling Kabinett SD ♀ $$$ Frequently as low as 8% alcohol, this unabashedly fruity yet totally refreshing and distinctively mineral-tinged Kabinett is irresistible for simply sipping solo.

WEINGUT STEIN *(Mosel)*

Riesling trocken ♀ $$$ Redolent of lime and tangerine; tingling and refreshing yet possessed of real "stone soup," palate-saturating minerality; this adamantly dry Riesling has only 10.5% alcohol yet tastes ripe.

GÜNTER STEINMETZ *(Mosel)*

Mühlheimer Sonnenlay Riesling feinherb ♀ $$$ This cask-matured Riesling displays the Steinmetz style: amplitude, textural richness, and relatively low acidity (by Mosel standards), with memorable suggestions of mineral matter and sheer length.

Veldenzer Graftschafter-Sonnenberg feinherb ♀ $$$ A richly expressive, versatile, virtually dry-tasting, pit-fruit- and nut-oil-saturated Riesling the likes of which would for most of the last century have been labeled and celebrated as classic Spätlese.

J. & H. A. STRUB *(Rheinhessen)*

Niersteiner Brückchen Kabinett SD ♀ $$ Typically stuffed full of orchard fruits and sweet corn, often with suggestions of vanilla, talcum, and chalk dust, this luscious, sappy Kabinett is irresistible in quality and price.

Niersteiner Paterberg Spätlese S ♀ $$$ Sauvignon-like in its essence of aromatic herbs, and with bright citrus and saline minerality keeping it invigorating despite its sweetness. Don't simply savor this wine on its own, take it to the table!

Riesling Soil to Soul SD ♀ $$ This latest incarnation of Strub's discreetly sweet house wine marries two sites, achieving synergies of citrus, pit fruits, aromatic herbs, chalk, and talcum.

ST. URBANS-HOF *(Mosel and Saar)*

Ockfener Bockstein Riesling Kabinett 🆂🅳 ⊻ **$$$** Orange blossom scented, spicy, loaded with orchard and tropical fruits, and unabashedly sweet.

Piesporter Goldtröpfchen Kabinett 🆂🅳 ⊻ **$$$** Cassis, tropical fruit, and nut oil laden, this exemplar of its famous site is lavishly rich yet light in weight.

Riesling 🆂🅳 ⊻ **$$** This estate Riesling is impeccably sourced and vinified, full of flowers, herbs, ripe pit fruits, citrus, salt, and crushed stone.

Urban Riesling ⊻ **$** Urbans-Hof owner-winemaker Nik Weis's impeccably balanced new bottling from purchased fruit is archetypally dry-tasting, refreshing Mosel at an incredibly low price.

DANIEL VOLLENWEIDER *(Mosel)*

Wolfer Goldgrube Riesling Kabinett 🆂🅳 ⊻ **$$$** Youthfully yeasty, delicate, spritzy, yet satin textured, like Vollenweider's other bottlings, this makes a clear case for his single-handed revival of a once renowned vineyard.

VAN VOLXEM *(Saar)*

Riesling Saar ⊻ **$$$** Young outsider Roman Niewodniczanski's ambitions and unorthodox (low-acid, creamy, dense) style have shaken up the Saar and are on fine display in this flower-tinged, texturally alluring basic bottling.

DR. HEINZ WAGNER *(Saar)*

Saarburger Rausch Riesling Kabinett 🆂🅳 ⊻ **$$$** This pit-fruit- and citrus-laden, light yet extract-rich Kabinett isn't typical for Wagner (most of whose wines are dry) but is typical for the portion of his portfolio that's exported.

WAGNER-STEMPEL *(Rheinhessen)*

Riesling trocken ⊻ **$$** Try this bright, apple-y, subtly stony and saline refresher, and you might conclude that the reason it's sold in liter bottles is 750 milliliters would never be enough!

Silvaner trocken ♀ $$$ Simply one of the world's most amazing white wine values, young star Daniel Wagner's Silvaner offers luscious pear and apple underlain by nut-oil richness and shot through with salinity and pungent smoke.

WEEGMÜLLER *(Pfalz)*

Riesling Kabinett trocken ♀ $$$ Most years, there are three single-vineyard dry Riesling Kabinett bottlings from Stephanie Weegmüller, any of which offer clarity, refreshment, and an abundance of citrus, pit fruits, spice, and mineral salts.

Scheurebe trocken ♀ $$$ Expect mint, sage, black currant, and pink grapefruit from this glossy, quite full-bodied, dry rendition of an audaciously aromatic and astonishingly versatile grape that's nowadays usually vinified sweet.

Weisser Burgunder trocken ♀ $$$ This rich and nutty yet elegant and refreshing Pinot Blanc offers exceptional versatility and quality-price rapport.

DR. WEHRHEIM *(Pfalz)*

Riesling Kabinett trocken Bundsandstein ♀ $$$ This offers clear, penetrating citrus and pit-fruit character and a positive sense of sheer stuffing, as well as consistent invigoration and refreshment.

Silvaner trocken ♀ $ This liter bottling must be numbered among a handful of the world's most amazing vinous bargains: unusually bright, vivacious, and mineral tinged for Silvaner, yet plush and palpably extract rich.

FLORIAN WEINGART *(Mittelhrein)*

Schloss Fürstenberg Riesling Kabinett SD ♀ $$$ Consistently floral; light yet mysteriously, palpably full of stuffing; and animated by ripe acidity, this offers a clear window onto the vinous charms of these Lorelei slopes and the talents of young Florian Weingart.

WEINS-PRÜM *(Mosel)*

Graacher Domprobst Riesling Kabinett SD ♀ $$$ Demonstrating the difference location makes, this displays the typical nutty richness and pit fruits of the great Domprobst site.

Graacher Himmelreich Riesling Kabinett ⬚SD ⚗ **$$$** Transparency, delicacy, and overt sweetness are common denominators in all Weins-Prüm wines. From Himmelreich, expect apple, citrus, and black fruits with a bright, tangy finish.

Wehlener Sonnenuhr Riesling Kabinett ⬚SD ⚗ **$$$** Here is the apple and vanilla, creaminess and polish (by no means precluding refreshment) typical of the site, in an especially effusive form.

WEISER-KÜNSTLER *(Mosel)*

Enkircher Ellergrub Riesling Kabinett ⬚SD ⚗ **$$$** Redolent of herbs and flowers typical for this steep, long-neglected site, along with pure pear nectar, a lovely silken texture, and wafting lightness, this finishes with impeccably judged, scarcely noticeable sweetness and a vivid invocation of wet stone.

Riesling feinherb ⚗ **$$** This virtually dry Riesling displays juicy licorice, crushed stone, and lemon zest–suffused honeydew melon and retains youthful notes of yeast and CO_2 typical for this estate.

Trabacher Gaispfad Riesling Kabinett ⬚SD ⚗ **$$$** This husband-and-wife collaboration (since 2005) is restoring dignity to unjustly neglected sites, and if you tread Trabach's steep "goat path," you will get a delicious look at Mosel Riesling's delicate virtues.

ZILLIKEN *(Saar)*

Ockfener Bockstein Riesling Kabinett ⬚SD ⚗ **$$$** This orange blossom– and tropical fruit–scented Bockstein epitomizes the electrically charged, impeccably balanced although hugely high-sugar Riesling for which Zilliken is renowned.

Riesling Butterfly ⚗ **$$$** Sourced entirely from Zilliken's steep, slate Saarburg vineyards, this versatile wine is plush in texture, virtually dry (at around 11.5% alcohol), and calls forth a range of mineral vocabulary.

Saarburger Rausch Riesling Kabinett ⬚SD ⚗ **$$$** Typically redolent of cherry, almond, citrus, and spice, this invigorating and remarkably affordable tonic is a marvel of balance.

GREECE

GREEK WINE VALUES

by Mark Squires

Greece is a bargain hunter's treasure trove. There are a few trophy wines, but even most of the better wines come in at under $50. It is easy to find quality bargains under $25, particularly in whites and dessert wines. Consumers do need to invest a little effort in one respect, though. They must become familiar with popular indigenous grapes, particularly the "big four"—Xinomavro (skee-NO-mah-vro) and Agiorgitiko (ay-yor-YEE-tee-ko), both red; and Assyrtiko (uh-SEER-ti-ko) and Moschofilero (mos-ko-FEEL-er-o), both white. Although you will certainly find many winemakers effectively using international grapes, including Sauvignon Blanc, Syrah, and Cabernet Sauvignon, the local grape varieties have their own personalities and offer new flavors.

A word of warning: Transliteration from Greek is tricky and alternative spellings are common. While "Assyrtiko," "Xinomavro," and "Agiorgitiko" are more or less standard, it sometimes it seems like anything goes and you will also see "Xynomavro," "Asirtiko," and "Asyrtico," and so on. There is some talk of the need to standardize spellings. I generally use whatever is on the label to avoid consumer confusion.

Regions and Grapes

There are bargains everywhere in Greece. For a small country, it is geographically spread out, with many appellations, so take this as just a snapshot of some of the more popular areas relating to the big four rather than an exhaustive explanation of Greece's classification system and *terroir*. **Santorini** is known for Assyrtiko. By custom and by law, a white wine labeled simply Santorini will be dominated by Assyrtiko. Unoaked Assyrtiko from Santorini's pre-phylloxera vineyards is one of Greece's best wines and also one of its best buys. It is often exceptional and mostly within our $25 price cutoff, even from top producers. It can be a powerful, ageworthy white wine. In other incarnations, Assyrtiko can project fine depth and a friendlier, more gentle feel.

Nemea is one of Greece's most important red wine appellations, famed for Agiorgitiko. Agiorgitiko is often fruity and bursting with flavor, a tasty, crowd-pleasing wine that is hard to resist. In the hands of good producers, these bottlings also have structure and become more than a simple, fruity little wine, but complexity, to be sure, is not the main virtue here. The best of them are simply delicious. The high-elevation region of **Mantinia** is the go-to region for Moschofilero. Moschofilero wines are generally charming, elegant, and delicate, perfect summer wines, perhaps a competitor to Vinho Verde. In the north, **Naoussa** is known for Xinomavro and is another of Greece's notable red wine appellations. Xinomavro can produce powerful and intense wines with lots of acidity and tannin. It is a difficult grape that can sometimes be rustic.

The dessert wine category produces some of Greece's best wines. There are the charming and usually very inexpensive Beaumes-de-Venise–style Muscats that are often steals, usually delightful and often running around $10; stunning Vinsantos that can age, although it is harder here to find bargains; and aromatic Mavrodaphnes, among others. They are as a group a pleasure to drink.

Vintage Smarts

It is difficult to generalize about Greek vintages without becoming very specific, down to the producer. This takes into account both that Greek wines and wineries are improving and that there is a lot of diversity in Greek *terroir*, which is spread out over a large and often mountainous area. In some years and regions, it might depend on when one picked. Some regions, like Santorini, are more consistent than others. I've generally seen a lot to like in '05–'07 reds and whites and '07 and '08 whites, which as of this writing currently dominate the marketplace. The '07 reds look especially good in the north with Xinomavro. The vintage most likely to be criticized in recent times is 2002. You won't likely see many bargain wines still on the shelves from this vintage.

Drinking Curves

Greece's popular indigenous grapes are very different in terms of cellaring potential. Moschofilero (and similar whites like Athiri and Roditis) should be drunk young. Most should be drunk on release or within 1–3 years of their vintage date. Agiorgitiko from good producers can hold well, but at the bargain end, expect many of them to be in a relatively soft and fruity style, best drunk within 3–6 years of their vintage date. Assyrtiko is a white wine that can age—although it often doesn't. From top producers, it might last a decade or more and it often needs a year or two to show its best. It is a grape that has a tendency to oxidize, though, and it needs careful handling. Xinomavro should age well in most of its incarnations. Even many very inexpensive wines might hold well for 5–8 years or more. There are, of course, exceptions to everything.

Greece's Top Wine Values by Winery

ACHAIA CLAUSS *(Patras)*

Muscat of Patras ⑤ $ This has a Beaumes-de-Venise feel to it, sweet but not overly so, with some modest intensity and good depth.

BOUTARI *(Santorini, Mantinia, and Naoussa)*

Grand Reserve Naoussa ♥ $$$ The midpalate is modest, but this has better structure and a better finish than the regular Naoussa, leaving it elegant, earthy, and bright, with a somewhat rustic edge.

Moschofilero ♀ $$ Light and bright, with only 11% alcohol, delicate in body, delightfully fruity, and quite appealing, with a nice, flavorful finish.

Naoussa ♥ $$ All Xinomavro, this can seem a bit older than its vintage date would suggest, but it is elegant and bright, with some tannin on the finish at the outset and earthy nuances.

Santorini ♀ $$ This Assyrtiko has a nice, bright finish, a bit of herbaceousness, and some bursts of acidity around the edges, making it persistent, sunny, and charming.

Vinsanto ⑤ $$$ Sweet, rather decadent, ageworthy, and simply delicious, this lush, unctuous wine grabs the palate and dribbles sugar and fruit all over it.

COSTA LAZARIDIS *(Drama)*

Amethystos ♀ $$ Mostly Sauvignon Blanc, with some Assyrtiko and Sémillon, light, very racy, and very grassy.

Chardonnay (Château Julia) ♀ $$ Fresh and relatively light, open, and accessible, this fleshes out a bit as it airs out, becoming fruitier and tastier.

Sauvignon Blanc "Amethystos" ♉ **$$** Oak-fermented and aged *sur-lie,* this pure Sauvignon Blanc is relatively laid-back, ripe, and plump, and surprisingly less grassy than the Amethystos Sauvignon Blanc blend, above.

EMERY *(Rhodes)*

Athiri Mountain Slopes ♉ **$$** More penetrating and focused than the Rhodos version (below), but not necessarily better every year.

Athiri "Rhodos" ♉ **$** There is some elegant power here; a fine job with a delicate grape.

GAI'A *(Peloponnese and Santorini)*

Nótios ♉ **$** A blend of Moschofilero and Roditis, with a pungent nose projecting some herbaceousness, a delicate midpalate, and a crisp, mouthwatering, perhaps even mouth-puckering finish.

Thalassitis ♉ **$$** One of Greece's best bargains in Assyrtiko; on the steelier side, powerful and piercing. Prices have increased to the $$$ level as of the 2008 vintage.

GENTILINI *(Cephalonia)*

Aspro Classic ♉ **$$** This wine has some character and distinctiveness, as the Sauvignon Blanc component is moderated by other grapes, turning it more to dry melon than grassy and herbaceous exuberance.

GREEK WINE CELLARS *(Patras)*

Muscat-Samos Ⓢ **$** A lovely Beaumes-de-Venise–style Muscat, aromatic and rather sweet, with some acidity, too.

Roditis "Asprolithi" (Oenoforos) ♉ **$** Unoaked, light, crisp, and pungent, with nice floral aromas.

HATZIDAKIS *(Santorini)*

Santorini ♉ **$$$** Bright and lively, full in the mouth, with a lingering finish, this has some power.

Vinsanto Ⓢ **$$$** Very sweet, rich, and delicious, coming in at 13% alcohol, with a first rush of fruit and sugar that is enthralling.

DOMAINE HATZIMICHALIS *(Atalanti Valley and Opontia Locris)*

Domaine Hatzimichalis Estate ♀ $ A blend of Athiri, Assyrtiko, and Robola, this is a well-constructed wine that has some body, a nice finish, and a certain mouth-coating quality that engages the whole palate initially.

Veriki ♀ $$$ An equal blend of Chardonnay and Robola, this unoaked wine can be distinguished as well as reasonably priced, with fine depth, a feeling of substance, and gravitas.

DOMAINE KARYDAS *(Naoussa)*

Xinomavro ♀ $$$ A beautiful wine from a small boutique producer, combining fine fruit and a certain suave feel while retaining all the typical aspects of this grape.

MERCOURI ESTATE *(Pisatis and Ilia)*

Antares ♀ $$$ Mostly Mourvèdre, this is gamy on the nose, which follows through strongly on the palate, and it seems like very typical Mourvèdre with a very French demeanor.

Folói ♀ $$ A blend of Roditis (85%) and Viognier, this is light and bright, a bit delicate, but simply charming, a wine that tastes delicious and has a crisp, mouthwatering finish.

Rosé "Lampadias" ♀ $ In perfect balance, medium bodied, dry, and crisp, but ripe, fruity, and flavorful.

MORAITIS *(Paros)*

Parios Oenos ♀ $$ All Monemvasia, fresh, pure, delicate in the midpalate, pristine, and sunny.

Sillogi Moraiti ♀ $$ An Assyrtiko-Malagouzia blend, this is pungent, light, low in alcohol (12.5%), and crisp, a rather lively and sunny wine that is charming and refreshing.

CHRISTOFOROS PAVLIDIS *(Drama)*

"Thema" ♀ **$$** This wine is largely dominated by Sauvignon Blanc, with the classic cut-grass nuances in the foreground here, but the Assyrtiko stops it from spinning out of control and gives the wine some body and distinction.

SANTO WINES *(Santorini)*

Assyrtiko ♀ **$$$** Laid-back and fruity for Santorini, with little of the steely austerity one often encounters, it has good depth and a certain pleasing roundness.

SEMELI *(Peloponnese)*

Agiorgitiko Rosé ♀ **$** A dry, piercing pink on opening, but that power is deceptive because this in fact is rather friendly.

Mountain Sun ♀ **$** A blend of high-altitude Roditis (10%, over 900 feet) and Moschofilero (over 400 feet), it is herbaceous, quite pungent, light, and bright, a warm-weather wine that is best served and drunk young and well chilled.

DOMAINE SIGALAS *(Santorini)*

Asirtiko/Athiri ♀ **$** This has good depth and a fat feel to it, with intensity at the end from the acidity.

Santorini ♀ **$$$** All Assyrtiko, this adds depth to the blend above, and it feels rich.

SKOURAS *(Peloponnese and Nemea)*

Moscofilero ♀ **$** Light and bright, more intense than the basic white blend, Skouras white, reviewed below, with a much better finish, yet still delicate . . . and quite delicious.

Saint George ♀ **$** Impeccably balanced, this has an ethereal feel to it; it is bright, sunny, charming, and tasty, with some grip on the finish, a Beaujolais without the carbonic maceration.

Skouras white ♀ **$** A blend of Roditis and Moschofilero, this is bright and a touch grassy, but with decent depth and some succulence on the finish.

Viognier "Cuvée Larsinos" ♀ $$ Light and a bit delicate, this nonetheless feels more ethereal than ephemeral and is stylistically true to Viognier, with lovely aromatics and good focus.

THIMIOPOULOS *(Macedonia)*

"Uranos" Xinomavro ♥ $$$ This is a somewhat modern style of Xinomavro, but still distinctive and a wine that can grow on you, as it becomes more complex with about 2 hours of decanting.

TSELEPOS *(Mantinia)*

Moschofilero ♀ $$$ Crisp, succulent, a little grassy, and rather light, the persistent acidity here lifts up the fruit around it.

UNION OF WINEMAKING COOPERATIVES OF SAMOS *(Samos)*

Muscato "Vin Doux" Ⓢ $$ A bit higher priced than many Greek Muscats, this is also a cut above the ordinary in quality, surprisingly viscous and honeyed, with simply delicious fruit.

Samena Golden ♀ $ Made from Muscat, it is typically pungent, light on its feet, dry, and rather crisp.

VAENI NAOUSSA *(Naoussa)*

Damascenos (a.k.a. Damaskinos) ♥ $$$ All Xinomavro, meant to be a somewhat more individualistic product in Vaeni's lineup, ripe and oak-aged, a sedate and modern style for Xinomavro.

Xinomavro ♥ $$ Light, bright, and relatively low in alcohol, this is one of the best intersections of value and price in their lineup.

VATISTAS *(Laconia)*

Asproudi/Assyritko ♀ $$ Rather straightforward, but round, with a nice mouth-feel, reasonable depth, and decent acidity.

VOLCAN WINES *(Santorini)*

Koutsoyiannopoulos ♀ $$$ All Assyrtiko, this is full in the mouth, with a velvety texture, yet also sunny and rather crisp, with a fine, lingering finish.

ITALY

ITALIAN WINE VALUES

by Antonio Galloni

Few, if any, countries offer consumers a breadth of value-priced wines that can match that of Italy. From the crisp, minerally whites of Alto Adige to the perfumed Nebbiolos of Piedmont to the rich, bold reds of Campania, Italy produces a wide range of wines for every palate and budget. Seeking out the best values often means looking beyond the most coveted varieties and regions. Of course, this plays perfectly to the strengths of a country with somewhere between 1,000 and 2,000 indigenous grape varieties, most of which remain undiscovered by consumers on a wide scale. In addition, consider the diversity of Italy's wine-producing regions, which encompass everything from the dry, desert-like heat of Sicily all the way to the Alpine microclimates of Alto Adige, and everything in between. Add to that a series of strong vintages, and the marketplace today is literally awash with hundreds of compelling wines that can be had for $25 or less, yet will deliver tremendous pleasure.

Understanding Italian Wine Culture

As outstanding as Italy's wine can be, readers should note that in Italy, wine and food are inextricably linked to an extent that is perhaps matched only in France. Italians rarely drink wine outside of mealtimes, and even the occasional glass of wine consumed as an *aperitivo* is always accompanied by food. This is important to keep in mind, as one of the secrets of enjoying Italian wines to the maximum is to pair them with dishes from the same region. It is tough to beat a glass of fine Chianti alongside a plate of pasta with boar sauce or a Vermentino with fresh fish or shellfish, to cite just two examples. Readers who are looking for wines to serve at the table will find much to consider in the coming pages, but if the goal is to find wines that can be enjoyed alone, consumers may find that wines from other regions deliver more immediate pleasure.

Piedmont

When it comes to sheer diversity, it's awfully hard to beat Piedmont for value. That may sound hard to believe considering the prices top Barolos and Barbarescos fetch in today's market, but the fact remains that Piedmont offers extraordinary quality at the budget level. When looking for value in Piedmont a good rule of thumb is to stick with entry-level wines of the best estates whenever possible. More often than not top Barolo and Barbaresco producers treat their Dolcettos and Barberas with the same care that they lavish on their higher-end bottlings, and these entry-level wines make a great introduction to the various producers' styles.

Arneis is a perfect aperitif or summertime wine, but its floral qualities and delicate fruit are best enjoyed up to one year after the harvest. Dolcetto is the everyday red wine of Piedmont. The best versions are so packed with dark ripe fruit, minerals, and spices that they often leave me wondering why on earth I don't drink the wines more often. Most of the Barberas in the under-$25 price range are typically made in a fresh style, with little or no oak. In a ripe year like 2006 the wines are especially generous and fleshy. Barberas from the towns around Alba are often rounder and more supple than the more minerally versions from around Asti, but at their best, both areas produce wines of notable quality. The finest Nebbiolos offer all of the qualities of their bigger siblings, Barolo and Barbaresco, but in miniature. Finally, there are few better ways to end a meal than with a glass of Moscato. Unfortunately there is an ocean of Moscato in the marketplace, and the long-standing assumption is that all of the wines are essentially the same. Nothing could be farther from the truth. Great Moscato requires all of the same things needed to make any important wine: a first-class site, low yields, and most important of all, the vision and passion of a dedicated grower.

Tuscany

Although Tuscany doesn't offer the sheer varietal diversity of Piedmont, Campania, Sardinia, and other regions, it compensates for that with an enormous number of delicious, value-priced wines. Tuscany's strong suit is reds, particularly those where Sangiovese is the principal grape. Readers will find a vast number of choices from all of Tuscany's appellations.

Northern Italy

With the exception of Campania, I can think of no better region to explore the breadth of Italian whites than **Trentino–Alto Adige.** Alto Adige excels in a wide range of both indigenous and international varieties. The wines tend to be steely and minerally, with gorgeous aromatics and tons of varietal character. Highlights are Pinot Bianco, Pinot Grigio, Sylvaner, Kerner, and Gewürtztraminer, a variety that was discovered in the town of Termeno.

Veneto is home to a number of compelling wines. For starters, the sparkling Prosecco is a delicious aperitif wine that embodies the joy of the Italian lifestyle, also known as *la dolce vita*. Veneto's other great white is the Garganega-based Soave. Much maligned in the past, today Soave produces a number of gorgeous whites that merit consideration. Of course, Veneto also boasts Valpolicella, Amarone, and a number of magnificent sweet wines. While many of these fall outside the budget level, readers will find a number of delicious Valpolicellas in the under-$25 category. Like Soave, Valpolicella is a wine with a checkered past, but today's wines are building a new and well-deserved reputation for quality.

Friuli has been in the spotlight for some time, and as a result, it is harder to find value-priced wines. The main grapes grown in Friuli are Ribolla, Friulano (the grape previously known as Tocai), Sauvignon, Chardonnay, and Pinot Grigio among the whites; Merlot, Cabernet, Refosco, Schioppettino, and Pignolo among the reds; and Picolit (also known as Ramandolo) among the varieties used for sweet wines. **Lombardy** has two important appellations: Franciacorta, for sparkling wines, and Valtellina, where the local Chiavennasca (Nebbiolo) is customarily air-dried, Amarone-style, to make rich wines that at their best offer tons of personality. Sadly, the vast majority of these wines fall outside our $25 price range. **Emilia-Romagna** is a region that doesn't get a lot of attention in serious wine circles, yet each year I taste a number of interesting offerings that merit consideration. Lambrusco is a wine that is often dismissed, but at its best it is well worth discovering. Emilia-Romagna is also capable of producing good to excellent Sangiovese.

Central and Southern Italy

Campania is a region that fascinates to no end. Blessed with an extraordinary range of highly expressive indigenous varieties, unique *terroirs*, and an oenological history that dates back several thousand years, Campania is a gem waiting to be discovered. Among the whites, the fruity Falanghina can be a standout, but only when made by quality-minded producers. The intensely mineral-driven Greco di Tufo is a great food wine, particularly with raw fish and seafood. Fiano di Avellino is typically rounder and softer than Greco, yet it, too, can offer notable complexity. Among the reds, Aglianico reigns supreme. Readers will find a number of entry-level bottlings that capture the unique qualities of this compelling indigenous grape.

Sicily is another region that is capable of making a wide array of compelling wines. Among the whites, readers should focus on distinctive native varieties like Inzolia and Catarratto, which yield perfumed, aromatic wines. Nero d'Avola is a red grape whose potential has barely been mined. Nero d'Avola can be light colored and delicate, almost like Pinot Noir, but it can also produce big, full-bodied, gamy wines. Nerello Mascalese, which flourishes on the high-altitude slopes of Etna, is capable of reds that resemble Pinot or Nebbiolo, but sadly, these wines remain hard to find in the value space. I continue to be amazed by the stunning quality of the wines of **Sardinia**. Nowhere is the white Vermentino as convincing as it is in Sardinia. A perfumed, floral white, at its best, Vermentino delivers tremendous pleasure for the money. The island's array of native red varieties is truly stunning. Monica, Carignano, Bovale Sardo, and above all, Cannonau (Grenache) yield wines of notable richness and depth.

The **Marche** is most famous for the white Verdicchio, yet the region is also capable of making delicious reds as well. **Abruzzo** is a great source for value-priced wines. Montepulciano, the main red variety grown there, has come a long way from the harsh, rustic wines that were common years ago. Today's best Montepulcianos are juicy, plump, and full of fruit. Cerasuolo, the rosé from Montepulciano, can be quite special. The white Trebbiano is also yielding increasingly noteworthy results, but the wines need to be drunk young. **Umbria** excels most with reds, with the exception of Orvieto, which can be interesting on occasion. The most interesting appellation in Umbria is Montefalco, where the native Sagrantino is capable of wines imbued with character. Unfortunately, these wines cost well above $25, but top estates' entry-level *rossos* can be delicious introductory wines.

Puglia is one of the most fascinating emerging regions in Italy. The native Negroamaro and Primitivo (Zinfandel) are among the red varieties whose full potential has yet to be fully tapped. In **Basilicata** it is the red Aglianico, especially when grown in the Vulture district, that is worthy of consideration. **Calabria** is another of the regions of southern Italy that is off the beaten track, but in recent years a number of wines made from the native Gaglioppo have been very delicious.

Vintage Smarts

Broadly speaking, Italian reds are very successful in both 2006 and 2007. The 2006s are big, bold wines loaded with ripe fruit backed up by plenty of structure. The 2007s are more aromatic and also softer, largely because the acidities are lower. Both vintages are first rate for the wines of Piedmont and Tuscany. 2005 is a cooler vintage and requires a more selective focus on top producers. The reds of southern Italy tend to be less variable with regard to vintage because the weather is more consistent. Both 2006 and 2007 yielded a number of outstanding whites from all of Italy's main regions, with 2006 offering a touch better balance than the riper 2007s. Early indications are that 2008 is an above-average vintage in most of Italy's main winemaking regions.

Drinking Curves

For the most part, Italy's value-priced wines are meant to be enjoyed upon release. The reds can age for a few years, and the occasional Chianti or Nebbiolo can surprise at age 10 or beyond, but these are exceptions. Italy's entry-level whites are meant to be consumed young, preferably upon release. Most wines will benefit from being opened at least 30 minutes prior to serving.

Italy's Top Wine Values by Winery

ABBAZIA DI NOVACELLA *(Alto Adige)*

Sylvaner ♀ $$$ A wine that reveals lovely detail and nuance in a layered expression of varietal fruit.

ABBAZIA SANTA ANASTASIA *(Sicily)*

Nero d'Avola ♟ $$ A pretty, layered offering that shows plenty of dark fruit, licorice, and mint along with the notes of gaminess that are typical of Nero d'Avola.

Passomaggio ♟ $$$ An impressive red loaded with jammy dark fruit, smoke, and tar on a full-bodied, structured frame. This blend of Nero d'Avola and Merlot is seductive stuff.

ABBONA *(Piedmont)*

Dogliani Papa Celso 🍷 **$$** A deeply colored wine packed with layers of ripe dark fruit supported by a firm tannic structure that ensures a minimum of several years of very fine drinking after release. Without question one of the finest Doglianis being made today.

Barbera d'Alba Rinaldi 🍷 **$$$** Reveals considerable weight and richness in its layers of dark red fruit, toasted oak, and spices. Aged first in French oak and then in larger Slavonian oak casks.

ACCORDINI *(Veneto)*

Valpolicella 🍷 **$$$** An absolutely beautiful, joyous wine bursting with perfumed, fresh fruit, earthiness, and tar. First-class Valpolicella.

Valpolicella Ripasso 🍷 **$$$** Full bodied, expansive, with plenty of black cherries, tobacco, sweet toasted oak, and grilled herbs.

ALARIO *(Piedmont)*

Dolcetto di Diano Montagrillo 🍷 **$$** No-holds-barred style, with plenty of intense, superripe blackberries, blueberries, cassis, minerals, and spices. One of the finest Dolcettos on the market.

ALLEGRINI *(Veneto)*

Soave 🍷 **$$** A lean, focused style of Soave (80% Garganega, 20% Chardonnay.)

Valpolicella Classico 🍷 **$$** This Valpolicella offers up an attractive array of wild herbs, rosemary, and cherries in a medium-bodied style.

Palazzo della Torre 🍷 **$$$** An opulent, generous red loaded with jammy dark cherries, chocolate, spices, and sweet toasted oak. (70% Corvina Veronese, 25% Rondinella, and 5% Sangiovese made from partially dried grapes.)

La Grola 🍷 **$$$** Enticing notes of crushed flowers, raspberries, minerals, and sweet spices, with outstanding length and silky-textured tannins. (70% Corvina Veronese, 15% Rondinella, 10% Syrah, and 5% Sangiovese.)

GIOVANNI ALMONDO *(Piedmont)*

Roero Arneis Vigne Sparse ♀ $$$ This Arneis offers ripe peaches, almonds, smoke, and minerals in a medium-bodied style.

Langhe Nebbiolo ♟ $$$ Perfumed red fruits and spices come together in a lithe, feminine style framed by firm yet elegant tannins. This needs a year or so of bottle aging after release to drink at its best.

ELIO ALTARE *(Piedmont)*

Dolcetto d'Alba ♟ $$$ This full-bodied Dolcetto packed with jammy dark blueberries, licorice, and tar is a serious wine from one of Piedmont's top producers.

ALTESINO *(Tuscany)*

Rosso di Altesino ♟ $$ An accessible, fresh red with attractive notes of dark fruit, earthiness, and herbs. (80% Sangiovese and 20% Merlot and Cabernet Sauvignon aged in stainless steel.)

AMBRA *(Tuscany)*

Trebbiano ♀ $ This accessible, easygoing white offers typical varietal notes of honeyed peaches and cantaloupe.

Rosato di Toscana ♀ $ The Rosato is a delicious, fresh wine to enjoy in the summer months.

Barco Reale di Carmignano ♟ $$ This weighty, brooding wine is packed with intense black cherries, smoke, and earthiness. (75% Sangiovese, 10% Cabernet Sauvignon, 10% Canaiolo, and 5% Merlot.)

Carmignano Santa Cristina in Pilli ♟ $$$ A very pretty, graceful wine with layers of sweet perfumed fruit, earthiness, smoke, and tobacco that flow onto the palate in a weightless, delicate style. A beautiful smaller-scaled expression of Carmignano.

Carmignano Montefortini ♟ $$ This Carmignano reveals superior density and concentration in its mentholated, balsamic profile, along with notes of earthiness, leather, smoke, and dark ripe fruit that open in the glass. A big, rich wine.

ANSELMI *(Veneto)*

San Vincenzo ♀ $ A perfumed, floral white with a generous expression of honey, flowers, apricots, and minerals. (80% Garganega, 15% Chardonnay, and 5% Trebbiano.)

Capitel Foscarino ♀ $$ This pretty, layered white possesses notable inner perfume of flowers, melon, smoke, and apricots. (90% Garganega and 10% Chardonnay.)

Capitel Croce ♀ $$$ This oak-aged offering is honeyed and perfumed, with plenty of apricots and an additional layer of volume from the oak.

ANTICHI VIGNETI DI CANTALUPO *(Piedmont)*

Nebbiolo Il Mimo ♀ $ This rosé Nebbiolo from the northern reaches of Piedmont offers gorgeous inner sweetness in its subtle notes of earthiness, red cherries, rose petals, and minerals. A classy rosé with tons of elegance, complexity, and sheer breed to spare.

ANTONIOLO *(Piedmont)*

Nebbiolo Coste della Sesia ♥ $$ Typical aromas of mountain herbs, mint, and pine complement a core of plump fruit. An overachiever in its category and a great introduction to the Nebbiolos of the Gattinara, in the north of Piedmont.

ARALDICA *(Piedmont)*

La Luciana ♀ $$ This nice, midweight Gavi reveals attractive notes of flowers, white peaches, and honey.

Barbera d'Asti Albera ♥ $ This Barbera from Asti reveals a core of dark red fruits, with suggestions of tar and licorice that add complexity and the minerality that is typical of the wines of this part of Piedmont.

ARGIANO *(Tuscany)*

Non Confunditur ♥ $$$ A fat and superripe wine packed with dark plums, cherries, smoke, tar, herbs, and licorice from one of Montalcino's top estates. (40% Cabernet Sauvignon, 20% Sangiovese, 20% Merlot, and 20% Syrah.)

ARGILLAE (Umbria)

Grechetto ♀ $$ A lovely, harmonious white with gorgeous inner perfume to its fruit.

Sinuoso ♂ $$ This plump, juicy red possesses tons of superripe black fruits, earthiness, chocolate, and toasted oak. Hillside Cabernet Sauvignon and Merlot aged in French oak.

ARGIOLAS (Sardinia)

Selegas ♀ $$ Made from the indigenous Nuragus grape, this medium-bodied white opens with expressive aromatics that meld into rich, honeyed fruit.

Costamolino ♀ $$ A very pretty white with layers of perfume-laced fruit and minerals that flow from the glass. Primarily Vermentino with a small addition of other local varieties.

Is Argiolas ♀ $$$ This 100% Vermentino from hillside vineyards is gorgeous and soft textured, with plenty of volume and depth.

SerraLori ♀ $$ This blend of indigenous red varieties (Cannonau, Monica, Carignano, Bovale Sardo) is powerful in its exotic, wild expression of ripe fruit, sweet herbs, and licorice.

Perdera ♂ $$ A delicious, hearty red loaded with dark red cherries, cracked black pepper, spices, licorice, and herbs (90% Monica, 5% Carignano, and 5% Bovale Sardo, all indigenous varieties.)

Costera ♂ $$ This massive, generous wine is packed with dark fruit, game, earthiness, mint, spices, herbs, and bacon fat. (90% Cannonau, 5% Carignano, and 5% Bovale Sardo.)

AZELIA (Piedmont)

Dolcetto d'Alba Bricco dell'Oriolo ♂ $$ An elegant, floral Dolcetto that often shows an almost Pinot-like expression of red fruit.

BADIA A COLTIBUONO (Piedmont)

Chianti Classico ♂ $$$ This pretty, delicate wine typically offers excellent clarity in its vibrant dark cherries, earthiness, spices, leather, and tobacco. (90% Sangiovese, 10% Canaiolo.)

BAGLIO DI PIANETTO *(Sicily)*

Ficiligno ♀ $$ This blend of Viognier and Insolia reveals pretty floral notes in its suggestions of peaches, melon, and zesty lemon peel.

BARBA *(Abruzzo)*

Montepulciano d'Abruzzo Vasari ♀ $ A full-bodied, generous red that offers superb purity, plenty of black fruit, and terrific overall balance.

Montepulciano d'Abruzzo Colle Morino ♀ $ The Colle Morino, made in a riper style of Montepulciano than the Vasari, is loaded with an engaging mix of smoke, licorice, earthiness, tar, and black cherries in a medium-bodied yet richly flavored style.

BASTIANICH *(Friuli Venezia Giulia)*

Friulano ♀ $ A very pleasant, soft-textured white with pretty varietal notes of ripe peaches, mint, and flowers.

BATZELLA *(Tuscany)*

Bolgheri Mezzodì ♀ $$$ A perfumed expression of Granny Smith apples, minerals, and flowers, with lovely mineral notes that frame the wine. (70% Viognier and 30% Sauvignon Blanc that was partly aged in oak, with frequent *bâtonnage.*)

Bolgheri Peàn ♀ $$$ Dark fruit, plums, smoke, and wild herbs, with a soft-textured, accessible personality. (70% Cabernet Sauvignon and 30% Cabernet Franc that sees 12 months in oak.)

BENANTI *(Sicily)*

Bianco di Caselle ♀ $$$ Made from the native Carricante, this white reveals a beguiling mix of richly textured fruit, minerals, smoke, and roasted nuts on a focused, medium-bodied frame.

Rosso di Verzella ♀ $$$ This red from the slopes of Mt. Etna offers up sweet cherries and flowers with the delicate, feminine personality that is typical of the wines from this part of Sicily. (Nerello Mascalese and Nerello Cappuccio.)

BERTANI *(Veneto)*

Valpolicella Valpantena Secco-Bertani ♟ $$ This Valpolicella reveals gaminess, smoke, scorched earth, spices, and dark cherries in a medium-bodied style. The wine undergoes a secondary fermentation *ripasso* on the skins that are left over from the vinification of the estate's Amarone.

BISCI *(Marche)*

Verdicchio di Matelica ♟ $$ This richly textured, full-bodied white changes constantly in the glass, revealing new dimensions to its honeyed fruit with every taste. The high-altitude vineyards give this wine gorgeous aromatics and notable freshness.

BISOL *(Veneto)*

Jeio Valdobbiadene Brut Prosecco ♟ ♟ $$ A Prosecco that shows notable freshness, vibrancy, and crispness in its green apples, flowers, and sweet spices, with terrific energy and harmony.

BOCCADIGABBIA *(Marche)*

Rosso Piceno ♟ $$ A generous, hearty red imbued with dark fruit, earthiness, grilled herb, and smoke nuances. (Equal parts Sangiovese and Montepulciano that spends 10 months in used French oak barrels.)

IL BORRO *(Tuscany)*

Pian di Nova ♟ $$ This poised, feminine wine reveals a floral, perfumed profile, with expressive aromatics that meld into notes of ripe red fruit, spices, and sweet toasted oak. (Syrah and Sangiovese.)

F. BOSCHIS *(Piedmont)*

Barbera del Piemonte ♟ $$ Superripe dark fruit and spiced, mentholated overtones flow from this fruit-driven, rustic Barbera.

Dogliani Vigna dei Prey ♟ $$$ This powerful, structured Dolcetto is loaded with fruit. It offers a more immediate, up-front personality, if slightly less complexity than the San Martino bottling.

Dogliani Sorì San Martino 🍷 $$$ The San Martino is more reticent at first than the Vigna dei Prey, but then explodes onto the palate with masses of mineral-infused dark fruit. It offers superb length and richness in a textbook expression of Dolcetto from Dogliani.

BRAIDA *(Piedmont)*

Barbera d'Asti Montebruna 🍷 $$$ This fresh, vibrant Barbera is loaded with gorgeous black cherries, menthol, and minerals followed by balsamic notes that develop in the glass. It is the estate's entry-level Barbera and also the most classic of the wines, as it is aged in cask.

Il Bacialè 🍷 $$$ A soft-textured, ripe wine with plenty of fruit and an accessible personality. (60% Barbera, 20% Pinot Noir, 10% Cabernet Sauvignon, and 10% Merlot.)

Moscato d'Asti Vigna Senza Nome 🍷 Ⓢ 🍷 $$ Crisp green apples, spices, and flowers flow from this generous, creamy-textured wine. A gorgeous version of Piedmont's most famous dessert wine.

Brachetto d'Acqui 🍷 Ⓢ 🍷 $$$ Brachetto is not as well known as Moscato, but it, too, is capable of producing wonderful wines. This pretty, red sparkling wine offers up sweet candied red fruits, berries, cinnamon, and licorice on a medium-bodied frame. It can be used for slightly richer dishes than Moscato, such as chocolate-based desserts or cooked (as opposed to fresh) fruit sweets.

BRANCAIA *(Tuscany)*

Tre 🍷 $$ A blend of 80% Sangiovese, 10% Merlot, and 10% Cabernet Sauvignon sourced from the estate's three properties in Chianti Classico and Maremma. This pretty wine is loaded with attractive notes of dark fruit, leather, spices, and French oak.

BRICCO MONDALINO *(Piedmont)*

Barbera del Monferrato Superiore 🍷 $$ This cask-aged Barbera is an intriguing wine. It reveals a generous expression of ripe fruit with the mineral edge that is common in the wines from this part of Piedmont.

BRIGALDARA *(Veneto)*

Valpolicella Classico ♟ **$** This soft, voluptuous Valpolicella reveals dark red cherries intertwined with tobacco and earthiness in an accessible, easygoing style.

BRUNI *(Tuscany)*

Syrah ♟ **$$** A rich, fruity red with dark plum, tar, bacon, and game notes that flow from the glass.

Poggio d'Elsa ♟ **$** Sangiovese and Cabernet loaded with dark red fruit, herbs, and spices.

Morellino di Scansano Marteto ♟ **$$** A full-bodied, powerful Morellino, the Marteto offers terrific persistence in its expression of black cherries intermingled with sweet toasted oak. (85% Sangiovese, 15% Merlot aged in French oak.)

BUCCI *(Marche)*

Verdicchio Classico dei Castelli di Jesi � **$$$** This mineral-driven, pure Verdicchio delivers plenty of varietal expression in its floral aromatics and white peach fruit, with a focused personality. A lovely introduction to the house style.

Rosso Piceno Pongelli ♟ **$$$** A tasty, fruit-driven red that is perfect for lighter, simpler fare. (Sangiovese and Montepulciano.)

CA' BIANCA *(Piedmont)*

Gavi ♗ **$$** Perfumed aromatics lead to a honeyed expression of apricots and peaches as this inviting white opens up in the glass. A rich, generous style of Gavi.

Barbera d'Asti Ante ♟ **$$** Sweet, ample, and expressive, this dense, fruit-driven Barbera offers plenty of floral, red fruit, with excellent length and fine overall balance.

Barbera d'Asti Superiore Chersi ♟ **$$$** A dark, brooding wine imbued with the essence of road tar, black cherries, spices, and toasted oak.

CABERT *(Friuli Venezia Giulia)*

Pinot Nero ♟ $$ Offers clean, varietal fruit in a soft-textured style with attractive inner sweetness and few of the hard edges or herbal notes that are common in reds from this part of Italy.

Refosco dal Peduncolo Rosso ♟ $ Dark red fruit, spices, wild herbs, and roasted coffee beans all flow from this tasty, accessible Refosco.

CAGGIANO *(Campania)*

Aglianico dell'Irpinia Taurì ♟ $$ This beautiful entry-level red offers up dark fruit, leather, tobacco, sweet spices, and herbs, all of which come together with unusual grace.

LE CALCINAIE *(Tuscany)*

Vernaccia di San Gimignano ♙ $$ Offers notable complexity in its white peaches, minerals, smoke, and earthiness. This is just about as good as Vernaccia gets.

Chianti Colli Senesi ♟ $$ Vibrant black-cherry fruit on a medium-bodied, classically structured frame. Made from biologically farmed Sangiovese, Colorino, and Canaiolo.

CAMIGLIANO *(Tuscany)*

Rosso di Montalcino ♟ $$$ This soft, easygoing Rosso offers ripe dark fruit, leather, and spices.

CANELLA *(Veneto)*

Prosecco Conegliano ♙ ♙ $$ Floral, perfumed apricots and spices flow from this precise, well-delineated Prosecco.

CANTELE *(Puglia)*

Negroamaro Rosato ♙ $ Sweet red cherries, strawberries, and herbs emerge from this finessed, versatile rosé.

Salice Salentino Riserva ♟ $ A plump, juicy, superripe red that offers terrific quality for the money. (85% Negroamaro and 15% Malvasia aged in used oak.)

Primitivo ♀ $ An engaging wine that flows with plenty of sweet, ripe fruit.

CANTINA DEL TABURNO (*Campania*)

Falanghina ♀ $$ A pretty, aromatic white with notable inner perfume and lovely balance.

Fiano Beneventano ♀ $$ Combines a generous expression of fruit with the unique, mineral-driven notes that make the wines of Campania so irresistible.

Greco ♀ $$ The most taut and focused of the estate's whites.

Rosso Beneventano Torlicoso ♀ $ A pretty, soft-textured wine that shows the delicate, graceful side of Aglianico in its fresh berries and flowers.

Aglianico Fidelis ♀ $$ This pleasing Aglianico offers plenty of dark red fruit and tobacco with superb purity and length on the palate. (90% Aglianico, 10% Sangiovese.)

CANTINA DI TERLANO (*Alto Adige*)

Pinot Bianco ♀ $$ Consistently one the finest of the entry-level wines from Terlano. Sweet, inviting aromatics meld into white peaches in a focused, minerally style as this beautiful wine opens up in the glass.

Pinot Grigio ♀ $$$ A very pleasant, perfumed Pinot Grigio that captures the essence of Alto Adige with a touch more weight and roundness than the Pinot Bianco.

Chardonnay ♀ $$$ A steely, taut Chardonnay that gains weight and volume in the glass. This remains a quintessential expression of Alto Adige minerality and *terroir*.

Müller Thurgau ♀ $$$ Another of the highlights of the entry-level wines, this white possesses gorgeous, floral aromatics that meld into peaches and mint, with a delicate, subtle note of petrol that lingers on the close.

Terlaner ♀ $$ A blend of 60% Pinot Bianco, 30% Chardonnay, and 10% Sauvignon Blanc, the Terlaner Classico reveals jasmine, honey, and sweet fruit, with the Sauvignon dominating the wine's aromatic profile and Chardonnay providing the body.

CANTINA ROTALIANA *(Alto Adige)*

Teroldego Rotaliano ☐ $$$ A rich, full-bodied offering loaded with dark fruits, smoke, minerals, iron, and game. Some of the heartier elements in this wine need food to be at their best.

CAPRAI *(Umbria)*

Montefalco Rosso ☐ $$$ A pretty, feminine wine that reveals perfumed aromatics and soft red fruit in a polished style. This is a great introduction to the wines of Marco Caprai, one of the leading producers in the Montefalco appellation of Umbria.

LA CARRAIA *(Umbria)*

Orvieto Classico Superiore Poggio Calvelli ☐ $$ A blend of 50% Grechetto, 25% Chardonnay, and 25% Procanico aged briefly in French oak. As one might expect, this is an especially rich, generous style of Orvieto, with pleasing honeyed overtones that add complexity to the fruit.

Tizzonero ☐ $ This French-oak-aged Montepulciano-Sangiovese blend reveals aromas and flavors that tend toward the darker side of the spectrum, with notes of earthiness, leather, and smoke.

CASCINA BONGIOVANNI *(Piedmont)*

Langhe Arneis ☐ $$ A fairly rich, textured style of Arneis, with pretty notes of honeyed fruit, flowers, and smoke that emerge from its lush frame.

CASCINA CHICCO *(Piedmont)*

Roero Arneis Anterisio ☐ $$ Offers notable complexity and focus in its white peaches, mint, and minerals.

CASCINA TAVIJN *(Piedmont)*

Barbera d'Asti ☐ $$$ This Barbera shows some of the gamier elements of the grape, yet it offers excellent complexity and balance in a hearty, rustic style.

CASCINA VAL DEL PRETE *(Piedmont)*

Barbera d'Alba Serra de' Gatti ♛ **$$$** This soft-textured, juicy Barbera offers pretty, floral aromatics and plenty of fruit in a pleasing, affable style.

CASTELLO BANFI *(Tuscany)*

Rosso di Montalcino ♛ **$$$** A delicious, fragrant *rosso* with generous red fruits and an engaging personality.

CASTELLO DELLE REGINE *(Umbria)*

Rosso di Podernovo ♛ **$** An attractive blend of 80% Sangiovese, 10% Syrah, and 10% Montepulciano. This flavorful Umbrian red is loaded with dark red fruit, which is given an additional layer of depth and roundness from the Syrah.

CASTELLO DI BOSSI *(Tuscany)*

Chianti Classico ♛ **$$** Sweet dark fruit, spices, tobacco, and toasted oak are some of the nuances that emerge from this Chianti Classico, a 100% Sangiovese that is aged for longer than normal prior to being released.

CASTELLO DI FONTERUTOLI *(Tuscany)*

Poggio alla Badiola ♛ **$$** A blend of 70% Sangiovese and 30% Merlot made in a soft-textured, pleasing style loaded with ripe dark fruit.

CASTELLO DI LUZZANO *(Emilia-Romagna)*

Tasto di Seta ♛ **$$$** Wild, perfumed aromatics are beautifully woven into green apples, jasmine, flowers, and honey as this unique, compelling white opens in the glass. (Malvasia di Candia.)

"Carlino" Bonarda Oltrepò Pavese ♛ ♛ **$$** A selection made from the estate's best Bonarda fruit. This red offers terrific harmony and balance in its dark fruit, spices, chocolate, and minerals, with a soft-textured, totally engaging personality.

Bonarda Oltrepò Pavese 🍷 🥂 **$$** This quirky red possesses plenty of fruit and a joyful, winsome personality. Bonarda Oltrepò Pavese is a sparkling red wine that is often consumed in these parts.

CASTELLO DI MONSANTO (*Tuscany*)

Chianti Classico 🍷 **$$** A classy and elegant Chianti at this level, the wine offers lovely weight in its sweet, ripe fruit.

Chianti Classico Riserva 🍷 **$$$** Reveals a profile of red berries, herbs, crushed flowers, and spices with finessed tannins and more density and depth than the straight Chianti Classico.

CASTELLO DI NIPOZZANO (*Tuscany*)

Chianti Rúfina Riserva 🍷 **$$$** This Chianti from the high-altitude Rúfina district is at its best in top vintages such as 2004, where it offers well-delineated dark cherries, menthol, spices, earthiness, and smoke, but in cooler vintages such as 2005 the fruit can struggle to ripen.

CASTELLO MONACI (*Puglia*)

Primitivo Piluna 🍷 **$** This vibrant, pure red shimmers on the palate with layers of dark cherries, sweet herbs, licorice, and tobacco. Readers who haven't discovered Primitivo, Italy's version of Zinfandel, owe it to themselves to do so, and this is a great starting point. This is a wine of uncommon harmony.

Negroamaro Maru 🍷 **$** Dried figs, plums, cherries, spices, herbs, and tobacco flow from this exotic red that delivers plenty of varietal character.

Salice Salentino Liante 🍷 **$** This blend of 80% Negroamaro and 20% Malvasia is another beauty. Made in a very sweet, ripe style, it offers notes of plums, prunes, leather, tar, smoke, and earthiness.

CASTELVERO (*Piedmont*)

Cortese 🥂 **$** A fresh and zesty wine redolent of green apples, pears, and flowers, perfect for casual drinking.

Barbera 🍷 **$** This Barbera offers varietal dark red fruits in a plump, easygoing style. As is typical of Barberas at this price point, some rustic elements are present, but this is still a very pleasing wine.

CATALDI MADONNA (*Abruzzo*)

Trebbiano d'Abruzzo ♟ **$$$** This Trebbiano reveals a mineral-driven style along with hints of white peaches and jasmine that remain in the background.

Cerasuolo ♟ **$$$** This gorgeous, well-articulated rosé typically displays attractive aromas and flavors that recall rose petals, minerals, and earth, with excellent depth and refreshing, bracing acidity that rounds out the long, satisfying finish.

Montepulciano d'Abruzzo ♟ **$$$** A delicious, mouth-filling red that offers terrific density and persistence in its ripe dark fruit, earthiness, and licorice. This is an especially harmonious Montepulciano.

CAVALLOTTO (*Piedmont*)

Dolcetto d'Alba Vigna Scot ♟ **$$** A terrific Dolcetto from the hillside vineyard in Castiglione Falletto that is the source of the estate's signature Barolos. The wine typically offers masses of ripe dark fruit that sweep across the palate, yet persistent notes of minerality give the wine a gorgeous sense of balance and proportion.

Dolcetto d'Alba Vigna Melera ♟ **$$$** This big, full-bodied Dolcetto is loaded with superripe dark fruit, chocolate, licorice, and spices. It offers terrific density with a touch less elegance and harmony than the estate's Dolcetto d'Alba Vigna Scot. The Vigna Melera is made from vines averaging 40 years of age and is aged in cask.

Langhe Freisa Bricco Boschis ♟ **$$$** This Freisa flows from the glass with a sweet, refined expression of ripe red fruit, mint, spices, and minerals. Freisa is a variety that often shows gamy notes, yet none of those qualities are present here.

Langhe Nebbiolo Bricco Boschis ♟ **$$$** A fresh, perfumed Nebbiolo full of varietal character that is perfect for near-term drinking.

CECCHI (*Tuscany*)

Chianti ♟ **$** This fresh, floral Chianti displays bright red cherry fruit and a delicate, feminine personality.

Chianti Classico ♟ **$$** The Chianti Classico reveals a darker profile than the regular Chianti, with a generous expression of black cherries, tar, and licorice.

CESANI *(Tuscany)*

Vernaccia di San Gimignano ♀ $$ A fairly rich, honeyed style of Vernaccia that offers notable ripeness and a generous, soft-textured personality.

CEUSO *(Sicily)*

Scurati Rosso ♀ $$ This compelling Nero d'Avola is packed with jammy black fruits, licorice, cassis, and wild herbs. Plump, full-bodied, and intense, it delivers plenty of pleasure.

MICHELE CHIARLO *(Piedmont)*

Gavi ♀ $$ A fairly full-bodied style of Gavi that favors textural richness over clarity and detail.

Barbera d'Asti Superiore Le Orme ♀ $ This delicious, fragrant Barbera offers notable harmony in its ripe red fruit, minerals, and spices.

Moscato d'Asti Nivole ♀ ⑤ ♀ $ White peaches, jasmine, and mint flow from this tasty version of Piedmont's most famous dessert wine.

CHIONETTI *(Piedmont)*

Dolcetto di Dogliani Briccolero ♀ $$$ A mineral-infused expression of ripe dark fruit, cherries, tar, smoke, and flowers emerges from this tasty Dolcetto.

Dolcetto di Dogliani San Luigi ♀ $$ A more plump, unctuous style of Dolcetto that emphasizes generous fruit in a structured, harmonious style.

CIACCI PICCOLOMINI D'ARAGONA *(Tuscany)*

Poggio della Fonte ♀ $ This is an especially plump, juicy wine loaded with fruit from one of Montalcino's leading estates. (Sangiovese, Cabernet, and Merlot aged in used French oak barrels.)

LE CINCIOLE *(Tuscany)*

Chianti Classico ♀ $$$ Floral aromatics lead to bright red fruit, with undertones of tobacco, autumn leaves, and menthol that develop in the glass in this pretty Chianti Classico.

DOMENICO CLERICO *(Piedmont)*

Langhe Dolcetto Visadì ♟ **$$** A deeply colored, full-bodied Dolcetto loaded with dark jammy fruit that captures the style of one of Barolo's legendary producers.

COCCI GRIFONI *(Marche)*

Pecorino Colle Vecchio ♟ **$$$** A simply wonderful Pecorino for its layered expression of minerals, sage, mint, and ripe fruit.

Rosso Piceno Le Torri Superiore ♟ **$$** This delicious, vibrant red is loaded with red cherries, earthiness, licorice, wild herbs, minerals, and tobacco, all framed by firm but silky tannins. (Montepulciano and Sangiovese.)

ELVIO COGNO *(Piedmont)*

Dolcetto d'Alba ♟ **$$$** A fresh bouquet and ripe dark fruit framed by sturdy tannins are just some of the elements to be found in this terrific, delicious Dolcetto.

COL DI BACCHE *(Tuscany)*

Morellino di Scansano ♟ **$$** A delicious, mouth-filling red loaded with fresh, vibrant fruit and an inviting, vinous personality. This sweet, tasty wine is what Morellino is all about.

COL D'ORCIA *(Tuscany)*

Rosso di Montalcino ♟ **$$$** A fresh, vinous *rosso* with pretty, ripe red fruit and an accessible personality from one of Montalcino's leading estates.

COL VETORAZ *(Veneto)*

Prosecco di Valdobbiadene Brut ♟ ♟ **$$** This pure, joyous Prosecco is loaded with perfumed peaches, crisp green apples, and sweet spices. A reliably delicious version of Veneto's famous sparkling wine.

COLLE MASSARI *(Tuscany)*

Montecucco Rosso Rigoleto ♟ **$$** This Sangiovese-based wine offers perfumed, bright red fruits, spices, and tobacco with excellent length and an attractive floral lift on the finish.

COLLESTEFANO *(Marche)*

Verdicchio di Matelica ♀ $$ A bright, high-toned white that possesses well-defined aromatics and plenty of crisp, zesty fruit. A terrific example of the Marche's best-known white.

COLOSI *(Sicily)*

Sicilia Rosso ♟ $ The estate's entry-level Nero d'Avola is an awesome, mouth-filling red loaded with dark fruit, chocolate, and gorgeous aromatic intensity.

Nero d'Avola ♟ $$ A notable, full-bodied Nero d'Avola bursting with sweet dark cherries, menthol, sage, and flowers that offers notable clarity and elegance. Made from the property's best fruit.

COLTERENZIO *(Alto Adige)*

Pinot Grigio Classic ♀ $$ A joyous Alto Adige white endowed with soaring aromatics and clean, well-articulated fruit that blossoms on the palate with notable expansiveness.

Pinot Bianco Classic ♀ $ Green apples, peaches, earthiness, minerals, and smoke flow from this beautiful, energetic white.

Pinot Bianco Weisshaus ♀ $$ A taut, focused expression of green apples, flowers, smoke, and minerals with a vibrant, refreshing finish.

Pinot Grigio Puiten ♀ $$ A generous and lush Pinot Grigio that boasts layers of perfume-laced fruit. This is a wine that will make readers forget the overly commercial Pinot Grigios that have given the varietal its dubious reputation.

COLTIBUONO *(Tuscany)*

Cancelli ♟ $ A plump, juicy red with attractive, perfumed fruit perfect for casual drinking. (Sangiovese and Syrah.)

Chianti Cetamura ♟ $ Sweet dark fruit, leather, spices, and tobacco emerge from this medium-bodied wine. (Sangiovese and Canaiolo.)

Chianti Classico Selezione RS ♟ $$ This tasty, easygoing Chianti Classico offers notable vibrancy and a layered expression of vibrant dark fruit.

CONTERNO FANTINO *(Piedmont)*

Dolcetto d'Alba Bricco Bastia 🍷 $$$ This medium- to full-bodied, fleshly Dolcetto offers gorgeous length and elegance to spare in its fragrant ripe, dark fruit, spices, and minerals. A great Dolcetto from one of Barolo's top estates.

Barbera d'Alba Vignota 🍷 $$$ A fruit-driven wine loaded with character from this admirable property.

CONTINI *(Sardinia)*

Tonaghe Cannonau di Sardegna 🍷 $$$ This hearty, delicious red is rustic yet pleasing in its vibrant black cherries and herbs.

COPPO *(Piedmont)*

Gavi La Rocca 🍷 $$$ A pretty, perfumed white that reveals plenty of varietal character in a refreshing, bright style.

Barbera d'Asti L'Avvocata 🍷 $$ This medium-bodied, cask-aged Barbera displays layers of vibrant red fruit, earthiness, smoke, and menthol, with terrific balance and poise.

Barbera d'Asti Camp du Rouss 🍷 $$$ This superripe Barbera, from the estate's best vineyards, comes across as juicy and forward, with leather, spices, and sweet toasted oak that complement the generous fruit. It provides a fascinating contrast to the Avvocata, in that it is a different—but not necessarily better—wine.

GIOVANNI CORINO *(Piedmont)*

Barbera d'Alba 🍷 $$ This plump, generous red is packed with superripe dark fruit, graphite, and spices, with an additional dimension of sweetness that comes from the few months the wine spends in French oak.

RENATO CORINO *(Piedmont)*

Barbera d'Alba 🍷 $$ A fresh, vibrant Barbera that offers plenty of sweet dark fruit intermingled with toasted oak in an incredibly delicious style.

MATTEO CORREGGIA *(Piedmont)*

Roero Arneis 🍷 $$ A tightly wound, mineral-driven Arneis, with prominent notes of flint, menthol, and smoke.

Barbera d'Alba 🍷 $$ A sweet, succulent Barbera packed with jammy dark fruit, minerals, smoke, licorice, and road tar. The wine spends one year in used French oak barrels, which contributes to its voluptuous, generous texture.

Anthos 🍷 Ⓢ 🍷 $$ This exotic red made from Brachetto floats on the palate with ethereal notes of candied cherries, sweet medicinal herbs, and spices. The sandy soils of Roero give this wine a feminine, floral quality that is absolutely irresistible.

CORTE DEI PAPI *(Lazio)*

Cesanese del Piglio 🍷 $$ A flavorful red packed with fruit made from Cesanese d'Affile and Cesanese Comune, 2 varieties that are native to Lazio.

CORTE GIARA *(Veneto)*

Soave Pagus 🍷 $ A silky, finessed Soave made in a modern style that incorporates 20% Chardonnay with the indigenous Garganega.

Valpolicella Ripasso 🍷 $$$ Hints of new leather, spices, and toasted coffee beans emerge from the Valpolicella Ripasso.

GIUSEPPE CORTESE *(Piedmont)*

Dolcetto d'Alba Trifolera 🍷 $$ A forward, fragrant style of Dolcetto with plenty of red fruit and spices.

Barbera d'Alba 🍷 $$ This Barbera offers up gorgeous superripe aromas along with tons of fleshy, ripe fruit.

Langhe Nebbiolo 🍷 $$ The Langhe Nebbiolo reveals fragrant aromatics, along with sweet red cherries, flowers, and spices in a medium-bodied style, showing all of the qualities one expects in young Nebbiolo.

COSTARIPA *(Lombardy)*

Pievecroce Lugana ♀ **\$\$** This Trebbiano di Lugana offers attractive, perfumed fruit balanced by lively acidity. A touch of oak gives the wine additional roundness. A terrific example of the white from Lake Garda.

CUSUMANO *(Sicily)*

Nero d'Avola ♥ **\$** This fresh, accessible Nero d'Avola flows with an attractive core of ripe red fruit and some of the wilder notes that are typical of this grape.

Benuara ♥ **\$\$** The Benuara (Nero d'Avola, Syrah) presents a darker profile of fruit, licorice, and tar, as well as greater body than the Nero d'Avola.

D'ALESSANDRO *(Tuscany)*

Cortona Syrah ♥ **\$\$\$** A fresh, vinous Syrah with attractive dark fruit, flowers, spices, and menthol from one of the appellations best suited to this variety in Italy.

DAMILANO *(Piedmont)*

Barbera d'Alba ♥ **\$\$\$** This soft, caressing Barbera offers notable delineation in its aromas and flavors.

Nebbiolo d'Alba ♥ **\$\$\$** This is a pretty, fruit-driven Nebbiolo that offers good varietal character intermingled with sweet scents of French oak.

DI GIOVANNA *(Sicily)*

Gerbino Rosso ♥ **\$\$** This gorgeous wine offers layers of dark fruit, spices, sweet herbs, cassis, and minerals in an elegant style. (Cabernet Sauvignon, Merlot, Nero d'Avola, and Syrah aged in French oak.)

Nerello Mascalese ♥ **\$\$** An especially generous, deeply flavored expression of this rediscovered native variety. Displays pretty notes of dark fruit, underbrush, earthiness, and smoke, with a supple personality and well-integrated tannins.

DI MAJO NORANTE *(Molise)*

Sangiovese ♀ $ This superripe, racy Sangiovese offers plenty of forward, plump fruit, along with notes of earthiness, spices, and tobacco.

Ramitello Rosso ♀ $$ A pure, engaging red that reveals sweet perfumed aromatics and layers of dark cherries, smoke, earthiness, and tar. (Prugnolo and Aglianico aged in large neutral casks and steel.)

Aglianico Contado ♀ $$ A great example of Aglianico from Molise, with plenty of dark fruit, black pepper, and wild herbs. The estate gives the Contado 18 months in oak barrels of various sizes.

Cabernet ♀ $ A tasty offering with plenty of plump fruit, menthol, and underbrush made in a supple, juicy style.

CAMILLO DONATI *(Emilia-Romagna)*

Malvasia dell'Emilia ♀ $$$ This sparkling dry white made from Malvasia Candia reveals plenty of varietal aromas and flavors, but with fizz. The color is somewhat cloudy, as is common for wines made in this very natural style.

Lambrusco dell'Emilia ♀ ♀ $$$ A big, fruit-driven style of Lambrusco that offers a level of intensity that is quite rare.

EINAUDI *(Piedmont)*

Dolcetto di Dogliani ♀ $$$ A fragrant, perfumed offering bursting with sweet varietal fruit. Despite the wine's sumptuous dark fruit, this is an especially elegant and refined style of Dolcetto from one of the leading estates in Dogliani.

FALESCO *(Umbria and Lazio)*

Vitiano Rosso ♀ $ This blend of Sangiovese, Merlot, and Cabernet Sauvignon possesses layers of plump, ripe fruit intermingled with sweet scents of French oak with a sleek, stylish personality.

Merlot ♀ $$ A wine that shows good depth and inner sweetness, with waves of dark fruit, chocolate, spices, and French oak that flow from its full-bodied, richly textured frame. Riccardo Cotarella is known for his work with Merlot, and the wine is proof of his mastery of the grape.

FANTI *(Tuscany)*

Sant'Antimo Rosso ♇ $$ This inviting, racy wine is loaded with superripe fruit on a soft-textured, generous frame. (Sangiovese, Merlot, Syrah, and Cabernet Sauvignon, aged in French oak.)

Rosso di Montalcino ♇ $$$ An attractive, fleshy wine with a plush core of sweet dark fruit from vineyards in Montalcino.

FARNESE *(Abruzzo)*

Pecorino Casale Vecchio ♈ $$ A generous, caressing white that reveals notable richness in its soft-textured expression of ripe peaches, flowers, and minerals.

Cerasuolo ♈ $ This rosé made from Montepulciano d'Abruzzo possesses lively minerality underpinning bright red fruit.

Montepulciano d'Abruzzo ♇ $ This vibrant, joyful red is packed with spiced dark cherry fruit.

FATTORIA DEI BARBI *(Tuscany)*

Rosso di Montalcino ♇ $$ A gorgeous wine that literally sparkles with bright red fruit supported by a fresh vein of acidity, from a historic property in Montalcino that is making terrific wines.

FATTORIA DEL CERRO *(Tuscany)*

Rosso di Montepulciano ♇ $$ A medium-bodied offering with a soft-textured core of ripe red fruit from Montepulciano, one of Tuscany's historic appellations.

FATTORIA DI FÈLSINA *(Tuscany)*

Chianti Classico ♇ $$$ A beautiful, plump Chianti loaded with vibrant, sweet, ripe fruit that offers lovely depth in an engaging style. A great effort from one of Tuscany's elite producers.

FATTORIA DI MAGLIANO *(Tuscany)*

Morellino di Scansano Heba ♇ $$$ This serious Morellino bursts from the glass with tons of sweet red fruit, raspberries, flowers, and spices. The tannis are firm yet also well integrated into the wine's full-bodied fabric. Consistently top-notch.

FATTORIA BRUNO NICODEMI *(Abruzzo)*

Cerasuolo ♀ $$ A rosé loaded with explosive aromatics, gorgeous texture, and plenty of focused fruit.

Montepulciano d'Abruzzo ♀ $$ This deeply colored, full-bodied wine is packed with ripe dark fruit, earthiness, and sweet toasted oak. It offers superb balance and tons of personality in an immensely pleasing style.

Montepulciano d'Abruzzo Notari ♀ $$$ This generous Montepulciano bursts from the glass with tons of jammy dark fruit, chocolate, vanilla, and sweet toasted oak.

FATTORIA LA PARRINA *(Tuscany)*

Rosso Parrina ♀ $$ A pretty, feminine Sangiovese with silky tannins that frame small red fruits.

FATTORIA LA RIVOLTA *(Campania)*

Taburno Falanghina ♀ $$ This Campanian white offers unusual complexity in its citrus-peel, mint, and mineral flavors, with terrific energy and vibrancy.

FATTORIA LE PUPILLE *(Tuscany)*

Poggio Argentato ♀ $$$ This steely, mineral white offers excellent length and an inviting finish. (Sauvignon and Traminer.)

FATTORIA LE TERRAZZE *(Marche)*

Rosso Conero ♀ $$$ This Rosso Conero is made in a fresh, fruit-forward style that reveals violets, smoke, earthiness, cured meats, and dark fruit. (Montepulciano aged in cask.)

FATTORIA SAN LORENZO *(Marche)*

Verdicchio Classico di Gino ♀ $$ This richly flavored, full-bodied white offers appealing notes of honeyed fruit and an engaging, irresistible personality. The slightly late-harvest style contributes to the wine's richness.

Verdicchio dei Vign Castelli di Jesi Classico Superiore delle Oche
♟ $$$ A sweet, polished, and refined Verdicchio, with generous ripe
fruit and a full-bodied personality.

FATTORIA ZERBINA *(Emilia-Romagna)*

Sangiovese di Romagna Ceregio ♟ $ A soft, pleasing red from
Emilia-Romagna. Attractive red cherry, spices, tobacco, and
earthiness emerge from this pretty, medium-bodied Sangiovese.

Sangiovese di Romagna Superiore Torre di Ceparano ♟ $$$ A
drop-dead gorgeous wine of notable pedigree that reveals plenty of
dark fruit layered with notes of toasted oak, mint, smoke, and tar in a
remarkably complete, harmonious style.

FERRARI *(Trentino)*

NV Brut ♟ $$$ This medium-bodied sparkler from Trentino offers
up notes of white peaches, flowers, smoke, and minerals in a taut,
focused style.

FEUDI DI SAN GREGORIO *(Campania)*

Fiano di Avellino ♟ $$$ This Campanian white reveals a gorgeous
fabric of ripe yellow peaches with lovely harmony.

Aglianico Rubrato ♟ $$ This is a pretty, soft-textured red that
flows from the glass with layers of dark fruit, smoke, tar, and sweet
toasted oak.

FEUDO MONTONI *(Sicily)*

Grillo ♟ $ A beautiful, perfumed white loaded with ripe white
peaches, mint, and flowers.

Catarratto ♟ $$ A decidedly riper style than the Grillo. Attractive
notes of yellow peaches intermingled with subtle notes of earth and
minerals emerge from the glass.

Nero d'Avola ♟ $$ A delicate wine with pretty notes of ripe red
fruits, spices, and mint on a medium-bodied, weightless frame.

IL FEUDUCCIO *(Abruzzo)*

Montepulciano d'Abruzzo Fonte Venna ♟ $$ This generous, plump red offers classic Montepulciano notes in its superripe red cherries, earthiness, and smoke.

FIRRIATO *(Sicily)*

Nero d'Avola Chiaramonte ♟ $$ This sweet, plump wine offers plenty of fruit in an accessible, juicy style.

FONTALEONI *(Tuscany)*

Vernaccia di San Gimignano ♟ $ This pretty wine reveals notes of honeyed white peaches and cantaloupe, with a generous, up-front personality.

Chianti Colli Senesi ♟ $ This tasty Chianti is made in a style similar to the Vernaccia, as plenty of plump, juicy fruit is intermingled with floral aromas.

NINO FRANCO *(Veneto)*

Prosecco di Valdobbiadene Rustico ♟ ♟ $$$ A reference-point Prosecco that offers classic notes of white peaches, flowers, and sweet spices. This is just about as good as Prosecco gets at the nonvintage level.

FROZZA *(Veneto)*

Prosecco di Valdobbiadene Spumante Extra-Dry Col dell'Orso ♟ ♟ $ This richly textured Prosecco flows onto the palate with layers of perfumed fruit. It is one of the finest versions of Veneto's sparkling wine readers are likely to come across.

ETTORE GERMANO *(Piedmont)*

Dolcetto d'Alba Pra di Pò ♟ $$ A Dolcetto with notable clarity and definition in its varietal aromas and flavors.

Barbera d'Alba ♟ $$ This soft-textured, vinous offering is loaded with plump red fruit.

BRUNO GIACOSA *(Piedmont)*

Dolcetto d'Alba ♀ $$$ A lovely wine redolent of crushed flowers, raspberries, and minerals. Made in a simple, easygoing style, it nevertheless offers plenty of detail with excellent length and a clean finish.

Dolcetto d'Alba Falletto ♀ $$$ A rich Dolcetto jam-packed with vibrant, shimmering fruit supported by notable structure. Licorice and menthol nuances emerge, adding further complexity. This Dolcetto is made from the same vineyard in Serralunga that is the source of Giacosa's legendary Barolos.

GINI *(Veneto)*

Soave Classico ♀ $$ Perfumed aromatics lead to apricots and minerals as this gorgeous wine opens up in the glass. (100% Garganega.)

BIBI GRAETZ *(Tuscany)*

Bianco di Casamatta ♀ $ Mint, minerals, white peaches, and spices are just a few of the aromas and flavors that emerge from this delicious white. (100% Vermentino sourced from vineyards in Bolgheri, on Tuscany's coast.)

Casamatta ♀ $$ An absolutely delicious Sangiovese that offers a pretty expression of ripe red fruits intermingled with fresh floral notes.

ROCCOLO GRASSI *(Veneto)*

Soave Superiore Vigneto La Broia ♀ $$$ This compelling white from Veneto reveals the essence of crushed rocks, minerals, white peaches, and smoke in a focused, linear style that recalls Chablis.

SILVIO GRASSO *(Piedmont)*

Dolcetto d'Alba ♀ $$ This delicious Dolcetto is packed with varietally true fruit and is exactly what Dolcetto should be, nothing more, nothing less.

Barbera d'Alba ♀ $$ A fresh, vinous wine with a pretty expression of flowers and small red fruits.

GIACOMO GRIMALDI *(Piedmont)*

Dolcetto d'Alba ♟ $$ A powerful, structured Dolcetto packed with mentholated dark fruit, licorice, and spices that captures the essence of these old vineyards in the town of Monforte.

GULFI *(Sicily)*

Carjcanti ♀ $$ This racy, generous white opens with explosive aromatics that meld into ripe yellow apricots and peaches, with underlying notes of smoke and toasted oak that add complexity. (Carricante and Albanello.)

Nero d'Avola Rossojbleo ♟ $ A chunky red from Sicily loaded with dark cherries, mint, flowers, spices, and licorice.

HILBERG-PASQUERO *(Piedmont)*

Barbera d'Alba ♟ $$$ An accessible, vinous wine bursting with blueberries, blackberries, tar, and licorice.

Vareij ♟ Ⓢ ♀ $$ This absolutely pristine, beautiful wine caresses the palate with silky-textured fruit intermingled with typical Brachetto varietal notes of wild herbs, mulling spices, and flowers.

ICARDI *(Piedmont)*

Barbera d'Asti Tabarin ♟ $ This delicious Barbera reveals plenty of fragrant dark fruit with elegant tannins and impressive roundness for a wine from Asti.

Barbera d'Asti Surì di Mù ♟ $$$ A juicy, full-throttle, modern-style Barbera redolent of tar, licorice, superripe dark fruit, and toasted oak.

ICARIO *(Tuscany)*

Rosso di Montepulciano ♟ $$ This generous red reveals superripe dark fruit intermingled with scents of sweet toasted oak and flowers with notable depth and harmony.

INAMA *(Veneto)*

Soave Classico ♀ $$ The Soave Classico reveals apricots, honey, flowers, and almonds on a richly textured frame. This is a fairly generous style of Soave that sacrifices a touch of aromatic complexity, but it is absolutely delicious all the same.

Sauvignon Vulcaia ♀ $$$ This unique Sauvignon melds subtle varietal notes of green apples, mint, and flowers with a distinctly Veronese sense of minerality.

Carménère Più ♟ $$$ A delicious, harmonious red that possesses an attractive array of ripe dark fruit, earthiness, tobacco, leather, and spices. (Carménère, Merlot, and Raboso Veronese.)

LATIUM MORINI *(Veneto)*

Soave Campo Le Calle ♀ $ A delicious, joyous Soave. Perfumed, honeyed aromatics waft from the glass, followed by rich, ripe yellow peaches.

Valpolicella Superiore Campo Prognài ♟ $$$ This intense yet soft-textured wine reveals gorgeous aromatics, superripe dark fruit, and plenty of toasted oak.

MACULAN *(Veneto)*

Pino & Toi ♀ $ This attractive wine offers plenty of perfumed fruit in a friendly, light-bodied style. (Tocai, Pinot Bianco, and Pinot Grigio.)

Costadolio ♀ $ A delicate, fragrant rosé to enjoy as an aperitif in the warm summer months.

Brentino ♟ $$$ Elegant aromatics meld into a palate of sweet dark fruit, herbs, and toasted oak. (Merlot and Cabernet Sauvignon.)

Dindarello ♀ ⑤ $$$ An exciting array of citrus, orange peel, spices, acacia, and honey develops in the glass as this beautiful wine reveals the depth of its personality. Made in a style that combines the floral aromas of the Moscatos of Piedmont with the textural richness of the sweet wines of Veneto. (Moscato Fior d'Arancio.)

MALVIRÀ *(Piedmont)*

Roero Arneis Renesio ♀ $$$ A flinty, mineral-driven white with a focused expression of white peaches, flowers, and smoke.

Roero Arneis Trinità ♀ $$$ The Trinità reveals an additional layer of sweetness and ripeness in its apricots, smoke, and sweet toasted oak.

GIOVANNI MANZONE *(Piedmont)*

Dolcetto d'Alba Le Ciliegie 🍷 $ A very pretty, straightforward Dolcetto with an attractive juiciness to its plummy dark fruit and violets.

Dolcetto d'Alba Superiore La Serra 🍷 $$ Manzone's bigger Dolcetto. This beautifully balanced, structured wine reveals pretty balsamic overtones that complement a core of dark fruit, spices, and tar.

MARCARINI *(Piedmont)*

Dolcetto d'Alba Fontanazza 🍷 $$ A round, caressing style of Dolcetto, with generous dark red fruit, mint, and spices all woven into the wine's medium-bodied frame.

Moscato d'Asti 🍷 S 🍷 $$ Offers good length and balance in its floral aromatics, spices, and crisp green apples.

Barbera d'Alba 🍷 $$ A soft, fruity red with pleasant suggestions of flowers, spices, dark fruit, and herbs.

Langhe Nebbiolo Il Crutin 🍷 $$$ Dried roses, cherries, and sweet herbs emerge from this medium-bodied wine.

GIUSEPPE MASCARELLO *(Piedmont)*

Dolcetto d'Alba Santo Stefano di Perno 🍷 $$$ This traditionally made Dolcetto from one of Barolo's top producers needs quite a bit of air for the richness of its fruit to shine through.

MASSOLINO *(Piedmont)*

Dolcetto d'Alba 🍷 $$ Clean, refreshing mineral notes frame this very pretty, generous Dolcetto that is often among the finest versions in the region.

Barbera d'Alba 🍷 $$$ A plump, juicy red loaded with fruit that shows unusual grace and elegance.

Moscato d'Asti 🍷 S 🍷 $$$ Offers up pretty varietal aromas and flavors with good overall balance.

MASTROBERARDINO *(Campania)*

Greco di Tufo Novaserra 🍷 $$$ A clean, focused Greco di Tufo with prominent notes of flinty minerality, white peaches, grapefruit, mint, and flowers.

Fiano di Avellino Radici 🍷 $$$ Reveals a distinctly earthy, smoky profile with sweet ripe fruit buffered by a lively note of minerality that carries through to the long finish. Typically more generous on the palate than the Greco di Tufo Novaserra.

MAZZEI *(Sicily)*

Zisola 🍷 $$$ A dark, brooding wine that shows the wilder, animalistic side of Nero d'Avola in its dark fruit, earthiness, sage, and mint.

MAZZI *(Veneto)*

Valpolicella Superiore 🍷 $$ This is a lovely Valpolicella that offers excellent balance and proportion in its candied red fruits, raspberries, flowers, toasted oak, and spices.

LA MEIRANA *(Piedmont)*

Gavi di Gavi La Meirana 🍷 $$$ A generous, medium-bodied Gavi made in a richly textured yet crisp style with gorgeous inner perfume in its honeyed apricots, flowers, and spices.

MOCALI *(Tuscany)*

Morellino di Scansano Suberli 🍷 $$ Dark cherries and sweet toasted oak emerge from this plump, juicy red.

I Piaggioni 🍷 $$ A delicious Sangiovese loaded with dark cherries, toasted oak, smoke, tar, and spices made in a rich, weighty style.

MOCCAGATTA *(Piedmont)*

Barbera d'Alba 🍷 $$$ Perfumed aromatics are laced throughout this rich, fruit-driven Barbera from one of Barbaresco's leading properties.

MOLETTIERI *(Campania)*

Irpinia Aglianico Cinque Querce 🍷 **$$$** This bold, racy Aglianico is loaded with dark red fruit, flowers, spices, leather, and black pepper. The Cinque Querce is a great introduction to the virtues of Campania's most noble red grape from one of the region's leading producers.

MAURO MOLINO *(Piedmont)*

Langhe Rosso Dimartina 🍷 **$$** This delicious, beautifully balanced red is loaded with fruit. (Barbera.)

Barbera d'Alba 🍷 **$$** A soft-textured, plump Barbera packed with dark red fruit in a fresh style.

IL MOLINO DI GRACE *(Tuscany)*

Chianti Classico 🍷 **$$** A fresh, perfumed Chianti Classico with lovely balance and poise in its red berry fruit.

MONTE ANTICO *(Tuscany)*

Monte Antico 🍷 **$** This forward, juicy red offers tons of dark fruit in a generous, inviting style, with notable depth and plumpness. Year after year Monte Antico is an incredible value from Tuscany.

MONTI *(Abruzzo)*

Montepulciano d'Abruzzo 🍷 **$$** This plump, juicy, cask-aged Montepulciano is loaded with jammy dark cherries, spices, and underbrush.

MORGANTE *(Sicily)*

Nero d'Avola 🍷 **$$** A delicious, full-throttle wine imbued with jammy dark fruit, minerals, mint, spices, tar, and chocolate, from one of Sicily's top producers.

GIACOMO MORI *(Tuscany)*

Chianti 🍷 **$$$** This medium-bodied, delicate Chianti offers bright red fruit intermingled with floral, perfumed aromatics and refreshing acidity.

MORISFARMS *(Tuscany)*

Vermentino ♀ **$$$** A fairly full-bodied style of Vermentino loaded with green apples, smoke, mint, and wild herbs.

Morellino di Scansano ♟ **$$** This Morellino is an engaging red packed with plump, ripe fruit. A quintessential wine from Scansano, one of Tuscany's most promising emerging appellations.

LA MOZZA *(Tuscany)*

Morellino di Scansano I Perazzi ♟ **$$** This sexy, juicy Morellino is loaded with fruit, underbrush, smoke, and licorice nuances that emerge from its generous, plump frame. An unusually complex and well-balanced Morellino.

MURI-GRIES *(Alto Adige)*

Müller-Thurgau ♀ **$$** An accessible, soft-textured white with lovely detail in its aromas and flavors.

Lagrein Rosato ♀ **$** This deceptively medium-bodied wine reveals layers of sweet fruit, flowers, and spices that gradually emerge from its soft-textured frame. Year in and year out, this is one of Italy's most enticing and delicious rosés.

Lagrein ♟ **$$** A generous, forward Lagrein endowed with generous fruit and a soft, plush personality.

MUSELLA *(Veneto)*

Valpolicella Superiore Vigne Nuove di Musella ♟ **$** This Valpolicella exhibits remarkable clarity and focus in its bright red cherry fruit.

Valpolicella Superiore Ripasso ♟ **$$** Another incredibly harmonious wine from Musella packed with ripe dark fruit, leather, spices, and licorice. A dash of French oak and the secondary fermentation on the Amarone lees (also known as the *ripasso* method) gives this wine an attractive fleshiness and inner sweetness that is irresistible.

Monte del Drago 🍷 $$$ This dark, superripe wine offers notable depth and richness in its jammy blackberries, wild herbs, melted road tar, and spices. With air this soft-textured wine reveals notable inner sweetness and tons of overall harmony. (Cabernet and Corvina.)

NINO NEGRI *(Lombardy)*

Valtellina Superiore Quadrio 🍷 $$$ Perfumed cherries, spices, and wild herbs are delicately woven into this medium-bodied, ethereal wine from Valtellina, in the Lombardy region. An intriguing blend of Chiavennasca (the local name for Nebbiolo) and Merlot aged in cask.

ANDREA OBERTO *(Piedmont)*

Dolcetto d'Alba 🍷 $$$ This rich, concentrated Dolcetto possesses notable depth and purity in its dark fruit, along with notes of menthol and spices that add complexity.

Barbera d'Alba 🍷 $$$ This Barbera sparkles on the palate with sensations of dark raspberries, licorice, and spices.

OCONE *(Campania)*

Falanghina 🍷 $$ This Falanghina offers gorgeous aromatics that lead to a generous core of apricots, peaches, and jasmine supported by a very pretty note of minerality that gives the wine its sense of balance and harmony.

Aglianico 🍷 $$ An accessible style of Aglianico that emphasizes dark berries, spices, minerals, and herbs, with an inviting, fresh finish.

PAITIN *(Piedmont)*

Dolcetto d'Alba Sori Paitin 🍷 $$ A pretty, medium-bodied Dolcetto with expressive aromatics and attractive dark red fruit from one of Barbaresco's top wineries.

IL PALAZZINO *(Tuscany)*

Chianti Classico Argenina 🍷 $$$ This medium-bodied Chianti Classico offers excellent clarity and definition in its fruit with a fresh, floral personality.

PALAZZONE *(Umbria)*

Orvieto ♀ $ A crisp, mineral offering that captures the essence of Umbria's most famous white wine.

Grechetto ♀ $ Reveals an added dimension of textural weight and ripeness in an engaging and generous style that is sure to find many admirers.

Orvieto Classico Superiore Terre Vineate ♀ $$ This richly textured wine reveals layers of fruit and a long, clean finish. (A selection of Procanico, Grechetto, Verdello, Malvasia, and Drupeggio, all indigenous varieties.)

PALLADIO *(Tuscany)*

Chianti ♥ $ This Tuscan red offers plenty of dark ripe fruit with an accessible, easygoing personality.

MARCHESI PANCRAZI *(Tuscany)*

San Donato ♥ $$ An unusual blend of Pinot Noir and Gamay with bright, high-toned aromas and flavors.

PARUSSO *(Piedmont)*

Langhe Bianco ♀ $$$ A richly textured, generous Sauvignon loaded with ripe peaches, mint, smoke, and subtle oak.

Dolcetto d'Alba Piani Noce ♥ $$$ Floral red berries, smoke, and earthiness emerge in an almost Burgundian style of Dolcetto. A pretty wine from Marco Parusso.

PECCHENINO *(Piedmont)*

Dolcetto di Dogliani San Luigi ♥ $$$ This pretty, fresh Dolcetto reveals clean varietal fruit and lovely overall balance. A delicious introduction to the style of one of the top producers of Dolcetto.

PEDERZANA *(Emilia-Romagna)*

Lambrusco Grasparossa ♥ ♀ $$ An explosive, fruit-driven wine that flows onto the palate in stunning style. This is about as good as it gets for Lambrusco, Emilia-Romagna's dry sparkling red wine.

PELISSERO *(Piedmont)*

Dolcetto d'Alba Munfrina 🍷 $$ A vibrant, pure Dolcetto that offers notable complexity in its dark fruit, spices, and menthol.

Dolcetto d'Alba Augenta 🍷 $$ This beautifully perfumed, full-bodied Dolcetto marries generous fruit with firm structure. Aged in cask, the Augenta is the more classic of the estate's Dolcettos.

Barbera d'Alba Piani 🍷 $$$ A full-bodied, superripe Barbera, the Piani possesses notable concentration in its dark jammy fruit and sweet toasted oak, with silky tannins.

PERRINI *(Puglia)*

Salento 🍷 $$ An incredibly appealing red loaded with dark wild cherries, raspberries, sweet herbs, and spices. (Negroamaro and Primitivo.)

Primitivo 🍷 $$$ The Primitivo has more varietal character, if not quite the textural richness of the Salento. Pretty notes of tobacco, smoke, sweet herbs, and wild cherries with terrific clarity and precision.

ELIO PERRONE *(Piedmont)*

Barbera d'Asti Tasmorcan 🍷 $$ This Barbera literally bursts from the glass with an explosion of primary ripe red fruits and minerals.

Moscato d'Asti Sourgal 🍷 Ⓢ 🍷 $$ A creamy-textured Moscato that offers outstanding length and finesse in its classic varietal notes of crisp green apples, mint, flowers, and spices. Simply put, this is as good as Moscato gets.

Moscato d'Asti Clarté 🍷 Ⓢ 🍷 $$$ This is an intensely mineral-driven Moscato that emphasizes notes of smoke, earthiness, and ash over a more typical floral expression of fruit. A rich, full-bodied style of Moscato.

Bigaro 🍷 Ⓢ 🍷 $$$ This rosé-colored dessert wine (Moscato and Brachetto) offers up floral red raspberries, cinnamon, flowers, sweet herbs, and a host of other aromas and flavors. A perennial favorite.

PETILIA *(Campania)*

Greco di Tufo 🍷 **$$** Offers notable intensity in a round, fruit-driven style of Greco that nevertheless shows plenty of the linear thrust that makes Greco such a compelling white.

Fiano di Avellino 🍷 **$$** This wine of uncommon elegance and distinction reveals awesome richness in its ripe fruit, along with subtle notes of smoke and mint that add further complexity.

PETRA *(Tuscany)*

Zingari 🍷 **$** A delicious, easygoing wine with pretty aromatics and an attractive core of dark red fruit, smoke, tar, and licorice. (Merlot, Syrah, Petit Verdot, and Sangiovese.)

Ebo 🍷 **$$$** Exotic aromas that recall wild herbs, earthiness, and autumn leaves lead to layers of ripe dark fruit, licorice, tar, new leather, smoke, and black pepper. (Cabernet Sauvignon, Sangiovese, and Merlot aged predominantly in large casks, with a touch of used French oak.)

PIAZZANO *(Tuscany)*

Chianti 🍷 **$** A fresh, vinous Chianti with plummy dark fruit, chocolate, and spices.

Chianti Rio Camerata 🍷 **$$** This harmonious, beautiful Chianti is plump and engaging, with plenty of sweet dark fruit.

PIEROPAN *(Veneto)*

Soave Classico 🍷 **$$** This classy, elegant Soave is redolent of ripe peaches, smoke, and earthiness. A reference-point wine from one of Soave's leading producers. (Garganega and Trebbiano di Soave.)

PODERE LA MERLINA *(Piedmont)*

Gavi di Gavi 🍷 **$$** Perfumed aromatics lead to an elegant, restrained expression of fruit that impresses with its clarity and precision in this inviting, soft-textured wine.

PODERI COLLA *(Piedmont)*

Dolcetto d'Alba Pian Balbo 🍷 **$$** A delicate, feminine Dolcetto with pretty notes of red berries, flowers, menthol, and spices.

PODERI SAN LAZZARO *(Marche)*

Rosso Piceno Superiore Podere 72 ♀ **$$$** A juicy, generous red packed with sweet dark fruit made in a plump, accessible style. (Sangiovese and Montepulciano aged in French oak.)

POGGIO AL TESORO *(Tuscany)*

Vermentino Solosole ♀ **$$$** A silky, generous white loaded with expressive, perfumed fruit supported by an underlying vein of acidity that provides balance and length. From Tuscany's coastal Maremma region.

POGGIO ARGENTIERA *(Tuscany)*

Morellino di Scansano Bellamarsilia ♀ **$$** A vibrant, tasty wine with plenty of dark fruit, licorice, sweet herbs, and tobacco.

POGGIO BERTAIO *(Umbria)*

Stucchio ♀ **$$$** This medium- to full-bodied wine reveals well-defined aromatics along with a generous expression of leather, earthiness, dark cherries, and spices. (100% Sangiovese aged in French oak.)

POGGIO SAN POLO *(Tuscany)*

Rubio ♀ **$$** A fresh, plump wine bursting with sweet dark fruit in a warm, generous style. (100% Sangiovese.)

Rosso di Montalcino ♀ **$$$** This delicate, floral Sangiovese offers pretty notes of small red fruits and spices.

POGGIONOTTE *(Sicily)*

Nero d'Avola ♀ **$$** This sleek, stylish red from Sicily reveals an elegant expression of ripe dark cherries layered with sweet toasted oak, tar, and licorice. A beautiful, refined Nero d'Avola.

POLIZIANO *(Tuscany)*

Rosso di Montepulciano ♀ **$$** This pleasing, accessible Tuscan red presents fresh, perfumed aromatics and delicate notes of small red fruits.

PRA *(Veneto)*

Soave Classico ♀ $ This is a delicate, feminine Soave redolent of green apples, flowers, and spices framed by pretty notes of minerality.

Soave Staforte ♀ $$$ Six months of aging on the lees with frequent stirring gives the wine a richer and more intense expression of varietal Garganega aromas and fruit.

PRATESI *(Tuscany)*

Locorosso ♀ $ This pretty, aromatic wine offers lovely clarity and freshness in its perfumed black cherries. (100% Sangiovese from the Carmignano district, aged in French oak.)

PRUNOTTO *(Piedmont)*

Dolcetto d'Alba ♀ $$ A big, full-bodied Dolcetto loaded with perfumed dark fruit.

Barbera d'Asti Fiulot ♀ $$ This pretty, engaging Barbera offers up ripe red fruits, with excellent length and the bright acidity that is the hallmark of the wines of Asti.

Morellino di Scansano ♀ $$ A juicy, medium-bodied Morellino that offers plenty of ripe fruit with the telltale warmth and volume of Tuscany's Maremma.

QUATTRO MANI *(Abruzzo)*

Montepulciano d'Abruzzo ♀ $ A powerful, mouth-filling wine loaded with dark cherries and earthiness.

LE RAGOSE *(Veneto)*

Valpolicella Classico Superiore Ripasso Le Ragose ♀ $$$ Dark cherries, plums, baking spices, smoke, and earthiness emerge from this beautiful cask-aged Valpolicella from one of Veneto's leading properties.

Valpolicella Classico Superiore Ripasso Le Sassine ♀ $$$ A delicate, understated Valpolicella with pretty red cherries, earthiness, and tobacco.

Valpolicella Classico Superiore 🍷 $$$ This simply joyous Valpolicella is loaded with clean, superripe flavors in a refined, harmonious style.

FRATELLI REVELLO *(Piedmont)*

Barbera d'Alba 🍷 $$$ This glorious Barbera from one of Piedmont's top producers offers tons of purity and harmony in its juicy red fruit.

BARONE RICASOLI *(Tuscany)*

Chianti Classico 🍷 $$ A plump, generous wine with soft-textured dark fruit and an easygoing, accessible personality.

RIECINE *(Tuscany)*

Chianti Classico 🍷 $$$ A modern Chianti Classico that offers plenty of dark red fruit intermingled with toasted oak in a soft-textured, ripe style.

RIETINE *(Tuscany)*

Chianti Classico 🍷 $$ This weighty, modern-style wine is loaded with sweet dark fruit, toasted oak, and spices in a full-bodied, fruit-driven style.

ROAGNA *(Piedmont)*

Dolcetto d'Alba 🍷 $$ This understated Dolcetto favors tertiary, ethereal notes of menthol, licorice, and spices rather than the more overt expression of fruit that is more typical of Dolcetto. A delicious wine from one of Piedmont's most staunchly traditional producers.

ALBINO ROCCA *(Piedmont)*

Rosso di Rocca 🍷 $$ This compelling red from one of Barbaresco's top producers possesses an expressive bouquet and plenty of ripe fruit in a medium-bodied, accessible style. (Nebbiolo, Barbera, and Cabernet Sauvignon.)

Dolcetto d'Alba Vignalunga 🍷 $$ A soft, caressing wine loaded with dark red fruits and an engaging personality.

Barbera d'Alba Gepin 🍷 $$$ Clean, perfumed aromatics meld seamlessly into a core of ripe dark in this gorgeous, silky Barbera.

GIOVANNI ROSSO *(Piedmont)*

Dolcetto d'Alba Le Quattro Vigne 🍷 $$ A big, full-bodied Dolcetto made very much in the style of the wines of Serralunga, where Rosso is based.

SALADINI PILASTRI *(Marche)*

Rosso Piceno 🍷 $ A soft-textured red that caresses the palate with waves of ripe fruit, tobacco, and spices.

Rosso Piceno Superiore Vigna Piediprato 🍷 $ Vibrant dark cherries, plums, licorice, tobacco, and tar emerge from this deep, flavorful wine. (Montepulciano and Sangiovese.)

Rosso Piceno Superiore Vigna Montetinello 🍷 $$ A more brooding wine than the Piediprato, with notes of earthiness, iron, tobacco, menthol, and dark cherries. (Montepulciano and Sangiovese aged in cask.)

Rosso Piceno Superiore Vigna Monteprandone 🍷 $$$ The most structured of the estate's Rosso Picenos, the Monteprandone possesses notable vibrancy in its dark cherries, plums, spices, and sweet toasted oak. (Montepulciano and Sangiovese aged in medium-size French oak barrels.)

Rosso Pregio del Conte 🍷 $$ Sweet, open aromatics lead to a soft-textured expression of superripe dark red fruits, spices, and toasted oak in this voluptuous, late-harvest red. (Montepulciano and Aglianico aged in French oak.)

SALCHETO *(Tuscany)*

Chianti Colli Senesi 🍷 $ An easygoing, fruity Chianti with lovely balance.

Rosso di Montepulciano 🍷 $$$ This generous Rosso is layered and sweet in its expression of dark fruit, spices, menthol, and earthiness.

LE SALETTE *(Veneto)*

Valpolicella 🍷 $$ Sweet, engaging aromatics lead to a soft-textured core of ripe red fruits in this caressing, harmonious wine. Everything a great Valpolicella should be.

SAN FABIANO (*Tuscany*)

Chianti Putto 🍷 **$$** A fresh, vinous Chianti with good overall balance.

SAN FELICE (*Tuscany*)

Chianti Classico Riserva Il Grigio 🍷 **$$$** A medium-bodied, easygoing Chianti with suggestions of berries, flowers, and spices that typically offers good freshness and vibrancy.

Poggibano 🍷 **$$$** Offers excellent length and inner sweetness in its dark fruit, smoke, licorice, and tar. (Merlot and Cabernet aged in French oak from Tuscany's Maremma district.)

SAN FRANCESCO (*Calabria*)

Cirò Rosso Classico 🍷 **$** An absolutely delicious, exotic wine made from the native Gaglioppo grape that possesses notable inner sweetness in its notes of cinnamon, incense, red cherries, and dried figs.

SAN GIORGIO A LAPI (*Tuscany*)

Chianti Classico 🍷 **$$$** This pretty, midweight Chianti Classico flows with attractive ripe red fruit.

SAN MICHELE APPIANO (*Alto Adige*)

Pinot Bianco 🍷 **$$** An aromatic, crisp Pinot Bianco with perfumed white peaches and persistent mineral notes.

Pinot Bianco Schulthauser 🍷 **$$** A rounder, richer style of Pinot Bianco, with layers of smoke and earthiness that add complexity.

Pinot Grigio Anger 🍷 **$$** A round, soft style of Pinot Grigio with excellent definition and clarity.

Riesling Montiggl 🍷 **$$$** A unique wine that expresses more Alto Adige character than varietal aromas and flavors. With some time in the glass pretty notes of ripe peaches, citrus, and lime zest emerge with lovely inner sweetness.

LUCIANO SANDRONE *(Piedmont)*

Dolcetto d'Alba 🍷 **$$$** Expressive aromatics and a sweet core of dark fruit flow from this deeply colored, intense Dolcetto from one of Barolo's legendary producers.

SANTADI *(Sardinia)*

Vermentino Villa Solais 🍷 **$** A Vermentino that offers lovely elegance, balance, and poise. Beautifully expressive aromatics lead to ripe peaches framed by silky, refined tannins.

Vermentino Cala Silente 🍷 **$$** This white reveals a sweet, layered expression of ripe fruit supported by a lovely underlying note of minerality. A more full-bodied style than the Villa Solais.

Carignano del Sulcis Tre Torri 🍷 **$** A beguiling rosé imbued with the essence of sweet candied fruit, herbs, mint, and spices, and the weight to stand up to richly flavored foods.

Monica di Sardegna Antigua 🍷 **$** A refined, elegant red that flows from the glass with a multitude of dark cherry, earth, and smoke flavors.

Carignano del Sulcis Grotta Rossa 🍷 **$** A big, fruit-driven wine loaded with character and personality. It is perhaps a little more soft textured and seamless than the Monica di Sardegna Antigua, but every bit as exciting.

PAOLO SARACCO *(Piedmont)*

Moscato d'Asti 🍷 ⑤ 🍷 **$$** This reference-point Moscato offers an exciting array of lime peel, pears, green apples, flowers, and minerals in a focused, incredibly pure style. A benchmark Moscato from one of the region's most inspired producers.

Moscato d'Autunno 🍷 ⑤ 🍷 **$$** A unique and compelling version of Piedmont's famous dessert wine made in a generous style that seeks great textural richness in its ripe fruit, smoke, earthiness, and minerals.

SCACCIADIAVOLI *(Umbria)*

Montefalco Rosso 🍷 **$$** This engaging red from Umbria's Montefalco district offers up an irresistible array of crushed flowers, red cherries, spices, and wild herbs on a medium-bodied frame. (Sangiovese, Sagrantino, and Merlot.)

PAOLO SCAVINO *(Piedmont)*

Langhe Bianco ♀ $$$ A unique blend of Sauvignon and Chardonnay that offers up plenty of minerals, sage, and white peach nuances intermingled with varietal Sauvignon aromatics.

Rosso ♟ $$ This plump, juicy red reveals attractive jammy red fruits and spices in a very pleasing, harmonious style. A great value from one of Piedmont's most consistently outstanding producers. (Nebbiolo, Dolcetto, Barbera, and Cabernet aged in used oak barrels.)

Dolcetto d'Alba ♟ $$$ A generous, full-bodied wine with floral and spice notes that add complexity to the overtly fruit-driven style.

SCUBLA *(Friuli Venezia Giulia)*

Friulano ♀ $$$ A mineral-driven, focused white that reveals excellent persistence and balance. Notes of white peaches intermingled with flowers and herbs emerge from this pure, gorgeous wine.

Sauvignon ♀ $$$ Made in a similarly taut style as the Friulano. Varietal aromatics meld into a fabric of expressive fruit.

FRATELLI SEGHESIO *(Piedmont)*

Dolcetto d'Alba Vigneto della Chiesa ♟ $$ A drop-dead gorgeous wine. This big, full-bodied red bursts from the glass with loads of vibrant dark cherries in a superripe yet beautifully balanced style.

Barbera d'Alba ♟ $$$ This richly textured wine is made in the fruit-driven style that is the estate's calling card.

SELLA E MOSCA *(Sardinia)*

Vermentino di Sardegna La Cala ♀ $ A classic Vermentino with its soaring, perfumed aromatics and crisp, clean fruit.

Cannonau di Sardegna Riserva ♟ $ A light- to medium-bodied style that emphasizes ethereal, perfumed aromatics rather than an overt expression of fruit.

Carignano del Sulcis Riserva Terre Rare ♟ $$$ This Carignano features a wild, gamy set of aromas and flavors that dominate the sweet red fruit.

SELVAPIANA *(Tuscany)*

Chianti Rufina 🍷 $$$ A purebred Chianti of notable finesse with exceptional complexity and nuance in its black cherries, leather, licorice, tar, mint, and spices. This wine has it all and in top vintages is also capable of aging gracefully.

SOTTIMANO *(Piedmont)*

Dolcetto d'Alba Bric del Salto 🍷 $$ This elegant and finessed Dolcetto reveals balsamic overtones wrapped around a core of dark red fruits, spices, and minerals. A first-rate wine from one of Barbaresco's finest young producers.

Maté 🍷 Ⓢ 🍷 $$ An exotic array of strawberry jam, spices, sweet *amaro* medicinal herbs, and pink peppercorns emerge from this medium-bodied yet intense wine. The wine is best served slightly chilled and is an ideal match to fine *salumi* and *prosciutti*. (Brachetto.)

Langhe Nebbiolo 🍷 $$$ Red cherries, flowers, and spices are some of the flavors that are typically found in this Langhe Nebbiolo, a wine that would give many producers' Barbarescos a run for their money.

LA SPINETTA *(Piedmont and Tuscany)*

Moscato d'Asti Bricco Quaglia 🍷 Ⓢ 🍷 $$ An expressive wine endowed with perfumed fruit and a generous, engaging personality. A reliably outstanding wine from one of Piedmont's top producers.

Il Nero di Casanova 🍷 $$$ This medium- to full-bodied red possesses an engaging, generous personality loaded with ripe dark fruit.

SPORTOLETTI *(Umbria)*

Assisi Rosso 🍷 $$ This compelling wine offers up attractive bright red fruits intermingled with spices, tobacco, and scents of sweet toasted oak. (Sangiovese, Merlot, and Cabernet Sauvignon.)

STELLA *(Abruzzo)*

Trebbiano d'Abruzzo 🍷 $ White peaches, flowers, and earthiness all come through in this small-scale but tasty Trebbiano.

Montepulciano d'Abruzzo 🍷 $ This plummy, harmonious wine offers up attractive notes of smoke, tar, ash, and dark cherries, with good length and balance.

SUAVIA *(Veneto)*

Soave Classico 🍷 $$ A generous, full-bodied style of Soave that shows the complexity and character of this hillside site in its ripe yellow fruits, smoke, earthiness, and minerals.

TAMELLINI *(Veneto)*

Soave 🍷 $$ A gorgeous wine endowed with elegant, rich fruit. Notes of earthiness and smoke emerge with air, adding further complexity as this taut, focused Soave reveals the full breadth of its personality.

Soave Classico Le Bine de Costiola 🍷 $$$ This medium- to full-bodied, soft-textured Soave reveals an expansive core of ripe candied apricots and flowers, with subtle notes of French oak in the background. (100% Garganega from 35-year-old vines.)

TASCA D'ALMERITA *(Sicily)*

Regaleali Bianco 🍷 $ A soft-textured, generous white with pretty notes of jasmine, white peaches, and sweet spices. (Inzolia, Catarratto, and Grecanico.)

Leone 🍷 $$ A French-oak-aged blend of Catarratto and Chardonnay. The Catarratto gives the wine its aromatics while the Chardonnay provides an additional level of fatness in its fruit.

Nozze d'Oro 🍷 $$$ This blend of Inzolia and Sauvignon is floral, aromatic, and richly textured in its soft, honeyed fruit.

Nero d'Avola Regaleali 🍷 $$ This hearty red reveals an attractive plumpness to its dark fruit, herbs, and earthiness, with plenty of juiciness and style.

Nero d'Avola Lamuri 🍷 $$$ A silky-textured red that reveals an almost Pinot-like expression of red fruits, flowers, spices, and toasted oak. Here the fruit is especially perfumed, while the finessed tannins frame the fruit with uncommon grace.

TENIMENTI ANGELINI *(Tuscany)*

Vino Nobile di Montepulciano Tre Rose 🍷 **$$$** Fresh, perfumed aromatics meld into a well-delineated core of dark red fruit as this medium-bodied Vino Nobile reveals outstanding length and complexity.

TENUTA BELGUARDO *(Tuscany)*

Serrata 🍷 **$$** This plump, juicy wine is loaded with dark red fruit intermingled with sweet toasted oak. (Sangiovese and Alicante aged in French oak.)

TENUTA DI CAPEZZANA *(Tuscany)*

Sangiovese 🍷 **$** A fun, juicy wine bursting with dark fruit.

Barco Reale di Carmignano 🍷 **$$** A pretty wine that offers an attractive array of ripe dark fruit, earthiness, and minerals in a medium-bodied style. (Sangiovese with Cabernet and Canaiolo.)

TENUTA DI GHIZZANO *(Tuscany)*

Il Ghizzano 🍷 **$$** This tasty red possesses a core of plump dark fruit, new leather, and spices, with an engaging personality. (Sangiovese and Merlot.)

TENUTA LE QUERCE *(Basilicata)*

Aglianico del Vulture Il Viola 🍷 **$$** This medium-bodied red presents the untamed side of this unique variety in its dark cherries, wild herbs, and menthol, with excellent persistence and a long, clean finish.

TENUTA RAPITALA *(Sicily)*

Nero d'Avola Campo Reale 🍷 **$** A fresh, vinous wine bursting with perfumed, sweet red fruit and a silky-textured, open personality.

Nadir 🍷 **$$** This generous, deeply flavored Syrah is loaded with dark cherries, underbrush, licorice, earthiness, herbs, and sweet toasted oak.

Nuhar ♟ $$ Fragrant aromatics lead to a core of sweet, almost candied fruit as the wine reveals its delicate, understated personality. (Nero d'Avola and Pinot Noir.)

TENUTA SAN GUIDO *(Tuscany)*

Le Difese ♟ $$$ A plump, juicy wine endowed with plenty of sweet, dark fruit, smoke, and underbrush nuances from one of Tuscany's leading estates.

TENUTA STATTI *(Calabria)*

Gaglioppo ♟ $$ This beautiful, elegant wine bursts from the glass with superripe dark cherries and remarkable clarity and transparency for a wine from the south.

Arvino ♟ $$$ Mint, cassis, spices, and sweet dark fruit emerge from this poised, plummy red. (Gaglioppo and Cabernet Sauvignon aged in French oak.)

TENUTA DI TAVIGNANO *(Marche)*

Verdicchio dei Castelli di Jesi Misco ♟ $ This Verdicchio offers gorgeous textural richness in its perfumed peaches, apricots, and mint. It strikes a lovely balance between ripeness and elegance, with notable purity and a long, clean finish.

Verdicchio dei Castelli di Jesi Classico Superiore Misco Riserva ♟ $$ An expansive, full-bodied Verdicchio loaded with sweet apricots, mint, and honey. More intense than the regular Misco bottling.

TERRE DEI RE *(Basilicata)*

Aglianico del Vulture Vultur ♟ $$$ This big, beefy Aglianico from the Vulture district is made in a generous, fruit-driven style. An excellent example of Aglianico from Basilicata.

TENUTA DELLE TERRE NERE *(Sicily)*

Etna Bianco ♟ $$ The Etna Bianco is made in a ripe style, with notes of smoke and earthiness that gradually emerge with time in the glass. (Carricante, Catarratto, Grecanico, and Inzolia, all native varieties.)

Etna Rosso ♥ $$ A very pretty, midweight effort with attractive notes of tobacco, earth, and black cherries, and an accessible personality. (Mostly Nerello Mascalese, from the estate's youngest vines.)

TERREDORA *(Campania)*

Falanghina ♀ $$ A fairly full-bodied expression of Falanghina that offers rich, almost tropical fruit laced with perfumed aromatics in an extroverted style.

Greco di Tufo Loggia della Serra ♀ $$$ A racy, laser-like wine imbued with grapefruit, melon, mint, and minerals, and tons of class.

Aglianico ♥ $$ A soft-textured, generous red that flows from the glass with notable harmony.

Lacryma Christi del Vesuvio Rosso ♥ $$$ This delicious red made from the Piedirosso grape comes across as a little more angular than the Aglianico, but it, too, is delicious, with plenty of dark red fruit, licorice, and minerals.

TIEFENBRUNNER *(Alto Adige)*

Pinot Bianco ♀ $ This Pinot Bianco possesses gorgeous textural richness, along with layers of smoke and earthiness that emerge, adding further complexity and nuance.

TORMARESCA *(Puglia)*

Primitivo Torcicoda ♥ $$$ A big, jammy offering with lovely nuances of herbs, tobacco, leather, licorice, and toasted oak that play off the wine's ripe dark fruit.

TORRE QUARTO *(Puglia)*

Negroamaro Sangue Blu ♥ $$ Spices, wild herbs, tobacco, dried cherries, and plums all make an appearance in this delicious red.

Uva di Troia Bottaccia ♥ $$ This pretty wine is packed with wild cherries, tobacco, herbs, and sweet toasted oak. A firmer and slightly fresher style than the Primitivo Tarabuso.

Primitivo Tarabuso ♥ $$ Reveals a darker, richer profile than the Uva di Troia Bottaccia, with aromas of smoke, licorice, and herbs that complement the ripe, generous fruit. Outstanding density and depth.

TOSCOLO *(Tuscany)*

Chianti � $ This Chianti offers notable freshness and vibrancy in a plump, fruit-driven style. A consistent overachiever in its class.

Chianti Classico � $$$ A pretty, accessible wine with floral red fruits, smoke, and licorice.

TRABUCCHI *(Veneto)*

Valpolicella Superiore Terre del Cereolo � $$ A deeply colored wine packed with black cherries, wild herbs, earthiness, and tobacco made in an imposing, superconcentrated style.

TRAMIN *(Alto Adige)*

Pinot Grigio ♗ $ A delicious white with clean, refined aromas and flavors.

Pinot Bianco ♗ $ Floral notes, mint, and white peaches are all intermingled in this tasty, taut white. A slightly fatter style than the Pinot Grigio.

Sauvignon ♗ $$ Expressive varietal notes of mint, tomato leaf, and peach emerge from this delicious white. A reference-point Sauvignon from Alto Adige.

Gewürztraminer ♗ $$$ Clean and focused in its exotic notes of passion fruit, spices, and flowers. Sourced from vineyards in Termeno, where Gewürztraminer was first discovered.

TRAPPOLINI *(Umbria)*

Orvieto ♗ $ A delicious Umbrian white endowed with pretty notes of melon, jasmine, and minerals that shows remarkable finesse at this level.

TUA RITA *(Tuscany)*

Rosso dei Notri ♗ $$$ A big, bold wine loaded with superripe dark fruit, sweet spices, leather, and chocolate made in a dense, richly textured style. A delicious entry-level red from one of Tuscany's most accomplished producers.

G. D. VAJRA *(Piedmont)*

Dolcetto d'Alba 🍷 **$$** This Dolcetto possesses awesome richness in its dark fruit, along with mineral and balsamic nuances that add complexity. A powerful and serious style of Dolcetto from one of Piedmont's finest growers.

Dolcetto d'Alba Coste & Fossati 🍷 **$$$** An incredibly pure, full-bodied Dolcetto packed with fruit that offers remarkable clarity and compelling overall balance.

Langhe Nebbiolo 🍷 **$$$** This graceful, vibrant Nebbiolo walks a tightrope balancing fruit and structure with notable finesse. A poor man's Barolo of the highest level.

VALDIPIATTA *(Tuscany)*

Rosso di Montepulciano 🍷 **$$** A fragrant, accessible red with attractive dark red fruit and a medium-bodied personality. (Sangiovese, Canaiolo, and Mammolo.)

LA VALENTINA *(Abruzzo)*

Montepulciano d'Abruzzo 🍷 **$** This Montepulciano offers plenty of sweet, ripe fruit in a plump, juicy style. Absolutely delicious.

Montepulciano d'Abruzzo Spelt 🍷 **$$$** A big, full-bodied wine. Floral, spiced aromatics lead to a core of raspberries intermingled with sweet toasted oak.

VALLE REALE *(Abruzzo)*

Trebbiano d'Abruzzo Vigne Nuove 🍷 **$** This Trebbiano exhibits terrific intensity in its deeply layered fruit, with expressive aromatics and notable energy.

Cerasuolo Vigne Nuove 🍷 **$** Consistently one of Italy's finest rosés.

Montepulciano d'Abruzzo Vigne Nuove 🍷 **$** A fresh, vinous offering loaded with plummy dark fruit that offers excellent balance and tons of style.

Montepulciano d'Abruzzo 🍷 **$$** A more serious Montepulciano that spends 12 months in used French oak barrels. Shows lovely depth in its expression of dark cherries, licorice, smoke, and toasted oak, in an elegant, harmonious style.

VAONA *(Veneto)*

Valpolicella Classico ♀ $$ Made in a midweight style, this graceful wine possesses notable clarity and precision in its sweet red cherries, earthiness, and wild herbs. It is a small-scale Valpolicella of uncommon elegance and finesse.

VELENOSI *(Marche)*

Pecorino Villa Angela ♀ $$ A big, full-bodied white redolent of ripe, honeyed fruit, roasted nuts, and mint. This lovely, expressive Pecorino is a beautiful example of this newly rediscovered variety.

I VERONI *(Tuscany)*

Chianti Rufina ♀ $$ This medium-bodied Chianti reveals a lush expression of dark red fruit, with underbrush, licorice, and tar overtones that linger on the finish. An unusually generous wine from one of Tuscany's cooler microclimates.

VESEVO *(Campania)*

Sannio Falanghina ♀ $$ A perfumed wine with pretty notes of tropical fruit and a soft, easygoing personality.

Fiano di Avellino ♀ $$$ Sweet, layered fruit is enhanced by subtle tones of earth and minerals in this rich, generous Fiano di Avellino.

Aglianico Beneventano ♀ $$ A fresh, perfumed wine bursting with dark fruit and sweet toasted oak, with a gorgeous inner sweetness that carries through from start to finish.

VIETTI *(Piedmont)*

Barbera d'Alba Tre Vigne ♀ $$$ This Barbera offers up layers of superripe dark fruit, leather spices, smoke, and earthiness with awesome textural depth and richness. Made in the soft, round style that is typical of the wines of Alba.

Barbera d'Asti Tre Vigne ♀ $$ Perhaps a little more linear than its sibling from Alba, this Barbera reveals greater complexity in its sweet dark fruit, with a persistent note of minerality that gives the wine length and a clean, refreshing finish.

Langhe Nebbiolo Perbacco 🍷 $$$ This exceptional wine reveals expressive aromatics and a lovely core of perfumed ripe fruit on a medium-bodied frame. Made from Barolo-designated vineyards, the wine has all the hallmarks of its big sibling, but in miniature.

VILLA CARAFA *(Campania)*

Aglianico Sannio 🍷 $$ The Aglianico Sannio is a big, dark, brooding wine loaded with dark fruit, licorice, and toasted oak, not to mention considerable character.

VILLA MALACARI *(Marche)*

Rosso Conero 🍷 $$ This hearty, rustic red is loaded with dark cherries, spices, herbs, licorice, and underbrush. (Montepulciano aged in cask.)

VILLA MATILDE *(Campania)*

Falanghina 🍷 $$$ A pretty, medium-bodied wine laced with perfumed ripe fruit.

Falerno del Massico Bianco 🍷 $$$ This drop-dead gorgeous white from Campania reveals a soft-textured, layered expression of honeyed peaches and pears intermingled with spice, mineral, and acacia overtones. Falerno del Massico is an ancient clone of Falanghina with a lineage that goes back several thousand years.

Aglianico 🍷 $$$ This generous Aglianico is loaded with ripe dark fruit, spices, and sweet toasted oak.

VILLA MEDORO *(Abruzzo)*

Chimera 🍷 $$$ A racy, full-bodied white with a pretty core of tropical fruit, jasmine, French oak, and spices. (Trebbiano d'Abruzzo and Falanghina.)

Montepulciano d'Abruzzo 🍷 $ This red offers much up-front appeal in its plummy dark fruit, with excellent length on the palate and good overall balance.

Montepulciano d'Abruzzo Rosso del Duca 🍷 $$$ The Rosso del Duca presents attractive sweet dark fruit intermingled with toasted oak nuances in an open, generous style.

VINI BIONDI *(Sicily)*

Gurna Bianco ♀ $$ This medium-bodied wine reveals notable complexity in its expression of white peaches, earth, flowers, smoke, minerals, and acacia, all of which are delicately woven into its fabric. (Carricante, Catarratti, Minella, Malvasia, and Muscatello dell'Etna.)

Outis ♀ $$ A silky, soft-textured wine with a pretty core of bright red fruit. (Nerello Mascalese.)

Gurna Rosso ♀ $$$ The Gurna Rosso reveals a dark core of fruit, with subtle notes of smoke, earth, spices, leather, and licorice that gradually emerge from its structured frame. (Nero d'Avola and Cabernet Sauvignon.)

VINOSIA *(Puglia)*

Essenza di Primitivo ♀ $ A delicious wine packed with generous, superripe fruit in a full-bodied style.

ZARDETTO *(Veneto)*

Prosecco Brut ♀ ♀ $$ A Prosecco that bursts from the glass with an engaging array of aromas and flavors.

Prosecco Zeta ♀ ♀ $$$ Made from the property's best fruit, the Prosecco Zeta offers an additional level of weight and depth in its creamy texture, with a touch more residual sugar.

ZENATO *(Veneto)*

Lugana San Benedetto ♀ $ The Lugana reveals a delicate expression of ripe peaches, mint, and sage, with lovely balance and poise. The indigenous Trebbiano di Lugana is especially aromatic here, where it is grown on the shores of Lake Garda.

Valpolicella Classico Superiore ♀ $ A dark, brooding wine loaded with character. An array of smoke, earth, game, and dark cherry emerges from this hearty, classically styled Valpolicella that also happens to be a great introduction to the wines of the region.

NEW ZEALAND

NEW ZEALAND WINE VALUES

by Neal Martin

New Zealand is the new kid on the block, as it is only since the early 1990s that the country has established a successful wine industry, and boy, has it striven to make up for lost time. In Sauvignon Blanc they nurtured a grape variety that soon became a welcome, value-driven alternative to the omnipresent Chardonnay, and the United Kingdom lapped up its crisp, gooseberry-tinged flavors and tittered when they heard descriptions like "cat's pee"—that was all part of its charm. Coupled with slick marketing campaigns based around the image of New Zealand as an unspoiled rural paradise, evocatively depicted by the iconic label of Cloudy Bay, it is unsurprising that from virtually nothing there are now just shy of 62,000 acres under vine.

In the USA, just like in the UK, Sauvignon Blanc remains the grape that consumers have taken to their heart, and most retail for between $14 and $18 per bottle. Many criticized it for being excessively herbaceous and underripe, and while those problems have been tackled head-on, New Zealand sought a more "noble" variety, and that came in the form of Pinot Noir, hitherto the bastion of Burgundy. It offered a refreshing, cheaper alternative centered upon Martinborough and Central Otago and slaked the thirst of Pinot lovers frustrated by the inconsistency and complexity of the Côte d'Or. The last decade has witnessed an explosion of boutique wineries that have eked out any available patch of suitable *terroir*. It has been extraordinarily successful, perhaps so extraordinarily that many have effectively priced themselves beyond the scope of a book that is dedicated to value wines below $25 per bottle.

This is a pity because relative to much of Burgundy, New Zealand Pinot Noir remains great value, and as their infant vines mature, the wines will inevitably improve. Over the last six years, New Zealand's producers have managed to maintain price stability in the U.S. market, having resisted price rises with the weakening U.S. currency. With the current strengthening of the dollar, prices could soften but that will depend on how the present recession will affect demand. The current vogue is for aromatic varieties such as Riesling, Gewürztraminer, and most popular of all, Pinot Gris, perhaps to the chagrin of quality-motivated producers who learned from the mistakes that Australia made in unwittingly basing its reputation on too many volume-led brands. While I can sympathize with their concern, there is no doubt that the success of Sauvignon Blanc and more recently Pinot Gris has allowed producers the financial means to pursue more challenging, rewarding varieties. I would not anticipate winemakers relinquishing their cash cows in the near future.

On the other hand, I hope that New Zealand is not misconceived as reliant upon just one or two styles of wine. On the contrary, it is an incredibly dynamic country that is only just beginning to explore its terrain and produce a potpourri of wines, from herbaceous Sauvignon Blancs to exemplary honeyed sweet wines, some of which represent good value.

Drinking Curves

Most of New Zealand's white wines are made to be drunk immediately, in particular nearly all Sauvignon Blancs and Pinot Gris, although the best cool-climate Chardonnay and Rieslings from top producers can be aged 5–6 years. Likewise a majority of New Zealand red wines should be consumed within 1–2 years, although the best Pinot Noirs from Central Otago—and perhaps even more so from Martinborough and Canterbury—can evolve wonderfully over 5–6 years, occasionally longer. Bordeaux blends should be consumed within 3–4 years of purchase, but the top wines from areas such as Gimblett Gravels in Hawke's Bay may last up to 10–12 years, while the best Syrahs benefit from 1–2 years cellaring and can last well for 6–8 years. New Zealand is such a young, dynamic wine-producing country that there is very little track record upon which to make concrete recommendations, notwithstanding the fact the nearly all wines are bottled under screw cap, whose influence upon long-term aged wine is yet to be evaluated on a countrywide scale.

Regions

New Zealand is basically two islands, the North Island, which is home to Northland, Auckland, Gisborne, Hawke's Bay, and Wairarapa (including Martinborough), and the South Island, which includes Nelson, Marlborough, Canterbury/Waipara, and the most southerly region, Central Otago. I will summarize each from north to south, with the exception of Northland, which is a more peripheral region.

AUCKLAND

Just 3% of New Zealand's vineyards lie within the ambit of the country's major cosmopolitan area, Auckland. Improvements in vineyard techniques have boosted the quality in subregions such as Waiheke Island, Clevedon, and Matakana, including some fine Bordeaux-style blends. Principal grape varieties include Chardonnay and some Bordeaux.

Location: On the North Island, with Kumeu and Huapai northwest of the city and Henderson due west from it; Matakana north of Auckland on the east coast; and Waiheke Island around 10 miles directly east of the city.

Acres Under Vine: 1,317

Subregions: Matakana, Waiheke Island, Clevedon

Average Annual Production: 1,241 tons

Principal Grape Varieties: Chardonnay and Bordeaux varietals

Principal Soil Type: Around Kumeu, heavy alluvial clay, while on Waiheke Island there is "stony batter clay loam" that is rich in volcanic ash and can produce some superb wines when coupled with steep terrain.

GISBORNE

Lying on the east coast of the North Island, this region was severely affected by phylloxera. The silver lining of that epidemic is that vast tracts of Müller-Thurgau were replaced by Chardonnay, which veers toward a more tropical style and is also a prime source for domestic sparkling production. These plantings have since been complemented by Gewürztraminer.

Location: North Island, eastern coast

Acres Under Vine: 5,268

Subregions: Ormond, Central Valley, Waipaoa, Golden Slope, Patutahi, Riverpoint, Manutuke

Average Annual Production: 26,034 tons

Principal Grape Variety: Chardonnay (much used for sparkling wine production)

Principal Soil Type: Fertile alluvial clay/loams and silt loam

HAWKE'S BAY

Hawke's Bay, on the east coast of the North Island, is New Zealand's largest red wine region with 42% dedicated to red varieties. An esoteric array of wines are produced in Hawke's Bay thanks to a complex mosaic of soil and meso-climates, plus a topography that ranges from vast fertile plains to well-drained, gravelly soils with a propensity to nurture high-quality fruit, most notably the Gimblett Gravels. A large percentage of rich, plummy Merlot is cultivated here, the cool climate engendering a slight herbaceous quality to some of the more Cabernet-based Bordeaux blends, plus some exciting, peppery Syrah. The Sauvignon Blanc tends to have less pungency on the nose and lower acidity than its Marlborough counterparts. The most recognized subregion is the Gimblett Gravels, and others include Esk Valley and Whakatu.

Location: Eastern coast of the North Island

Acres Under Vine: 11,525

Subregions: Esk Valley, Gimblett Gravels, Mangatahi, Roys Hill, Dartmoor Valley, Meeanee, Whakatu, Te Awanga

Average Annual Production: 41,963 tons

Principal Grape Varieties: Chardonnay, Bordeaux varieties, Syrah, and Sauvignon Blanc

Principal Soil Type: Extremely varied, mainly volcanic loess, alluvial silts, and deep river gravels

WAIRARAPA

Lying at the southern extreme of the North Island, Wairarapa is home to the well-known region of Martinborough and a plethora of boutique wineries striving for low yields and high quality. The climate is a little cooler than that of Marlborough, with greater diurnal temperature variation. Here one finds some of the best Pinot Noirs and high-performing, relatively tannic Cabernet Sauvignon that often impart meaty, sometimes chocolate-tinged flavors.

Location: Southern end of the North Island

Acres Under Vine: 2,044

Subregion: Martinborough

Average Annual Production: 1,949 tons

Principal Grape Varieties: Pinot Noir and Sauvignon Blanc

Principal Soil Type: Well-drained gravel soils on river terrace (known as the Martinborough Terrace)

NELSON

Nelson is the most northerly wine region of the South Island, the warmest region in New Zealand with the surrounding mountains creating a mild, sunny climate. It is home to Sauvignon Blanc, augmented by Pinot Noir, Chardonnay, and a little Riesling. Wines tend to be fragrant and supple with signature flavors of cherry, wild strawberry, and plum.

Location: Northern tip of the North Island in the rain shadow of western mountains

Acres Under Vine: 1,932

Subregion: Waimea Plains

Average Annual Production: 5,190 tons

Principal Grape Varieties: Sauvignon Blanc

Principal Soil Type: Clay-loam

MARLBOROUGH

Marlborough on the South Island is the largest, sunniest wine region in New Zealand, and its vineyards occupy the Wairau and Awatere valleys. The region found international fame in the mid-1980s thanks to Cloudy Bay. The region is known for its intense gooseberry, lime, and tropical fruit–infused Sauvignon Blanc, with Pinot Noir now more widely cultivated than Chardonnay. The Pinots tend toward raspberry and plum flavors, with well-defined structures and tannic backbone.

There are also expanding plantations of Riesling, while some of the Chardonnay and Pinot Noir is used to make sparkling wine.

Location: South Island, eastern coastal valleys

Acres Under Vine: 32,585

Subregions: Wairau Valley and Awatere Valley

Average Annual Production: 120,888 tons

Principal Grape Variety: Sauvignon Blanc

Principal Soil Type: Complex array of soil profiles, including old glacial and young riverbed deposits

CANTERBURY

Centered around the town of Christchurch, Canterbury is a cool, dry region that makes it susceptible to early- and late-season frost. It is most widely known for its subregion Waipara, its cool climate suitable for growing Chardonnay and Pinot Noir, with small parcels of Riesling and Pinot Gris.

Location: Eastern side of the South Island

Acres Under Vine: 741

Subregions: Waipara and the plains around Christchurch

Average Annual Production: 1,699 tons

Principal Grape Variety: Pinot Noir, Chardonnay, Riesling

Principal Soil Type: Waipara—chalk loam, rich in limestone; southern areas more alluvial silt-loam soils

CENTRAL OTAGO

As one of the most southerly wine regions in the world, it should be noted that Central Otago is the only New Zealand wine region influenced by a continental rather than a maritime climate, marked by high hours of sunshine and high diurnal-temperature variations. Its hillsides are home to Pinot Noir, which constitute around three-quarters of plantings. The wines tend toward the more intense, fruit-driven style, especially in the Bannockburn and Lowburn areas. There is immense variation in microclimate between subregions. For example,

Bendigo is the warmest, Gibbston the coolest (other subregions include Wanaka, Cromwell, Bannockburn, Lowburn. and Alexandra).

Location: South Island, in fact the world's most southerly vineyards, in valleys protected by 6,500-foot mountains, the only region influenced by a continental climate rather than a maritime one

Acres Under Vine: 3,496

Subregions: Gibbston, Wanaka, Cromwell, Bannockburn, Lowburn, Bendigo, Alexandra

Average Annual Production: 3,434 tons

Principal Grape Variety: Pinot Noir

Principal Soil Types: Loess and alluvial deposits with underlying gravels, plus some glacial deposits in the west

New Zealand's Top Wine Values by Winery

ALLAN SCOTT WINES *(Marlborough)*

Hounds Pinot Noir ♆ $$$ A competitively priced Pinot with an engaging brambly nose of mulberry and wild hedgerow, complemented by a soft, sensuous palate with hints of bitter dark chocolate toward the finish. Superb.

Moorlands Riesling ♆ $ This is an outstanding Riesling from 30-year vines; it has a minerally, apple-scented nose with beautiful definition accompanied by a crisp, lively palate with subtle green fruits and a subtle touch of passion fruit. Delicious!

Sauvignon Blanc ♆ $ This "Savvy" is imbued with flinty/smoky aromas with an elegant, understated palate—a Savvy with panache, one might say.

Sparkling Blanc de Blancs Brut ♆ $$$ This has an attractive flinty nose with a reserved, Chablis-like palate that would be a perfect match for fresh oysters.

Wallops Chardonnay ♆ $ A delightful nose of white peach and nectarines with the definition of a premier cru Burgundy; the palate has an almost Meursault-like persona with subtle floral notes on a beautifully poised finish.

ALPHA DOMUS *(Hawke's Bay)*

Alpha Domus Navigator ♟ **$$** This Bordeaux-style blend has a slightly herbaceous, tobacco-infused nose, the kind of new-world wine that could easily serve as an alternative to a fine Left Bank cru bourgeois: a little tannic, a touch of greenness, slightly austere, but refreshing and satisfying all the same.

Alpha Domus Viognier ♟ **$$** Everything you could wish for in the bouquet of this aromatic variety: white peach, apricot, and passion fruit, all well defined and not as blowsy as some Viogniers tend to be. The palate is well balanced and surprisingly reserved: a perfect wine for chilling slightly and serving with lightly spiced Asian cuisine.

Chardonnay ♟ **$** A crisp, oyster-shell-tinged nose, and a citrus palate inflected by tropical fruits with a smooth, easy-drinking finish.

AMISFIELD *(Central Otago)*

Pinot Gris ♟ **$$$** This Pinot Noir can be more phenolic, with touches of orange blossom on the nose and an attractive oily texture.

Sauvignon Blanc ♟ **$$$** Amisfield's Sauvignon Blanc can often pack a punch and offer impressive minerality.

AURUM WINES *(Central Otago)*

Riesling ♟ **$$** A delightful Central Otago–meets-Mosel-style affair.

BABICH *(Marlborough and Hawke's Bay)*

Black Label Sauvignon Blanc: ♟ **$$** A little barrel fermentation lends this Sauvignon a more floral nose, while the palate is imbued with good minerality and freshness.

Irongate Unoaked Chardonnay ♟ **$$** Hailing from the renowned Gimblett Gravels in Hawke's Bay, this Chardonnay has a petrol-tinged nose with lots of green apples and orange peel on the palate.

Dry Riesling ♀ $$ A commercial Riesling, but refreshingly crisp.

Pinot Gris ♀ $$ This is a Wairau Valley–sourced charmer with a sassy peach and apricot nose coupled with a relatively aromatic palate.

Pinot Noir Winemakers' Reserve ♥ $$ Plumes of red cherry and raspberry on the nose; the palate tends toward the lighter, leafier style of Pinot.

Sauvignon Blanc ♀ $$ A more herbaceous Sauvignon with touches of gooseberry on the nose and vibrant, racy acidity on the sharp but taut palate.

Syrah Winemakers' Reserve ♥ $$ Lean and focused on the nose with a sprinkle of white pepper; allow this Syrah to unfurl in the glass.

STEVE BIRD WINERY *(Marlborough)*

Steve Bird's wines sport the "Old Schoolhouse Vineyard" moniker.

Big Barrel Pinot Noir ♥ $$$ An engaging Pommard-like profile on both nose and palate, this Pinot should drink nicely over 5–6 years.

Pinot Gris ♀ $$ This Pinot Gris has a floral nose with hints of quince and apricot, and a well-balanced palate laced with orange blossom.

Riesling ♀ $$ This can be leafy on the nose but often shows tension and ripeness on the slightly herbaceous palate.

Sauvignon Blanc ♀ $$ This is your typically herbaceous, gooseberry-flavored Savvy with crisp acidity on the finish.

CLOUDY BAY WINERY *(Marlborough)*

Sauvignon Blanc ♀ $$$ Cloudy Bay is better known for their Chardonnay; this has gooseberry and cut grass on the sharp, zesty nose, and the palate often brims with green apple and kiwi fruit. It is certainly a well-crafted Sauvignon Blanc, but not exactly the cheapest New Zealand Sauvignon.

CRAGGY RANGE *(Hawke's Bay)*

Fletcher Family Vineyard Riesling ♀ $$$ This has tropical scents on the nose and a very harmonious palate with a well-judged, seemingly dry finish.

Kidnappers Vineyard Chardonnay ♀ $$$ This Chardonnay can develop an intriguing Meursault-like hazelnut aroma, and the judicious use of new oak really allows the fruit to express itself unimpeded.

Te Muna Road Sauvignon Blanc ♀ $$$ Cut grass and lime aromas with a grassy, citrus-led palate.

Yacht Club Vineyard Sauvignon Blanc ♀ $$$ This has a more complex nose, with touches of pink grapefruit and crisp green apples thrilling the palate.

THE CROSSINGS *(Marlborough)*

Sauvignon Blanc ♀ $$$ This can be complex on the nose with undertones of passion fruit and apricot, vibrant on the entry; brimming with vigor on the apple- and lime-infused palate.

Unoaked Chardonnay ♀ $$$ An enticing melon- and mango-scented nose, and a palate imbued with unashamed tropical notes of mango, pear, and mandarin with a dry but refreshing finish.

DELTA VINEYARD *(Marlborough)*

Pinot Noir ♀ $$$ A modern-style Pinot with pure raspberry and cranberry on the nose and a supple, lithe palate that is both generous and approachable.

Sauvignon Blanc ♀ $$$ A typical gooseberry-tinged nose with touches of herbaceous green fruits on the crisp, lively palate.

DOG POINT VINEYARD *(Marlborough)*

Sauvignon Blanc ♀ $$ Dog Point's regular Sauvignon Blanc has a well-defined herbaceous nose complemented by lime and gooseberry; the crisp and focused palate has green apple and fresh gooseberry at center stage, with apricot and pineapple applauding from the side.

GROVE MILL *(Marlborough)*

Pinot Noir ♗ $$$ This has great complexity on the nose with semblances of Pommard; cranberry and raspberry leaf are followed by a taut, red cherry and cranberry palate that has a surfeit of tension and poise. Top-class.

Riesling ♗ $$ This Wairau Valley Riesling brims with gooseberry and cut grass on the well-defined nose; floral and peachy on the palate; commercial but certainly pretty.

Sauvignon Blanc ♗ $ This is crisp and focused on the herbaceous, capsicum-tinged nose with a lovely marriage of sharp limes and tropical fruits such as passion fruit and apricot on the palate, all with great length and class.

HUIA *(Marlborough)*

Gewürztraminer ♗ $$$ This sees a little French oak and displays a light Alsatian nose with white peach and touches of beeswax, with the palate a little waxy in texture, well balanced, focused, with an appealing sense of harmony on the finish.

Pinot Gris ♗ $$ Intense on the nose with pear and passion fruit and a touch of minerality; the palate is yeasty, with all the lees stirring with dried fruits on the finish.

Sauvignon Blanc ♗ $$ A pretty, floral nose that is crisp and well defined, simple but harmonious on the palate, with lime and citrus fruits toward the pert finish.

HUNTERS *(Marlborough)*

Sauvignon Blanc ♗ $ A crisp, well-defined bouquet with granite tones and cut grass, and a palate zesty with lively gooseberry with a touch of orange zest leading to a sharp, bitter lemon finish.

JACKSON ESTATE *(Marlborough)*

Sauvignon Blanc ♗ $$$ This has a slightly herbaceous nose, often with touches of limestone, with an unashamedly zesty citrus palate.

Shelter Belt Chardonnay ♗ $$$ This excellent barrel-aged Chardonnay is imbued with a lovely beeswax aroma with subtle tropical fruits on the palate.

KEMBLEFIELD ESTATE *(Hawke's Bay)*

Distinction Chardonnay ♀ $$ This nose is inflected with touches of tropical fruit, such as guava and peach, and would appeal to those with a penchant for California Chardonnay.

Distinction Gewürztraminer ♀ $$ Packed full of oily, lychee-tinged fruit, not a subtle wine but one perfect if slightly chilled for a summer's day.

Distinction Sauvignon Blanc ♀ $$ Tropical overtones, with touches of passion fruit and grapefruit on the nose, developing a floral note with time. The palate is well balanced with a peachy, soft finish.

Reserve Merlot ♟ $$ Matured for 18 months in French barrels and has sappy cranberry fruit on the nose with a grainy, Right Bank Bordeaux personality on the palate.

Reserve Zinfandel ♟ $$ Roasted chestnuts and dark melted chocolate on the nose; rich and gamy on the palate.

KIM CRAWFORD *(Various)*

Kim's Favourite Chardonnay ♀ $$$ A Gisborne-sourced Chardonnay that comes packed with kiwi and pink grapefruit on the nose and a crisp, well-defined palate.

Marlborough Pinot Noir ♟ $$ Crawford's entry-level Pinot Noir is more Central Otago in style than Marlborough, with bright black cherries and blueberries.

Marlborough Sauvignon Blanc ♀ $$ This displays a slightly herbaceous nose leading to a citrus and passion fruit palate.

Marlborough Unoaked Chardonnay ♀ $$ This has a floral nose with touches of guava and a crisp honeysuckle palate.

Rory Brut ♀ $$$ This Pinot Noir and Chardonnay blend has a crisp, yeasty nose and a lush, creamy palate. It is commercial but well crafted.

SP Anderson Vineyard Bone Dry Riesling ♀ $$$ The handpicked Riesling has subtle mango and apricot on the nose, married to an intriguing kerosene-tinged palate.

KUMEU RIVER *(Auckland)*

Estate Chardonnay ♀ **$$$** From one of New Zealand's best exponents of the variety, their entry-level Chardonnay has a very Meursault-like nose with a spellbinding minerally palate and develops some lovely hazelnut flavors with time.

Pinot Gris ♀ **$$$** The Pinot Gris has an aromatic, lees-scented nose with touches of white peach and guava on the palate.

LAWSON'S DRY HILLS *(Marlborough)*

Pinot Noir ♟ **$$** A light-bodied Pinot with a fragrant red cherry and strawberry nose; taut and crunchy on the palate.

Sauvignon Blanc ♀ **$$** An attractive grassy, apple-y nose with a citric, lively palate that would appeal to those who like their Savvy razor-sharp.

LINDAUER *(Marlborough)*

Blanc de Blancs Non-Vintage Sparkling ♀ **$** One of New Zealand's most successful sparkling exports, with a simple but clean nose inflected with green apples and a touch of white flowers; the palate is sharp, clinical, and bursting with zingy green fruits with a minerally finish.

MAHI *(Marlborough)*

Sauvignon Blanc ♀ **$$** A fine source of subtle, tropical-tinged Marlborough-style Savvy, the Francis Vineyard is a little more extroverted, with mango and pineapple scents on the nose.

Ward Farm Pinot Gris ♀ **$$$** This beautiful wine is understated and very feminine; subtle rosewater scents on the nose with great purity on the palate.

Francis Vineyard Sauvignon Blanc ♀ **$$$** An extrovert Sauvignon Blanc with attractive mango and pineapple scents on the nose.

MANU *(Marlborough)*

Sauvignon Blanc ♀ **$$** A joint venture of David Duckhorn and Steve Bird, this has a vibrant nose of green apple and kiwi fruit, the palate bright and zesty; uncomplicated but utterly refreshing.

MATUA VALLEY *(Various)*

Estate Marlborough Pinot Noir 🍷 $$$ Aged on its lees, this Pinot has lovely notes of black cherries and wine gums on the nose with a touch of iodine on the linear, off-dry palate, once again not a complex wine, but well crafted and clean.

Marlborough Sauvignon Blanc 🍷 $ This is adorned with a pungent, herbaceous nose, with the palate full of fresh kiwi fruit and gooseberry; a simple but well-crafted white for weekday drinking.

Paretai Sauvignon Blanc 🍷 $$$ Certainly a step up from the entry-level Sauvignon Blanc, with a greater sense of minerality on the nose and touches of limestone interlaced with lime and apple; the palate is finely tuned with a more reserved stony finish.

MILLS REEF WINERY *(Hawke's Bay)*

Elspeth Merlot/Malbec 🍷 $$ This is very well balanced with succulent, polished black fruit.

Sauvignon Blanc 🍷 $$ This has a typically zesty, gooseberry-scented nose with tropical tones on the palate.

MILLTON VINEYARD *(Gisborne)*

Opou Vineyard Chardonnay 🍷 $$$ This fabulous Chardonnay is blessed with Burgundy-inspired aromatics and captures the minerality of a great Meursault.

Riverpoint Chardonnay 🍷 $$ From biodynamist James Millton, this has wonderful balance and definition with delicate apricot flavors on the finish.

Te Arai Chenin Blanc 🍷 $$$ This Chenin can be drunk in the flush of youth, although it is worth laying down for 3–4 years, whereupon it can develop a complex nose of wet wool, greengage, and white flowers, the palate crisp but silky with touches of clementine and pink grapefruit.

MONTANA (BRANCOTT) *(Various)*

Marlborough Barrel Aged 🍷 $$$ A step up from the South Island Pinot (below), this offers more aromatic complexity with violets and wild strawberries, and crunchy cranberry on the palate.

Reserve Sauvignon Blanc ♀ $$ This is sourced almost entirely from their own vineyards and is less overtly herbaceous than some of their other brands.

South Island Pinot Noir ♥ $ This offers a wallet-friendly introduction to New Zealand's signature red grape; no-frills, simple, fresh, and crisp.

MT. DIFFICULTY *(Central Otago)*

Pinot Gris ♀ $$$ Mt. Difficulty's Pinot Gris can veer toward Viognier on the apple-blossom-tinged nose with white peach and green apple flavors on the crisp palate.

Riesling ♀ $$$ A superb Riesling with its zingy, lime- and petrol-tinged nose and great *nervosité* on the palate.

Roaring Meg Pinot Noir ♥ $$$ A popular entry-level Pinot Noir, this is blessed with a vibrant cranberry bouquet, with Doris plum and bright red cherries on the vivacious palate.

MUD HOUSE *(Marlborough)*

Chardonnay ♀ $$$ Mud House's Chardonnay has a buttery nose and is rounded and slightly honeyed on the palate with a dry finish.

Pinot Noir ♥ $$ This Pinot has a lifted cherry and red currant nose with a spiky, crunchy palate that leaves the mouth fresh and reinvigorated.

Sauvignon Blanc ♀ $ A simple, zippy, gooseberry-scented, herbaceous wine to quaff with friends.

MUDDY WATER *(Canterbury)*

Chardonnay ♀ $$$ This barrel-fermented Chardonnay is highly recommended, with great minerality suffusing both nose and palate.

James Hardwick Riesling ♀ $$$ This has a complex, beeswax-tinged nose and is slightly viscous on the well-balanced palate, with honey tones toward the finish.

MURDOCH JAMES *(Martinborough)*

Blue Rock Sauvignon Blanc ♀ **$$** This is a more neutral, mineral/stony style with a sharp twist of lime on the finish.

NEUDORF *(Nelson)*

Brightwater Pinot Gris ♀ **$$** This can be quite spicy in its youth, a simple, commercial, but well-crafted entry-level Pinot Gris.

Brightwater Riesling ♀ **$$** This is crisp and bright with a steely off-dry finish.

Chardonnay ♀ **$$$** This comes highly recommended, with a honeyed nose and orange zest on the vibrant, racy palate.

Sauvignon Blanc ♀ **$$** One of New Zealand's best Sauvignons, this brilliantly marries the herbaceous elements of Hawke's Bay with the tropical hints of Marlborough.

Tom's Block Pinot Noir ♥ **$$$** Neudorf's Pinot Noir can be a bit sullen in its youth and develops a more Martinborough, Côte de Beaune–style personality with age.

OYSTER BAY *(Marlborough)*

Chardonnay ♀ **$** Seductive scents of mango and apricot on the nose; very commercially driven but cleanly made with a lovely creamy texture on the palate.

Sauvignon Blanc ♀ **$** Although this popular brand can be slightly vegetal on the palate, it is undeniably crisp and refreshing, with strong gooseberry and lime flavors.

PALLISER ESTATE *(Martinborough)*

Pencarrow Sauvignon Blanc ♀ **$** An excellent commercial Savvy with an attractive gooseberry-scented nose and crushed stones on the palate.

Pencarrow Pinot Noir ♀ **$$** Quintessential Martinborough: an almost rustic, cherry-scented nose and cranberry-flavored palate that can become very refined on the finish.

Sauvignon Blanc ♀ **$$** For just a few dollars more than the Pencarrow, Palliser produces one of New Zealand's best Sauvignons, with its herbaceous, elderflower-scented nose and crisp, zesty palate.

PEGASUS BAY *(Canterbury)*

Dry Riesling ♀ **$$$** This Riesling often adopts a reserved, granite-scented bouquet, clearly influenced by the Mosel and shockingly similar in style; the wine is so well balanced that you might fail to notice how dry the finish actually is!

Riesling ♀ **$$$** Like the Dry Riesling, this is in the vein of the Mosel, with hints of honeysuckle and apricot on the nose, the palate crisp and as light as a daisy. To put it prosaically, it is simply delicious.

Sauvignon Blanc/Sémillon ♀ **$$$** This can be scintillating: vibrant and animated on the nose and developing lovely scents of yellow flowers and lemon curd with a little age.

SAINT CLAIR *(Marlborough)*

Marlborough Pinot Noir ♟ **$$** Broody and introverted on the nose, dense and masculine on the palate, with a plum-flavored, herbaceous finish.

Marlborough Sauvignon Blanc ♀ **$$** This has an intriguing nose of granite; quite herbaceous with a vibrant, capsicum-tinged palate.

Vicar's Choice Pinot Noir ♟ **$$** Taut dark cherry and boysenberry bouquet and a palate that veers toward the more rugged, rustic style, with black brambly fruit and a dry finish. Not the most sophisticated Pinot Noir in the world, but it has bags of charm.

Vicar's Choice Sauvignon Blanc ♀ **$$** Saint Clair's entry-level Sauvignon, which comes with a light grassy nose and crisp palate infused with apple and gooseberry.

DANIEL SCHUSTER *(Waipara)*

Sauvignon Blanc ♀ **$$$** Sourced from gravelly soils, this has a waxy, nutty bouquet with a slightly oxidative palate that lends it an almost Meursault-like character.

Waipara Riesling ♀ **$$** A marriage between two bouquets: Mosel and Alsace. Very aromatic with touches of pear and kerosene and just a dab of ginger.

SEIFRIED (Nelson)

Gewürztraminer ♀ $$ This has a light peachy nose with touches of lychee and white flowers, leading to a lively palate with peach and nectarine notes on the entry with a touch of jasmine toward the finish. It is commercial and yet very well crafted.

Riesling ♀ $ Seifried's Riesling is quite grassy in style but with subtle tropical fruit in the background, with a hint of pear drop on the floral palate. An easy drinker that should be consumed within a couple of years.

Sauvignon Blanc ♀ $$ This has a pleasant nose with chalk dust and freshly mown grass and an attractive capsicum-tinged palate that zings about the mouth.

Sweet Agnes Riesling [S] $$$ This botrytized Riesling can top 200 grams of residual sugar. It is well worth seeking out: a luscious honeyed, beeswax-scented nose is the mere introduction to a viscous, honeyed palate with sufficient acidity to leave the palate tasting fresh and ready for another sip.

SERESIN (Marlborough)

In addition to the following, there are labels that would retail above, but not far above, $25, and I would also look out for their second-label range entitled Momo.

Gewürztraminer ♀ $$$ Up-front peach aromas on the nose complemented by mango and apricot; an extroverted wine but certainly not blowsy or over-the-top, with a hint of beeswax toward the finish.

Memento Riesling ♀ $$ Quite delicate on the nose with touches of apple blossom and apricot, with hints of pear drop and, again, apricot on the well-balanced, crisp palate leading to a sweet, slightly honeyed finish.

Sauvignon Blanc ♀ $$$ A superb Marlborough Sauvignon blended with a little Sémillon that has an intense nose of gooseberry, limestone, and cut grass, and a palate crisp with lively acidity, with a judicious amount of herbaceous elements toward the finish.

SHERWOOD ESTATE *(Waipara)*

Laverique Méthode Traditionelle Réserve ♀ **$$** A bargain price for a great kiwi sparkler. An equal blend of Chardonnay and Pinot Noir with 18 months resting on its lees, it has a crisp, citrus nose with granite and green apple aromas and an expressive minerally palate that will make you question your purchases of Champagne over the years.

Riesling ♀ **$** Great clarity on the nose with hints of an English garden lawn and apple blossom, with subtle orange zest on the palate.

STAETE LANDT *(Marlborough)*

Chardonnay ♀ **$$** Staete Landt's Chardonnay can be quite reserved at first, encouraging you, the drinker, to seek out its captivating *nervosité* and its minerality, which becomes more pronounced with aeration.

Pinot Gris ♀ **$$$** Comparatively reserved, less phenolic than its peers, with attractive apple-blossom notes on the palate and a neutral palate that has semblances to the western Loire Valley.

Sauvignon Blanc ♀ **$** A typical zesty, gooseberry-scented nose, less herbaceous than others, with a crisp, vivacious palate.

STONELEIGH *(Marlborough)*

Classic Chardonnay ♀ **$$** Aromas of wet stones with a touch of honeysuckle on the nose; the palates commercial but with an undeniably attractive buttery, slightly honeyed finish.

TE MATA ESTATE *(Hawke's Bay)*

Cape Crest Sauvignon Blanc ♀ **$$$** This sees one-third new oak and is therefore creamier, perhaps more internationally styled than the Woodthorpe Chardonnay, developing a smoky, almost hazelnut tang with a little bottle aging.

Woodthorpe Vineyard Chardonnay ♀ **$$** Touches of limestone and white peach on the nose, well defined and lifted with lush tropical fruits inflecting the palate.

Woodthorpe Vineyard Gamay Noir 🍷 $$ A crisp green-pepper-tinted nose with a fresh, vibrant, rounded palate that you could almost describe as bouncy!

Woodthorpe Vineyard Merlot/Cabernet 🍷 $$ This tends to develop hints of Christmas cake on the nose with a broody, chewy palate that might benefit from a few months' bottle aging.

Woodthorpe Vineyard Sauvignon Blanc 🍷 $$ A citrus-driven nose with touches of lime, well balanced and straightforward on the palate, and does everything you expect a Sauvignon Blanc to do.

Woodthorpe Vineyard Viognier 🍷 $$$ This is 80% barrel-fermented and comes replete with a spicy, aromatic nose with lush floral fruit on the palate, the kind of ostentatious Viognier that does not care whether you love or loathe it.

TOHU *(Marlborough and Gisborne)*

Gisborne Unoaked Chardonnay 🍷 $ This offers great value: touches of coconut and pine on the nose, a palate imbued with slightly honeyed fruits and a touch of apricot on the finish.

Mugwi Sauvignon Blanc 🍷 $ A vineyard selection that has an herbaceous nose with tinned pear and guava on the palate.

Pinot Gris 🍷 $ Sourced from Marlborough and Nelson with its well-defined nose of pear and melon, not too phenolic as some Pinot Gris can be; the palates refined, with a surprisingly complex finish of lanolin and dried pineapple.

VAVASOUR *(Marlborough)*

Dashwood Sauvignon Blanc 🍷 $ A clean, crisp Sauvignon with lime and gooseberry on the nose, simple but fresh and invigorating, and at 10 bucks a bottle, you can't go wrong.

Vavasour Pinot Noir 🍷 $$$ Brims with red berries and cranberry fruit on the nose, with a very polished, modern-style palate.

Vavasour Sauvignon Blanc 🍷 $ One of Marlborough's finest, with typical gooseberry and cut-grass notes complemented by nuances of passion fruit and peach. It builds nicely on the palate to reveal a minerally core of fruit—just a very well-crafted Sauvignon that deserves more than just quaffing.

VILLA MARIA *(Various)*

At the time of this writing, criminally few of these find themselves crossing the Pacific Ocean, though I suspect this will change as Americans embrace New Zealand's wines.

Cellar Selection Sauvignon Blanc ♀ **$$** This comes highly recommended: fresh and lively on the nose, superb definition on the citrus-driven palate, and great length.

Cellar Selection Syrah/Viognier ♟ **$$$** Rather coarse and chunky but full of mouth-coating brambly black fruits that pack a punch.

Private Bin Sauvignon Blanc: ♀ **$$** A typically herbaceous, gooseberry-scented nose and zesty, apple-y palate; a simple but sprightly wine for weekday quaffing.

WAIMEA ESTATES *(Nelson)*

Pinot Gris ♀ **$$$** Very attractive on the nose with hints of rosewater and peony; the palate has a good sense of minerality and tropical fruits—very pretty and a great value.

Sauvignon Blanc ♀ **$$$** Grassy and herbaceous with good definition; the palate is never complex but is well balanced, with green apples and a touch of capsicum on the finish.

WAIRAU RIVER *(Marlborough)*

Sauvignon Blanc ♀ **$$** Flint and granite on the nose that has as much in common with the herbaceous Hawke's Bay take on the grape as Marlborough; the palate is zesty and minerally with crisp apples on the finish.

WITHER HILLS *(Marlborough)*

Sauvignon Blanc ♀ **$** A quintessential gooseberry-scented nose with great crispness and zest, followed by a vibrant palate that is bursting with crisp green apple and citrus fruits. It is nothing spectacular, but it does everything one would expect from a Sauvignon Blanc.

PORTUGAL

PORTUGUESE TABLE WINE VALUES

by Mark Squires

Portugal is full of fine values that manage to make it to international markets despite exchange rate fluctuations that wreak havoc on retail pricing here. Prices do seem to be trending up and some wines that were once great values are now merely good ones, in part because of those exchange rate problems. Overall, though, the prices are still reasonable and values are easy to find. Plus, they come in distinctive blends that are hard to replicate elsewhere. Where else but the Douro will you get a blend of Touriga Nacional, Tinta Roriz, and Touriga Franca? Where else but southern Portugal will you get blends comprised of grapes like Syrah, Alicante Bouschet, and Castelão? That gives Portugal an advantage if you like the style and flavors. It is something different and distinctive, as well as reasonably priced for the most part.

Regions

While some are more important for values than others, it is a mistake to ignore any region. The **Douro**, in northeastern Portugal, is Portugal's best and most famous wine region. In 2006, it celebrated its 250th anniversary as a demarcated and regulated wine region. It has a cachet that is unmatchable by any other region in Portugal—although much of that stems from the port connection. A typical Douro red blend will likely center around grapes like Touriga Nacional, Tinta Roriz, and Touriga Franca. Whites will be blends of grapes like Códega, Malvasia, Rabigato, and Viosinho. While the heart of the Douro's reputation within Portugal is not centered on values, it in fact produces some good value wines, particularly reds. As in any region, you have to look past the trophies.

Alentejo is the best-known competitor to the Douro at the moment. It is at the opposite end of the country, a vast region in Portugal's south, Portugal's Châteauneuf-du-Pape, if you will, to the Douro's Bordeaux. Alentejo's wines are immensely popular in Portugal. Traditionally, it is one of the go-to regions for value wines. The wines here are frequently called "international" for their tendency to blend red grapes like Cabernet Sauvignon and Syrah with local grapes like Trincadeira, Alicante Bouschet (French, but perhaps at its best in southern Portugal), and others. White wines are likely blends of Antão Vaz, Roupeiro, Arinto, and others.

Turning to less famous regions is often the ticket to getting the best buys in many countries. Certainly, regions like Bairrada, Dão, Estremadura, Ribatejo, and Vinho Verde are fertile ground for bargain hunters. In fact, if you are a white wine fan, note that the continuing **Vinho Verde** quality revolution has resulted in some of the best values in Portugal. The 100% Alvarinhos, made right across the border from their Spanish Albariño counterparts, are often outstanding. These wines can age a little, too. They aren't the simple, fizzy little Vinhos Verdes that are here today, gone tomorrow. For the entire Vinho Verde region, it is hard to find much *over* this book's cutoff of $25, let alone worry about finding good wines that can be had for $25. In **Dão**, which celebrated its one hundredth year as a classified subregion in 2008, you will find familiar grapes from the Douro—Touriga Nacional and Tinta Roriz—in heavy use. The wines can be superb and inexpensive, elegant and graceful. Other popular grapes include Jaen and Alfrocheiro. The fine white of note is Encruzado. There is a lot of quality available in this region for modest money. **Bairrada** is, with Dão, the other important DOC-classified subregion of Beiras. It is a split-personality region—many producers are using international grapes, but the difficult, signature red grape for which it is famous (or infamous) is Baga. Bical is a popular and well-structured white that has considerable potential. **Ribatejo** and **Estremadura,** like Alentejo, use a variety of local and international grapes. The wines are usually very well priced.

Vintage Smarts

In most places in Portugal, the 2006 vintage was beset with difficulties. In general, I've liked the vintage a little better in Dão than in Douro, and the whites overall a little better than the reds, although the final verdict is not yet in. Most everyone suffered, though. It is a typical theme of the '06 Portuguese reds I tasted that they start out well but quickly thin and ultimately seem a bit short and hollow. Exchange rate fluctuations may actually make many 2006s as or more expensive than better recent vintages like the rich 2003s, the dense 2004s, and the lighter-styled, elegant 2005s. It is too early to evaluate fully the 2007s, which are just starting to arrive in the market, but they look very good in most places. The best recent vintage is 2004, which is producing concentrated, ageworthy, and intense wines with excellent fruit that generally still retain their balance and focus.

Drinking Curves

Generalizations in vintages or drinking curves are by nature never precise, but from the Douro Valley, with its port traditions, to the acidic Baga-based reds of Bairrada, to Dão's Touriga Nacionals, Portuguese reds usually hold well. There are, of course, exceptions to every rule, as well as many ultra-low-end wines specifically meant to be very early maturing, but Portuguese producers usually provide some structure. Even many bargain wines should be able to hold for 5–8 years gracefully—more in some cases and in some vintages. Portuguese whites are much more likely to be early maturing, although there are exceptions to everything. Vinho Verde, for example, is by reputation particularly likely to be early maturing and usually needs to be drunk within a year or two of its release, but new-wave Vinhos Verdes can age a few years longer in many instances.

Portugal's Top Table Wine Values by Winery

ADEGA COOPERATIVA DE BORBA (Alentejo)

Aragonês/Cabernet Sauvignon (Adegaborba.Pt) ♀ $ This blend has very attractive red berry notes.

Aragonez & Touriga Nacional ♀ $ Fruity, soft, and lively, with sweet, easy fruit, it has enough structure to make it seem like real wine.

Reserva (Adegaborba.Pt) ♀ $ Denser and more ageworthy than the regular bottlings, this uses a fair bit of American oak but absorbs it well with some air.

Touriga Nacional ♀ $ Fragrant and beautifully balanced, with ripe tannins sufficient to provide support.

ADEGA DE MONÇÃO (Vinho Verde)

Muralhas de Monção ♀ $ Mostly Alvarinho with some Trajadura blended in, it is delicate but persistent.

CAMPOLARGO *(Bairrada)*

Arinto ♀ $$ This is fermented in barrels, very different than the high-acid Arintos one finds elsewhere.

"Os Corvos da Vinha da Costa" ♥ $ A lush blend of international grapes like Tinta Roriz, Syrah, and Merlot.

CARM (CASA AGRICOLA ROBOREDO MADEIRA) *(Douro)*

Grande Reserva Branco ♀ $$$ This typical Douro blend of Códega, Rabigato, and Viosinho is oak aged but remains crisp most years.

Reserva (Quinta do Côa) ♥ $$$ Deeper and better structured than the regular Tinto, this retains a lush feel with sweet fruit.

Tinto ♥ $$ This typical Douro blend is usually well balanced, a bit compact, but flavorful and charming with an obvious backbone.

Tinto (Quinta do Côa) ♥ $$ This single-quinta wine often seems lusher and richer than the multiquinta Tinto and it is always bursting with flavor.

CASA DE CELLO *(Vinho Verde and Dão)*

Branco (Quinta de Sanjoanne) ♀ $ This crisp and flavorful Vinho Verde is unoaked, ageworthy, and piercing.

"Porta Fronha" (Quinta da Vegia) ♥ $$ This is a young-vines Tinto that is clean and pure, with ripe tannins for support.

Tinto (Quinta da Vegia) ♥ $$$ This is typically a Touriga Nacional–Tinta Roriz blend, fruity, elegant, and fresh, with ripe tannins and a lively feel.

CASA ERMELINDA FREITAS *(Terras do Sado)*

Reserva ♥ $$ A blend of grapes like Touriga Nacional, Syrah, and Castelão, the latter from 50+-year-old vines, this shows lovely fruit and nice structure, with some intensity on the finish.

Tinto ♥ $ The Castelão here is from 40+-year-old vines and is about one-third of the blend.

CASA DE VILA VERDE *(Vinho Verde)*

Branco 🍷 $ A single-estate wine that is awfully friendly, fruity, and easy to drink. Their 100% Alvarinho is better, if a couple of dollars more.

CAVES ALIANÇA *(Dão and Bairrada)*

Quinta da Garrida Estate 🍷 $$ This graceful, elegant wine has lovely aromatics and fruit.

Tinto (Quinta das Baceladas) 🍷 $$$ This is a rather elegant, very bright, and modern-style Bairrada, a blend of Cabernet Sauvignon, Merlot, and "a limited quantity" of Baga.

CAVES TRANSMONTANAS *(Douro)*

Espumante Bruto Super Reserva (Vértice) 🍷 $$ This wine, aged for years on the lees, provides considerable depth and lots of toast for the money.

Espumante Reserva (Vértice) 🍷 $ Lighter and easier drinking than the Super Reserva, and a couple of bucks less.

CHURCHILL GRAHAM *(Douro)*

Tinto 🍷 $$$ A very elegant Douro blend, bright and sunny, with good flavor and some intensity on the finish.

COLINAS DE SÃO LOURENÇO (SILVIO CERVEIRA) *(Bairrada)*

Chardonnay/Arinto 🍷 $ Bright and crisp, with the Arinto providing good acidity.

Private Collection 🍷 $$$ A blend of local and international grapes, it adds a layer of depth to the regular Tinto, while retaining a rather elegant and suave style.

Tinto 🍷 $ A blend of local and international grapes, this is a sunny, fairly high-acid wine with a succulent finish and an elegant midpalate.

DÃO SUL (*Dão*)

Touriga Nacional (Quinta de Cabriz) ♟ $$$ A classic Dão in many respects, elegant in midpalate weight, increasingly aromatic as it opens up.

DOMINGOS ALVES DE SOUSA (*Douro*)

Caldas Reserva ♟ $$ A well-balanced Douro blend, with a little intensity and rather delicious plum-nuanced flavors.

Estação ♟ $ This is one of those low-end wines that can surprise you; bright, with some persistence on the finish and a nice, sunny demeanor.

Reserva (Quinta do Vale da Raposa) ♟ $$ This typical Douro blend is a friendly, easy-drinking wine that has lovely aromatics, an elegant midpalate, a lush feel, sweet up-front fruit, and refined tannins.

JOSÉ MARIA DA FONSECA (*Terras do Sado and Douro*)

Domini ♟ $$ Fonseca's Douro entrant, it is usually on the lighter side, bright and elegant, with some character and some persistent flavors.

Periquita Reserva ♟ $$ A Portuguese classic, this is bright, elegant, and charming, with succulent, juicy fruit that has a certain blueberry overlay.

FUNDAÇÃO EUGÉNIO DE ALMEIDA (ADEGA DE CARTUXA) (*Alentejo*)

Branco "Cartuxa" ♙ $ A blend of grapes like Arinto, Antão Vaz, and Roupeiro, it is light and easygoing, with enough persistence on the finish to seem a little lively.

Branco "EA" ♙ $ This is a mass-market classic but quite charming, clean, and tasty, with some brightness around the edges.

Foral de Évora Tinto ♟ $$$ This can be a powerful midlevel wine with some depth and ability to age.

HERDADE DO ESPORÃO *(Alentejo)*

Alandra ♟ $ Soft, grapy, and easygoing, this is Esporão's mass-market table wine, an attractive blend of Moreto, Castelão, and Trincadeira.

Aragonês ♟ $$$ Good structure, grip on the finish, good acidity, and some early power.

"Monte Velho" Branco ♟ $ A familiar mass-market classic that is usually a good value, if rather delicate.

Touriga Nacional ♟ $$$ Elegant, with a lovely floral nose.

Verdelho ♟ $$ Exuberant and a bit grassy, with a lemony note at first on the finish, it is crisp and pungent, with a rather gripping finish and reasonable depth.

Vinha da Defesa Branco ♟ $$ More herbaceous than the Monte Velho (above), it is crisp and steely, made in stainless steel.

HERDADE SÃO MIGUEL *(Alentejo)*

Tinto ♟ $ A blend of local and international grapes, this is a flavorful and well-structured wine that can age a bit and develop in the cellar.

HOTEL DO REGUENGO DE MELGAÇO *(Vinho Verde)*

Alvarinho ♟ $$ In good vintages, this deep Vinho Verde may sometimes show better after 6–12 months of cellaring.

JOÃO PORTUGAL RAMOS *(Alentejo and Ribatejo)*

Loios Tinto ♟ $ A blend of typical southern grapes like Aragonez, Trincadeira, and Castelão, fermented in stainless-steel tanks, it is light and bright, pointed and focused.

Reserva "Conde de Vimioso" (Falua) ♟ $$$ A blend of grapes like Touriga Nacional, Cabernet Sauvignon, and Tinta Roriz from a single vineyard, it is ageworthy as well as flavorful.

Tinto "Marquês de Borba" ♟ $$ Bright, with good acidity, big red fruit flavors, and a luscious finish.

Tinto (Vila Santa) ♟ $$$ A blend of local and international grapes, it is fruity but well structured, needing some cellar time to allow the oak to integrate.

LAVRADORES DE FEITORIA *(Douro)*

Tinto "Três Bagos" ♟ $$ This brand provides a nice rush of easygoing fruit, but it has enough depth and structure that it can take an hour or so to show its best on release.

MONTE DA CAPELA *(Alentejo)*

Reserva ♟ $$ A typical southern blend, it is bright and elegant, with reasonably complex flavors, ripe tannins, some good red fruit, a touch of herbs, and some earthiness.

PAULO LAUREANO VINUS *(Alentejo)*

Dolium Branco Escolha ♟ $$$ Likely all Antão Vaz, this has heavy notes of hazelnuts and a *sur-lie* influence. It is a very Burgundian style.

Dolium Reserva ♟ $$$ Call this the Singularis (below) with more of everything, including flavorful fruit and good structure.

Singularis Tinto ♟ $ Rather elegant; a lighter style, with bright red berry notes.

ANSELMO MENDES (ANDREZA) *(Vinho Verde)*

Alvarinho ♟ $$$ This powerful Vinho Verde, around 13% alcohol, can seem remarkable in its depth and intensity.

Loureiro "Escolha" (Andreza) ♟ $ This "special selection" is 100% Loureiro, a delicate grape that makes a fine wine; crisp, aromatic, and refreshing.

PINHAL DA TORRE *(Ribatejo)*

"2 Worlds Reserva" (Quinta do Alqueve) ♟ $$ Usually the steal of the lineup, a well-structured blend, 50% each of Cabernet Sauvignon and Touriga Nacional, representing the New and Old Worlds.

POÇAS *(Douro)*

Coroa d'Ouro Reserva Branco ♉ **$** Grassy, refreshing, and rather lively.

Novus ♉ **$$** A typical Douro blend in a sexy, lush, easily approachable style.

Tinto "Coroa d'Ouro" ♉ **$** Nicely constructed and flavorful, with some intensity on the finish and a solid feel to the midpalate.

Vale de Cavalos ♉ **$$$** Better structured than the Novus, this wine still features lovely sweet fruit.

QUANTA TERRA *(Douro)*

Reserva "Terra a Terra" ♉ **$$$** This Douro blend has a rather suave feel to it; supple, with ripe tannins and impeccable balance.

QUINTA DA ALORNA *(Ribatejo)*

Tinto ♉ **$** Aromatic and very fruity in an obvious way, maybe too obvious for some.

Touriga Nacional/Cabernet Sauvignon Reserva ♉ **$$** Tightly wound on release, with the texture oak softened, the palate delivers ripe and fresh fruit.

QUINTA DA AVELEDA *(Vinho Verde and Bairrada)*

Alvarinho ♉ **$** This has a solid feel, projecting depth and concentration unusual for Vinho Verde at its modest price point.

"Follies" Chardonnay/Maria Gomes ♉ **$** An unusual grape combination that works pretty well, this has depth and crispness, and a nice finish that can project a lot of flavor.

Touriga Nacional/Cabernet Sauvignon "Follies" ♉ **$$** This can project a tannic punch and has good depth for its price range.

QUINTA DA CORTEZIA *(Estremadura)*

Reserva ♉ **$** Smoothly textured and easygoing, it nonetheless has a little intensity and focus on the finish, and reasonably good structure for a wine this cheap.

Touriga Nacional ♉ **$$** A charming wine, elegant, aromatic, and graceful, if a bit lacking in midpalate concentration.

QUINTA DA ROMANEIRA *(Douro)*

"R" de Romaneira 🍷 $$$ Touriga Franca dominated, elegant in the midpalate, with a graceful feel and well-integrated tannins on the finish.

QUINTA DE CHOCAPALHA *(Estremadura)*

Tinto 🍷 $$ A blend of various grapes, sometimes Tinta Roriz, Touriga Nacional, Alicante Bouschet, and Castelão, it has a rather creamy texture, but the fruit pops up immediately and there is good structure.

QUINTA DE RORIZ *(Douro)*

Prazo de Roriz 🍷 $$ Utterly charming, round, and velvety, with a little bite on the finish.

QUINTA DE VENTOZELO *(Douro)*

Tinta Roriz 🍷 $$ Elegant, bright, and well structured, with tasty fruit.

Touriga Nacional 🍷 $$ Bright, persistent flavors and good structure, too.

QUINTA DO AMEAL *(Vinho Verde)*

Loureiro 🍷 $$ Bright, somewhat mouthwatering, and delicate, as most Loureiros are.

QUINTA DO CASAL BRANCO *(Ribatejo)*

Branco (Capoeira) 🍷 $ A blend of Fernão Pires from 25-year-old vines and Sauvignon Blanc, it is perky, exuberant, and refreshing.

Branco (Falcoaria) 🍷 $ I wonder how many people drinking one blind would think this charming, dirt-cheap wine was the equivalent of a $25 California Chardonnay.

Branco (Quartilho) 🍷 $ All Fernão Pires from a single plot of 25-year-old vines, it is unoaked, refreshing, and bright, if a little light.

Castelão & Cabernet Sauvignon "Terra de Lobos" 🍷 **$** Fruity and accessible, it offers pleasant flavors, with a certain sharp, pointed red berry nuance.

Reserva (Falcoaria) 🍷 **$$** This Reserva isn't that much more expensive or that much better than the Tinto, but it is a bit tighter, with a slightly fuller feel, while the Tinto is fresher and livelier.

Tinto (Falcoaria) 🍷 **$$** Smooth and lushly textured, it finishes a bit tight, with some grip.

QUINTA DO FEITAL *(Vinho Verde)*

Auratus 🍷 **$$** An unoaked blend of Alvarinho and Trajadura with a steely midpalate.

QUINTA DO MOURO (MIGUEL LOURO) *(Alentejo)*

Reserva "Casa dos Zagalos" 🍷 **$$** Flavorful, softly textured, elegant, and beautifully balanced, it has just enough intensity and verve and a pretty decent finish.

QUINTA DO NOVAL *(Douro [Duriense])*

Cedro do Noval 🍷 **$$$** Aromatic, rich, and delicious; Noval started adding Syrah as about half the blend of this second wine in 2005.

QUINTA DO PORTAL *(Douro)*

Reserva 🍷 **$$$** A typical Douro blend, it retains the lovely fruit of the regular bottlings but adds more structure.

Tinto 🍷 **$$** Modest in the midpalate, with ripe tannins providing some intensity and vibrancy, it is quite charming.

Tinta Roriz 🍷 **$$** Bright with some overt red fruit flavor up front, this has a fair bit of power lurking underneath.

QUINTA DO VALE MEÃO *(Douro)*

Meandro do Vale Meão 🍷 **$$** This second wine is a typical Douro blend, bright, elegant, and refreshing, yet with some power.

QUINTA DO VALLADO *(Douro)*

Tinto 🍷 $$ This is among the Douro's better and most consistent bargains; round, ageworthy, and smooth, with some modest power lurking underneath. About a third of the blend in most years comes from old vines (70+ years), with the rest young vines.

QUINTA DOS ROQUES *(Dão)*

Encruzado 🍷 $$ An elegant white, clean and friendly.

QUINTA VALE DAS ESCADINHAS *(Dão)*

T-Nac (Quinta da Falorca) 🍷 $$ A rather soft Touriga Nacional, with delicious fruit and a modest midpalate.

RAMOS PINTO *(Douro)*

Adriano Branco 🍷 $$ This develops a certain roundness as it gets a little age, but it is perky and bright when young, as well as refreshing.

ROQUEVALE (SOC. AG. DE HERDADE DA MADEIRA) *(Alentejo)*

Tinto da Talha Syrah/Touriga Nacional "Grande Escolha" 🍷 $ Smooth and refined, and tasting mostly of oak at first, but its parts integrate very well.

SOCIEDADE AGRICOLA DE SANTAR *(Dão)*

Tinto (Casa de Santar) 🍷 $$ A blend of grapes like Touriga Nacional, Alfrocheiro, and Tinta Roriz, it is elegant, flavorful, and graceful, with some intensity on the finish.

SOGRAPE VINHOS *(Douro, Alentejo, and Dão)*

Callabriga Alentejo 🍷 $ Lush and tasty, with a little grip on the finish and a bright demeanor.

Callabriga Dão 🍷 $ Fruity, elegant, and tasty, it is an easygoing wine with a little brightness on the finish.

Callabriga Douro 🍷 $ Light and bright, it has some of those sweet 'n' sour plum notes from Touriga Nacional, a modest midpalate, and modest structure.

Pena de Pato ♟ $ A respectable little wine, albeit very light in the midpalate, that is more than the Beaujolais-esque quaffer that one usually sees in this price range. It is focused, elegant, and pristine, with good structure.

SYMINGTON FAMILY ESTATES *(Douro)*

Altano Reserva ♟ $$ Also a blend, but more likely to be reliant on Touriga Franca, it is a step up on the regular Altano and it is a step up on the regular Altano and the Vale do Bomfim in terms of depth and structure, but it can be significantly marked by oak some years.

Reserva "Vale do Bomfim" (Dow) ♟ $ This Douro blend has ripe tannins, but this wine is notable for easygoing fruit and a very elegant midpalate.

TERRAS DE ALTER *(Alentejo)*

Branco "Fado" ♟ $ A typical southern white blend of grapes like Antão Vaz and Roupeiro, resulting in a rather charming wine with some roundness in the texture, a feeling of depth, and some grip on the finish.

VINHO ALVARINHO DE MONÇÃO *(Vinho Verde)*

Alvarinho "Solar de Serrade" ♟ $$ Crisp, with lemon-lime notes on the mouthwatering finish, but quite fruity after a few months as it comes around quickly.

SOUTH AFRICA

SOUTH AFRICAN WINE VALUES

by David Schildknecht

In the 15 years since the abolition of apartheid, a renaissance of South African wine and a new level of international recognition have paralleled the country's political rebirth. In addition to long-established viticultural areas (South Africa has been home to serious wine-growing for a century longer than Australia or the United States), many exciting opportunities are opening up in formerly obscure or entirely new sectors of the country. Major challenges remain to be tackled, ranging from inferior and diseased vine stocks—in large part a legacy of the long period of antiapartheid sanctions—to an ever more crowded market, reflecting not only competition from other countries, but also the new brands that South Africa has been bringing to market at a frenetic pace. While many of these wines lack distinctive character or memorable flavor intensity, or suffer from a common new-world malady of vegetal flavors combined with noticeably high alcohol, the great news is that some—including, of course, the value wines featured in this guide—are truly outstanding.

Regions

South Africa's two oldest and most prestigious regions—Constantia and Stellenbosch—are directly adjacent to Cape Town itself. But nearly all of South Africa's wine-growing regions parallel the Atlantic and Indian Ocean coasts north and east of Cape Town, many in immediate proximity to the cooling deep waters and maritime breezes. North of Stellenbosch, the best-known region is Paarl, one of several that lie on the edge of a vast area—extending well into the interior—known as Swartland. Southeast of Cape Town and Stellenbosch, hugging the Atlantic Coast, are among others the districts of Walker Bay and Cape Agulhas, the latter named for the point that divides the Atlantic and Indian oceans. Among the interior districts east of Stellenbosch whose wines are most often encountered on labels stateside are Robertson and Calitzdorp. The broadest regional designation to be found on South African labels is "Western Cape," referring collectively to all of the above districts, and more besides. (A distant, smaller, and much less important wine-growing region is the Northern Cape.)

Grapes

Based on its uniqueness and prevalence, Pinotage—a cross between Cinsault and Pinot Noir—is treated as South Africa's national grape, although in truth it tends a bit toward rough and rustic, at times pungently sweaty, and most of South Africa's best reds originate with grapes familiar from Bordeaux, Burgundy, and the Rhône. Sauvignon, Sémillon, and Chenin Blanc (here known also as Steen and seldom displaying much in common with its distant Loire cousins) are especially prevalent among white grapes, and all three are capable of distinction. In warmer areas, Grenache Blanc and Viognier, among others, have recently shown potential. The length of supply chains leading from South Africa and no doubt other factors, too, result in an unusually broad range of vintage dates in the American market at any time. But with few exceptions (and allowing for a harvest 6 months ahead of that in the Northern Hemisphere), inexpensive South African white wines that reach our shores should be enjoyed within one calendar year of their vintage date. With inexpensive reds, the situation is too complicated to support broad generalizations, but it is not a bad rule of thumb to favor wines within 3 years of their vintage date when possible. Give the vast areas and range of grape varieties involved, it is best within the scope of this guide not to attempt generalizations about vintage character.

South Africa's Top Wine Values by Winery

AVONDALE (Paarl)

Chenin Blanc ♉ $ Quince and faintly wet wool aromas and a ripe, bittersweet quince- and lime-zest palate impression with a hint of sweetness are all enlivened by an attractive hint of CO_2 and good acidity.

Cabernet Franc ♉ $ Possessed of a faintly smoky overlay in the nose, this satisfyingly supple and tartly refreshing, organically grown red features ripe mulberries with hints of sage and fresh green beans.

BACKSBERG *(Paarl)*

Chenin Blanc ♀ **$** This exhibits lovely fresh apple and floral scents, a subtly sweet nuttiness balanced by insistent lemon citricity on the palate, and a clean, low-key, but persistent finish.

Klein Babylons Toren ♟ **$$$** Michael Back's superb-value blend of Cabernet Sauvignon, Merlot, and a bit of Shiraz offers a rich, polished, barrel-enhanced mélange of tobacco, sealing wax, plum, blackberry, humus, iodine, underbrush, and sweetly floral notes, all suggesting a Bordeaux wine that would cost at least three times its price.

GRAHAM BECK *(Robertson)*

Viognier ♀ **$** With an ultratypical nose of acacia, peach, cress, and white pepper, this smells set to make a dramatic palate impression but comes up very slightly metallic and bitter. Still, at its price it's a bargain.

Syrah The Ridge ♟ **$$$** Faintly stewed red fruits are tinged with rose hip, saddle leather, licorice, smoky black tea, and vanilla in this satisfying concentrated, fine-grained Syrah.

BILTON *(Stellenbosch)*

Matt Black ♟ **$$** This blend of Bordeaux varieties with Syrah displays lightly cooked blackberry and blueberry accented by mint, tobacco, and black pepper; sappy persistence; and ample brightness.

BLACK PEARL *(Paarl)*

Oro ♟ **$$** A blend of Shiraz and Cabernet, this blackish, seamlessly rich wine exudes dried black currants, tar, baking spices, tea, mint, and black olives, finishing with generous fruit and unobtrusive tannins.

BRAMPTON *(Stellenbosch)*

Sauvignon Blanc ♀ $ This mouth-filling, invigoratingly zesty, versatile second-label Sauvignon of well-known Rustenberg offers pungent grapefruit and lime zest and herbs with invigorating tartness and tactile chew.

Shiraz ♟ $ A nose of black raspberry, sage, and black pepper introduces a ripe but lively palate with pungent pepper and herbs persisting into a finish of slight astringency and heat.

BUITENVERWACHTING *(Constantia)*

Sauvignon Blanc Beyond ♀ $ This second-label Sauvignon is brimming with gooseberry and herb aromas and faintly bitter and tart red berry and citrus flavors. Firm, brisk, saline, chalky notes accompany its tactile finishing pungency.

Sauvignon Blanc ♀ $ This smells outrageously of gooseberry, sage, boxwood, and lime zest. Stony, saline, and chalky undertones accompany correspondingly intense flavors on a subtly oily palate, and it has a tactile, bracing finish.

Chardonnay ♀ $$ An expressive nose of pear drop, vanilla, and toasted almond leads to a palate-balancing sap and freshness of fruit against the toasty but slightly drying effects of new wood and a lightly caramelized, faintly bitter finish.

CAPAIA WINES *(Stellenbosch)*

Sauvignon Blanc Blue Grove Hill ♀ $$ Manfred Tement (see "Austria") advises on this second label of Stephan von Neipperg of St.-Émilion's Capaia. Salted grapefruit, passion fruit, green herbs, gooseberry, and black currant inform a bright, impressively sleek, refined, juicy, and persistent Sauvignon.

Blue Grove Hill ♟ $$ This polished, elegant blend generally of two-thirds Merlot with Cabernet Sauvignon, features tobacco, herbs, and black currant, with toasted nuts, dark chocolate, and a suggestion of floral perfume.

DURBANVILLE HILLS *(Durbanville)*

Sauvignon Blanc ♀ $ This is dominated by passion fruit, peach, and grapefruit, with a brisk, bright, zesty personality and hints of bitterness.

Pinotage ♀ $ A rare inexpensive and wholeheartedly recommendable example of this widely planted South African variety, with fresh red raspberry augmented by subtle smokiness and integrated herbal-vegetable aspects.

EDGEBASTON (FINLAYSON FAMILY VINEYARDS) *(Stellenbosch)*

The Pepper Pot ♀ $$ From one of South Africa's leading wine-growing families, this generous and unusual blend of Mourvèdre with Tannat and Syrah is a fascinating stew of red meat, blackberries, spinach, herbs, and black pepper.

Shiraz ♀ $$$ With air, this opens to reveal copious bittersweet black cherry fruit, black pepper, asphalt, and bitter herbs. Literally and figuratively opaque, it is powerful, rich, and suffused with fine-grained tannin, and finishes with smoky pungency and tarry cling.

EXCELSIOR ESTATE *(Robertson)*

Cabernet Sauvignon ♀ $ This smells of tobacco, hemp, cassis, and toasted pralines; offers quite mouth-filling ripeness; and finishes with sappy cling and just a hint of roughness and heat.

FAIRVALLEY *(Coastal Region)*

Chenin Blanc ♀ $ The wine from the decade-old Fairvalley Workers Association is delightful: lovely white peach, pineapple, and bittersweet floral aromas lead to a juicy and refreshing palate and finish.

FLEUR DU CAP *(Stellenbosch)*

Sauvignon Blanc Unfiltered ♀ $$ This juicy, generous, succulent Sauvignon offers honeydew melon, celery, and just a hint of passion fruit.

Merlot Unfiltered ♟ **$$$** Ripe red cherry and tomato foliage aromas mingle in the nose, while ample richness, supple tannins, and subtle dark chocolate, toasted nut, and bitter herbal nuances emerge on the satisfyingly juicy palate.

THE FOUNDRY *(Coastal Region)*

Viognier ♟ **$$** Avoiding frequent pitfalls of canned fruit, heaviness, or excessive astringency, this offers aromas of acacia, white peach, apricot kernel, and roasted pistachio and an enveloping, rich, subtly creamy yet refreshing palate tinged with cress, fruit pits, and white pepper.

GLEN CARLOU *(Paarl)*

Grand Classique ♟ **$$** Black currant, stewed mulberry, tar, and tobacco comprise an impressive aromatic opening gambit to a blend of Bordeaux grapes that's bright and gripping, if slightly sweet-sour and a touch warm.

DE GRENDEL *(Durbanville)*

Sauvignon Blanc ♟ **$$** Sneeze-inducing peppermint and grasses with a hint of passion fruit mark the nose, and a brisk, refreshing palate leads to interesting suggestions of nut oils, salts, and wet stone in a finish of impressive tenacity.

INDABA *(Western Cape)*

Chardonnay ♟ **$** Among Indaba's truly mind-boggling values, it would be hard to imagine a better-balanced or more succulent rendition of the world's most ubiquitous white variety than this, with spiced apple, pineapple, and pear truly framed, not overwhelmed, by a bit of oak.

Chenin Blanc ♟ **$** Suggesting watermelon, grapefruit, and pineapple, this pleasantly tart, invigorating, very inexpensive wine finishes with attractive bittersweetness.

Sauvignon Blanc ♟ **$** This nicely balances its variety's weedy and herbal side with succulent grapefruit and restrained gooseberry. Pungent and lively, it marries textural richness to bracing, ripe acidity, finishing with invigorating hints of peppermint and white pepper.

Merlot 🍷 $ Mouth filling and seamlessly ripe, this relatively light-bodied rendition of a ubiquitous variety features ripe cherry, beetroot, dark chocolate, and licorice.

KANU (Stellenbosch)

Chenin Blanc 🍷 $ An offshoot of well-known Mulderbosch, Kanu's Chenin displays clarity and freshness; luscious melon fruit laced with pungent herbs and cress; and a zesty, faintly bitter finish.

DE KRANS (Calitzdorp)

Tawny Port $ 🍷 S These fortified-wine specialists have (re-) introduced the classic Portuguese varieties. This smells of dried strawberries, sultanas, toasted walnuts, and cocoa powder; is surprisingly bright and tangy on the palate; and displays uncanny balance, finishing with discreet sweetness and nutty, chocolate-like richness.

LYNX (Franschhoek)

Cabernet Sauvignon 🍷 $$ Flirting with hyperconcentration, this tannic, black wine displays crème de cassis, elderberry preserves, tobacco, resin, and mint on the nose. A pure core of very ripe black fruit on the palate remains unperturbed by a firm but fine-grained corset of tannin.

Shiraz 🍷 $$ Restrained aromas of blackberry preserves and leather inform this dense and opaque, sappy, faintly oily Syrah deserving of high marks for sheer pepper- and vanilla-tinged black fruit concentration and clean, seamless ripeness.

CATHERINE MARSHALL (Paarl)

Shiraz 🍷 $$$ Smoky, herbal pungency, desiccated black fruits, and a wild, gamy side remind one of the Languedoc. On the palate, this preserves admirable clarity of fruit and refinement of tannins, with hints of bitter herbs and black pepper.

MISCHA ESTATE (Wellington)

Shiraz Eventide 🍷 $$ This second-label Syrah offers generous aromas and flavors of cassis, prune, and beef jerky. Quite densely concentrated for a wine of its price, its sheer ripeness runs no danger of becoming simply sweet, as there is plenty of finishing verve and saline brightness as well as a fine-grained frame of tannin.

Shiraz 🍷 **$$$** This smells of cassis and blackberry preserves with hints of bay, black pepper, soy, and sweat. It is impressively dense, bright, mouth coating, and gripping, and its jam-like black fruit finish benefits from black pepper pungency, a saline tang, and cooling herbal overtones.

OVERGAAUW *(Stellenbosch)*

Tria Corda 🍷 **$$$** This blend of Bordeaux varieties offers generous aromas of black currant, mulberry, peat, tobacco, and tomato foliage, with smoky, stony suggestions to its rather stewed fruit and a faintly dry and rustic finish.

PAINTED WOLF *(Coastal Regions)*

Painted Wolf 🍷 **$** This blend (principally of Shiraz and Pinotage) is pungently smoky, peppery, and herbal, with solid black fruit and raw meat informing a particularly sappy, fine-grained palate.

RAATS FAMILY *(Stellenbosch)*

Chenin Blanc Original 🍷 **$** This "unwooded" version of a prominent South African variety brims with melon and pineapple, offering a simple, generously juicy, if slightly bitter finish.

Chenin Blanc 🍷 **$$$** Spiced pear and musk melon aromas usher in a lushly textured, subtly yeasty, smoke-tinged, but rather bitter palate and an undeniably lasting if faintly warm finish.

RIETVALLEI ESTATE *(Robertson)*

John B. Cabernet Sauvignon—Tinta Barocca 🍷 **$** Smelling of black raspberry jam and milk chocolate, this soft, fruity red evinces sufficient brightness in its finish to ward off heat or palate boredom.

RUPERT & ROTHSCHILD *(Western Cape)*

Classique 🍷 **$$$** This blend of Cabernet Sauvignon and Merlot (in collaboration with Bordeaux's Baron Benjamin de Rothschild) mingles cooked purple plum and red raspberry with sealing wax, flowers, bittersweet herbal concentrate, iodine, green peppercorn, and stone.

SPRINGFONTEIN ESTATE *(Walker Bay)*

Pinotage Unfiltered Terroir Selection 🍷 $$$ This boasts a clarity of fruit and lift seldom encountered with Pinotage. Bitter black currant, black olive, and beetroot inform this dark yet not heavy red, whose silken texture and long, bittersweet finish introduce suggestions of wet stone and toasted nuts.

Springfontein 🍷 $$$ Springfontein's eponymous flagship Bordeaux blend is among the most fascinating South African wines for its price. Black currant, smoky Latakia tobacco, cedar, mint, dark chocolate, roasted red peppers, and black pepper encounter a bright, saline, chalky side that keeps its richness enticing and refreshing.

Ulumbaza 🍷 $$$ This wooded 100% Shiraz mingles sweet-tart blackberry and cassis with fennel, pepper, and cinnamon. Satisfying, sappy freshness and refined tannins in the finish are accompanied by some vegetal notes.

STELLENRUST *(Stellenbosch)*

Sauvignon Blanc 🍷 $ A nose of honeydew melon, white peach, and mint leads to a light, refreshing palate impression and pleasing hints of citrus zest and pungently herbal bitterness in a thirst-quenching finish.

THELEMA *(Stellenbosch)*

Sauvignon Blanc 🍷 $$ This is pungently scented with gooseberry, grapefruit rind, and fennel. Rather adamant and slightly bitter in the mouth, but impresses with its sheer intensity and bracingly salty, pungent finish.

TWO OCEANS *(Western Cape)*

Sauvignon Blanc 🍷 $ Gooseberry, passion fruit, and lime are thankfully not accompanied by any aggressively vegetal traits or bitterness in this clean, bright, refreshing wine.

Shiraz 🍷 $ This soft, generously juicy, and surprisingly polished as well as inexpensive Syrah is dominated by ripe black raspberry fruit, with notes of chocolate, black pepper, and a slight greenness in the finish.

UKUZALA *(Western Cape)*

Chenin Blanc ♀ $ Despite its garish label, improbably low suggested retail price, and label subtitle "wooded," this is full of fresh apple, winter pear, and pungent green herbs; juicy and refreshing, with a mere hint of wood.

VINUM SOUTH AFRICA *(Stellenbosch)*

Cabernet Sauvignon ♀ $$$ A nose of cassis, humus, black walnut husks, and green peppercorns leads to a well-concentrated palate mingling stewed black fruits and bitter herbs, and a sappy finish with notes of tobacco and juniper berry.

DANIE DE WET *(Robertson)*

Chardonnay Limestone Hill ♀ $$ This understated, unoaked Chardonnay offers impeccably pure, refreshing apple, peach, and lemon fruit, a lovely leesy richness of texture, and a nutty, chalky, fruit-filled finish of imposing length.

DE WETSHOF ESTATE *(Robertson)*

Chardonnay Lesca ♀ $$$ This barrel-fermented Chardonnay displays baked apple, salt-tinged toasted nuts and grains, lime and tangerine zest, and a clarity of fruit and refined expression of lees and barrel such as one too seldom encounters with this ubiquitous grape variety.

SPAIN

SPANISH WINE VALUES

by Dr. Jay Miller

Spain is best known as a treasure trove for red wine values. However, crisp, refreshing white wines have made major inroads over the past several years. The most prominent are the tasty whites made from the Albariño grape in Rías Baixas, the Verdejo grape from Rueda, and the Godello grape from Valdeorras. And while the booming Spanish sparkling wine business continues to percolate, few makers of sparkling wine actually produce exceptional wine; most of it is reliably pleasant and very inexpensive, under $25—hence the appeal.

Red wine is king in Spain, with the country increasingly realizing its vast potential. The best red wines come predominantly from northern Spain. The two areas best known for quality are Rioja and Ribera del Duero. Yet these traditional bastions of Spanish wine are being rivaled, and in come cases surpassed, by upstart regions. Priorat, Montsant, Bierzo, and Toro are today's overachievers, and Jumilla, Calatayud, and Yecla are beginning to attract attention. Overall, Spain has more than 60 viticultural regions (DOs).

Vintage Smarts

Spain is a large and diverse country, making it difficult to generalize about vintages. Virtually all of the wines noted here come from the 2005, 2006, and 2007 vintages, with a sprinkling of 2008 white wines and rosés that do not require upbringing in oak barrels. These were all good to excellent vintages in Spain.

Drinking Curves

The vast majority of wines in the under-$25 category from Spain are meant to be drunk in their first few years of life. The notable exceptions are the Tempranillo-based wines from Rioja and Toro, and the Garnacha-Cariñena blends from Montsant and Priorat. The best of these will reward several years of bottle aging and drink well for 4–6 years.

Spain's Top Wine Values by Winery

A COROA (Valdeorras)

Godello ♀ $$$ The Godello is medium straw colored, with an expressive bouquet of mineral, pear, white peach, and melon. This is followed by a voluminous wine with tons of flavor, excellent grip, and a long, complex finish. Drink this vibrant effort during its first 2–3 years.

BODEGA DEL ABAD (Bierzo)

Abad Dom Bueno Godello Joven ♀ $$ Offers an attractive nose of baking spices, mineral, and citrus. Mouth filling, intense, and vibrant, it has superb grip and length.

ACUSTIC (Montsant)

Acustic ♀ $$ A blend of Samsó (Cariñena) and Garnacha offering up an alluring perfume of smoke, mineral, underbrush, blueberry, and black cherry. This is followed by a full-bodied wine with tons of blue and black fruit, spice and mineral notes, and enough structure to evolve for 2–3 years. It is an excellent introduction to the style of the region.

AGUSTÍ TORELLO MATÁ (Cava-Penedès)

Reserva Brut ♀ ♀ $$$ A blend of Macabeo, Parellada, and Xarel-lo, offering up an alluring nose of yeast, Wheat Thins, biscuit, green apple, and mineral notes. Dry, crisp, and refreshing on the palate, it has excellent grip, concentration, and depth, leading to a lengthy, pure finish.

Rosat-Trepat Reserva Brut ♀ ♀ $$$ It has a lovely bouquet of rose petals, strawberry, and raspberry. It reveals a steady stream of small, persistent bubbles, a crisp, refreshing midpalate, and outstanding depth of flavor. It is the perfect match for *jamón ibérico* when DP Rosé or Cristal Rosé have gone missing from your cellar.

BODEGAS ALTO MONCAYO (Campo de Borja)

Veraton ♀ $$$ Veraton is the winery's entry level and is 100% Garnacha sourced from vines ranging in age from 35 to 92 years. It offers up a sensational aromatic array of smoke, pencil lead, earth notes, wild black cherry, and black raspberry. Dense, layered, and full-flavored, this hedonistic effort is balanced enough to evolve for several years but can be enjoyed now.

FINCA DE ARANTEI *(Rías Baixas)*

Albariño ♉ $$$ This Albariño is sourced entirely from estate-grown fruit, a relative rarity in Rias Baixas. It exhibits an enticing nose of spring flowers, mineral, green apple, lemon, and a hint of tropical aromas in the background. Round on the palate, it has lively acidity, a sense of elegance, and spritely flavors.

BODEGAS ATECA *(Calatayud)*

Atteca ♉ $$ Atteca is sourced from 80- to 120-year-old head-pruned Garnacha vines. It exhibits an impressive nose of crushed stone, black cherry, and plum. This is followed by a full-bodied wine with layers of savory fruit, spice notes, and silky tannin.

CELLER BARTOLOMÉ *(Priorat)*

Finca Mirador ♉ $$$ Finca Mirador is a blend of Garnacha and Cariñena offering up an alluring bouquet of crushed stone, scorched earth, violet, black cherry, and blueberry. Thick and rich on the palate, the wine has outstanding depth and concentration, savory flavors, excellent balance, and a pure finish. It is as good a value as you are likely to find from the pricey DO of Priorat.

CELLER BATEA *(Terra Alta)*

Las Colinas del Ebro ♉ $ 100% varietal exhibits an attractive perfume of mineral, spring flowers, white peach, and melon that jumps from the glass. On the palate it is exceptionally concentrated, mouth filling, and vibrant, with plenty of spicy fruit, good depth, and a fruit-filled finish.

BELLUM-SEÑORÍO DE BARAHONDA *(Yecla)*

Bellum Providencia ♉ $$ 100% Monastrell offering up an alluring bouquet of cedar, tobacco, underbrush, and blueberry. This leads to a layered, full-flavored, vibrant wine with excellent balance, superior grip, and a pure finish. This pleasure-bent effort will develop in the bottle for another 2–3 years but can be enjoyed now.

BODEGA BERROJA (*Txakoli*)

Berroia Chacolí de Bizkaia ♀ $$ Berroia is a blend of 90% Hondarribi Zuri, 6% Folle Blanche, and 4% Riesling. It exhibits an enticing nose of spring flowers, mineral, apple, and anise. Round on the palate with good acidity, the wine has excellent grip, balance, and length. It is an excellent value in Txakoli for drinking during its first 1–2 years.

CELLER LA BOLLIDORA (*Terra Alta*)

Plan B ♀ $$$ Plan B is composed of 60% Garnacha Negra, 15% Samsó (Cariñena), and the balance Syrah and Morenillo. It exhibits a brooding bouquet of crushed stone, scorched earth, black cherry, blackberry liqueur, and licorice. On the palate it has outstanding depth, excellent grip, savory flavors, and enough structure to mandate 5–7 years of additional cellaring.

BODEGAS BORSAO (*Campo de Borja*)

Tres Picos Garnacha ♀ $$$ The Tres Picos Garnacha offers up sexy aromas of cedar, underbrush, mineral, and black cherry. This leads to a layered, intense, spicy, rich Garnacha with gobs of succulent fruit, excellent balance, and a plush finish.

CELLER CAL PLA (*Priorat*)

Black Slate ♀ $$ Black Slate is a blend of Garnacha and Cariñena exhibiting aromas of spice, mineral, underbrush, black licorice, and blueberry. Elegant on the palate, it has tons of sweet black fruit, ripe flavors, outstanding depth and concentration, and several years of aging potential.

CALLEJO (*Ribera del Duero*)

Cuatro Meses en Barrica ♀ $$ 100% Tempranillo from estate vineyards. It delivers a fragrant perfume of smoke, earth notes, spice box, black cherry, and blackberry. This leads to a medium- to full-bodied wine with loads of succulent red and black fruit, a smooth texture, excellent balance, and a seamless finish.

CELLER CAPÇANES *(Montsant)*

Costers del Gravet ♟ **$$** This is an unusual Montsant blend in that it contains 50% Cabernet Sauvignon as well as the more typical 30% Garnacha and 20% Cariñena. A flamboyant nose of *framboise* leaps from the glass of this purple-colored wine, accompanied by notes of mineral and underbrush. Supple textured, intense, and loaded with vibrant red fruits, this well-balanced, full-flavored wine will drink well for 5–6 years.

Mas Donís Barrica ♟ **$** The Mas Donis Barrica is a blend of Garnacha (from vineyards over 80 years of age) and Syrah. It offers up an alluring bouquet of smoke, pencil lead, earth notes, clove, cinnamon, and black cherry. This leads to a wine with remarkable depth and concentration for its humble price, savory flavors, and a fruit-filled finish.

CASA CASTILLO *(Jumilla)*

Las Gravas ♟ **$$$** Composed of Monastrell and Cabernet Sauvignon, offering an enticing aromatic array of smoke, pencil lead, black raspberry, and blueberry that jumps from the glass. This leads to an opulent, dense wine with complex flavors, a smooth texture, and a lengthy, fruit-filled finish.

Valtosca ♟ **$$$** The Valtosca is 100% Syrah, revealing a flamboyant, kinky nose of wild blueberry accompanied by notes of smoky new oak, pencil lead, and Asian spices. On the palate it shows off a voluptuous personality, layers of succulent fruit, superb depth and concentration, and a 40-second finish.

CASADO MORALES *(Rioja)*

Reserva White ♙ **$$** The Reserva White is a blend of 90% Viura and 10% Malvasia offering up a complex bouquet of buttered toast, baking spices, melon, and white peach. This is followed by a wine with ample ripe fruit, good acidity, and an elegant personality that overdelivers for the modest asking price.

ADEGA O CASAL *(Valdeorras)*

Casal Novo Godello 🍷 **$$$** The medium-straw-colored Godello delivers a fragrant savory/spicy bouquet with notes of minerality, melon, and white peach. Layered and round on the palate, it is loaded with succulent white fruits, and has vibrant acidity and a lengthy, pure finish.

BODEGAS CASTAÑO *(Yecla)*

Solanera 🍷 **$** A blend of Monastrell, Cabernet Sauvignon, and Garnacha Tintorera. It reveals an expressive perfume of underbrush, licorice, graphite, blueberry, and black cherry. This is followed by an elegant, intense, smooth-textured wine with tons of red and black fruit, excellent balance, and a lengthy finish.

CASTILLO LABASTIDA *(Rioja)*

Reserva 🍷 **$$$** The Labastida Reserva is a traditionally styled Rioja made from 100% Tempranillo. It is bright cherry red in color, and the nose reveals smoke, mineral, leather, and black cherry. This leads to an elegantly styled wine with nicely integrated oak, wild berry flavors, excellent depth, and enough structure to evolve for another 2–3 years.

CASTRO VENTOSA *(Bierzo)*

El Castro de Valtuille Mencía Joven 🍷 **$** This 100% Mencía reveals an enticing perfume of baking spices, eucalyptus/pine notes, black cherry, and black raspberry. This leads to a smooth-textured, sweet, forward wine with no hard edges. It is a terrific introduction to the Mencía grape and the Bierzo region.

BODEGAS J.C. CONDE *(Ribera del Duero)*

Vivir, Vivir 🍷 **$** 100% Tempranillo featuring racy aromatics of mineral, spice box, black cherry, and blackberry. Silky on the palate with no hard edges, this tasty wine will provide pleasure over the next 3 years.

El Arte de Vivir 🍷 **$$** El Arte de Vivir is also 100% Tempranillo sourced from older vines. It is more substantial and structured than the Vivir, Vivir cuvée, with layers of fleshy fruit, excellent concentration, and 1–2 years of aging potential. The finish is lengthy and sweet. Drink this pleasure-bent wine over its first 6 years.

CONDE DE SAN CRISTOBAL *(Ribera del Duero)*

Conde de San Cristobal 🍷 $$$ A blend of Tinta Fino (Tempranillo), Merlot, and Cabernet Sauvignon exhibiting an expressive nose of cedar, tobacco, mineral, spice box, blackberry, and black currant. Full-bodied and dense on the palate, it has tons of savory black fruits; earth, mineral, and spice notes; and enough structure to evolve for 3–5 years.

CONDE DE VALDEMAR *(Rioja)*

Reserva 🍷 $$ A blend of 90% Tempranillo and 10% Mazuelo. Dark crimson colored, it reveals an alluring nose of cedar, spice box, tobacco, black cherry, and blackberry. On the palate it displays considerable finesse along with plenty of ripe, spicy red and black fruit, a silky texture, and excellent balance.

CUATRO PASOS *(Bierzo)*

Cuatro Pasos 🍷 $ Cuatro Pasos (100% Mencía) has an enticing perfume of smoke, blueberry, and black raspberry. Elegant and smooth-textured, this flavorful, pleasure-bent effort will go down easily during its first 4 years.

DESCENDIENTES DE JOSÉ PALACIOS *(Bierzo)*

Petalos del Bierzo 🍷 $$$ Descendientes de José Palacios's entry-level wine is Petalos del Bierzo, 100% Mencía from vineyards ranging in age from 40 to 90 years. It offers up a superfragrant bouquet of smoke, violet, mineral, wild blueberry, and black raspberry. Fruity yet complex on the palate, it has superb depth, grip, and balance.

EDULIS *(Rioja)*

Crianza 🍷 $$$ The Crianza is 100% Tempranillo exhibiting an attractive nose of cedar, spice box, tobacco, earth notes, and blackberry. This leads to a medium-bodied, elegant wine with plenty of ripe fruit, spice notes, and 2–3 years of aging potential.

EGIA ENEA TXAKOLINA *(Txakoli)*

Txakoli de Biskaia ♀ $$ The Egia Enea Txakoli reveals an expressive nose of mineral, lime, melon, and petrol. Smooth-textured, bracing, and racy on the palate, this flavorful effort will drink well during its first 2 years.

CELLER DE L'ENCASTELL *(Priorat)*

Marge ♀ $$$ A blend of Garnacha, Syrah, Merlot, and Cabernet Sauvignon. It is a glass-coating opaque purple with legs that ooze down the glass. The brooding nose reveals crushed stone, spice box, violet, tar, black cherry, and blueberry. This is followed by a dense, rich, structured Priorat with 1–2 years of aging potential.

BODEGAS ESTEFANIA *(Bierzo)*

Tilenus Tinto Roble ♀ $$$ Tilenus is 100% Mencía. It delivers a floral, cherry- and raspberry-accented bouquet. On the palate it reveals an elegant personality, a velvety texture, ripe red fruit flavors, spice notes, and a hint of minerality. It has a lengthy finish with no hard edges.

EXOPTO CELLARS *(Rioja)*

Big Bang de Exopto ♀ $$ The entry-level B.B. (Big Bang) de Exopto is composed of 50% Garnacha, 40% Tempranillo, and 10% Graciano. Dark ruby colored, it offers up an exceptionally spicy nose (from the Graciano) along with floral notes, underbrush, cassis, cherry, and plum. It has layers of flavor, excellent acidity, savory fruit, and enough structure to evolve for 2–3 years.

FALSET-MARÇÀ *(Montsant)*

Falset Old Vines ♀ $$ The Falset Old Vines is composed of 85% Garnacha and 15% Cabernet. It emits a superb aromatic array of slate/mineral, dried herbs, spice box, and black cherry. Full bodied and layered, it has vibrant acidity and well-integrated oak. Rich, succulent, and pleasure bent, it can be enjoyed now but will improve in the bottle over the next several years.

FILLABOA *(Rías Baixas)*

Selección Finca Monte Alto 🍷 $$$ This single-vineyard Albariño offers up an alluring bouquet of honeysuckle, mineral, and lemon-lime. Nicely focused, concentrated, and well balanced, it has plenty of vibrant fruit and should drink well for 2–3 years.

FINCA SOBREÑO *(Toro)*

Crianza 🍷 $$ Purple colored, with a fragrant nose of cedar, damp earth, pencil lead, black cherry, and blackberry. On the palate it is smooth-textured, ripe, and easygoing, leading to a finish with no hard edges. It can be enjoyed during its first 5 years.

O. FOURNIER *(Ribera del Duero)*

Urban Ribera 🍷 $ Made from 100% Tinta del Pais (Tempranillo), the wine spends four months in French oak. Purple colored, it offers up a fragrant bouquet of scorched earth, violet, and black cherry that leaps from the glass. Smooth-textured and suave on the palate, it has loads of succulent black fruit, silky tannins, excellent depth and grip, and a juicy finish.

BODEGAS SILVANO GARCÍA *(Jumilla)*

Viñahonda Crianza 🍷 $$$ The Crianza is a blend of Monastrell and Cabernet Sauvignon, and exhibits a complex aromatic array of cedar, tobacco, mineral, black cherry, and blueberry. Layered on the palate, it has tons of ripe fruit, plenty of spice notes, excellent balance, and a pure finish.

Viñahonda Monastrell 🍷 $$ The Viñahonda Monastrell (100% varietal) offers up a fragrant nose of underbrush, mineral, spice box, and blueberry. Layered, mouth filling, and succulent, this forward effort will offer much pleasure during its first 4 years.

GUITIAN *(Valdeorras)*

Godello Joven 🍷 $$$ A medium straw colored wine, with a slight green tint. It offers up a fragrant bouquet of baking spices, spring flowers, green apple, and melon with a hint of chamomile in the background. Crisp and well balanced, the wine has an elegant personality and a lengthy finish.

VIÑA HERMINIA *(Rioja)*

Reserva ♥ $$$ Is a traditionally styled Rioja composed of 85% Tempranillo and 15% Garnacha. It offers up an enticing bouquet of cedar, leather, earth notes, black cherry, and cassis leading to a finesse-styled, concentrated wine with excellent depth, plenty of spice, and a seamless finish.

BODEGAS Y VIÑEDOS DEL JARO *(Ribera del Duero)*

Sembro ♥ $$ Sembro is 100% Tempranillo with a superfragrant bouquet of cedar, forest floor, wild cherry, and blackberry. This is followed by a full-flavored, mouth-filling, easygoing wine with tons of savory fruit and no hard edges.

LADERA SAGRADA *(Valdeorras)*

Castelo do Papa ♀ $ 100% Godello. Medium straw colored, with plenty of glycerin oozing down the glass, it reveals an alluring nose of mineral/slate, white peach, lime, and melon. Crisp and vibrant on the palate, it has exceptional volume in the mouth and a long, fruit-filled finish.

LAGAR DE COSTA *(Rías Baixas)*

Albariño ♀ $$$ Lagar de Costa is a small winery producing Albariño from an estate-grown 50-year-old vineyard. It exhibits an expressive nose of mineral, spring flowers, and lemon meringue. On the palate it is creamy textured, rich, vibrant, and well balanced.

CAVAS LLOPART *(Cava-Penedès)*

Llopart Brut Rosé ♀ ♀ $$$ Produced by the traditional Champagne method and composed of Monastrell, Garnacha, and Pinot Noir. Salmon pink colored, it has a lovely perfume of strawberry, rhubarb, and biscuit. Crisp on the palate with a persistent stream of small bubbles, this tasty Cava would be the ideal match for Spain's legendary Joselito *jamón*.

BODEGAS LOS 800 (Priorat)

Los 800 🍷 $$$ Los 800 is a blend of Garnacha, Cariñena, Syrah, and Cabernet offering up a roasted bouquet of cedar, pencil lead, earth notes, cherry, and blueberry. Elegant on the palate, it conceals a bit of structure under the fruit and should evolve for 2–3 years. It is a very good introduction to the wines of Priorat.

LUNA BEBERIDE (Bierzo)

Finca la Cuesta 🍷 $$$ Finca la Cuesta (100% Mencía) reveals a complex aromatic array of mineral, spice box, pomegranate, and black cherry. This leads to a smooth-textured, suave wine with tons of fruit, excellent density, and enough structure to evolve for 2–3 years.

CELLER MALONDRO (Montsant)

Latria 🍷 $$ The Latria exhibits an expressive nose of mineral and black cherry. Ripe, full flavored, and seamless on the palate, it was designed for pleasure. Drink it over the next 4 years.

Malondro 🍷 $$$ The Malondro offers up an alluring bouquet of cedar, smoke, mineral, black cherry, and blueberry compote. Layered, dense, succulent, well balanced, and long, it will drink well over the next 6 years.

MANGA DEL BRUJO (Calatayud)

Manga del Brujo 🍷 $$$ This wine is a blend of Garnacha, Syrah, Tempranillo, and Mazuelo. It offers up a toasty, smoky bouquet with aromas of mineral, black cherry, and blueberry. This is followed by a wine with an elegant personality; a silky texture; intense, savory blue and black fruit flavors; superb balance; and 2–3 years of aging potential.

MAS IGNEUS (Priorat)

Barranc dels Closos 🍷 $$$ It is a blend of Garnacha and Cariñena offering up an expressive perfume of earth, slate, espresso, black cherry, blueberry, and licorice. This leads to a full-bodied wine with intense liquid mineral and black fruit flavors, outstanding depth, and enough ripe tannin to support an additional 2–3 years of cellaring.

BODEGAS MAS QUE VINOS *(La Mancha)*

Ercavio Roble 🍷 **$** Made up of 100% Cencibel (Tempranillo), this wine delivers an expressive nose of cedar, earth notes, black cherry, and blackberry liqueur. Thick, dense, and opulent on the palate, it has gobs of savory black fruit, licorice, and spice notes, enough structure to evolve for 1–2 years, and a lengthy finish. It totally overdelivers for its humble price.

CELLER EL MASROIG *(Montsant)*

Sycar Les Sorts 🍷 **$$$** Sycar Les Sorts is a blend of Samsó (Cariñena) and Syrah offering up an intriguing bouquet of underbrush, spice box, toast, blueberry, and blackberry jam. This leads to an elegantly styled wine with plenty of ripe fruit, succulent flavors, 1–2 years of aging potential, and a lengthy finish.

BODEGAS MATARREDONDA *(Toro)*

Juan Rojo 🍷 **$$$** Dark ruby colored, with an enticing nose of cedar, tobacco, spice box, black cherry, and blackberry. On the palate it reveals an elegant personality, succulent flavors, a smooth texture, and enough silky tannin to evolve for another 3–4 years. This lengthy effort can be enjoyed now but will be at its best from 2011 to 2020.

BODEGAS MAURODOS *(Toro)*

Prima 🍷 **$$$** Prima is a blend of 90% Tinta de Toro (Tempranillo) and 10% Garnacha revealing an expressive nose of smoke, pencil lead, tobacco, spice box, black cherry, and blackberry. Supple and round on the palate, it has layers of ripe fruit, savory flavors, and enough soft tannin to improve for another 3–5 years. It is a serious example of Toro at a nearly frivolous price.

VIÑA MEÍN *(Ribeiro)*

Viña Meín 🍷 **$$$** A blend of multiple indigenous grape varieties, the principal component is Treixadura. Medium straw colored, it offers up a complex aromatic array of mineral, slate, white peach, melon, and baking spices. Round and creamy on the palate, it has excellent depth of flavor and a lengthy, refreshing finish.

BODEGAS EMILIO MORO *(Ribera Del Duero)*

Emilio Moro 🍷 **$$$** This wine has a superb bouquet of smoke, roasted herbs, scorched earth, and blackberry. Layered on the palate, it has tons of fruit, plenty of spice box notes, a firm structure, and 2–3 years of aging potential.

Finca Resalso 🍷 **$** Sourced from younger vines, this wine emits an enticing perfume of mineral, violet, black cherry, and blackberry. On the palate it reveals an elegant personality; savory, spicy flavors; good depth; and a fruit-filled finish.

CAVES NAVERÁN *(Cava-Penedès)*

Naverán Dama 🍷 **$ $$** A blend of Chardonnay and Pinot Noir offering up a complex aromatic array of freshly baked biscuit, green apple, and mineral. It has an attractive *mousse* and a persistent stream of tiny bubbles. Smooth textured and vibrant, this classy Champagne look-alike is a great value in sparkling wine.

NITA *(Priorat)*

Nita 🍷 **$$$** A blend of Garnacha, Cariñena, Cabernet Sauvignon, and Syrah exhibiting a fragrant bouquet of crushed stone, underbrush, spice box, black cherry, and blueberry jam. Silky textured, forward, succulent, and well balanced, this charming effort can be enjoyed now but should provide pleasure for another 5 years.

BODEGAS O'VENTOSELA *(Ribeiro)*

Viña Leiriña 🍷 **$** A blend of Treixadura and Albariño, Viña Leiriña exhibits a delicate aromatic array of mineral, sea salt, spring flowers, white peach, and lime. Clean and crisp on the palate with bracing acidity, it calls out for clams and oysters.

Gran Leiriña 🍷 **$$$** Gran Leiriña is a blend of Treixadura, Albariño, Lado, and Torrontés from older vines than the Viña Leiriña. It has a distinctive smoky, stony bouquet as well as honeysuckle, citrus, and pit-fruit notes. Mouth filling, vibrant, concentrated, and impeccably balanced, it may well evolve for several years. It is Ribeiro's take on grand cru Chablis.

PAGO FLORENTINO *(La Mancha)*

Tinto ♀ **$$** It is 100% Tempranillo revealing an enticing perfume of cedar, pencil lead, leather, chocolate, and black cherry. On the palate it has loads of ripe fruit, a smooth texture, succulent flavors, and a 40-second finish. Drink this tasty effort over its first 6 years.

PAPA LUNA *(Calatayud)*

Papa Luna ♀ **$$$** This wine is a blend of Garnacha, Monastrell, and Mazuelo offering up an alluring bouquet including *garrigue* notes, spice box, lavender, black cherry, and blueberry. This is followed by a velvety-textured wine with layers of savory fruit, a sense of elegance, complex flavors, and a lengthy, pure finish. Drink this hedonistic effort during its first 6 years.

PORTAL DEL MONTSANT *(Montsant)*

Brunus Rosé ♀ **$$$** The delightful Brunus Rosé is composed of 100% Garnacha grown specifically for this purpose. Dark pink colored, it offers up a serious bouquet of mineral, spice box, and red cherry. This leads to an elegant, smooth-textured, flavorful wine with gobs of succulent cherry-flavored fruit, vibrant acidity, and a lengthy, pure finish.

PRODUCCIÓNS A MODINO *(Ribeiro)*

San Clodio ♀ **$$** San Clodio is a blend of Treixadura, Godello, Loureiro, Torrontés, and Albariño offering up an intriguing perfume of mineral, citrus, and white peach. On the palate it is smooth and creamy with an almond-paste character that sets it apart. This elegant effort is impeccably balanced and long.

LA RIOJA ALTA *(Rioja)*

Viña Alberdi Reserva ♀ **$$** Viña Alberdi is a classically styled Rioja with a nose of earth, mushroom, mineral, cherry, and blackberry. This is followed by an elegant wine with a silky texture, good depth and concentration, considerable complexity, and a seamless finish. It is at its peak now and will continue to drink well for another 5 years. It personifies finesse.

BODEGAS SAN ALEJANDRO *(Calatayud)*

Las Rocas Garnacha 🍷 $ This Garnacha delivers alluring aromas of spice box, mineral, cherry, and black raspberry. Layered on the palate, it has superb depth, succulent flavors, and a pure, lengthy finish. It will provide pleasure during its first 3 years.

Las Rocas Rosado 🍷 $ The deep pink colored Rosado offers a fragrant bouquet of strawberry, cherry, and rhubarb leading to a fleshy wine with tons of flavor, excellent depth, and a vibrant personality. It will be versatile with a wide range of cuisine.

Las Rocas Vinyas Viejas 🍷 $$ The old-vine cuvée has a cedary, spicy, cherry and cranberry bouquet. More structured than the "regular" bottling, it has layered fruit, savory flavors, excellent depth, and a fruit-filled finish. Drink it during its first 3–4 years.

CELLERS SANT RAFEL *(Montsant)*

Solpost 🍷 $$$ Solpost is a blend of Garnacha, Cariñena, and Cabernet Sauvignon with an enticing perfume of mineral, earth notes, cassis, and black cherry. Smooth textured, on the palate it has outstanding depth and concentration, savory red and black fruit flavors, and a long, fruit-filled finish.

VIÑA SASTRE *(Ribera del Duero)*

Roble 🍷 $$$ The entry-level Roble is 100% Tempranillo offering up an intriguing nose of fungus/mushroom, cedar, espresso, and blackberry. This is followed by a wine with concentrated, spicy black fruit flavors, excellent depth, enough structure to evolve for 2–3 years, and a pure finish.

SEÑORÍO DE BARAHONDA *(Yecla)*

Barahonda Barrica 🍷 $ Barahonda Barrica is a blend of 70% Monastrell and 30% Cabernet Sauvignon. It exhibits a bouquet of cedar, spice box, scorched earth, black currant, and blueberry. This leads to a dense, structured wine with savory flavors, an assertive personality, and 2–3 years of aging potential.

Heredad Candela 🍷 $$$ Heredad Candela is 100% Monastrell offering up an alluring perfume of toast, mineral, violet, black cherry, and blueberry. Velvety on the palate, it has layers of savory dark fruit, rich flavors, excellent balance, and a pure finish.

Nabuko 🍷 $ Nabuko is composed of 50% Monastrell and 50% Syrah. Purple colored, it reveals a fragrant nose of smoke, underbrush, blueberry, and blackberry jam. On the palate spice notes and black licorice emerge along with layers of savory blue fruit. Well balanced and lengthy, this seamless effort can be enjoyed during its first 4 years.

SOLAR DE URBEZO *(Cariñena)*

Crianza 🍷 $$$ The Crianza is a blend of Tempranillo, Cabernet Sauvignon, Merlot, and Syrah that offers up an attractive nose of cedar, mineral, tobacco, cassis, blueberry, and blackberry. This leads to a smooth, easygoing, spicy wine with savory flavors, good balance, and a seamless finish. Drink this pleasure-bent wine during its first 5 years.

VIÑA SOMOZA *(Valdeorras)*

Classico 🍷 $$ The Classico is 100% Godello (Spain's most interesting white grape). It offers up an expressive bouquet of mineral, baking spices, citrus, melon, and hints of tropical aromas in the background. Round, concentrated, and loaded with spicy white fruits, this vibrant wine will provide pleasure during its first 3 years.

FINCA TORREMILANOS *(Ribera del Duero)*

Los Cantos de Torremilanos 🍷 $$$ 100% Tempranillo. The nose reveals wood smoke, lavender, pencil lead, black cherry, and blackberry. Firm and structured on the palate with an elegant personality, this lengthy effort will improve in the bottle for 2–3 years after the vintage.

TRASCAMPANAS (*Rueda*)

Verdejo ♀ $$ Medium straw colored with a green tint, this Verdejo offers up a superexpressive nose of fresh herbs, baking spices, citrus, and floral notes. On the palate melon, peach, mineral, and lemon-lime flavors emerge. Creamy and deep, this impeccably balanced, vibrant wine will provide pleasure during its first 3 years.

TXAKOLI TXOMIN ETXANIZ (*Txakoli*)

Txakoli de Guetaria ♀ $$$ Features a nose of slate/mineral, white peach, and green apple. This is followed by a crisp, dry, vibrant, light-bodied white that calls out for some of Spain's great shellfish. Balanced and lengthy, it should be drunk during its first 12–18 months.

BODEGAS Y VIÑEDOS VALDERIZ (*Ribera del Duero*)

Valdehermoso Crianza ♀ $$$ The Valdehermoso Crianza offers up cedar, scorched earth, pencil lead, and fragrant black cherry and blackberry notes. Firm and structured on the palate with an elegant personality, it will evolve for another 3–5 years in the bottle.

VALDUMIA (*Rías Baixas*)

Selección de Añada ♀ $$ The Selección has an attractive bouquet of mineral, floral notes, lemon curd, and white peach. Mouth filling and with an extra dimension of complexity from old vines, this vibrant Albariño can be enjoyed during its first 2–3 years.

VALTOSTAO (*Ribera Del Duero*)

Legón Roble ♀ $ The Legón Roble is 100% Tinto Fino (Tempranillo) offering up an enticing bouquet of cedar, spice box, earth notes, black cherry, and blackberry. This is followed by a smooth-textured, ripe, juicy wine with loads of fruit, an easygoing personality, and a seamless finish.

VEIGADARES *(Rías Baixas)*

Veigadares ♉ **$$$** Veigadares is composed of 85% Albariño, 10% Treixadura, and 5% Loureiro. This ambitious Albariño offers up an attractive bouquet of baking spices, mineral, and lemon meringue with the oak nicely integrated. It has a creamy texture, excellent depth of flavor, and a fruit-filled finish.

VETUS *(Toro)*

Vetus ♉ **$$$** Vetus is sourced from a single 50-acre estate vineyard planted with Tinta de Toro. Purple colored, it exhibits an alluring nose of balsam wood, cinnamon, clove, violet, and black cherry. This is followed by a medium- to full-bodied wine with tons of spicy fruit, savory dark fruit flavors, excellent depth and grip, and a lengthy finish.

BODEGAS VIÑAGUAREÑA *(Toro)*

Eternum Viti ♉ **$$$** Glass-coating opaque purple in color. It offers up a fragrant bouquet of earth notes, mineral, spice box, and blackberry. This leads to a dense, ripe, powerful wine that manages to keep its tannins under control.

VINOS DE ARGANZA *(Bierzo)*

La Mano Roble ♉ **$** This is about as good as it gets for 10 bucks. La Mano Roble is 100% Mencía from the increasingly prestigious DO of Bierzo. It delivers a fragrant perfume of earth notes, mulberry, and blueberry. Layered on the palate, it has extraordinary depth and concentration for its humble price.

CELLER VINOS PIÑOL *(Terra Alta)*

Ludovicus ♉ **$** The Ludovicus is a blend of 35% Garnacha, 30% Tempranillo, 25% Syrah, and 10% Cabernet Sauvignon. It has a glass-coating deep crimson hue with an expressive nose of cherry, blueberry, and blackberry. Mouth filling, succulent, and flavorful, this tasty effort is a sensational value for drinking during its first 1–2 years.

Portal Tinto 🍷 \$\$ The Portal Red is a blend of equal parts Cabernet Sauvignon, Garnacha, Merlot, Tempranillo, and Syrah. It is dark ruby colored, with a nose that exhibits earth notes, cedar, tobacco, cassis, cherry, and blackberry. It is ripe and sweet on the palate, and licorice, dried herbs, and mineral notes make an appearance leading to a lengthy, pure, fruit-filled finish.

Portal Blanco 🍷 \$ Composed of 70% Garnacha Blanco, 20% Sauvignon Blanc, and the balance Macabeu and Viognier. It delivers a complex nose of mineral, dried herbs, fresh apple, and gooseberry. This is followed by a vibrant, intense, spicy wine with superb balance and length. It defines the word "overdelivering."

BODEGAS VIRGEN DEL VALLE *(Rioja)*

Cincel Gran Reserva 🍷 \$\$\$ This winery specializes in old vintages of Rioja. Their wines offer elegance and complexity as well as a glimpse into Rioja's past.

VIRXEN DEL GALIR *(Valdeorras)*

Godello 🍷 \$\$ Light gold colored with a slight green tint, the nose exhibits spring flowers, lime, and poached pear aromas that jump from the glass. This leads to a rich, full-flavored wine in which tropical flavors and mineral notes emerge on the palate. Ripe, dense, and long, this superb Godello will provide pleasure during its first 3 years.

VITICULTORS DEL PRIORAT *(Priorat)*

Vega Escal 🍷 \$\$\$ The purple-colored Vega Escal is a blend of Cariñena, Garnacha, and Syrah exhibiting an alluring bouquet of smoke, crushed stone, lavender, leather, black cherry, and blueberry. Elegantly styled on the palate, it has layers of savory fruit, good depth and concentration, and a lengthy finish.

BODEGAS VOLVER *(La Mancha)*

Volver 🍷 \$\$ Volver is sourced from a single 72-acre vineyard that was planted in 1967 with head-pruned Tempranillo. It offers up an alluring aromatic array of toast, smoke, violet, black cherry, and blackberry that jumps from the glass. On the palate it has gobs of ripe fruit, succulent flavors, soft tannins, and excellent balance.

XARMANT TXAKOLINA *(Txakoli)*

Arabako Txakolina ♉ **$$** Arabako is the newest of Txakolina's DOs, having been formed in 2003, and is considered to produce rounder, warmer wines. Xarmant Txakolina is composed of 80% Hondarribi Zuri and 20% Hondarribi Zuri Zerratía, both indigenous to the region. It offers an enticing nose of mineral, citrus, and lemon zest. This is followed by a light- to medium-bodied dry wine with mouthwatering fruit and excellent length.

UNITED STATES

CALIFORNIA WINE VALUES

by Robert M. Parker, Jr.

Trying to find values in California is perhaps more difficult than in any other wine region in the world. Most of the finest Cabernet Sauvignons, Chardonnays, and Pinot Noirs are well above the $25 break point for this book. In addition, the most prestigious areas, such as the Napa and Sonoma Valleys, as well as the Santa Cruz Mountains south of San Francisco, and even farther south, Santa Barbara, fetch very high prices because of the high fashion and popularity of these areas. Since most wines are named after the grape variety they are produced from, it's important to go outside of the very popular chocolate and vanilla flavors of Cabernet Sauvignon and Chardonnay (throw Pinot Noir in there as well) and look for other varietals that are well made. For white wine, there is not a lot out there, but Colombard, Chenin Blanc, Pinot Blanc, and of course, the workhorse white that still can be found at very attractive prices, Sauvignon Blanc, offer plenty of appeal for value-conscious consumers. For red wines, the very top level of Cabernet Sauvignon, Merlot, and Pinot Noir is frightfully expensive, and you can even add Syrah and the best Zinfandels to that category. However, Zinfandels can still be found for $25 and under, as can some Syrahs and Rhone Ranger blends from south of San Francisco. This seems to be where the best values exist. It's very hard to produce high-quality Pinot Noir for under $25, although some can be found. Again, the best bargains will be Zinfandel, Syrah, occasionally Petite Sirah, and Rhone Ranger blends of these grapes. Another important strategy is to search out the best-made wines from viticultural areas that are not as much in demand and are considered somewhat backwater areas. Lodi, Paso Robles, Lake County in the north, and from the Central Coast, Livermore Valley, Santa Clara Valley, and Arroyo Seco often are the areas that produce good values. From the interior appellations, El Dorado, the Shenandoah Valley, and Clarksburg are areas to seek out.

Vintage Smarts

Vintages differ in California as they do elsewhere in the world, but the extreme highs and lows that exist in most of Europe are rarely seen in California. For whites and rosés, 2008, 2007, and 2006 (whites only) are the vintages of choice, and for red, just about anything produced since 2002, even in the under-$25 category, should be attractive and appealing when made by conscientious producers.

Drinking Curves

Most wines designed to sell for under $25 are meant to be drunk immediately upon release. This does not mean they can't age, but to be on the safe side, every white wine should be consumed during its first 3 years of life, and rosés should be consumed within 18 months of the vintage. For example, the 2008 rosés should be drunk by late spring of 2010. White wines can last 2–3 years, and most of the inexpensive, high-quality red wines can easily keep for 5–7 years. I would have no difficulty drinking any of the following producers' reds from as far back as 2002.

California's Top Wine Values by Winery

ADELAIDA CELLARS *(Paso Robles)*

Schoolhouse Crush 🍷 $ This Côtes du Rhône blend displays supple tannins, medium body, and superficial concentration in a pleasant bistro style.

Schoolhouse Crush 🍸 $ A pleasant white best consumed in its first year.

Schoolhouse Syrah-Crush 🍷 $ Medium bodied with abundant tannin and a monolithic personality.

ALEXANDER VALLEY VINEYARDS *(Alexander valley)*

Cabernet Franc 🍷 $$$ Cabernet Franc is rarely inexpensive, but this spicy, medium-bodied, silky-textured red is a deliciously fruity, value-priced effort.

Dry Rosé of Sangiovese 🍸 $ A terrific dry, medium bodied rosé to enjoy within 6 months of its release.

Sin Zin 🍷 $$ This delicious, medium-bodied 100% Zinfandel exhibits southern Rhône-like characteristics of pepper, briar, and berry fruit.

Syrah Estate 🍷 $$ Monolithic, simple, straightforward, and narrowly constructed.

Viognier Estate 🍷 $$$ Offers notions of honeysuckle, apricot, and white peaches, but falls off quickly in the mouth.

DOMAINE ALFRED *(Edna Valley)*

Rosé Chamisal Vineyard 🍷 $$$ With fresh acidity and medium body, this is a delicious, top-flight Grenache-based rosé that should be consumed over its first 6 months.

ANGLIM *(Central Coast)*

Grenache 🍷 $$$ Starts well, but falls off on the palate. Drink within a year.

Viognier Bien Nacido Vineyard 🍷 $$$ Offers good acidity, hints of wet stones and minerals, a medium- to full-bodied texture, and terrific purity.

ARCADIAN WINERY *(Santa Ynez)*

Syrah Santa Ynez Valley 🍷 $$$ Represents a California imitation of a good Crozes-Hermitage.

ARROWOOD VINEYARDS AND WINERY *(Russian River)*

Côte de Lune Blanc Saralee's Vineyard 🍷 $$$ A great bargain in dry white wines, medium to full bodied, with loads of personality and fruit.

Gewürztraminer Saralee's Vineyard 🍷 $$ Gewürztraminer has never done really well in California, but this one from Saralee's Vineyard is elegant, displaying a hint of rosewater in a medium-bodied, dry style.

AVALON *(Napa)*

Cabernet Sauvignon California 🍷 $ An elegant, medium-weight, attractive red to enjoy over its first several years.

Cabernet Sauvignon Napa ♀ $ Medium bodied and pure with silky tannins as well as a surprisingly long finish.

L'AVENTURE *(Paso Robles)*

Côte à Côte Rosé ♀ $$$ This seriously endowed rosé offers lovely fruit in a dry, medium-bodied, nearly austere personality that is loaded with character. Drink within 8–12 months.

BECKMEN VINEYARDS *(Santa Ynez Valley)*

Cuvée Le Bec ♀ $$ A blend of Rhône varietals and one of the wine world's finest bargains, this is an ideal bistro red, delicious and personality filled.

Grenache Rosé Purisima Mountain Vineyard ♀ $$ A medium-bodied, refreshing rosé meant to be consumed within 8–12 months.

Marsanne Purisima Mountain Vineyard ♀ $$ Exhibits medium body, fine ripeness, a hint of minerality, and good underlying acidity.

Syrah Estate ♀ $$$ This supple-textured, mouth-filling Syrah has a savory, fleshy personality.

BERINGER *(Napa)*

Alluvium Blanc ♀ $$ There is not a better value in California dry whites. A blend of several white varietals, it is a distinctive, dry, medium- to full-bodied white compatible with an assortment of foods.

Cabernet Sauvignon ♀ $$$ Cabernet Sauvignon is one of Beringer's strengths; this is medium to full bodied, with a seductive, round, silky texture.

Chardonnay Napa ♀ $$$ Crisp and lean, this is a medium-weight, dry, refreshing white to enjoy in its first 1–3 years.

Chardonnay Stanly Ranch ♀ $$ Exhibits more minerality and elegance than one expects in a Chardonnay of this price range.

BONNY DOON VINEYARD *(Central Coast)*

Le Cigare Blanc Beeswax Vineyard ♀ $$$ This delicious white displays a medium-bodied, delicate personality.

Vin Gris de Cigare Rosé ♀ **$** This consistently well-made rosé is fresh, lively, and medium bodied. Enjoy it within 6–12 months.

BREGGO CELLARS *(Anderson Valley)*

Gewürztraminer ♀ **$$$** Displays terrific fruit, medium to full body, and a dry, long finish.

Pinot Gris Wiley Vineyard ♀ **$$$** Gorgeously rich, zesty, and pure, this sensational Pinot Gris possesses amazing flavor intensity, yet it's light on its feet.

Sauvignon Blanc Ferrington Vineyard ♀ **$$$** Dry and medium bodied with superb fruit, depth, and richness, this is a provocative, gorgeous expression of dry Sauvignon.

BRIDLEWOOD ESTATE WINERY *(Central Coast)*

Viognier Reserve ♀ **$$$** Possesses classic notes of apricots and honeysuckle as well as good fruit, acidity, and freshness.

BROC CELLARS *(Monterey)*

Grenache Ventana Vineyard ♥ **$$$** From a cool-climate Monterey site, this round, lush white is best drunk during its first several years.

BUEHLER VINEYARDS *(Russian River)*

Russian River Chardonnay ♀ **$** This white possesses plenty of tropical fruit notes, medium body, and a fresh, lively personality.

CARLISLE *(Sonoma)*

Syrah Sonoma ♥ **$$$** An outstanding value in top-class Syrah and a 400-blend of different sites, this wine is soft, round, and clearly dominated by the black side of the fruit spectrum.

Zinfandel Sonoma ♥ **$$** Flashy aromatics, a full-bodied mouthfeel, good underlying acidity, and its lushness and intensity make this quite a stunning wine.

CARTLIDGE & BROWNE *(California)*

Cabernet Sauvignon ♥ **$** A fruit-driven, medium-bodied, soft wine to consume during its first 2–3 years.

Chardonnay ♀ $ There is no evidence of oak in this lovely Chardonnay, which displays medium body, crisp acidity, and fine purity as well as freshness.

Merlot ♟ $ Monolithic, straightforward, and short.

Pinot Noir ♟ $ Cartlidge & Browne's Pinot Noir is better than many that sell for 5 times the price, with good size, medium body, excellent purity, and a generous, savory texture.

Rabid Red ♟ $ A blend of Cabernet Sauvignon and Petite Sirah with small amounts of Merlot and Syrah, this wine is medium bodied, with excellent texture, good purity, and a decent finish.

Sauvignon Blanc Dancing Crow ♀ $ A medium-bodied white loaded with melony fruit notes, crisp acidity, freshness, and a true Sauvignon character.

CLINE CELLARS *(Contra Costa)*

Ancient Vines Carignane ♟ $$ Reveals a dark ruby color, an earthy, dusty texture, and a Provençal-like character.

Ancient Vines Mourvèdre ♟ $$ Exhibits a subtle touch of oak along with medium body, excellent ripeness, decent acidity, and fine purity.

CLOS MIMI *(Paso Robles)*

Petite Rousse Syrah ♟ $$$ A lovely interpretation of a Paso Robles–style French Crozes-Hermitage, this provocative red exhibits medium to full body, silky tannins, and a broad, savory mouth-feel.

CONSILIENCE *(Santa Barbara)*

Syrah Santa Barbara ♟ $$ This red possesses a fat, fleshy personality that is very much in keeping with this estate's signature, but while mouth filling, it does not display the complexity of the top efforts.

COPAIN *(Anderson Valley)*

Pinot Noir Saisons des Vins l'Automne ♟ $$$ Medium bodied with crisp acidity, this is a tasty, straightforward, easygoing Pinot Noir to drink over its first 1–2 years.

CREW WINES *(Russian River)*

Chardonnay Mossback ♈ $$ Crisp, elegant poached pear, crushed rock, and white currant notes characterize this Chardonnay, which appears to have more in common with a low-level French Chablis than a California Chardonnay.

DASHE CELLARS *(Dry Creek)*

Zinfandel Dry Creek ♈ $$$ Blended with a bit of Petite Sirah, this impeccably well-made, medium- to full-bodied, lush, tasty Zin should provide plenty of pleasure over its first 2–3 years.

DI ARIE VINEYARD *(California)*

Zinfandel Amador ♈ $$ A blend of Petite Sirah, mixed blacks, and Zinfandel, this is an excellent, medium- to full-bodied wine with no hard edges, displaying good purity and an attractive finish.

Zinfandel Shenandoah Valley ♈ $$$ A combination of primarily Zinfandel and a little Petite Sirah, exhibiting medium to full body, a soft texture, and a good finish.

DRY STACK

See Grey Stack.

DUCKHORN VINEYARDS *(Napa)*

Sauvignon Blanc ♈ $$$ One of California's finest Sauvignons is consistently the offering from Duckhorn Vineyards, a flavor-filled, complex white to drink over its first year.

EDMEADES *(Mendocino)*

Zinfandel ♈ $$ Medium to full bodied, ripe, and altogether a hedonistic mouthful of big Zinfandel.

ENKIDU WINE *(Northern California)*

Humbaba Rhône Blend ♈ $$$ The full-bodied, opulent, juicy, and succulent Humbaba is drinkable for 3–4 years.

Shamhat Rosé ♈ $$ Enkidu's delicious Shamhat rosé is a dry, medium-bodied rosé best enjoyed over its first 6–8 months.

EPIPHANY *(Santa Barbara)*

Gypsy Proprietary Red 🍷 **$$$** Medium bodied, compact, and foursquare, with attractive notes of fresh mushrooms, forest floor, tree bark, blueberries, and cherries, this wine's finish is tannic and austere.

ETUDE *(Carneros)*

Pinot Gris 🍷 **$$$** Crisp, with surprising fruit intensity, good texture, and a dry finish, this white can be enjoyed over its first year.

ROBERT FOLEY VINEYARDS *(Napa)*

Pinot Blanc 🍷 **$$$** A delicious, screw cap–finished Pinot Blanc that offers scents of apple skins and tropical fruits in a crisp, light- to medium-bodied style.

FOXGLOVE *(San Luis Obispo)*

Chardonnay 🍷 **$$** From fruit accessed in California's Edna Valley, this is a remarkable effort that is fresh, lively, and best drunk over its first 1–2 years.

FREI BROTHERS RESERVE *(Russian River)*

Chardonnay Reserve 🍷 **$$** This is a well-made, midweight Chardonnay made in a medium-bodied, fresh, lively style with a subtle influence of wood.

GALLO FAMILY VINEYARDS *(Sonoma)*

Pinot Gris Sonoma Reserve 🍷 **$** Exhibiting medium body; light, dry flavors; and surprising intensity for a relatively lighter style of wine, the fruit is pure and the wine impeccably well made.

GIRARD *(Russian River)*

Chardonnay 🍷 **$$$** This brilliant Chardonnay boasts abundant amounts of honeysuckle and tropical fruits in a medium-bodied, pure, crisp format. Only a light touch of wood is noticeable.

JOEL GOTT *(California)*

Cabernet Sauvignon ♟ $$ Made from 100% Cabernet Sauvignon, this medium-bodied, richly fruity, clean, pure red will drink well for 5–6 years.

Sauvignon Blanc ♟ $ Plenty of fig, flint, honeyed grapefruit, and lemon-zest characteristics in a medium-bodied, crisp personality.

Zinfandel ♟ $$ This brilliant Zinfandel boasts fabulous ripeness along with a full-bodied, tarry, briary nose.

GRAYSON CELLARS *(Paso Robles)*

Cabernet Sauvignon ♟ $ A medium-bodied, fruit-driven effort, with silky tannin, excellent purity, and a real personality.

Chardonnay ♟ $ A medium-bodied, fruit-driven, tasty Chardonnay, best consumed over its first 1–2 years.

GREY STACK *(Bennett Valley)*

Sauvignon Blancs Rosemary's Block ♟ $$ A wine with remarkable texture, a dry, crisp, seriously endowed mouth-feel, and a fresh finish; the overall impression is of a honeyed ripeness and headiness with superb precision and definition.

HALTER RANCH *(Paso Robles)*

GSM Rosé Halter Ranch Vineyard ♟ $ This excellent rosé exhibits delicious notes of strawberries and cherries along with medium body, good freshness, and exuberance. Enjoy it over its first 6–9 months.

HAVENS WINE CELLARS *(Napa)*

Albariño ♟ $$$ This steel-fermented and -aged white exhibits elegant, crisp tropical fruit notes offered in a light-bodied, zesty style. Drink it over its first year.

HENDRY *(Napa)*

Unoaked Chardonnay ♟ $$ A good California imitation of a fine French Chablis, with zesty acidity, medium body, and excellent freshness.

Pinot Gris ♀ $$ The Pinot Gris possesses crisp acidity presented in a medium-bodied, richly fruity, fresh, lively style.

HOLLY'S HILL VINEYARDS *(El Dorado)*

Syrah Wylie-Fenaughty Vineyard ♀ $$$ Medium bodied and exhibiting plenty of black currant and cherry characteristics along with notions of loamy soil, damp earth, pepper, and roasted herbs.

Viognier Holly's Hill Vineyard ♀ $$ While straightforward and one-dimensional, this white will provide pleasant, uncritical quaffing over its first year.

HONIG *(Napa)*

Sauvignon Blanc ♀ $$ A classic, fresh, lively example in a light- to medium-bodied style, this white offers outstanding flexibility with food and is best drunk over its first year.

Sauvignon Blanc Reserve ♀ $$$ A bigger-style yet fresh, impressive Sauvignon that can drink well for a minimum of 1–2 years.

HUSCH VINEYARDS *(Mendocino)*

Chenin Blanc ♀ $ A thoroughly delectable aperitif wine, richly fruity and best consumed in its exuberant youth.

Muscat Canelli Ⓢ ♀ $ Slightly sweet but also very low in alcohol, this wine is probably best as an aperitif or served with light desserts.

Sauvignon Blanc ♀ $ The medium-bodied Sauvignon Blanc possesses delicious, pure fruit and a fresh finish.

JADE MOUNTAIN *(Contra Costa)*

Mourvèdre Ancient Vines, Evangelho Vineyard ♀ $$ Medium bodied and pleasant, but lacks serious concentration.

La Provençale ♀ $$ A medium-bodied Côtes du Rhône look-alike that can be enjoyed over its first several years.

JAFFURS WINE CELLARS *(Santa Barbara)*

Syrah Santa Barbara ♀ $$$ A beautiful, lush, sexy effort with pure fruit, medium to full body, and a lush texture.

JC CELLARS *(Various Regions)*

Syrah California Cuvée ♀ **$$$** Made in an up-front, supple, fruity style, this Syrah offers abundant amounts of fleshy, peppery, sweet cherry and black currant fruit along with hints of smoke and earth.

JUSLYN *(Napa)*

Sauvignon Blanc ♀ **$$$** In the best vintages, this fine Sauvignon Blanc can even be Bordeaux-like, with a perfumed nose of grapefruit, lemon zest, and a touch of herbs.

KALEIDOS *(Paso Robles)*

Oakrock Proprietary Red ♀ **$$$** The Oakrock reveals aromas of spicy oak, new saddle leather, black currants, and a touch of tobacco leaf.

KENDALL-JACKSON *(Various Regions)*

Chardonnay Camelot Highland Estates ♀ **$$$** Fleshy, rich, pure, and a total delight to drink.

Grand Reserve Chardonnay ♀ **$$$** This beauty is a pure, rich wine exhibiting subtle oak but dominated by its fruit.

Grand Reserve Pinot Noir ♀ **$$$** This red offers crisp underlying acidity that focuses the plum, black cherry, and earthiness of the wine as well as the dark ruby color and soft tannins.

Vintner's Reserve Meritage ♀ **$$$** A soft, medium-bodied, stylish Californian take on a good Bordeaux.

Vintner's Reserve Chardonnay ♀ **$** Crisp orange marmalade and lemon oil notes as well as some tropical fruits always characterize this wine, which seems to show very little evidence of oak, with gorgeously lush fruit and zesty acidity in a fresh, lively style.

Vintner's Reserve Sauvignon Blanc ♀ **$** Offering the classic melon, fig, and lemongrass of Sauvignon, this is dry, medium bodied, and aromatic.

KIAMIE WINE CELLARS *(Paso Robles)*

Proprietary White Derby Vineyard ♀ $$$ This exotically scented blend of 65% Roussanne and 35% Viognier displays plenty of tropical fruit and melony notes buttressed by decent acidity as well as a medium-bodied mouth-feel.

KUNIN WINES *(Central Coast)*

Pape Star Proprietary Red ♀ $$ This bistro-styled red is a very good California interpretation of a well-made Châteauneuf-du-Pape, with terrific fruit, medium body, and no hard edges.

LA SIRENA *(Napa)*

Moscato Azul Ⓢ ♀ $$ One of the more tasty aperitif wines in all of California, this is a relatively dry Muscat with crisp acidity, a gorgeous fruit cocktail–like nose, and light body in a refreshing, zesty style.

LARKMEAD *(Napa)*

Sauvignon Blanc ♀ $$ A medium-bodied wine with surprising intensity and length. Drink it over its first 1–2 years.

CLIFF LEDE *(Napa)*

Sauvignon Blanc ♀ $$ This Sauvignon Blanc has an aromatic, beautiful, melon-scented nose with loads of fruit, crisp acidity, and plenty of honeyed grapefruit along the way. Drink it over its first year.

J. LOHR VINEYARDS *(Paso Robles)*

Syrah ♀ $ This competent, deep ruby/purple-hued Syrah offers attractive black currant fruit, good acidity, and a medium-bodied palate impression.

LUNA VINEYARDS *(Napa)*

Sangiovese ♀ $$$ A sexy, medium-ruby-colored Sangiovese with the complexity and personality of a top-notch Pinot Noir. With beautiful berry fruit as well as some spice, it is an altogether friendly wine that is opulent but not heavy or tiring.

MARIETTA CELLARS *(Various Regions)*

Cabernet Sauvignon ♆ $$ A solid, competently made Cabernet Sauvignon to drink over its first 5–7 years.

Old Vine Red (lot numbers vary with year of release) ♆ $ One of those blends made from everything but the kitchen sink, including Carignane, Zinfandel, Petite Sirah, Alicante, and numerous mixed black varietals, this medium-bodied, soft effort can be superficial but will offer tasty drinking over its first year or two. In the best years it comes across like a California Côtes du Rhône.

Zinfandel ♆ $$ A surprisingly elegant Zinfandel offering up aromas and flavors of black cherries, strawberries, tar, and pepper.

MASON CELLARS *(Napa)*

Sauvignon Blanc ♆ $$ Always one of California's better Sauvignon Blancs, Mason's medium-bodied white possesses exuberant tropical fruit, honeyed melon, and spice characteristics.

MELVILLE *(Santa Rita Hills)*

Syrah Verna's Vineyard ♆ $$$ Exhibits definition and minerality as well as the classic opulence and suppleness that make Syrah such a captivating and endearing wine.

Viognier Verna's Vineyard ♆ $$$ Extraordinary minerality and precision, despite its enormous power, are what set this wine apart from most blowsy, loosely constructed Viogniers. The wine's well-delineated character is remarkable.

MICHAEL-DAVID WINERY *(Lodi)*

Incognito Proprietary Blend ♆ $$ A blend of Rhône varietals, this is a straightforward, Côtes du Rhône–style effort with pepper, herb, sweet cherry, and currant characteristics.

Petite Petit ♆ $$ Made from Petite Sirah in a medium- to full-bodied, richly fruity style with no hard edges, this wine is atypically soft and supple for a Petite Sirah.

Syrah 6th Sense ♆ $$ A wine with a beautiful texture, velvety tannins, a lovely, opulent mouth-feel, and a long finish.

Syrah Earthquake 🍷 **$$$** A dense, chewy, mouth-filling, and savory wine that should be drunk over its first 3–4 years.

Viognier Incognito 🍷 **$$** Exhibiting plenty of apricot and melony fruit as well as a hint of exotic tropical fruits, this wine represents a very good value for Viognier.

Zinfandel Windmill Old Vine 🍷 **$** This medium-bodied, pure, classic Zinfandel can be enjoyed over its first 1–2 years.

7 Deadly Zins 🍷 **$$** A very good wine showing plenty of oak in addition to abundant varietal character in its briary, cherry, raspberry, earthy personality.

CHATEAU MONTELENA *(Napa)*

Riesling Potter Valley 🍷 **$$** Relatively dry, fresh, and lively, this is a light- to medium-bodied, pure Riesling that makes a nice aperitif.

MORGAN *(Santa Lucia Highlands)*

Chardonnay Metallico 🍷 **$$** There is no evidence of oak in this fresh white. Made in a lovely, medium-bodied, lively style, it should be enjoyed over its first 12 months.

Pinot Gris 🍷 **$** This crisp, elegant, medium-bodied, fresh Pinot Gris should be consumed in its first year.

MURPHY-GOODE *(Sonoma)*

Zinfandel Liar's Dice 🍷 **$$$** The Zinfandel Liar's Dice offers some spicy pepper, herbal notes, and medium body, but in some vintages it can fall off in the mouth.

ANDREW MURRAY *(Santa Ynez)*

Camp Four RGB 🍷 **$$$** A Rhone Ranger blend of white varietals, the one-dimensional Camp Four RGB reveals crisp acidity and fresh white currant and apple-like fruit, but not much of a finish.

Espérance 🍷 **$$$** An attractive California version of a low-level Côtes du Rhône, this wine offers straightforward berry fruit with medium body and easy drinkability.

Syrah Tous Les Jours 🍷 **$$** A lighter-style Syrah that tastes like a French Crozes-Hermitage, this is a long, ripe, soft, delicious red to enjoy over its first several years.

ORTMAN FAMILY VINEYARDS *(San Luis Obispo)*

Cuvée Eddy 🍷 **$$$** A medium-bodied, soft red, ideal for drinking over its first 2–3 years.

FESS PARKER WINERY *(Santa Barbara)*

Chardonnay Ashley's Santa Rita Hills 🍷 **$$$** One of the finest Chardonnay values from the highly acclaimed Santa Rita Hills appellation, this serious, full-bodied, spicy, French-style Chardonnay exhibits lots of acidity along with hints of lemon custard, brioche, and apple pie.

Chardonnay Bien Nacido Vineyard Santa Barbara 🍷 **$$$** Perhaps the best buy from this famous Santa Barbara vineyard, this sensational Chardonnay sells at a 40% discount compared to other single vineyard offerings. It is a not-to-be-missed bargain.

Chardonnay Santa Barbara 🍷 **$$** This inexpensive, consistently well-made Chardonnay spends approximately 10 months in 100% French oak (very little new). Primarily from estate vineyards, it possesses notes of honeysuckle, pears, apples, and melons.

N.V. Frontier Red 🍷 **$** This nonvintage blend put together by Fess Parker's excellent Central Coast winery is a sensational bargain. A blend of Zinfandel, Carignane, Petite Sirah, Grenache, Syrah, and other assorted red wine grapes, the wine tends to be peppery, spicy, fruity, medium bodied, and consistently good.

Pinot Noir Santa Barbara 🍷 **$$** One of the best buys among Santa Barbara Pinot Noirs, and the venue for the movie *Sideways,* this is the real deal. Notes of pomegranates, sweet strawberries, raspberries, and cherries intermixed with hints of forest floor and herbs make for an authentic, modestly priced example of a very flavorful Pinot Noir.

Syrah Santa Barbara 🍷 **$$** One of the most attractively priced Syrahs from the Central Coast, this cuvée is loaded with barbecue spices, blackberries, and a robust meatiness.

PAVILION WINERY *(Napa)*

Cabernet Sauvignon 🍷 $ This medium-bodied, spicy, ripe wine should be drunk over its first 2–3 years.

Chardonnay Oakville 🍷 $ This lovely Chardonnay from Oakville offers a touch of toasty oak along with attractive honeysuckle and butterscotch characteristics, serious concentration, excellent acidity, and a rich, heady finish.

Merlot 🍷 $ Displays crisp, elegant black cherry and berry notes intermixed with notions of cocoa and caramel.

Pinot Noir 🍷 $ It is hard to find a Pinot Noir of this quality for under $30 a bottle. Briary berry fruit and forest floor–like characteristics are offered in a medium-bodied, silky style to enjoy over 1–2 years.

JOSEPH PHELPS VINEYARD *(Napa)*

Sauvignon Blanc 🍷 $$$ This white shows plenty of grapefruit in a crisp, elegant, light- to medium-bodied, nonmalolactic style.

PINE RIDGE *(Clarksburg)*

Chenin Blanc/Viognier 🍷 $ The light-bodied Chenin Blanc–Viognier is an ideal aperitif wine to consume over its first 6 months, very perfumed, medium bodied, superpure, with no oak and a dry, crisp finish.

QUPE *(Central Coast)*

Los Olivos Cuvée 🍷 $$$ Earthy, peppery, *garrigue*, cherry, plum, and spice characteristics emerge from the Los Olivos Cuvée, a stylish Côtes du Rhône look-alike.

Syrah Central Coast 🍷 $$ A charming Syrah exhibiting plenty of sweet cherries, an attractive earthy character, hints of licorice and roasted herbs, and a tasty, medium framework with pretty flavors as well as soft tannins.

RENARD *(Various Regions)*

Rosé Sonoma 🍷 $ This aromatic rosé offers up scents of *framboise* and cherry with soil undertones in a medium-bodied, dry, crisp style. Enjoy it over its first 6–7 months.

Roussanne Westerly Vineyard 🍷 $$$ The Alsatian-like Roussanne Westerly Vineyard is a pretty, albeit one-dimensional, Roussanne to drink over its first 1–2 years.

Syrah Unti Vineyard & Kick Ranch 🍷 $$ This outstanding Syrah from the Unti Vineyard and the Kick Ranch exhibits dense, medium- to full-bodied flavors, excellent chewiness, and a long, heady finish.

J. ROCHIOLI VINEYARDS *(Russian River)*

Sauvignon Blanc Estate 🍷 $$$ This old-vine Sauvignon Blanc possesses crisp melon and fig-like notes, fresh acidity, and medium body. It is an excellent white to enjoy over its first several years.

ROSENBLUM CELLARS *(Various Regions)*

Petite Sirah Heritage Clones 🍷 $$ A full-bodied, tannic, chewy, rich, pedal-to-the-metal Petite Sirah with low acidity as well as ripe tannin.

Petite Sirah Pato Vineyard 🍷 $$$ A wine of unbridled richness, huge tannins, massive fruit, earth, purity, and loads of blackberry, blueberry, incense, and graphite characteristics.

Petite Sirah Rhodes Vineyard 🍷 $$$ A deep, chewy, full-bodied, tannic, monolithic effort, the Petite Sirah Rhodes Vineyard can be excruciatingly tannic on release, but there is plenty of density.

Vintner's Cuvée XXIX 🍷 $ A tarry, herbal, peppery effort with soft fruit and an easy-to-drink style.

Zinfandel North Coast 🍷 $$ This is a lighter-styled, fruit-driven Zinfandel meant for casual quaffing. It does not possess the body or high-octane alcohol of other offerings from this producer.

Zinfandel House Family Vineyard 🍷 $$$ A spicy, medium- to full-bodied Zinfandel revealing zesty acidity as well as a moderate structure.

Zinfandel Planchon Vineyard 🍷 $$$ A richly fruited, straightforward, medium- to full-bodied, soft Zin that is ideal for near-term drinking.

ROUND HILL *(Various Regions)*

Chardonnay California 🍷 $ The Chardonnay California offers crisp, fresh honeysuckle and fruit notes, medium body, and a simple personality.

Chardonnay Oak Free 🍷 $ The Chardonnay Oak Free displays crisp orange- and lemon-blossom characteristics, medium body, good fruit and purity, and surprising character.

RUTHERFORD RANCH *(Napa)*

Cabernet Sauvignon 🍷 $ Richly fruity, with silky tannin and a lush finish, this is a perfect Cabernet for restaurants to sell by the glass.

Chardonnay 🍷 $ A well-made, fresh white; consume this beauty over its first 12–18 months.

Rhiannon Proprietary Red 🍷 $$ Medium to full bodied with silky tannin, loads of fruit, and surprising depth for a wine in this price range.

SADDLEBACK CELLARS *(Northern California)*

Chardonnay 🍷 $$$ This Chardonnay represents a Napa-style Chablis, with tart acidity and medium body, and its aging in 50% new French oak is completely concealed by its exquisite aromas and flavors.

Marsanne 🍷 $$$ Pleasant as well as fairly priced, this light, nonmalolactic white is meant to be drunk during its first several years of life.

Pinot Blanc 🍷 $$ The best of the Saddleback whites is the Pinot Blanc, a superb example of this varietal offering up notes of apple skin, orange blossom, and citrus oil.

Pinot Grigio 🍷 $$ A crisp, elegant, medium-bodied offering displaying hints of honeyed grapefruit and apple skin in a lively format.

Viognier 🍷 **$$$** This vibrant Viognier offers good acidity, medium body, a fresh character, and no noticeable oak.

Venge Family Reserve Bianco Spettro 🍷 **$$$** A delicious, exotic, food-friendly white made from Chardonnay, Sauvignon Blanc, and a bit of Viognier, this is a bone-dry, medium-bodied white boasting a fruit cocktail–like fragrance and loads of flavor as well as personality.

SAGE *(Napa)*

Sauvignon Blanc 🍷 **$$$** Brilliant but extremely limited in availability, this amazingly ripe, rich, zesty Sauvignon Blanc is medium bodied, fresh, and lively, with terrific texture and pretty good size and richness.

ST. CLEMENT *(Various Regions)*

Chardonnay 🍷 **$$** This midweight Chardonnay is made in a French Chablis-like style, with the wood toned down and the wine revealing lots of citrus, a steely backbone, and good acidity.

Sauyvignon Blanc Bale Lane Vineyard 🍷 **$$** The Sauvignon Blanc Bale Lane Vineyard reveals plenty of steely grapefruit and other citrus characteristics in a light- to medium-bodied, dry, elegant, refreshing style.

CHATEAU ST. JEAN *(Alexander Valley)*

Chardonnay Belle Terre Vineyard 🍷 **$$$** With terrific freshness, purity, and length, this Chardonnay exhibits abundant notes of honeysuckle, white peaches, and apricots in its medium- to full-bodied personality.

Chardonnay Robert Young Vineyard 🍷 **$$$** Readers who find California Chardonnays too exuberant and fruity will enjoy this wine, which reveals straightforward notes of lemon oil and crushed rocks in its austere, tightly knit, pure, medium-bodied style.

Fumé Blanc 🍷 **$** The Fumé Blanc exhibits beautiful aromas offered in a crisp, dry, light- to medium-bodied, tasty personality. Enjoy it over its first 12–18 months.

Fumé Blanc Le Petit Etoile ⚲ **$$** Always a winner, the Fumé Blanc Le Petit Etoile is fruity, with superb definition, light to medium body, and a clean, fresh finish.

Fumé Blanc Lyon Vineyard ⚲ **$$** With medium body, fine acidity, and surprising intensity as well as depth, the Fumé Blanc Lyon Vineyard can drink nicely for several years.

SARAH'S VINEYARD *(Santa Clara)*

Syrah Besson Vineyard ⚲ **$$$** A complex aromatic and flavor profile, sweet tannin in the finish, and broad, savory flavors all add to the appeal of this wine from the Santa Clara Valley.

SAUVIGNON REPUBLIC *(Russian River)*

Sauvignon Blanc ⚲ **$$** This lively, medium-bodied, fresh, stainless-steel-aged Sauvignon Blanc should be drunk in its first year.

SAVANNAH-CHANELLE VINEYARDS *(Monterey)*

Syrah Coast View Vineyard ⚲ **$$$** A reasonably good value in high-quality Syrah, this wine has good acidity, loads of aromatics, and is clearly a cool-climate but very tasty and elegant Syrah.

SBRAGIA FAMILY VINEYARDS *(Dry Creek)*

Merlot Home Ranch ⚲ **$$$** This lovely Merlot exhibits chocolate, mocha, caramel, and berry fruit characteristics, medium to full body, and silky tannins.

Zinfandel Gino's ⚲ **$$$** Sbragia's Zinfandel Gino's is good but not great.

75 *(Various Regions)*

Sauvignon Blanc ⚲ **$$** A lovely, honeyed, fruity, crisp, personality-filled Sauvignon Blanc best drunk over its first year.

Cabernet Sauvignon Amber Knolls Red Hills ⚲ **$$** An attractive Cabernet with good ripeness and certainly a fair price.

SILVERADO VINEYARDS *(Yountville)*

Sauvignon Blanc Miller Ranch ♀ **$$** This lovely-scented Sauvignon Blanc exhibits loads of fig, melon, and honeyed grapefruit, followed by a dry, crisp finish. Enjoy it over its first year.

SKYLARK WINE COMPANY *(North Coast)*

Red Belly Proprietary Red ♀ **$$$** A California Côtes du Rhône if I have ever tasted one, Skylark's beautiful blend is an intriguing combination of Carignan, Syrah, and Grenache. Layered, ripe, and delicious, it can drink well for 1–2 years.

SNOWDEN *(Napa)*

Sauvignon Blanc ♀ **$$** Made from 100% Sauvignon Blanc, this wine offers crisp, elegant grapefruit and underripe pineapple notes, medium body, zesty acidity, and a fresh, nonmalolactic style that is undeniably food friendly. Drink it over its first 6 months.

CHATEAU SOUVERAIN *(Alexander Valley)*

Cabernet Sauvignon Alexander Valley ♀ **$$$** This richly fruity, straightforward Cabernet Sauvignon is a tasty, fruit-forward, reasonably good value.

SPENCER ROLOSON WINERY *(Napa)*

Palaterra Proprietary Red ♀ **$$$** The Palaterra, a blend of multiple varietals, is an excellent bistro-style red with loads of sweet fruit, medium body, good freshness, and a supple mouth-feel. Altogether, this is a very sensual wine.

STUHLMULLER VINEYARDS *(Alexander Valley)*

Chardonnay ♀ **$$$** This outstanding Chardonnay displays some mineral notes, crisp acidity, a medium-bodied style, and a judicious touch of oak. The result is a delicious white to drink over its first 1–2 years.

SUMMERS ESTATE WINES *(Various Regions)*

Chardonnay ♀ **$$$** With terrific fruit and no evidence of oak (30% new is used), this outstanding Chardonnay should be enjoyed over its first 1–2 years.

Merlot Reserve ♀ **$$$** Soft and round with velvety tannin as well as a lush finish, this attractive Merlot can drink well for 2–5 years.

Cabernet Sauvignon Adrianna's Cuvée ♀ **$$$** Finding a good 100% Napa Cabernet Sauvignon for under $50 a bottle is no easy task, and finding an excellent one is almost impossible, but that is exactly what this elegant, tasty Cabernet Sauvignon delivers. Classic Cabernet aromas are followed by a medium- to full-bodied wine with loads of fruit, soft tannin, and a long finish.

TABLAS CREEK *(Paso Robles)*

Côtes de Tablas ♀ **$$$** Tablas Creek's Côtes du Rhône effort is the exceptional Côtes de Tablas, a medium- to full-bodied wine displaying beautiful purity, fruit, and depth. The wine is a blend of such grapes as Grenache, Mourvèdre, Syrah, Cinsault, and Carignan.

Côtes de Tablas Blanc ♀ **$$$** The beautiful Côtes de Tablas Blanc is a medium-bodied, dry, personality-filled white best consumed in its first 2–3 years. It contains a blend of Roussanne, Marsaune, Viognier, and occasionally small percentages of other esoteric white grapes.

TALLEY VINEYARDS *(Various Regions)*

Bishop's Peak Syrah ♀ **$$** The Bishop's Peak Syrah is a fruit-driven California version of a Crozes-Hermitage, medium bodied, silky, and best drunk over its first several years.

Syrah Mano Tinta ♀ **$$** This wine, with its silky-smooth texture and red and black fruits, can drink nicely for 2 or so years.

10 KNOTS CELLARS *(Paso Robles)*

Beachcomber ♀ **$$$** A tasty, straightforward, well-made effort, enjoy this pleasant white over its first year.

Moonraker ♀ **$$$** This complex red is reminiscent of a good California-style Côtes du Rhône. Drink it over its first 2–3 years.

TERRE ROUGE *(Sierra Foothills)*

Côtes de l'Ouest 🍷 **$$** The delicious Côtes de l'Ouest, an elegant Rhone Ranger blend, is quite tasty and a heck of a fine value to drink over its first year.

Enigma Proprietary Blend 🍷 **$$$** The Enigma is a straightforward, attractive, light-to medium-bodied white that merits drinking over its first year or so.

Mourvèdre 🍷 **$$$** The most monolithic and least expressive wine of the Terre Rouge offerings; some dark fruits are there, but some hardness and austerity dominate the wine's finish.

Roussanne 🍷 **$$$** This white seems strikingly light in style for a wine from this varietal, but it is certainly competently made and pleasant.

Tête-à-Tête 🍷 **$** This Rhone Ranger blend is reminiscent of a classic southern Rhône Valley wine—textured, attractively pure, ripe, and delicious.

Viognier 🍷 **$$$** The best of the three whites from Terre Rouge, showing plenty of ripe peach, subtle apricot, and honeysuckle notes in a medium-bodied, pure, clean, unoaked style.

TRAVIS *(Monterey)*

Chardonnay Unfiltered 🍷 **$$** This unoaked Chardonnay exhibits plenty of crisp acidity as well as loads of tropical fruit in its medium-bodied, honeyed, rich, pure personality.

TRUCHARD VINEYARDS *(Carneros)*

Roussane 🍷 **$$** This straightforward, competent Roussanne is light, medium bodied, fresh, and zesty, but lacking substance.

TUTU *(Lodi)*

Pinot Grigio 🍷 **$** This tasty, fresh, light-bodied style of Pinot Grigio from Lodi exhibits good winemaking with loads of fruit. It is an ideal aperitif. Drink it over its first year.

VILLA CREEK CELLARS *(Paso Robles)*

Pink ♇ **$** The rosé offering from Villa Creek Cellars, the Pink, possesses crisp acidity (which provides freshness) as well as copious quantities of frothy strawberry and *framboise* fruit. It is a delicious value that is best consumed over its first 6–9 months.

Proprietary White Blend ♇ **$$$** The Proprietary White Blend exhibits an explosive bouquet followed by abundant quantities of ripe fruit, good acidity, and a fresh, lively style.

WINDSOR SONOMA VINEYARDS *(Russian River)*

Chardonnay ♇ **$$** This Chardonnay is classic California in its display of assorted tropical fruits, full-bodied opulence, superb purity, good acidity, and long finish.

Sauvignon Blanc ♇ **$** This stainless-steel-aged Sauvignon Blanc exhibits terrific fruit, medium body, and zesty acidity. It can provide plenty of pleasure over its first 1–2 years.

WYATT *(Various Regions)*

Cabernet Sauvignon ♇ **$** A knockout wine with loads of sweet fruit, medium body, velvety tannins, and a heady finish, this beauty can drink well for 5–7 years.

Pinot Noir ♇ **$$** This wine is a real winner, tasting like a delicious Côte de Beaune. Medium-bodied, with decent acidity, ripe tannin, and a nice, plush mouth-feel, this is a rather remarkable wine value for a Pinot Noir, which is always a fickle grape as well as expensive to produce. Drink it over its first 2–3 years, and buy it by the case.

Chardonnay ♇ **$** A medium-bodied, deliciously fresh, fruit-driven but stylish Chardonnay with no wood to be consumed over its first 1–2 years.

ZACA MESA *(Santa Ynez)*

Z Cuvée Estate ♇ **$$** A blend of Mourvèdre, Grenache, Cinsault, and Syrah, this medium-bodied, fruity effort is best consumed over its first 2–3 years.

OREGON WINE VALUES

by Dr. Jay Miller

The demand for Pinot Noir in the United States, ever since the film *Sideways,* appears to be insatiable, with no obvious signs that the bubble is going to burst, à la Merlot. The unanimous response when I asked producers if this was a good time to be in the Pinot business was a big grin. The bad news for consumers, however, is that the entry level for quality Pinot Noir begins at $35, beyond the purview of this handbook. On my most recent trip to Oregon, I was able to find nine Pinot Noirs under $25 that I could recommend out of hundreds tasted.

Vintage Smarts
2006, 2007, and 2008 are excellent to outstanding vintages for Oregon Pinot Noir.

Drinking Curves
Oregon Pinot Noir under $25 are designed for immediate drinking.

Oregon's Top Wine Values by Winery

A TO Z WINEWORKS *(Various Regions)*

Pinot Noir 🍷 $$ More than 40 vineyards from all over the state are represented in the blend. Medium ruby colored, it offers a pleasant bouquet of spice box and cherry fruit, medium body, sweet fruit, and a smooth texture. Overall, however, the wine is a bit superficial and lacking in serious flavor interest. That said, it looks like Pinot Noir, smells like Pinot Noir, and tastes like Pinot Noir, and at the asking price, as the retail saying goes, stack it high and watch it fly.

CANA'S FEAST WINERY *(Willamette Valley)*

Pinot Noir Bricco 🍷 $$$ Dark ruby colored, with an enticing nose of spice box and wild raspberries. On the palate the wine reveals a racy, elegant personality with a silky-smooth texture and savory flavors. Although in need of more depth and concentration, it is an excellent value.

J. K. CARRIERE WINES *(Willamette Valley)*

Pinot Noir Provocateur 🍷 $$$ Exhibits an expressive bouquet of cedar, spice box, and red fruits. On the palate, this medium-bodied effort has good depth of flavor and enough structure to evolve for 1–2 years.

CHEHALEM WINERY *(Willamette Valley)*

Cerise 🍷 $$$ Chehalem's Cerise is a blend of Gamay Noir and Pinot Noir (which in Burgundy is known as Passetoutgrains) that can be quite charming. It offers an excellent fruity nose featuring strawberry and cherry leading to a vibrant, flavorful wine with excellent balance and a lengthy finish.

ERATH WINERY *(Various Regions)*

Pinot Noir 🍷 $$ Erath Winery is one of Oregon's pioneers, with its first vintage occurring in 1972. Dick Erath sold the winery to Ste. Michelle Wine Estates recently but remains the largest grower for the winery (which owns no vineyards). Current production is at 125,000 cases with the Oregon Pinot Noir bottling accounting for almost two-thirds of that total. Light to medium ruby colored with pleasant red fruit aromatics, it is an easy-drinking, straightforward wine to drink over its first 4 years.

RANSOM WINE COMPANY *(Willamette Valley)*

Pinot Noir Love & Squalor 🍷 $$$ It is medium to dark ruby with an attractive nose of black cherry and black raspberry. The wine has good flavors and a smooth texture but lacks depth and has a truncated finish. Even so, it is a good Pinot Noir value.

STOLLER VINEYARDS *(Dundee Hills)*

Pinot Noir JV Estate 🍷 $$$ The Pinot Noir JV (junior vines) Estate offers up a nose of spice box and earth notes with a hint of red fruit aromas. This is followed by a smooth-textured wine that has ample savory red fruits on the palate but is a bit short on complexity.

SWEET CHEEKS WINERY *(Willamette Valley)*

Pinot Noir Estate ♀ $$ It may be the best value in the market for Oregon Pinot Noir. It has an expressive bouquet of spice box, cherry, and raspberry. Smooth textured and round on the palate, it has excellent concentration, balance, and length.

WILLAKENZIE ESTATE *(Willamette Valley)*

Estate Pinot Noir ♀ $$ It is a regional blend with a pleasant red fruit nose of cherry and raspberry. This leads to an easygoing, round, friendly wine for drinking during its first 4–5 years.

Postscript

As the above notes suggest, there are very few recommendable Oregon Pinot Noirs under $25 a bottle. Because Pinot Noir is what Oregon does best, that has been the focus of our coverage in recent years. However, Chardonnay, Riesling, Pinot Blanc, and Pinot Gris can do very well there, particularly in vintages in which vibrant acidity and ripeness go hand in hand—2007 and 2008 are the most recent such years. They are worth a try.

WASHINGTON WINE VALUES

by Dr. Jay Miller

Virtually all the wines described here are from the Columbia Valley appellation (which includes the Yakima and Walla Walla valleys). Primarily a desert, it is located in southeastern Washington and overlaps into Oregon. As one flies from Seattle to Walla Walla it is amazing to see the contrast between the lush green western slopes of the Cascades and the barren eastern side. From the tips of the Cascades all the way to Walla Walla, the only signs of vegetation are the trees bordering rivers and irrigated farms. One statistic dramatizes this weather pattern: Within the town of Walla Walla, on the eastern edge of the Columbia Valley appellation, annual rainfall increases by one inch per mile as one travels eastward. On the parched western edge of Walla Walla, abutting the l'Ecole No. 41 and Woodward Canyon wineries, are dusty asparagus fields. On the eastern edge, where Walla Walla Vintners and Leonetti's new vineyards are located, the rolling hills are lush and green.

Rain, the bane of wine producers the world over, is rarely a nuisance for Washington's main grape-growing region. Because Washington State vineyards are irrigated, viticulturalists can control the quantity of water each row of vines gets.

Readers should not assume that because Washington State borders Canada it has a cold climate. Once spring arrives, the Columbia Valley enjoys a grape-growing season that winemakers the world over would envy. Sun and heat are plentiful, evenings are cool—excellent for maintaining natural acidity levels.

This is not, however, a viticultural paradise. The winters and early springs can be a grape grower's nightmare. Why? The region is prone, on average once every 6 years, to "killer freezes" (as they are known in those parts), the last of which descended from the Arctic in late January and early February 1996 and devastated the vineyards. A less severe freeze in 2004 decimated much of the crop except at the highest elevations.

Vintage Smarts

Washington's high desert climate, marked by hot days and cool evenings, and lack of harvest rainfall, is remarkably consistent from year to year. 2005, 2006, 2007, and 2008 were excellent to outstanding in the Columbia Valley for both red and white wines.

Drinking Curves

The white wines in this chapter can be drunk upon purchase. Most of the red wines will evolve for 1–2 years and last for 4–5 years but can be enjoyed without additional cellaring.

Washington's Top Wine Values by Winery

AMAVI CELLARS *(Columbia Valley)*

Semillon ♀ $$ The Semillon offers aromas of citrus, spring flowers, and melon. This leads to a creamy-textured wine with ripe melon flavors buttressed by crisp acidity. The finish is medium long and refreshing.

BERGEVIN LANE *(Columbia Valley)*

Calico White ♀ $$ The Calico White is a blend of Chardonnay, Viognier, and Roussanne. It offers up aromas of fresh pear, spiced apple, peach, and melon. Nicely concentrated with an intense entry onto the palate, the flavors are ripe and dry, the finish crisp and refreshing.

BRIAN CARTER CELLARS *(Various Regions)*

Abracadabra—Columbia Valley ♀ $$$ A cuvée for declassified lots of pricier wines made up of seven grape varieties dominated by Syrah and Cabernet Sauvignon. Supple and easygoing, it offers up aromas and flavors of red cherries and raspberries.

Oreana White Wine Blend—Yakima Valley ♀ $$ The Oreana White Wine Blend is composed of Viognier, Roussanne, and Riesling. It exhibits a pleasant, fruity nose with notes of spring flowers, mineral, melon, and citrus. Crisp and balanced, in its first 2 years it will serve as an excellent aperitif or picnic wine.

CHATEAU ROLLAT *(Columbia Valley)*

Ardenvoir Semillon ♀ $$$ The Ardenvoir Semillon reveals floral notes, honey, and tangerine. Smooth on the palate, it has excellent concentration, good depth, lively acidity, some complexity, and a lengthy finish. Drink it with seafood during its first 2–3 years.

CHATEAU STE. MICHELLE *(Columbia Valley)*

Chateau Ste. Michelle, Washington's largest winery, continues to demonstrate that being big is not incompatible with high quality. Their portfolio of value-priced wines is exceptional.

Cabernet Sauvignon Indian Wells ♀ $$ Offers an enticing nose of wood smoke, blackberry, and black cherry. Firm on the palate, there is plenty of sweet fruit, light tannin, and attractive black fruit flavors.

Chardonnay Canoe Ridge Estate—Horse Heaven Hills ♀ $$$ This Chardonnay is made in a fruit-forward style. The nose offers toasty notes, white fruits, pear, and peach. This leads to a round, ripe wine with excellent texture and nicely integrated oak. The finish is lengthy and fruit filled.

Chardonnay Cold Creek Vineyard ♀ $$$ The nose reveals aromas of butterscotch, vanilla, apple, poached pear, and a hint of tropical fruits. Smooth textured and nicely balanced, the wine's finish is long and pure.

Dry Riesling ♀ $ A crisp, dry, vibrant effort with notes of mineral, petrol, and lemon-lime. This nicely balanced Riesling will pair well with Asian cuisine and the wild salmon of the Pacific Northwest.

Eroica Riesling ♀ $$$ Offers fragrant aromas of spring flowers, mineral, and honeysuckle. Crisp and just off-dry, in a Kabinett style, it delivers flavors of melon and pineapple. The wine is balanced and vibrant and may well evolve for several years in the manner of a top German Mosel Kabinett.

Merlot Canoe Ridge Estate—Horse Heaven Hills ♀ $$$ Reveals notes of cherry and black raspberry. It has a round mouthfeel and an elegant personality with attractive flavors and moderate length.

Pinot Gris ♀ $ The Pinot Gris contains 8% Viognier. It offers up earth notes, melon, and a hint of peach in the background. Just a touch off-dry, it has lively acidity, excellent balance, and a sprightly finish.

COLUMBIA CREST *(Columbia Valley)*

H3 Chardonnay Horse Heaven Hills ♀ $$ Offers up toasty apple and pear aromas with a bit of tropical fruit in the background. The wine is a bit short on depth and concentration, but it is pleasant and a good value nonetheless.

Merlot Reserve ♥ $$$ Purple colored with aromas of cedar, spice box, cassis, and black currant. There is more follow-through on the palate but the flavors are a bit austere.

Syrah Reserve ♥ $$ The Syrah Reserve offers up aromas of smoke, minerals, blueberry, smoke, and sausage. The flavors are classy but the finish is a bit compressed.

COUGAR CREST *(Walla Walla Valley)*

Chardonnay ♀ $$ The Chardonnay offers apple and pear aromas. On the palate it is crisp and straightforward with pleasant flavors. Drink it during its first 1–2 years.

Viognier ♀ $$ The stainless-steel-raised Viognier offers peach and apricot aromas followed by a flavorful, balanced wine with some elegance. Drink it during its first 12–18 months.

Vivacé ♀ $$ Vivacé is a blend of Viognier and Chardonnay with aromas of apple, peach, and apricot. This leads to a crisp, dry, tasty wine with good concentration and length. It is a very good aperitif wine to drink over its first 12–18 months.

FIDELITAS *(Columbia Valley)*

Semillon ♀ $$ The Semillon is barrel-fermented in seasoned oak. It offers aromas of melon, wax, and mineral. It exhibits good acidity and adequate fruit with good flavors leading to a medium-long finish.

ISENHOWER CELLARS *(Columbia Valley)*

Red Wine "The Last Straw" 🍷 $$ Predominantly Cabernet Sauvignon, Syrah, and a dollop of 7 other varieties. Tasty, forward, and pleasure-bent, it will make delightful drinking with bistro cuisine during its first 2–3 years.

Rosé 🍷 $$ The Rosé is an attractive blend of Grenache, Counoise, and Mourvèdre. Floral notes and chewy, crisp flavors do a fine impersonation of a top-level Côtes du Rhône. It should prove versatile with a wide range of picnic cuisine.

Snapdragon 🍷 $$ A tasty blend of Roussanne and Viognier aged in stainless steel. The nose offers up enticing notes of honey, peach, and melon. Crisp and refreshing on the palate, this nicely balanced wine has a fruity, pure finish.

JM CELLARS *(Columbia Valley)*

Bramble Bump Red 🍷 $$$ Made up of Cabernet Sauvignon, Merlot, Syrah, Malbec, and Cabernet Franc. This purple-colored effort has a fragrant perfume of spice box, clove, cinnamon, wood smoke, and earth notes. Easygoing and spicy on the palate, it has enough tannin to support 1–2 years of further cellaring.

KIONA *(Columbia Valley)*

Dry Riesling Reserve—Red Mountain 🍷 $ The nose offers up a lovely bouquet of spring flowers, mineral, and honey. This leads to a crisp, well-balanced Riesling with just a flicker of sweetness buttressed by lively acidity.

Ice Wine—Yakima Valley 🍷 $$$ The Ice Wine is a Chenin Blanc–Riesling blend with 20% residual sugar. The aromatics are heavenly, with notes of peach, tangerine, mango, and kiwi. On the palate the wine is smooth textured, racy, and nicely balanced. It should evolve for quite some time given the acid backbone. It is also a fabulous value in sweet wine.

White Riesling Late Harvest 🍷 $ The White Riesling Late Harvest is light gold colored, with a hint of petrol, tropical aromas, honeysuckle. Ripe and flavorful on the palate, it does a fine impersonation of a quality German Spätlese.

L'ECOLE NO. 41 *(Walla Walla Valley)*

Chardonnay Columbia Valley ♀ $$$ The Chardonnay comes from a cool site. It has tropical aromas and flavors, a creamy texture, savory flavors, and a lengthy, friendly finish.

Chenin Blanc Walla Voila Columbia Valley ♀ $ Offers a nose of fresh melon and spring flowers. It has lively acidity and excellent balance, and it is an ideal picnic or aperitif wine.

Semillon Columbia Valley ♀ $$ Contains 15% Sauvignon Blanc. Light gold colored, it offers fresh aromas of melons and honey. Smooth textured, concentrated, and balanced, this lengthy effort would be a fine match for sea bass or rockfish.

Semillon Estate Seven Hills Vineyard ♀ $$ Delivers aromas of melon, apple, and citrus. Round, full flavored, and ripe, this savory effort has superb balance and a long finish. Drink it over the next 3 years.

Semillon Fries Vineyard Wahluke Slope ♀ $$ Offers a similar profile as the Seven Hills Vineyard but with greater depth and concentration.

LONG SHADOWS *(Columbia Valley)*

Poet's Leap Riesling ♀ $$ Made by Armin Diel of the renowned Schlossgut Diel in the Nahe River Valley of Germany, it offers aromas of fresh apples, honey, and spring flowers. This splendidly balanced wine has lively acidity, crisp spicy flavors, and excellent length. This Kabinett-style Riesling should evolve for several years and drink well through 2015.

LOST RIVER WINERY *(Columbia Valley)*

Cabernet Sauvignon ♀ $$$ Reveals aromas of cedar, tobacco, earth, and black currant. Supple textured, forward, and uncomplicated, this nicely balanced, tasty wine will provide pleasure over its first 4–5 years.

Merlot ♀ $$$ The Merlot has an excellent bouquet of toast, smoke, black currant, and blackberry. This is followed by a layered wine with plenty of sweet fruit, enough structure to evolve for 1–2 years, and a long, pure finish.

Syrah ♀ $$$ The Syrah, sourced from the Walla Walla AVA, offers an enticing nose of mineral, earth, a hint of game, and blackberry. On the palate there are plenty of meaty flavors, good depth and concentration, and enough ripe tannin to support 1–2 years of further bottle aging.

McCREA CELLARS *(Red Mountain)*

Roussanne Ciel du Cheval Vineyard ♀ $$$ It is light gold colored, with a bouquet of mineral, melon, candle wax, and a hint of citrus. Ripe, layered, and balanced, the wine is an ideal match for Pacific Northwest salmon.

McKINLEY SPRINGS *(Horse Heaven Hills)*

Viognier ♀ $ The Viognier's expressive nose offers up peach, apricot, and floral notes leading to a rich, full-flavored wine with excellent balance and length.

MILBRANDT VINEYARDS *(Columbia Valley)*

Milbrandt has 2 lines of wine, Legacy for those made from estate fruit and Tradition for those from contracted fruit.

Pinot Gris Tradition ♀ $ The Pinot Gris Tradition offers aromas of mineral and pear leading to a crisp, dry wine with good grip and length. Drink it during its first 1–2 years.

Riesling Tradition ♀ $ The Riesling Tradition reveals scents of apple and spring flowers. Made in a Kabinett, barely off-dry style, the wine has refreshing acidity and flavors and could well evolve for 2–3 years.

Sundance Chardonnay Legacy ♀ $$ The Sundance Chardonnay Legacy resembles a village Chablis in its crisp, straightforward style. The nose offers apple, pear, and mineral notes leading to a wine with good acidity, balancing fruit, and moderate length.

Evergreen Chardonnay Legacy ♀ $$ The Evergreen Chardonnay Legacy raises the bar. More minerality and riper fruit lead to a longer, pure finish.

NOVELTY HILL *(Columbia Valley)*

Chardonnay Stillwater Creek Vineyard ♀ $$$ Offers toasty pear and apple aromas with some tropical fruits in the background. This leads to a focused, balanced Chardonnay with ripe flavors, a smooth texture, and excellent length.

Merlot ♀ $$$ Medium ruby colored, with aromas and flavors of red currants and cherry. Drink this solid, well-balanced effort over the 6 years following the vintage.

Roussanne Stillwater Creek Vineyard ♀ $$$ Reveals aromas of candle wax and melon. This leads to a wine with a ripe midpalate, concentrated flavors, excellent balance, and a crisp finish.

Sauvignon Blanc Stillwater Creek Vineyard ♀ $$ It features crisp lemon-lime aromas and flavors. The wine is well balanced with lively acidity and a refreshing finish.

Syrah ♀ $$$ A top-notch effort featuring aromas of game, bacon, black currant, and blueberry. Firm and structured on the palate, the wine has ample ripe, spicy black and blue fruit flavors and an elegant personality.

Viognier Stillwater Creek Vineyard ♀ $$$ Features peach and apricot aromas followed by a moderately intense, crisp wine lacking the creamy texture of the top examples of Viognier. Regardless, it is a solid example of Washington Viognier.

O · S WINERY *(Various Regions)*

Red—Columbia Valley ♀ $$ The Red is a blend of Cabernet Sauvignon, Cabernet Franc, Merlot, Syrah, and Petit Verdot. This easygoing wine has red fruit and plum aromas, a smooth texture, spicy flavors, and a medium-long finish.

Riesling Champoux Vineyard ♀ $$ An alluring perfume of spring flowers, mineral, and tropical aromas. Just off-dry, crisp, and refreshing, it is an ideal aperitif.

Sauvignon-Semillon Klipsun Vineyard ♀ $$ Consists of 55% Sauvignon and 45% Semillon. The blend works well, with expressive aromas of citrus, melon, and candle wax. This leads to a crisp, well-balanced wine with good depth, concentration, and a lengthy finish.

OWEN ROE   (*Various Regions*)

Riesling DuBrul Vineyard Yakima Valley ♀ **$$** This wine delivers a perfume of spring flowers, petrol, and white fruits. On the palate there is a touch of residual sugar with enough acidity for balance. This Kabinett-style Riesling can be enjoyed over the next several years.

Syrah Ex Umbris Columbia Valley ♀ **$$$** Offers superior aromatics of smoke, game, bacon, and blueberry. Smooth textured, on the palate this wine's fruit is layered and its flavors spicy and savory with some elegance.

ROSS ANDREW WINERY   (*Various Regions*)

Meadow—Oregon ♀ **$$** The Meadow is an intriguing blend of Pinot Blanc, Gewürztraminer, Riesling, and Pinot Gris sourced from Oregon's Willamette and Rogue Valleys. It has an enticing bouquet of mineral, spice box, floral notes, melon, and tropical fruits. Complex, ripe, and lively, it is an ideal aperitif wine reminiscent of the village blends produced by Marcel Deiss in Alsace.

Pinot Gris Celilo Vineyard—Columbia Gorge ♀ **$$** Exhibits aromas of apricot, tangerine, spring flowers, and mineral. On the palate, it is crisp, refreshing, vibrant, and balanced, and it is dry, mouth filling, and long. There are a great many Alsace wineries that would be proud to turn out a Pinot Gris of this quality.

SAINT LAURENT   (*Wahluke Slope*)

Merlot Mrachek Vineyard ♀ **$$** This wine unfolds on the palate revealing cedar, spice, and red fruits. Well balanced, it will drink well for several years.

Syrah Mrachek Vineyard ♀ **$$$** Offers aromas of blueberry, meat, and game, followed by an elegant wine with savory flavors and moderate length.

SNOQUALMIE VINEYARDS *(Columbia Valley)*

Naked Gewürztraminer ♀ $ This is from the winery's line of organic wines. Made in a dry style, the nose gives up rose petals and an amalgam of spices. Not bitter (as many dry Gewürztraminers can be), savory, and nicely balanced, it will make a fine match with Asian cuisine.

Sauvignon Blanc ♀ $ The Sauvignon Blanc delivers floral notes, fresh herbs, and melon in the aromatics and on the palate. Crisp and well balanced, it should be consumed during its first 12–18 months.

Winemaker's Select Riesling ♀ $ The Winemaker's Select Riesling is fruity and semidry. Floral aromas intermingle with tropical scents but the wine could use a bit more acidity to balance the sweetness.

STEVENS WINERY *(Yakima Valley)*

Viognier Divio ♀ $$$ The Viognier offers up an attractive bouquet of mineral, peach, and apricot. On the palate it has excellent concentration and depth, ripe flavors, and lively acidity. Drink this lengthy Viognier during its first 1–2 years.

SYZYGY *(Columbia Valley)*

Red Wine ♥ $$$ The Red Wine is a blend of Syrah, Cabernet Sauvignon, Merlot, and Malbec. It has an excellent bouquet of earth notes, black cherry, blackberry, and blueberry, and is layered on the palate; the fruit has excellent intensity, savory flavors, fine balance, and a lengthy finish.

TAMARACK CELLARS *(Columbia Valley)*

Chardonnay ♀ $$ The Chardonnay is barrel-fermented and goes through malolactic fermentation. It offers tropical fruit flavors and good balance, and is an excellent value.

Firehouse Red ♥ $$ The Firehouse Red is a seamless amalgam of 7 red grape varieties. It goes down easy, an excellent everyday quaffer.

WATERBROOK *(Columbia Valley)*

Chardonnay ♀ $ The Chardonnay spends time in new French oak, with some of the wine going through malolactic fermentation. It is a serious Chardonnay at a bargain price.

Mélange Blanc ♀ $ A blend primarily of Riesling and Gewürztraminer with the balance a mix of 4 other grape varieties. Just off-dry and pleasant, it is an ideal picnic wine.

Petit Verdot "1st & Main" ♀ $$$ The Petit Verdot is a powerful wine with aromas of cedar, wood smoke, earth notes, and blackberry. The wine has outstanding depth and concentration and should evolve for 3–4 years.

Pinot Gris ♀ $ The Pinot Gris is a pleasant fruity, forward wine with melon and tangerine aromas and flavors leading to a crisp, refreshing finish.

Riesling ♀ $ The Riesling is a fruity, crisp, off-dry wine with good acidity for balance.

Syrah ♀ $ The Syrah offers up smoke, meat, and blue fruit aromas. Soft, forward, and easy to understand, this tasty wine lacks only complexity.

CONTRIBUTORS

Robert M. Parker, Jr., is the only wine writer in history to be honored with both of France's presidential honors—knighthood in the National Order of Merit in 1992 from President Mitterand, and both knighthood and officier status in the Legion of Honor from President Chirac—as well as commander status in Italy's highest Presidential Order of Merit. He has also been named Marylander of the Year by Loyola College and Alumni of the Year by the University of Maryland. His books have been translated and published in many languages. He is a lifelong resident of Maryland.

David Schildknecht trained in philosophy and worked as a restaurateur before spending a quarter century in the wine trade. His tasting reports have been published regularly since the mid-1980s. Since 2007 he has been writing full-time for Robert Parker's *Wine Advocate,* covering in particular Austria, Germany, and much of France. A columnist for *The World of Fine Wine* (UK) as well as for *Vinaria* (Austria) and an occasional contributor of feature articles to *Wine & Spirits* (USA), he is a coauthor of the 7th edition of *Parker's Wine Buyer's Guide* and was responsible for the German wine entries in the third edition of *The Oxford Companion to Wine,* edited by Jancis Robinson. His life in wine occasionally permits him to pursue his passion for music, history, and his infinitely tolerant wife of 3 decades.

Antonio Galloni is widely recognized as one of the world's foremost experts on the wines of Italy and Champagne and has contributed his knowledge of those regions to this book. Antonio's passion for wine began as a teenager when he worked in his parents' wine and food business. Later, Antonio lived in Italy for a number of years, which allowed him to gain invaluable insight into the vastness of Italian wine culture. In 2005 he founded *Piedmont Report,* an independent publication that quickly established itself as a leading source for reviews on the wines of that important region. Antonio's work has appeared in a number of publications including the *Wine Advocate, The World of Fine Wine,* and *Parker's Wine Buyer's Guide,* seventh edition. Antonio has a BA from the Berklee College of Music and an MBA from the MIT/Sloan School of Management. He lives in New York City with his wife and son.

Dr. Jay Stuart Miller worked as a clinical psychologist specializing in child, adolescent, and family therapy until 2001. He holds a BA degree from the University of California in Los Angeles and an MS and PhD degrees from the University of Maryland at College Park.

Jay's wine-industry experience began in 1977 when he worked as a part-time wine consultant at Wells Discount Liquors, in Baltimore, Maryland, and later at Calvert Discount Liquors in Cockeysville, Maryland. In 1985 he became the part-time assistant to Robert M. Parker Jr. at the *Wine Advocate*. In 1998 he left to devote his full-time attention to wine sales at The Wine Source in Columbia, Maryland. In 2001 he became co-owner and manager of Bin 604 Wine Sellers in Baltimore. He currently covers the wines of Oregon, Washington, Spain, Australia, South America, and vintage ports.

Mark Squires was trained as a lawyer in Philadelphia, class of '78. Formerly the forum leader on Prodigy's Wine Forum, he has been teaching wine courses for over 15 years and has published numerous papers and articles in various magazines. In 1995 he began his own wine-appreciation website, which attracted international attention. Later, he added a popular bulletin board, which is now housed on eRobertParker.com. Mark sometimes organizes and presents wine seminars for organizations and individuals, and has also worked as an expert wine consultant. He has been reviewing wines professionally for approximately a decade, and his reviews have been cited in major publications. In 2006 he was assigned to cover Portugal's dry wines for the *Wine Advocate*. He now covers Israel, Greece, Lebanon, Cyprus, Bulgaria, and Romania as well.

Neal Martin is one of the world's authorities on fine wine, in particular those of Bordeaux, Burgundy, and New Zealand, although he did not drink wine, let alone write about it, until he was in his midtwenties. After gaining a BSc from the University of Warwick and working in Tokyo as an English teacher, he serendipitously gained employment as a fine-wine buyer in 1996 and made up for lost time through intense tasting and documenting of notes. These were the foundation for Wine-Journal, an independent website that he established in 2003, which rapidly gained worldwide popularity. Since 2007 its Wine-Journal has blazed an independent trail on eRobertParker.com, where Neal has published over 400 articles, as well as covering Sauternes and New Zealand for the *Wine Advocate*. His work has appeared in *Decanter, World of Fine Wine*, and *Parker's Wine Buyer's Guide*, seventh edition.

THE WINE ADVOCATE'S VINTAGE GUIDE 1994–2008

REGIONS		2008	2007	2006	2005	2004	2003	2002	2001	2000	1999	1998	1997	1996	1995	1994
BORDEAUX	St. Julien/Pauillac-St. Estephe	91E	86E	87E	95T	88T	95T	88T	88R	96T	88R	87T	84R	96T	92T	85C
	Margaux	90E	86E	88E	98T	87T	88I	88T	89E	94T	89R	86T	82R	88T	88E	85C
	Graves	91E	87E	87E	96T	88T	88I	87T	88R	97T	88R	94T	86R	86E	89E	88E
	Pomerol	96E	86I	90T	95T	88E	84E	85E	90E	95T	88R	86R	87R	85E	92T	89T
	St. Émilion	92E	86I	88E	99T	88E	90I	87E	90E	96T	88R	96T	86R	87T	88E	86T
	Barsac/Sauternes	87E	94T	88E	96T	82E	95E	85E	98T	88E	88E	87E	89E	87E	85E	78E
BURGUNDY	Côte de Nuits (red)	NT	NT	88I	98T	83R	93T	93T	86I	84R	92R	84I	89R	89T	90R	72C
	Côte de Beaune (Red)	NT	NT	82I	96T	79R	88T	90T	79I	80C	93R	82C	88R	89R	85R	73C
	White Burgundy	NT	88I	90E	90R	91T	84R	92R	86R	88R	89C	84C	89C	92C	93C	77C
RHONE	North–Côte Rôtie/Hermitage	NT	89E	92E	89T	85C	96T	78C	89T	87E	95T	90T	90E	86R	90T	88C
	South–Châteauneuf du Pape	NT	98E	90E	95T	90E	90I	58C	96T	98E	90E	98E	82C	82C	90T	86C
Beaujolais		85R	85R	89R	95R	81R	95I	86C	75C	91R	89R	84C	87C	82C	87C	85C
Alsace		NT	90R	79I	87R	86E	82R	86R	91R	90I	87R	90R	87R	87R	89R	90R
Loire Valley (White)		NT	84I	83E	94E	82C	82R	96R	82C	84R	84R	84C	88C	91R	88C	87C
Champagne		NT	NT	NT	NT	NT	86I	90T	83E	87E	87E	86C	86R	91T	90E	NV
ITALY	Piedmont	93T	92E	93T	92R	96T	90I	74C	96T	95T	95T	92T	93E	97T	87C	77C
	Tuscany	NT	93E	96T	92R	96T	92I	75C	94E	88E	94E	86C	95E	78R	88T	85C
Germany: Rhine (Riesling)		NT	92I	86I	93R	89I	91T	91I	69C	87E	93I	93T	87R	91T	86C	87C
Germany: Mosel, Saar, Ruwer		NT	92I	95I	96R	92I	91I	92T	95T	76C	86E	92T	88T	91I	90R	94I
Austria: Riesling, Grüner Veltliner		89I	90R	91I	87I	88I	89I	89T	88I	85C	95R	82C	96R	84C	90I	87C
Vintage Port		NT	NT	NT	NT	NT	90I	NT	NV	92T	NV	NV	89T	NV	NV	92T
SPAIN	Rioja	NT	89T	85T	92E	95E	87I	76C	94E	86E	86E	82C	86R	85R	90R	90R
	Ribera del Duero	NT	90I	93T	93T	95E	88I	78C	95E	87C	88C	88T	86R	92R	90R	90R
AUSTRALIA	S. Australia: Barossa/Clare/McLaren Vale	NT	85T	94T	96T	91E	90E	95T	95T	88C	88E	95E	88R	90E	87R	NT
	Western Australia	NT	86T	89T	91T	88T	89T	90T	90E	88E	89R	90R	87R	NT	NT	NT
New Zealand		NT	91R	90R	85R	83R	78I	87R	76I	81I	80I	90R	86I	89R	84I	87R
Argentina		NT	92T	94T	93T	91T	NT	NT	NT	NT	NT	NT	NT	NT	NT	NT
Chile		NT	88T	89T	90T	89T	NT	NT	NT	NT	NT	NT	NT	NT	NT	NT
CA. NORTH COAST	Cabernet Sauvignon	NT	96E	91E	95T	91R	92I	95E	96T	78C	88T	85R	94I	90T	94T	95E
	Chardonnay	NT	92I	87I	94E	92R	91R	90R	90C	87C	89R	89R	92C	87C	92C	88C
	Zinfandel	NT	88R	79I	78I	82I	93R	85R	90R	83C	87R	86C	85E	89C	87R	92C
	Pinot Noir	NT	90I	87I	90E	89I	90R	92E	92E	88R	90E	89R	90E	88R	88R	92R
California Central Coast Rhone Rangers		NT	94E	92E	92T	94R	92E	93E	89T	92R	88R	90R	90R	NT	NT	NT
Oregon Pinor Noir		NT	84T	93E	85T	86E	88E	92I	85E	86E	92E	89T	87C	83C	76C	91E
Washington Cabernet Sauvignon		NT	92I	91T	94T	91T	90T	89T	92T	89R	90I	90T	88T	88T	87R	90I
REGIONS		2008	2007	2006	2005	2004	2003	2002	2001	2000	1999	1998	1997	1996	1995	1994

96–100:	Extraordinary	70–79:	Average
90–95:	Finest	60–69:	Below Average
80–89:	Above Average to Excellent	Below 60:	Appalling

C: Caution, may be too old

E: Early maturing and accessible

I: Irregular, even among the best wines

T: Still tannic, youthful, or slow to mature

R: Ready to drink

NT: Not yet sufficiently tasted to rate

NV: Vintage not declared

INDEX OF THE BEST OF THE BEST

Red

MEDIUM BODIED (listed in order of appearance in text)

INDEX OF SPARKLING WINES

All of the following are dry white wines unless otherwise noted.

INDEX OF WINE PRODUCERS

eRobertParker.com

The Independent Consumer's Guide to Fine Wines

To help you further expand your wine horizons we're pleased to offer you a special bonus for buying *Parker's Wine Bargains*:

━ A COMPLIMENTARY ━ 30-DAY FREE SUBSCRIPTION TO EROBERTPARKER.COM!

eRobertParker.com is Mr. Parker's official website and the premier source of professional wine information on the Internet. In it Mr. Parker and his Wine Advocates offer:

- A searchable database of over 135,000 reviews from past issues of Mr. Parker's newsletter *The Wine Advocate*
- Thousands of articles about wine, wine producers, wine-producing regions, and other topics of interest to wine lovers everywhere
- *The Hedonist's Gazette,* a weekly feature that offers an insider's glimpse into the food and wine experiences of Mr. Parker and his Wine Advocates
- Up-to-date information about where you can purchase wines of interest to you at the best price
- Complimentary access from most Internet-enabled cell phones
- And much more!

To claim your complimentary 30-day subscription to **eRobertParker.com**, go to **www.eRobertParker.com/ValueWines/register .aspx**. You will be asked some questions to verify that you are a book purchaser, so please have this book with you when you register.